D0212784

THIS IS PEARL!

THIS IS PEARL!

THE UNITED STATES AND JAPAN—1941

by WALTER MILLIS

GREENWOOD PRESS, PUBLISHERS
WESTPORT, CONNECTICUT

Originally published in 1947 by William Morrow & Company, Inc.

Reprinted in 1971 by Greenwood Press
A division of Congressional Information Service, Inc.
88 Post Road West, Westport, Connecticut 06881

Library of Congress catalog card number 77-138594
ISBN 0-8371-5795-1

Printed in the United States of America

10 9 8 7 6 5 4 3 2

☞ FOR EUGENIA

CONTENTS

CHARTS

FOREWORD

From its inception this book has had but one aim—to tell the story of the Pearl Harbor attack and of the events, the policies and the popular attitudes of the year which led up to it in a single organized narrative. As the story was unfolded in the winter of 1945-46 before the Congressional Joint Committee investigation, it seemed to be of compelling dramatic interest in itself, quite aside from its political, diplomatic and military significance. It was, however, obscured by the very masses of evidence which were produced as well as by the political and other controversies which centered around the investigation. It seemed worth while to take the great wealth of material which had been made available and reduce it, as fairly and dispassionately as possible, to an ordered account of what actually happened and why it appears to have happened as it did. This is what I have here tried to do.

This book maintains no thesis; it is motivated by no impulse either to attack or to defend any of the many characters involved. I have done my best to let the facts speak for themselves. Obviously, however, any undertaking of this kind must reflect the author's own attitudes to some extent. I have not aimed at an appearance of bloodless (and in the nature of things impossible) "impartiality," nor attempted to conceal my own evaluations of the personalities and situations concerned. But I do not ask anyone to agree with these evaluations except in so far as the established facts may require.

It is plain that there can never be a final answer to the question of who was "responsible" for the Pearl Harbor disaster. It was the end result of a highly complex chain of actions, reactions, good decisions and bad ones, in which human foresight and failure were inextricably mingled; and the issue of responsibility, which in the last analysis is a moral rather than a factual issue, must turn in the end upon the particular standards which the observer applies to it. For myself, I find it difficult to see how Admiral Kimmel and General Short can escape the major responsibility for the military surprise, not because they were necessarily any more blind, less able or more negligent than others, but because as the commanding officers concerned it was on their shoulders that the burden lay. They were like the responsible captains of a ship told to navigate her through waters known to be highly dangerous. It is true that their equipment was inadequate, their charts, so to speak, unreliable and the information supplied them less complete in some ways than it might have been. But it is a captain's business to know when his charts are unreliable. These captains managed to run their ship squarely on just the kind of rock which all knew to exist. They were taken completely by surprise by a peril which had been repeatedly foreseen. Others may apply other standards of responsibility, but to me that is something which no military man, however deficient his support or uncertain his orders, can ever easily explain.

There were, of course, many mitigating circumstances. Nor can anyone say that the rough justice of war is anything but rough. Kimmel and Short were summarily "broken." MacArthur, whose generalship in the crisis was at least not above criticism, became a national hero. The contributory failures of the command system at Washington did not come to light until long afterward. But war is a rough business, and was at least no more so for the two commanders than for the 2,300 men who died at Pearl Harbor and whose careers were terminated as effectively as were those of Kimmel and Short.

There can be no final accounting. And merging with the question of immediate responsibility for the surprise there is the larger question of responsibility for the policies which led to it. Here again opinion will probably always differ. Many of the grosser suspicions which attained currency during the war and were kept alive afterward are emphatically dissipated by the evidence. The record offers no support for the view that the Roosevelt Administration plotted to invite a Pacific War or even wished for one. There is, on the contrary, overwhelming evidence that the guiding thought was to stave off a war as long as possible. Yet it is true that President Roosevelt and his advisers followed policies which, under all the circumstances, made the Japanese attack virtually inevitable. Why? The only valid answer must be sought in a consideration of the alternatives available at any given point in the process. To my mind, the Roosevelt Administration had no other choices than those which it successively took. Here, also, there is no doubt much room for disagreement. But sincere disagreement must demonstrate, not only that the courses followed eventuated in undesirable consequences, but that alternative courses would not have led to much worse ones. This is a canon of honest historical and political criticism which is not always observed.

These observations are set down simply to advise the reader of the point of view from which the story is told; I have tried to tell the story itself and let it stand on its own merits. As for my sources, they are, overwhelmingly, the forty volumes comprising the report, record and exhibits of the Joint Committee on the Investigation of the Pearl Harbor Attack (79th Congress, 2d Session; Senate Document No. 244 and accompanying "Hearings"). These volumes include the reports and records of all previous investigations; they also include a translation of the "Memoir" of Prince Konoye. In addition, Joseph C. Grew's *Ten Years in Japan* and the State Department's

Peace and War and *Foreign Relations of the United States, Japan,* 1931-1941, are a part of the official record, although not reprinted in these volumes. Among other official documents, I have also drawn on *The Campaigns of the Pacific War* and the two-volume *Interrogations of Japanese Officials* published by the Naval Analysis Division of the United States Strategic Bombing Survey (Pacific), and on the *War Reports* of Generals Marshall and Arnold and Admiral King (official documents, but republished in a single volume by J. B. Lippincott and Company).

Among unofficial sources I have used the files of *The New York Herald Tribune* and *The New York Times* and I am indebted for quotations or important suggestions to the following:

Lewis H. Brereton, *The Brereton Diaries,* New York, William Morrow and Company, 1946.

Galeazzo Ciano, *The Ciano Diaries,* New York, Doubleday and Company, 1946.

Forrest Davis and Ernest K. Lindley, *How War Came,* New York, Simon and Schuster, Inc., 1942.

Allison Ind, *Bataan, The Judgment Seat,* New York, The Macmillan Company, 1944.

Walter Karig and Welbourne Kelley, *Battle Report: Pearl Harbor to Coral Sea,* New York, Farrar and Rinehart, Inc., 1944.

Walter Karig, *Battle Report: The Atlantic War,* New York, Rinehart and Company, 1946.

Donald M. Nelson, *Arsenal of Democracy,* New York, Harcourt, Brace and Company, 1946.

John M. Raleigh, *Pacific Blackout,* New York, Dodd, Mead and Company, 1943.

Otto D. Tolischus, *Tokyo Record,* New York, Reynal and Hitchcock, Inc., 1943.

Jonathan M. Wainwright, *General Wainwright's Story,* New York, Doubleday and Company, 1946.

Amea Willoughby, *I Was on Corregidor*, New York, Harper and Brothers, 1943.

I also owe an acknowledgment to *The Smyth Report*, to an article by Richard A. Lauterbach in *Life*, March 4, 1946, and an article by Captain Homer N. Wallin in *United States Naval Institute Proceedings*, vol. 72, p. 1521. But while I must express my obligation to all these, the main reliance has been the report and record of the Congressional committee, an almost inexhaustible mine of often tragic, sometimes humorous and always fascinating material. And here I should make special mention of the paper which appears as "Appendix D" of the report of the committee. This "Review of the Diplomatic Conversations Between the United States and Japan," the work of Mr. John E. Masten, of the committee counsel, is an invaluable guide to the intricacies both of the actual events and of the committee record; it will be friend and helper to any who hereafter explore this history, as it has been to me. But I must absolve all official and unofficial sources of any responsibility for the chapters which follow. I have had no inspiration or assistance save that provided by the published record.

W. M.

THIS IS PEARL!

ONE

A GRIM YEAR BEGINS

I ☞

The year 1940 ran out in a holiday week which was much like its predecessors, yet not quite like them, either. "Christmas," said a front-page headline in the *New York Times* on December 26, "Is Gay in a Few Nations in a Blackout World." In New York, as through most of the Western Hemisphere, there was no doubt about the gaiety. The rail and air terminals were jammed with the holiday traffic. The stores had done a tremendous rush of business, responding to the first influence of the armament contracts which had been pouring out in growing volume since the black days of the preceding summer. If the stock market was still dullish, the indices of business activity were turning sharply upward. The theatrical and night-club worlds were flourishing. The Sunday newspapers were dropsical with advertising and extra sections, including the travel sections, in which the railroads still offered their luxury equipment and the steamship and air lines expatiated upon the glamors of the Caribbean and Latin America in competition with the resort hotels summoning vacationists to Quebec or Sun Valley. They pictured a fat and prosperous western world. But no advertisements invited tourists to the South of France or offered sailings to Bremen or Southampton.

Behind all the cheerfulness there was the dull, persistent tension of the war—the second great war which was tearing out Europe's vitals and one day might easily reach beyond that tortured continent. The newspapers said that over Christmas Day there had been a kind of unofficial truce in the strange air battle which was moving in fire and desolation across the face of Britain; but it was a truce for a day only. One could not glimpse the moon, shining peacefully above the city's lights, without thinking of it as a "bombers' moon," illuminating at that moment the treacherously revealing reaches of the Thames. There was the imagined stench of blood and wreckage in the nostrils of those buying holiday tickets for Mexico or the West Indies. There were photographs of gutted English homes and churches in the newspapers which reviewed the opening of John O'Hara's *Pal Joey*. And there were reports of huge Nazi legions massing against the Balkans side by side with forecasts of the enormous budget—ten billions for defense alone on top of seven billions for the ordinary expenses of government—which Franklin Roosevelt was about to send to Congress.

On Broadway *Life with Father* was on into its second year. Ethel Merman was the pleasantly ambiguous star of *Panama Hattie* and Ethel Barrymore was appearing in *The Corn Is Green*. Gaxton and Moore were available in *Louisiana Purchase* and Maurice Evans and Helen Hayes in *Twelfth Night*. One publisher announced that *For Whom the Bell Tolls* was in its 440th thousand; another proclaimed *Oliver Wiswell* as "the novel to give for Christmas." Thus realism contended, as usual, with romance for the holiday trade. But realism had not as yet got beyond Hemingway's dour account of that rather small and now distant war in Spain. There were no novels or plays so far about the titanic and decisive struggle which had been joined in the great cities of Europe, the near centers of our own western civilization.

There were, however, plenty of polemic books and articles arguing our difficult duty to that civilization. The Committee to Defend America by Aiding the Allies was fighting its fierce propaganda battle with the America First Committee. The venomously anti-Roosevelt and isolationist *Chicago Tribune* was filling the Middle West with its powerful appeals to retreat and appeasement; such leading newspapers as the *New York Herald Tribune*, the *New York Times*, and many others were, even when in political opposition to the President, urging him on in every bold step toward the support of Britain and the curbing of Nazi Germany. The greatly respected William Allen White led the "Committee to Defend" and had a host of eminent and passionately convinced men and women behind him. Colonel Lindbergh was lending his still potent name to the opposition, whose less numerous leaders were increasingly speaking with the jaundiced savagery of a losing minority. A red-headed young newspaper publisher, Mr. Verne Marshall, rose suddenly (and a little obscurely) out of the West to become, for a brief time, a bitterly sarcastic and vituperative voice of isolation. The one living ex-President, Mr. Herbert Hoover, hung ambiguously, but vocally, somewhere between the two parties; it was always clear that he was on the side of the angels, but rather less apparent just which angels he was siding with.

In Washington debate was violent. Senator Burton K. Wheeler, "fast emerging as one of the leaders of the peace group in Congress," was insisting that "we have got to look at this thing realistically." The Senator expanded on his concept of a "just peace":

> I think we are doing Great Britain a great disservice in urging her to go and fight until she is exhausted. . . . Peace has got to come sometime, and I don't think there is any sane, intelligent military or naval officer . . . who thinks that England can land troops on German soil and drive the Germans back to Berlin before that time arrives. And even if our own warmongers get us into the war, as it looks now they will, I doubt that the joint efforts of Great Britain and the United States could succeed in that project.

Passionate as the argument was growing, there was still

something theoretic about it, as if all sides were playing at a kind of game in which it was still open to this country to make its own rules, regardless of those which might be imposed by the grim imperatives of history. But it was not all theory, even then. In spite of holiday leaves from the new training camps, there must have been thousands of homes that Christmas with empty chairs at the table. Six months before, in May and June, there had come the giant tiger's spring upon the West and the shattering fall of France in six weeks' time. There had come those panic days of flight and foreboding, the swastika over Paris, the fall of Bordeaux, the beaches of Dunkerque, the first waves of refugees washing even to our own shores. There had come President Roosevelt's sudden demands for what then seemed stupendous sums for rearmament, and the instant votes of Congress granting them. In August there had come the induction of the National Guard into the Federal service; on September 16 the President had signed the first peacetime draft act in the nation's history. Several hundreds of thousands of men were already in uniform, learning their new and bloody trade. The echoes of 1917 were already insistent. The unfamiliar yet old, old training-camp jokes about top sergeants and kitchen police and awkward rookies, told no doubt since the time of Caesar's legions, were drifting about again; and many mothers were looking with an anxious mixture of emotions at new photographs of their sons wearing the strange clothes of war.

The uniforms, the training camps, the new weapons just beginning to trickle from the assembly line, were all, of course, strictly for defense. Officially we were preparing to repel the war, not to enter it. Yet no sane person could be unaware that the problem was less simple than that. There was no sharp dividing line between defense and participation, but only a hazy, uncertain tract where the publicists and politicians strove fiercely in the fogs of an impenetrable future. In the fall the country had stumbled through the third-term

Presidential election. Mr. Roosevelt had made his rash, and certainly rather less than completely ingenuous, promise that "your sons are not going to be sent into any foreign wars." But his opponent, Mr. Wendell Willkie, had in effect supported him. While the two candidates had duly hammered each other on "domestic" issues, there had been no real issue over foreign policy, which was so overwhelmingly the most important problem confronting the nation, alike for its domestic as for its international development. Both candidates had analyzed that problem in essentially the same terms. Both dedicated themselves to peace; both held that the support of the shattered British bastion of democracy against the cresting waves of German Nazism was vital to any peace worth having; both hoped to avoid a "shooting war" but believed that in any case a bold policy offered the best and safest defense for the essential national interest. On September 3, after receiving what amounted to Mr. Willkie's assent, Mr. Roosevelt had announced the agreement with Great Britain under which we provided 50 old American destroyers with which to reinforce the British Navy in its war on the German submarines in the Atlantic, in return for 99-year leases of British islands and coastal sites on which to build our own offshore bases against possible German attack. Mr. Willkie's refusal to make the famous "destroyer deal" an object of partisan attack was an act of high patriotism and conviction; but the deal itself obviously brought us close to an Anglo-American alliance against Hitlerism.

The newspapers had published photographs of the old "four-pipers" in Halifax harbor, of the American colors being lowered and the British white ensigns being run up, of American bluejackets instructing their British counterparts in the handling of the equipment. The ships had departed under their new names to take up at last the battle against the German U-boats for which they had been built twenty years before. And nothing very much had happened. Hitler, with the air Battle of Britain rising to its climax, had given no sign of responding with a declaration of war. Yet it was, to say the least, a drastic departure from accepted concepts of neutrality; and it had underlined the extent to which defense had already become actively aggressive. The men on the drill fields were being trained to defend the peace. None at home could be sure that they would not be required to fight a war in order to do so.

Nor was that all. A week before Christmas President Roosevelt had returned from a post-election vacation tour of the Caribbean. At his first press conference he had startled the reporters by outlining in a general way a proposal which he would submit to Congress in the new year. As everyone knew, the British were nearing the end of the financial resources with which they had been placing their big American contracts for planes and munitions. Some way, the President suggested, must be found by which the United States could in effect assume the British contracts and continue to supply the desperately needed instruments of war to those who were using them in the common cause, without the impediments involved by questions of money payment. Instead of lending money for weapons, this country could well lend the weapons themselves, to be returned after the war if they were still usable, to be written off if they had been expended in a struggle which was as much to America's interest as Britain's. It was an idea appealing in its logic and simplicity. But it would clearly align us irrevocably in the European struggle. It might suffice to secure Germany's defeat with no more than an economic contribution from the United States. If not, it would almost certainly mean that the United States would have to commit its blood.

Christmas that year fell upon a Wednesday. The nation enjoyed its trees and stockings in unseasonably mild weather, went back to work, and presently found itself in the week-end holiday. On Sunday evening, December 29, it was tuning its radios by the million to receive the "fireside chat" which had been announced from the White House. The high-pitched, familiar, and persuasive voice came on:

This is not a fireside chat on war. It is a talk on national security; because the nub of the whole purpose of your President is to keep you now, and your children later, and your grandchildren much later, out of a last-ditch war for the preservtaion of American independence. . . .

Tonight, in the presence of a world crisis, my mind goes back eight years ago to a night in the midst of a domestic crisis. . . . I well remember that while I sat in my study in the White House, preparing to talk with the people of the United States, I had before my eyes the picture of all those Americans with whom I was talking. I saw the workmen in the mills, the mines, the factories; the girl behind the counter; the small shopkeeper; the farmer doing his spring plowing; the widows and the old men wondering about their life's savings.

I tried to convey . . . what the banking crisis meant to them in their daily lives. Tonight I want to do the same thing, with the same people, in this new crisis which faces America. . . .

Never before since Jamestown and Plymouth Rock has our American civilization been in such danger as now. . . . The Axis not merely admits but proclaims that there can be no ultimate peace between their philosophy of government and our philosophy of government. . . . It can be asserted, properly and categorically, that the United States has no right or reason to encourage talk of peace until the day shall come when there is a clear intention on the part of the aggressor nations to abandon all thought of dominating or conquering the world. . . .

Some of our people like to believe that wars in Europe and in Asia are of no concern to us. But it is a matter of most vital concern to us that European and Asiatic warmakers should not gain control of the oceans which lead to this hemisphere. . . .

The British people are conducting an active war against this unholy alliance. Our own future security is greatly dependent on the outcome of that fight. Our ability to "keep out of war" is going to be affected by that outcome. . . . I make the direct statement to the American people that there is far less chance of the United States getting into war if we do all we can now to support the nations defending themselves against attack by the Axis than if we acquiesce in their defeat, submit tamely to an Axis victory, and wait our turn to be an object of attack in another war later on. . . .

There is no demand for sending an American expeditionary force outside our own borders. . . . You can, therefore, nail any talk about sending armies to Europe as a deliberate untruth. Our national policy is not directed toward war. Its sole purpose is to keep war away from our country and from our people. . . .

But all our present efforts are not enough. We must have more ships, more guns, more planes—more of everything. . . . Your Government, with its defence experts, can then determine how best to use them to defend this hemiphere. . . .

We must be the great arsenal of democracy. For us this is an emergency as serious as war itself. . . . There will be no "bottlenecks" in our determination to aid Great Britain. . . .

I believe that the Axis powers are not going to win this war. I base that belief on the latest and best information.* We have no excuse for defeatism. . . . I have the profound conviction that the American people are now determined to put forth a mightier effort than they have ever yet made. . . . As President of the United States I call for that national effort. . . .

The voice ceased, giving way to the announcer—"You have just heard the President of the United States"—and the conventional sound effects. But the impact sank home. The popular approval seemed overwhelming. The Republican *New York Herald Tribune* placed the text, double-leaded, on its front page and described it editorially as "one of the greatest efforts" of the President's career, "superb in its directness, its realism, its courage, and its purpose." In Congress, which throughout was more isolationist than the public, judging by opinion polls and similar indices, appeared to be, there were more dubious voices. Senator Bulow of South Dakota was

* This assurance, so contrary to all the appearances, made a deep impression at the time. I believe that it has never been explained on what it rested. According to Davis and Lindley, however, it was in "mid-January" that our Government warned the Soviet Union that Germany intended to attack Russia in June. If the President already felt certain of this, it would go far to explain his subsequent boldness.

unable to see how the address "squares with pre-election pledges to keep this country out of war," while Senator Capper of Kansas, though approving the call to preparedness, still felt that "we are nearer—pretty close—to war. I'm for keeping out of that war over there," he said. The idea that it might not be a matter of our own volition and that the war might come to us was still difficult to comprehend. But whether the end was to be peace or war, this address had clearly laid down the course which the Administration proposed to follow, and which it did follow consistently through the ensuing months to the consistent approval, at every decisive step, of Congress and the public. It explicitly defined the basic ideas, summarized the concepts of the international problem, and adumbrated the policies which were in fact to guide the American people through the vast crisis then confronting them. It is a document fundamental to the history which was to ensue.

At the moment that the radios were resounding to those tenor sentences, the people of London were struggling in the lurid inferno of the greatest fire raid they had yet sustained, the worst holecaust since the Great Fire of 1666. Half a dozen of the Wren churches, the graceful monuments to the earlier disaster, were destroyed in the new one; the Guildhall was gutted; whole blocks of the old city were swept away in the flames from the incendiary bombs, still rather new weapons then for which London was inadequately prepared. Yet terrible as such things seemed, they were still inevitably dulled by distance and censorship. On the American side of the Atlantic all indications pointed to "the most hilarious celebration" of the New Year the nation had ever known. In Europe on New Year's Eve Adolf Hitler was issuing another proclamation to his troops:

> It is the will of the democratic war inciters and their Jewish-capitalistic wire-pullers that the war must be continued. . . . We are ready! . . . The year 1941 will bring completion of the greatest victory in our history.

It did not dampen what one observer described as "one of the most colossal collective binges" in which Americans had ever indulged. It was a night of vast throngs, jammed theaters, roaring night clubs, and shrieking horns and whistles. How, in a world so dire, was one to explain the phenomenon? An editorial writer played with the idea that it was an expression of a doomed impulse to eat, drink, and be merry for tomorrow our world would die. But he put the thought aside. The more probable explanation, he concluded, was the new flood of armament money. Whatever the reason, it was the last peacetime New Year the country was to know, and it made the most of it.

II ☜

As the horns and whistles were still blaring in New York's Times Square, the first day of the New Year was already far advanced over the teeming roofs of Tokyo. In that moment of calm and new beginnings, the Honorable Joseph C. Grew, American ambassador to Japan, was sitting down in the embassy where he had worked for the past nine years to analyze and summarize the situation before him.

It was both obscure and difficult, imposing onerous demands upon the judgment of those in a position to exercise a responsible influence upon policy. Mr. Grew saw himself approaching the end of a long road—a road that went back at least to the days of Commodore Perry and his "black ships" ninety years before, and that wound down thereafter through all the turns and twists of Japan's remarkable rise to Great Power status.

The Japanese were the one Oriental people who had somehow contrived to use, as well as to be used by, the great outpouring of western energies in the nineteenth century. Nobody in the western world had ever quite understood them; nobody had trusted them; nobody had known just how far to fear them. The United States had sympathized with them, by and large, in their war against Russia in 1904-1905, and immediately thereafter had felt a certain alarm at this infant colossus which we had helped to raise out of the deeps of the western Pacific. At least since that day the theoretic problem of a Japanese-American war for the mastery of the Pacific had been a standard preoccupation of the staffs, the war colleges, and the more sensational publicists of both countries. The idea had tended to grow. In 1908 the ebullient elder Roosevelt had sent the United States Fleet around the world, ostensibly for good will but primarily to overawe the Japanese. There had been acrid issues of trade and immigration. We had intervened after the first World War to curb Japanese ambitions in Siberia and Shantung and to scale down their famous Twenty-One Demands imposed in 1915 upon China. Our effort to establish political and military stability in the Pacific with the Washington treaties of 1922 had constrained the Japanese Navy to a somewhat technical but nevertheless galling inferiority.

Western techniques had brought the same great increases of population to Japan which they had brought elsewhere, but a still feudal social structure had tended to channel their benefits into the hands of a few great industrial and banking families and into a hypertrophied militarism. The result was not only a heavy "population pressure" upon the poverty-stricken peasant masses, but also a powerful impulse toward the relief of that pressure through aggressive expansion and military conquest. By 1930 the great military, feudal, and industrial interests which controlled Japan were beginning to burst through the paper bonds imposed after the first World War. The London Conference of 1930 clearly foreshadowed the end of the naval limitation system; the conquest of Manchuria, announced by the "Mukden Incident" at the end of 1931 and the savage devastation of Shanghai in early 1932, meant the end of the Nine-Power Treaty and the other political settlements on which the naval treaty had been based. The

United States tried unsuccessfully to rouse the already decaying mechanisms of "collective security" against the growing threat of Japanese aggression; failing, we retired into the morally lofty, if somewhat futile, bastions of Mr. Henry L. Stimson's "non-recognition" policy. The Japanese were unimpressed, and went ruthlessly on with the rape of Manchuria. When in the spring of 1933 the League of Nations at last brought itself to a formal condemnation of Japanese action, the Japanese representative, Mr. Yosuke Matsuoka, stalked from the hall; and not long after Japan sent in her official notice of resignation from the League. It was the first definite break in the tottering "peace system" which had been set up at Versailles.

Adolf Hitler was by that time in power in Germany, and his own resignation from the League was to follow a few months later. The new totalitarian politics of brute military threat and violence were already well developed. In the hands of Mussolini and Hitler and Franco they were proving an effective weapon against the seemingly enfeebled forces of western capitalistic democracy; and it was the great democratic powers—Britain and the United States, France and the Netherlands—which had for so long held the dominant influence in the Far East and ringed the horizons of Japan. Japanese feudalism found both a model and an encouragement in the new methods of the totalitarians. In 1936 Japan signalized the trend by the more or less empty yet at the same time ominous gesture of joining Hitlerite Germany's "Anti-Comintern Pact." And then in 1937, at the Marco Polo bridge outside Peiping, she opened her brutal aggression upon the body of China proper.

It was apparent that the Japanese Empire was launching upon a vast and ambitious program of military aggression and conquest in the Far East. How far the Japanese might intend to press this grandiose undertaking no one knew; but it was also apparent that the United States could not remain passively indifferent to a development which threatened as drastic an overturn in the Far Eastern political structure as Hitler was already threatening in Europe. The United States put at least its "moral" support unreservedly behind the Chinese. In October, 1937, President Roosevelt made his celebrated suggestion of a "quarantine" for lawless and aggressor nations; and in July, 1938, the State Department imposed its "moral" embargo upon the export of airplanes to Japan. We had taken our first tentative steps upon the deceptive road of "peaceful" suasion.

In spite of them, the war in China dragged on, always inconclusive yet always expanding, steadily bringing larger territorial, political, and economic areas of Chinese life under the Rising Sun, and to the accompaniment of such appalling atrocities as the rape of Nanking. In the United States there appeared a vocal public sentiment for more effective economic sanctions against the Japanese war machine. In midsummer of 1939—that dark and sultry summer when all eyes were fastened upon the great thunderheads towering up over Europe and not many were troubling much about Far Eastern politics—the State Department remembered that the East and West were one problem on a global earth. On July 10 Secretary of State Cordell Hull called in the Japanese ambassador to tell him, among other things, that while our specific rights and interests in the Far East were important to us, the "big consideration" for the United States was that the whole of China and the Southwest Pacific should not be "Manchuriaized" by a process of lawless violence, treaty-breaking, and military conquest. The ambassador had little to answer. A few days later, on July 26, the United States formally denounced our commercial treaty with Japan. In itself only a warning gesture, the effect of the action would be to set us legally free in six months' time to apply discriminatory economic sanctions against this ambiguous power, which was threatening to disrupt the whole balance of power and of history in eastern Asia.

It was little over a month later that the great war in Europe broke at last, sending its violent shock through the foreign offices of the world. Poland was obliterated at a stroke in that bloody, dusty September; but then there ensued the six months of the "phony war," and it was not until the attack on Norway in April that the true measure of the crisis began to appear. When Hitler, on May 10, 1940, finally launched his crushing thunderbolt upon the West, it was the announcement to the eager soldiers and politicians everywhere that the old age was done, that the matted log-jam of the past had broken up, and that it was time for every alert mind to calculate the perils, and the opportunities, of the now uncertain future. After May 10, things in the Far East began very rapidly to happen.

The menace from Japan already seemed so alarming, in that disastrous hour, that the American War Department in June put its garrisons in Hawaii and the Panama Canal Zone on an all-out alert against a possible surprise raid across the Pacific. Except, no doubt, for the Japanese, no one knew much about this at the time—even the Navy, whom the garrisons were protecting, appears to have taken only a rather languid interest —but there was no mistaking the intention when in July the United States moved to the application of economic sanctions against Japan. Under the pretext (actually much less flimsy than this country may have realized at the time) that we had to conserve war supplies in the interests of our own rearmament program, an act of July 2, 1940, authorized the President to prohibit or curtail under license the export of strategic materials. It was announced that beginning in August the export to Japan of aviation gasoline and of most types of machine tools would no longer be permitted.

But this action was still no more than a gesture against a war machine already powerfully armed and stocked for great enterprises, and the Japanese were not interested in gestures. History was breaking up around them. Mussolini, with his "stab in the back" of France, had staked out his claim upon the new future, and it behooved the Japanese to do likewise.

It was in July that the militarist, pro-Axis, and "patriot" forces moved to action. The Cabinet of Admiral Yonai, a "liberal" of sorts, suddenly disappeared, to be replaced by one under Prince Fumimaro Konoye; and the American ambassador felt that a "typhoon" could not more effectively have wrecked the already shaky structure of Japanese-American relations.

Prince Konoye himself was a somewhat uncertain quantity. Head of the great house of Fujiwara, second only to that of the Emperor in the social hierarchy of Japan, he was deeply rooted in the feudal tradition but was at the same time western in training and outlook. Slim, elegant, with a touch of aristocratic delletantism and a tendency toward "diplomatic" hypochondria, he was probably suffering from a deep division between his western ideas and his ancient eastern loyalties. He was supposed to represent "moderate" and civilian influences as against the military fire-eaters; yet he was one of the chief inventors of the "New Order"—the Japanese variant of the Nazi German commodity of the same name—and of the "East Asia Co-Prosperity Sphere" which was its politico-economic expression. In his previous term as Prime Minister, in 1937, he had presided over the initiation of the "China Incident." He was afterward to claim that the militarists had embarked on the venture without his knowledge and against his wishes and that he had been a victim of army intrigue. Yet the possibility that he had been made Prime Minister at that time precisely in order to fulfill such a role could not be overlooked.

Nor was it Konoye alone who was ominous; it was his whole Cabinet and the wave of hot-headed enthusiasm for the Axis and for action on which it rode to office. His Foreign Minister was Mr. Matsuoka, who had been sent to Geneva to defend the rape of Manchuria and who had established his own career by marching out of the Assembly after the vote of censure, thus announcing Japan's withdrawal from the League. As a poor boy, he had managed to reach the United States; he had been picked up there by a Protestant minister who had befriended him and given him an American education. He was even more a western type than the Prime Minister, endlessly voluble, breezy, informal, indiscreet, and inclined to override the heavy etiquette of Japanese diplomacy. He was at the same time an unreliable opportunist and politician, who had linked his fortunes to the army and the Manchuria Gang, and Secretary Hull thought him "as crooked as a basket of fishhooks." The new War Minister was Lieutenant General Hideki Tojo, the "razor brains" of the Manchuria Gang, another opportunist and a political soldier who had worked himself up as a leader of the younger firebrands. The Konoye Cabinet, Ambassador Grew concluded in its first days, "gives every indication of going hell-bent toward the Axis and toward the establishment of the New Order in East Asia, and of riding roughshod over the rights and interests and the principles and policies of the United States and Great Britain."

The indications were soon being fulfilled. Within the month, the tiger of Japanese militarism, already standing with dripping jaws over vast areas of China, was reaching a stealthy and lethal paw around the Chinese flank into the French territory of Tonkin, in northern Indo-China. Early in September the demands were served on the wretched representatives of Vichy France—for ports, air bases, and the establishment of a large Japanese garrison on the railroad which ran through Hanoi into southern China. Berlin gave its imperious nod; and Vichy, powerless to do anything else, accepted. From Washington, where the transfer of destroyers to Britain had just been announced and the signature was scarcely dry on the selective service act, there issued a severely minatory State Department release:

> It seems obvious that the *status quo* is being upset and that this is being achieved under duress. The position of the United States in disapproval and in deprecation of such procedures has repeatedly been stated.

But "deprecation" was a less adequate instrument of policy in those grim times than even Washington may have appreciated. And Tonkin was only a part of it. In mid-September Herr Von Ribbentrop, then bestriding the earth as Hitler's Foreign Minister, paid an official visit to Rome. The Foreign Minister, much pleased by the spontaneous popular welcome which had been mobilized for him by the police and the "applauding squad," had a surprise for his Italian colleague, Count Ciano. Japan was about to join the Rome-Berlin Axis. It was a development, according to Von Ribbentrop, of "fundamental importance"; it would serve simultaneously to check the Russians, who were already looming rather ominously upon the Nazi horizons, and to give pause to the United States, which "under the threat of the Japanese Fleet will not dare to move." Count Ciano had his doubts. So far from damping American support for Britain, he feared it might have an opposite effect. And Hitler's promised reduction of Great Britain had not yet come off. Von Ribbentrop rather airily explained that the cross-Channel weather had been "very bad" of late, but that given a few good days the invasion would take place as advertised. Ciano still thought (or at any rate confided to his diary) that a break with the United States must be avoided "at all costs." But it made no difference what Ciano thought, or what Italy thought about this sudden extension of her "Pact of Steel"; and a few days later the Italian Foreign Minister was dutifully journeying up to Berlin for the ceremonies.

There it was, on September 27, 1940, that it fell to the lot of Mr. Saburu Kurusu, Japanese ambassador to Germany, to sign the death warrant of the Meiji Empire—and of Fascist Italy and Nazi Germany as well. Mr. Kurusu, a protectively colored career diplomat, naturally did not know that this was what he was doing. No one could know it then. Indeed, for so pregnant a moment in history the ceremonies were a trifle flat. The signing took place in the same room in Hitler's grandiose Chancellery (it is ruin now) in which the "Pact of Steel" had been concluded in 1939. But Ciano felt that the atmosphere was "cooler." The diplomatic corps was not invited; and the first public intimation of what was in the wind came when it was observed that the schoolchildren being mobilized ostensibly to welcome Ciano had been provided not only with German and Italian but also with Japanese flags. Ciano noted that "even the Berlin street crowd, a comparatively small one composed mostly of schoolchildren, cheers with regularity but without conviction. Japan is far away. Its help is doubtful. One thing alone is certain: that the war will be long." The signing took but a couple of minutes, and only at the end did Hitler emerge briefly from his study to give it his blessing.

Nobody knew exactly what the Tri-Partite Pact might portend. The treaty was brutally direct in its implications, but vague as to action. It provided:

1. Japan recognizes and respects the leadership of Germany and Italy in the establishment of a new order in Europe.

2. Germany and Italy recognize and respect the leadership of Japan in the establishment of a new order in Greater East Asia.

3. Germany, Italy, and Japan agree . . . to assist one another with all political, economic, and military means when one of the three contracting powers is attacked by a power at present not involved in the European War or in the Chinese-Japanese conflict.

A final, fifth clause crossed the t's and dotted the i's:

5. Germany, Italy, and Japan affirm that the aforesaid terms do not in any way affect the political status which exists at present between each of the contracting parties and Soviet Russia.

This obviously meant that the treaty was aimed directly at the United States, giving us warning to stay out of Hitler's war in Europe and the further wars the Japanese were preparing in Asia on penalty of combined attack by both powers. American opinion took it as such, and took it for the most part as a preposterous piece of bluff. "The reported agreement," declared Secretary Hull, authorizing direct quotation, "does not . . . substantially alter a situation which has existed for several years. Announcement of the alliance merely makes clear a relationship which has long existed." Editors and commentators were inclined to agree with him, and within a week or two the Tri-Partite Pact was for most Americans simply another leaf already whirled away down the rushing torrents of history.

Yet it did alter the situation, perhaps decisively. At every turn through the tortuous year that followed, Mr. Matsuoka's masterpiece was to arise to constrain the hand of statesmanship and to complicate every calculation. With Japan in formal alliance with Germany, American diplomacy could not risk the concessions it might otherwise have made; it was obviously doubly dangerous to give the Japanese a free hand to build up their strength in Asia when they were committed to throw that strength upon our rear should we become involved with the Germans. The Japanese, for their part, having pledged themselves just a little too soon to Hitler could never afterward quite take the risk of betraying him. And in the end even the Germans, instead of being protected by the Japanese alliance, were dragged by it into the global war which otherwise they might conceivably have avoided. Had Matsuoka and Von Ribbentrop been capable of writing a really firm alliance providing complete military and political unity of direction, they might have made the most out of the pact; indulging, as they did, in a form of words which each thought would trap the other into the service of his own interests, they ultimately got only the worst out of it. Had the Japanese ruling classes found the courage to go down the rapids alone, they might possibly have escaped the utter shipwreck which overtook them. But the signing of the Tri-Partite Pact made that impossible.

Even before the definitive conclusion of the pact, Ambassador Grew had summed up his estimate of the situation in a message, on September 12, 1940, which he was afterward to call his "green light" telegram. The ambassador had long been an opponent of the notion that Japan could be brought to a halt by the safe and easy application of economic embargoes. The great majority of Americans, ignorant of the East and misled by the slow and seemingly exhausting progress of the "China Incident," had no conception of the real power of the Japanese war machine or of the ruthless determination that its masters were prepared to put behind it. Mr. Grew, however, had steadily resisted the mounting pressure for "restraining" Japan by cutting off the scrap iron and petroleum imports with which she had been munitioning her aggressions. He knew that the Japanese stockpiles were large and that Japan had considerable reserves of unused military-economic power; and he believed that the resort to sanctions would be more likely to precipitate than to prevent a desperate bid for military and economic independence. The ambassador had not changed this estimate. But circumstances were changing its application.

While aware of the danger in an aggressive policy of sanctions, Mr. Grew had concluded that, on the other hand, "further conciliatory measures would appear futile and unwise." He reasoned that so long as American security was dependent on the survival of the British Empire—as he "emphatically" believed it to be—the United States must strive by all means in its power to maintain the *status quo* in the western Pacific. But this could no longer be achieved "merely by the expression of disapproval and carefully keeping a record thereof." A policy of yielding also had its perils. The time had come, Mr. Grew believed, for "firmness," because there was now no other way in which Japanese policy could be influenced. The ambassador's carefully balanced recommendations were somewhat elusive as to just what measure of "firmness" would be appropriate. But with this "green light" before it, with the Japanese advance into Tonkin, and with the signing of the Tri-Partite Pact, the State Department moved to further positive action. In the latter part of September it was announced that a total embargo would soon be laid down on the export of iron and steel scrap to Japan, and at about the same time American citizens were forcibly advised to evacuate the Far East.

On October 8 the Japanese ambassador, Mr. Kensuke Horinouchi, was at the State Department with a stiffly worded protest against the scrap embargo as a discriminatory and "unfriendly" act. These export restrictions, he observed, were causing a "feeling of tension among the people of Japan, who naturally presume that the system is intended to be a precursor of severance of economic relations between Japan and the United States"; and in view of this "high feeling" any further restrictions would render Japanese-American relations "unpredictable."

Mr. Horinouchi met with a scathing reception. Secretary Hull, after observing that he had been extremely "patient" with the Japanese, went on:

> It was clear now, however, that those who are dominating the external policies of Japan are . . . bent on the conquest by force of all worth-while territory in the Pacific Ocean area without limit as to extent in the South . . . and that we and all other nations are expected, as stated, to sit perfectly quiet and be cheerful and agreeable, but static, while most of Asia is Manchuria-ized. . . . I added that, of course, if any one country is sufficiently desirous of trouble, it can always find any one of innumerable occasions to start such trouble.

It was unheard-of, Mr. Hull caustically continued, for a nation engaged, in contravention of "all law and treaty provisions," in the rape of another to consider it an unfriendly act if a third power did not "cheerfully provide" the war materials required for the aggression; and he made it clear that in the view of the United States, both Germany and Japan were embarked upon a campaign of subjugation calculated to reduce Europe and Asia to the levels of "750 years ago." The ambassador "had little to say."

The Secretary was celebrated for the undiplomatic vigor of his language when vigor was thought necessary; and in this instance the tirade was no doubt premeditated. Hitler's invasion of Britain was still failing to proceed on schedule; there were indications that the Japanese might be having some second thoughts about the value of their new German alliance, and in American quarters Mr. Grew was by no means alone in his feeling that the "strong hand" might have its virtues. Across the street from the State Department on that same day, as it happened, there was a luncheon conference at the White House. The redoubtable Admiral J. O. Richardson, commander of the Pacific Fleet, who was in Washington for a brief visit, was protesting to the President against the existing naval dispositions. In the preceding spring, just before Hitler's great assault upon the West, President Roosevelt had moved the Pacific Fleet out of its long-established and commodious quarters in the San Diego area to base it permanently at Pearl Harbor. It was done as a gesture of "restraint" against Japan. "Jo" Richardson saw no sense in the policy. Pearl Harbor had not been fully developed as a permanent fleet base. It lacked the facilities for major repair and the unlimited fuel supplies of the West Coast; it also lacked recreation facilities for the crews and housing for their families. Basing at Pearl Harbor was complicating all the problems of supply, refit, training, and modernization with which the Navy, after twenty years of peace, was suddenly finding itself compelled to struggle. In the autumn of 1940 the Pacific Fleet (though very few Americans realized the fact) was simply not an effective instrument of war. Admiral Richardson, who did not believe that the Fleet in its unprepared state had much restraining value at best, wanted to withdraw to the lost comforts and conveniences of California.

The President was not favorably impressed. Even if keeping the fleet at Pearl would not restrain the Japanese, its withdrawal would vastly encourage them. With Secretary Hull exerting the "strong hand" across the street, with the embargo system about to be extended, with the President himself indulging in exaggerated ideas about establishing cruiser "blockade lines" across the Pacific, it was scarcely the moment for suggesting a retreat. The President seems to have sensed a negative and hostile attitude in his fleet commander. Mr. Frank Knox, the Republican newspaper publisher who had accepted Mr. Roosevelt's call to the Secretaryship of the Navy, was not pleased with the admiral. The latter was himself readily to grant afterwards that he was out of sympathy with the Administration's course to an extent which justified his replacement. At all events, the Fleet remained at Pearl Harbor; Admiral Richardson had effectively numbered his days as its commander, while the scrap-iron and steel embargo went into effect on October 16.

So the autumn waned, to the deadly rattle of machine-gun fire five miles above the peaceful and tidy fields of England, to the endless and aimlessly bloody patrolling of Japanese armies in China, to the bustle of troops and construction gangs establishing the new Japanese bases in Tonkin. In the United States the frenzy of the Presidential election rose to its climax; Mr. Roosevelt won his third term over the somewhat confused challenge of Mr. Willkie, and disappeared on his holiday in the Caribbean. American attention was preoccupied with the first air attacks on London, with Wavell's surprisingly successful shoestring offensive in North Africa against the Italians who had been massing for the conquest of Egypt, with the pitiful dilemmas of Vichy, with Hitler's grotesque attempts to stuff his "New Order" in Europe with reality. Americans were preoccupied as well with the formation of the new conscript armies and with the halting progress of industrial mobilization. The public was aware of some of the inordinate problems involved in both; of others it was wholly ignorant. It had never heard the word "radar" at that time and knew nothing of the Army's belated efforts to develop adequate radar warning systems; it knew nothing of the Navy's struggles to develop even approximately modern antiaircraft armament for its ships; it was unaware of how far our aviation doctrine and design was lagging behind the actual requirements of modern combat. Nor did it know anything whatever about a modest $40,000 contract between the National Defense Research Committee and Columbia University. Signed three days after the Presidential election, it represented the first sizable application of government funds to research upon the esoteric problems of atomic fission.

Though there was nothing of this last in the newspapers, they were too full of other matters for many to pay much attention to the remote antics of "the Japs." But Ambassador Grew, whose business it was to pay attention to them, had continued to reflect upon the problem, and as the weeks passed he became only more convinced of the necessity for a strong stand. In December he was writing a long letter to the President, addressed "Dear Frank." It put the situation baldly:

> It seems to me increasingly clear that we are bound to have a showdown someday, and the principal question at issue is whether it is to our advantage to have that showdown sooner or to have it later. . . . Only insuperable obstacles will now prevent the Japanese from digging in permanently in China and from pushing the southward advance. . . . Konoye and especially Matsuoka will fall in due course, but *under present circumstances* no Japanese leader or group of leaders could reverse the expansionist program and hope to survive. . . . It therefore appears that sooner or later, unless we are prepared . . . to withdraw bag and baggage from the entire sphere of "Greater East Asia including the South Seas" (which God forbid) we are bound eventually to come to a head-on clash with Japan.

Measures "short of war," Mr. Grew emphasized, would not do. Only if the United States were prepared to fight if necessary could the firm policy have any hope of success. Thus a "grim and cruel year" was running out. The autumn had faded into winter; winter had brought Christmas and the President's "arsenal of democracy" address; Christmas had given way to the roaring New Year's Eve, and Mr. Grew found himself sitting in his embassy on New Year's Day, 1941, reviewing a long, tangled past and trying to sum up the perilous future. There was nothing, he was now convinced, but "utter hopelessness" in any policy of appeasement toward Japan:

> The time for that has passed. . . . Only through the discrediting of the Japanese extremists by the failure of their plans can we hope to see peace in East Asia. Unarrested, the cancer will progressively invade everything within its reach. . . . It may become open to question whether we can afford to await a British victory [in Europe] and whether we should allow Japan to dig in throughout the areas where she now visualizes far-flung control. That question, I think, will depend upon the tempo of the Japanese advance. Meantime, let us keep our powder dry and be ready—for anything.

III ☞

"Let us keep our powder dry and be ready—for anything." It was excellent advice as the year 1941 opened upon us. But in Washington, still struggling with the underlying problem of basic national policy as well as with the innumerable preoccupations of the European war, of rearmament and mobilization, readiness of any kind was more easily recommended than achieved. On the 6th of January there came the President's annual message, sustaining the new program of leasing or lending the materials of war directly to those who could use them:

> I shall ask Congress for greatly increased new appropriations and authorizations to carry out what we have begun and to manufacture additional munitions and war supplies of many kinds to be turned over to those nations which are now in actual war with aggressor nations. They do not need manpower. They do need billions of dollars worth of weapons for defence. . . .

The United States, the President declared, would "not be intimidated by the threats of dictators that they will regard . . .

as an act of war our aid to the democracies which resist their aggression. . . . When the dictators are ready to make war on us, they will not wait for an act of war on our part." And the message ended with its famous proclamation of a future "founded upon four essential human freedoms. . . . This nation has placed its destiny in the hands and heads and hearts of its millions of free men and women; and its faith in freedom under the guidance of God."

Once more the public response seemed overwhelmingly favorable, and even the cautious Congressmen were for the most part enthusiastic. But Senator Robert Taft of Ohio could sourly observe that the President "is asking again for unlimited personal authority to loan abroad as much as he sees fit, without coming to Congress for appropriations or further authority, and confusing inextricably our already confused defense program with that of England." It was evident that isolationist and anti-Roosevelt opposition would be obstinate. Two days later, however, the $17,000,000,000 budget was brought in, carrying nearly $11,000,000,000 for defense; and then on January 10 the lend-lease bill was laid formally before the House. It bore, by what was unconvincingly declared to be a pure coincidence, the designation "H.R. 1776."

At the same time there was another lesser yet suggestive development. The Navy Department briefly announced that it was moving what would certainly be a "major force," including battleships and carriers as well as lesser types, into the Atlantic. Rear-Admiral Ernest J. King would be promoted to take over this new Atlantic Fleet; at the same time there were to be some other rearrangements in the higher command. A comparatively junior rear-admiral, Husband E. Kimmel, had been picked to replace the resistant Richardson in command of the Pacific Fleet at Pearl Harbor; while the Army was also changing its command in Hawaii, sending out Lieutenant General Walter C. Short to take over the garrison there. But what caught the eye was not these shifts in the remote central Pacific; it was the hint of growing menace on the Atlantic sea lanes.

Between the problems of Europe and the burdens of domestic popular and political leadership, President Roosevelt clearly had enough to absorb even his supple energies. But on January 21 he found time for a personal answer to Ambassador Grew's letter of the preceding month. He evidently agreed closely with "Dear Joe":

> I believe that the fundamental proposition is that we must recognize that the hostilities in Europe, in Africa, and in Asia are all parts of a single world conflict. We must, consequently, recognize that our interests are menaced both in Europe and in the Far East. . . . Our strategy of self-defense must be a global strategy.

Global strategy was not too easy. The President weighed the question of whether an entanglement in war with Japan would so "handicap" our aid to Britain as to threaten the British with defeat. But there was another side to the same shield. If Japan should seize the Netherlands East Indies and the Malay Peninsula, would not Britain's ability to sustain the war in Europe be even more gravely compromised? "Our strategy," Mr. Roosevelt concluded, "of giving [Great Britain] assistance . . . must envisage both sending of supplies to England and helping to prevent a closing of channels of communication to and from various parts of the world, so that other important sources of supply will not be denied to the British and be added to the assets of the other side." This was to "envisage" a policy of preventing any Japanese attack upon the British or Dutch possessions in the East. It would imply a commitment to keep Japan out of war upon the European democracies closely comparable to Japan's commitment, under the Tri-Partite Pact, to keep us out of a war with Germany. It was a bold suggestion; and one is forced to wonder whether the President had also envisaged the real costs and risks involved in a policy of bringing Japanese aggression to a halt. It was difficult in those days to take the Japanese, floundering as they seemed to be through their interminable and unsuccessful war with an almost unarmed China, very seriously. If only the great western democratic powers put up a really firm front, it was still hard to believe that Japan's shoestring militarism would ever actually have the audacity to challenge it.

Yet only a few days after the President's letter went off, the garrulous Mr. Matsuoka was talking again, and talking in terms which startled the already nervous American and British communities in the Far East. The Japanese Foreign Minister was in effect ordering the United States and Great Britain out of the western Pacific:

> The Co-Prosperity Sphere in the Far East is based on the spirit of Hakko Ichiu, or the Eight Corners of the Universe under One Roof. . . . The United States has apparently made England and Australia and New Zealand its first line of defense in Europe and the Pacific. While thus enlarging its own power, the United States repudiates Japan's right to control the western Pacific. We must control the western Pacific. . . . We must request United States reconsideration, not for the sake of Japan but for the world's sake. And if this request is not heard, there is no hope for improvement of Japanese-American relations.

The *New York Times* correspondent in Tokyo, Mr. Otto Tolischus, heard that the War Minister, the grim little General Tojo, had already told his high officers that the new year would bring Japan to "the gravest situation that has ever surrounded her since her foundation. High seas are running in the Pacific." The Navy Minister, Admiral Koshiro Oikawa, informed the Diet that "the Imperial Navy is fully prepared for the worst, and measures are being taken to cope with United States naval expansion." The Japanese press was filled with warlike propaganda. But the American people, far away beyond the world's widest ocean, took little notice of such utterances, which for years had seemed to be a more or less standard product of Japan's curious politics; and those who did notice them were still inclined to put them down to mere bluff and big talk.

At that stage perhaps they were bluff in some measure. The obscure processes by which policy was made in Imperial Japan had not yet ground to any irrevocable decisions; and Japanese statesmen were no less inclined than our own to hope that a sufficient show of threat and "firmness" might avert the necessity for more drastic measures to gain their ends. Yet the result was the same. On both sides of the Pacific the lines of policy had by early 1941 been clearly defined; projected, they were certain sooner or later to meet in violent collision. Only a radical change of course by one government or the other could now avert it. Either the Japanese militants must abandon their determination to seize the hegemony of East Asia and the western Pacific, or those in control of American policy must abandon the conviction that to yield that hegemony would be fatal, in this moment of desperate world crisis, to the American interest. Otherwise, war was the only outcome. But what would we have to fight it with?

One of the most curious features of the ensuing months was the fantastic underestimation of the Japanese and overvaluation of our own effective strength which ruled in the minds of the American public, of our policy-makers, and even, if to a lesser extent, of our military commanders. The President boldly assumed that it was essential to bring Japan to a halt, applied embargoes, and sketched far-flung plans for naval blockade without, apparently, any thorough analysis of what the Japanese might be able to do about it. Secretary Hull read his scathing lectures to Japanese diplomats as confidently as if the western Pacific were an American lake. Perhaps in the long view it was just as well; we might easily, like so many European states, have lost more through timidity than through our rash acceptance of the risks. It is still odd to find so little indication that the risks were ever seriously or scientifically calculated by those responsible for the shaping of our policy.

Perhaps it was that the enormous disparity between the ultimate American and Japanese war potentials was too obvious. In every basic element of military power—raw material, plant, technical knowledge, a skilled and highly productive population—the superiority of the United States was so overwhelming that it seemed impossible that necessitous Japan could ever challenge it. What this overlooked was, of course, the inordinate cost in effort, and in time, required to translate potential into actual military power. It also overlooked the fact that the Japanese military leaders could study the figures as easily as could we; and that if they proposed to make this seemingly reckless challenge they had probably been very careful to devise a solution for the problem it presented them which they believed would be successful. It overlooked the significant possibility that, when the Japanese Navy Minister declared that the Imperial Navy was "ready for the worst" and was "taking measures to cope with" our naval forces, he may have meant exactly what he said.

For the western Pacific was anything but an American lake. At the beginning of 1941 the United States was sensibly approaching war with Germany, Italy, and Japan. At that time the Germans had about 300 organized army divisions, the Italians about 70, and the Japanese about 120, for a total of nearly 500 divisions. The United States had 28. Many of the 120 Japanese divisions had received combat training in China, while the Japanese Army as a whole had behind it nearly four years' experience of large-scale military operations. Our Army had none. The 28 divisions at that time in formation were still seriously deficient in equipment, without training in war or even in combined maneuvers, and were, besides, in the United States, their energies fully absorbed by the great program of expansion only just getting under way.

Japanese spokesmen declared that their naval air force numbered about 4,000 operating aircraft, and it was believed that the army aviation was in about the same strength. The American naval air arm was efficient, but still very small; our Army Air Force was, as a combat organization, virtually nonexistent. Of this very serious deficiency the American public (misled, to some extent, by the Air Force's always expert attention to the publicity) was largely unaware. It had been told so much about America's pre-eminence in air development that it did not realize that some of our important military types, notably the fighters, were markedly inferior to foreign models, and that even such basically excellent designs as the four-engine bombers would call for much modification to make them into fully effective weapons. Even less was it realized that what we did have in the way of modern planes amounted to little more than pilot models. Despite the billions appropriated for rearmament there was still, in early 1941, no adequate standardization of planes or parts; the airplane industry had not yet been converted to deal with volume orders and the automotive and other industries had not yet been enlisted in that task, and nothing like mass production of combat types had been achieved. Finished combat planes were still coming only in dribbles; and many of these were to be drained off during the ensuing months by lend-lease requirements. There was a tremendous activity in expansion and training, but the results in the shape of organized combat squadrons, trained and equipped for action, were negligible. Even ten months later, as the Commanding General of the Army Air Forces was ultimately to confess, the crisis was to catch us "with plans but not with planes."

But if we had little at home, at the scene of probable action we had next to nothing. When, late in 1940, Major General Jonathan M. Wainwright arrived amid the pleasantly tropic languors of Manila to take command of the Philippine Division, he found that he would have under him a total ground army of about 7,500 men, the larger part of them Filipinos in the United States service. At that time General Masaharu Homma was already beginning to assemble in Formosa an invasion force subsequently estimated at some 150,000 men. Even the handful that Wainwright had was, of course, grossly lacking in such things as tanks, heavy and anti-aircraft artillery, land mines, transport, communications, and many other things which had been found useful in modern combat. But this force represented most of the available American contribution to the defense of the vast areas and teeming millions of Greater East Asia, which we were proposing to forbid to the hard-bitten samurai of Japan.

The air people had at that time only a few obsolescent fighters and bombers in the Philippines; the Asiatic Fleet, based on Manila, was purely a scouting or minor raiding force. In 1936 the curious, glamorous, and articulate Douglas MacArthur, having ended his tour as Chief of Staff of the United States and become the first field marshal of the Philippine Commonwealth, had begun the construction of a Philippine Army. By 1946 he proposed to have the islands in such a position of defense that it would cost the Japanese "at least half a million men as casualties and upwards of five billions of dollars in money" to invade "with any hope of success." Unhappily, however, 1946 was still a long way away. MacArthur's Philippine Army existed at this time only on paper and in organizational preliminaries; and it was not until that summer of 1941 that it would begin even small-unit training.

Our prospective allies had little more than we. There was a British handful at Hong Kong, and efforts were being made to reinforce Singapore, the great naval base which was to have controlled the Far East. The effort, drawn from the desperately hard-pressed resources of the Empire, did not amount to much. The Dutch in the Netherlands East Indies possessed a small cruiser and submarine fleet and were endeavoring to mobilize an army; but owing to the fact that they had almost no airplanes or modern weapons and no way of getting them save from the nonexistent supplies in the United States, the army's military value was severely limited. And for even these tiny American, British, and Dutch forces scattered around the vast periphery of the Japanese Empire, there was no unity of command, no concerted direction, and not even a common policy. Mr. Grew's advice to "keep our powder dry and be ready—for anything" was admirable. The difficulty was that at the time we had virtually no powder, wet or dry.

IV ☞

For this discrepancy, which seems so extraordinary in retrospect, between diplomatic purpose and military means, there was one justification. One additional factor there was, incapable, perhaps, of restoring a real military balance in the western Pacific, but powerful enough to make some semblance of reason out of the Allied hopes and dispositions. That was the United States Pacific Fleet, based at Pearl Harbor. With the detachments to the Atlantic which were about to take place it would be rather markedly inferior to the massed strength of the Japanese Combined Fleet. But its powerful battle line, its cruisers and aircraft carriers, were still a mighty weapon which could be thrown upon the flank of any Japanese advance, whether to the Indies or to Siberia, with serious effect. Far from the scenes of probable action, the Pacific Fleet might be incapable of preventing such an advance, but it would add very greatly to its risks and costs. The Pacific Fleet was the core of the only real opposition with which Japan was faced. That being the case, the Japanese strategists turned to examine it with particular care.

On January 27 (it was the day Mr. Matsuoka was issuing his bellicose edict to the United States and Great Britain) Ambassador Grew's staff was encoding a message for Washington:

> A member of the embassy was told by my Peruvian colleague that from many quarters, including a Japanese one, he had heard

that a surprise mass attack on Pearl Harbor was planned by the Japanese military forces, in case of "trouble" between Japan and the United States; that the attack would involve the use of all the Japanese military forces. My colleague said that he was prompted to pass this on because it had come to him from many sources, although the plan seemed fantastic.

The dispatch was ground through the official mills. Naval Intelligence scrutinized it; it went to Admiral Harold E. Stark, Chief of Naval Operations, and Admiral Stark duly forwarded it to Admiral Kimmel, just taking over command at Pearl. But the covering message explained that Naval Intelligence placed "no credence in these rumors." Furthermore, from known data on Japanese dispositions "no move against Pearl Harbor appears imminent or planned for in the forseeable future." The dispatch was forgotten; and only after the war was over was it learned that it was, in fact, in these last days of January that Admiral Isoroku Yamamoto, commander-in-chief of the Japanese Combined Fleet, initiated the serious study of the Pearl Harbor operation.

Admiral Yamamoto was a realist, destined to fall victim in a curious way to his realism and to the ineptitude of Japanese propaganda. On the morrow of Pearl Harbor he was to warn his countrymen that the war which they had started so auspiciously was unlikely to end until Japan could write the peace treaty in the White House. This was given to the world as a declaration that the admiral intended to write the peace in the White House. That supposed boast, together with the Pearl Harbor attack, made him an object of peculiar hatred to the Americans, and later in the war they were to go to great risk and trouble to mount the special operation which shot Yamamoto down in flames near Rabaul. But all that was in the future. In January, 1941, Admiral Yamamoto observed, quite correctly, that "if we have war with the United States we will have no hope of winning unless the United States Fleet in Hawaiian waters can be destroyed." And on that realistic appraisal of the problem he proceeded.

Ambassador Grew's telegram relaying the resultant rumors was discounted partly on the ground that the secretive Japanese would never let a Peruvian diplomat know what they really intended to do. But it probably failed to make an impression for another reason—the thing was too obvious. Naval Intelligence, as a matter of fact, was correct in its estimate that no attack was imminent; beyond that, the theoretic possibility of a surprise assault on Pearl Harbor was such a standard piece of currency in military and naval thought that its reappearance in this dispatch can scarcely have aroused much attention.

For the past twenty years the Japanese had been studying the problem of how to knock out the Pearl Harbor base and the Americans had been studying the problem of its defense. Since the famous surprise torpedo attack on the Russians at Port Arthur, two generations before, it had been an accepted principle of military planning that when Japan started a war she would strike without warning or declaration. In the early '30's the possibilities opened by the rapid development of aviation had begun to be apparent. As far back as the autumn of 1935 Major General Hugh A. Drum, at that time commanding the Army garrison in Hawaii, had pointed out the extreme vulnerability of the base to air attack and had accurately outlined the danger of surprise assault by carrier-borne aircraft. A considerable (but of course inconclusive) correspondence with the War Department had ensued. In this January of 1941 the gathering war clouds and the shift of both Army and Navy commands at Oahu had brought up the whole subject again, and once more there was considerable correspondence, in the midst of which the Grew telegram must have come as just another drop in a bucket.

One did not need to be a party to Admiral Yamamoto's secret thoughts in order to know the trend of Japanese strategy. One could buy books and articles on the streets of Tokyo discussing with the greatest freedom the manner in which Japan intended to win a Pacific war. There was, for example, *The Three-Power Alliance and a United States-Japanese War*, published in the preceding fall by Kinoki Matsuo, a liaison officer between the Admiralty and the Foreign Office. Like other such works, it clearly emphasized the critical importance of destroying the United States Fleet at the outset. These stimulating essays, to be sure, did not in terms call for the destruction of the Fleet while at anchor in Pearl Harbor by surprise air attack, but the possibility might have been—and in fact was—inferred.

The authorities both in Washington and Pearl Harbor, moreover, had a recent object lesson before them. In the preceding November the British, using only one aircraft carrier equipped with obsolescent torpedo planes, had gone into Taranto harbor at night and scuppered a large fraction of the Italian Navy as it lay at its moorings. In the light of that episode, Admiral Stark instructed Admiral Richardson to initiate a resurvey of Pearl Harbor's defenses. The results, as finally embodied in a letter of January 24 from the Secretary of the Navy to the Secretary of War, were grim. In this letter (dated, interestingly enough, three days before the receipt of the Grew telegram) the Navy observed that "if war eventuates with Japan, it is believed easily possible that hostilities would be initiated by a surprise attack upon the Fleet or the Naval Base at Pearl Harbor," with "inherent possibilities of a major disaster." The dangers envisaged were "in their order of importance and probability. . . : (1) Air bombing attack. (2) Air torpedo plane attack. (3) Sabotage. (4) Submarine attack. (5) Mining. (6) Bombardment by gunfire." Against all but the first two of these menaces the base was believed to be satisfactorily protected. But in face of the first two the situation was lamentable.

While the discovery and interception of an approaching carrier-borne attack was admittedly the Navy's function, Secretary Knox's letter observed that it might not be fulfilled "in case of an air attack initiated without warning prior to a declaration of war." That would throw the burden on the Army defenses, which were totally inadequate to meet it. The Army had only 36 fighter planes on Oahu; its anti-aircraft artillery was grossly deficient in numbers and power; it had no barrage balloons or smoke protection, and its only air warning system was dependent upon sound locators, which were good only up to four miles from the base. (In 1936 the War Department had sagely concluded that no warning system would be of any use unless it could detect an enemy up to 600 miles out, and since that was an impossibility at the time, had done nothing more about it.) Mr. Knox ended upon a note of utmost urgency. He demanded the "highest priority" for fighter planes, anti-aircraft artillery, a radar warning system, and for "joint exercises" by Army and Navy to prepare the Oahu forces "for defense against surprise aircraft raids."

Mr. Stimson, serving for the second time in his long and valuable career as Secretary of War, replied on February 7 with an expression of "complete concurrence" in these views. He recognized that it was the Army's business to give "full protection" to the Fleet, but the difficulties were formidable. No barrage balloons would be available until summer. He granted that seventeen of the fighter planes at Oahu were inferior (the nineteen good ones were P-36's, already obsolete at the time even if the Army did not fully realize it), but he was rushing more out and even hoped to have 50 P-40B's ready by March. More anti-aircraft artillery was on the way. No radar sets could be delivered until June, but he hoped by that time to have everything ready for their immediate installation. (The British, as the Secretary knew, though he did not say so, had begun their radar net in 1936; more than any other single factor it had won the Battle of Britain for them, but in early 1941 radar was still more or less an esoteric mystery to American military and naval men.) The Army was doing all in its power. In relation to the actual danger it was not, unfortunately, very much.

Admiral Stark, writing to Admiral Kimmel, the new Pacific Fleet Commander, on January 13 was prophetic:

In my humble opinion we may wake up any day . . . and find ourselves in another undeclared war. . . . I have told the gang here for months past that in my opinion we were heading straight for this war, that we could not assume anything else and personally I do not see how we can avoid [it] . . . many months longer. And of course it may be a matter of weeks or days. . . . I have been moving Heaven and Earth trying to meet such a situation, and am terribly impatient at the slowness with which things move here.

Evidently, the Chief of Naval Operations was thinking primarily of the danger in the Atlantic. He explained that "of course" he did not want to get involved in the Pacific if it was possible to avoid it, but he recognized that the country might have to face a two-front war and "to put it mildly, it will be one Hell of a job."

Admiral Kimmel, surveying the state of his new command and of its base defenses, could hardly have disagreed with that estimate. In view of what happened, the selection of this officer from well down on the admirals' list for the Navy's biggest and most critical field command was to be a subject of much subsequent innuendo and controversy. He was, however, one of four or five men whom Admiral Richardson had himself suggested, on an earlier occasion, as possible successors; the appointment, as the Chief of Naval Operations assured Kimmel, had "the overwhelming approval of the service," and there seem to have been no doubts at the time of "Mustapha" Kimmel's competence for the post. He now plunged with energy into its problems. In a confidential letter to his commanders on February 4, he emphasized the admirable principle that "current readiness plans . . . cannot be based on any . . . expectation . . . of improved conditions. Such plans must be based only on hard fact. They must be so developed as to provide for *immediate* action, based on materials and facilities that are *now* available." Meanwhile, however, his own first answering letter to "Betty" Stark began with an earnest complaint against the inadequacy of the Army's air defenses.

Admiral Stark took the complaint to his Army colleague, General George C. Marshall, the Chief of Staff. General Marshall, writing on his part to Lieutenant General Short on the latter's assumption of the Army command at Oahu, showed himself fully alive to the situation. The Chief of Staff's "impression of the Hawaiian problem" was that "if no serious harm is done us during the first six hours of known hostilities, thereafter the existing defenses would discourage an enemy against the hazard of an attack." The "real perils of the situation" lay in sabotage and in the risk of a surprise raid by air or submarine. General Marshall was aware that the Army's first duty in Hawaii was the protection of the Fleet, and he was conscious of the deficiencies in fighter planes and anti-aircraft guns. But, as he was forced to explain:

> What Kimmel does not realize is that we are tragically lacking in this matériel throughout the Army and that Hawaii is on a far better basis than any other command in the Army.
>
> The fullest protection for the Fleet is *the* rather than a major consideration for us, there can be little question about that; but the Navy itself makes demands on us for commands other than Hawaii, which make it difficult for us to meet the requirements of Hawaii. . . . You should make clear to Admiral Kimmel that we are doing everything that is humanly possible to build up the Army defenses of the Naval overseas installations, but we cannot perform a miracle.

Even the Navy could not always perform one itself. With Taranto vividly in mind, the Chief of Naval Operations on February 11 ordered the Bureau of Ordnance to develop torpedo nets for the protection of vessels anchored in harbor; "urgent" letters were sent on three subsequent occasions, but nine months later the nets had failed to materialize and this comparatively simple and obvious form of defense was lacking in the hour of crisis.

Miracles were to come hard and slowly all through that strenuous spring and summer and fall. But nobody seems to have doubted the desperate need for them. The fact was that by late January and early February all the responsible officers and officials plainly recognized, at any rate in theory, the nature of the Pacific strategic problem and the vital importance of the Fleet and of Pearl Harbor, which were the keys to the whole equation. The sources of the ultimate disaster are not to be found in any failure of theory; they lay in the inability to translate theory, at the moment of crisis, into effective action. Even General Marshall, in his letter to Short, was concerned about the "Japanese carrier-based pursuit plane." Between Admiral Yamamoto, already planning the destruction of the American Fleet at Pearl Harbor, and the Americans, frantically trying to scrape together the essentials for its defense while they were also trying to equip the nation for the larger crisis which impended, there was no great gap in the basic appreciation of the strategic problem of the Pacific.

TWO

MR. MATSUOKA'S ODYSSEY

I ☞

Even as our commanders were exchanging these harassed communications, something like a real war scare was developing in the Southwest Pacific to lend them a grimmer urgency. In the latter part of January Japanese naval forces were discovered to be active in the waters off southern Indo-China, the sensitive area directly threatening the British in Malaya and at Singapore and the Dutch in the Netherlands Indies. Japanese men-of-war were reported at Saigon, the principal port of southern Indo-China; in Camranh Bay, the magnificent natural harbor near by, which had long been regarded as a naval base site potentially rivaling Singapore itself; and even beyond Cape Cambodia in the Gulf of Siam. The pretext soon appeared. For some time an obscure and undeclared frontier war had been in progress along the jungle border between Siam and Indo-China, as the Thais sought to enforce old territorial claims against the now helpless pro-consuls of Vichy France. With a significantly imperial gesture, Japan was intervening in this fracas. On January 31 a dispatch from Saigon announced the conclusion of a Franco-Siamese armistice. It had been drafted by Japanese mediators and signed on board the Japanese light cruiser *Natori* *; the final peace, it provided, was to be negotiated in Tokyo.

* *Natori* was sunk off Samar on August 18, 1944, by an American submarine.

It cannot be said that this news made any great impression on the American public. Conveyed for the most part in brief telegrams on the far inside pages, it was well buried under the rising bitterness of the lend-lease debate, under the British advance on Bengasi in North Africa, the misadventures of Mussolini's luckless soldiery in Greece, the drama of Mr.

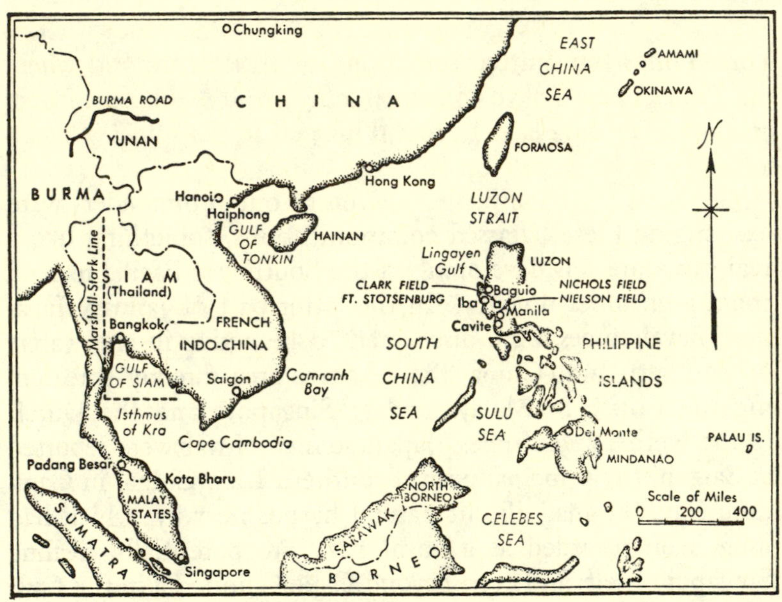

THE SOUTHWEST PACIFIC

Wendell Willkie's visit to bomb-wracked Britain. But in the Far East, still quivering to Mr. Matsuoka's imperious edict of a few days before, the effect was very different. It was not only that Japan was achieving an ostentatious prestige victory in this critical new territory. A flood of rumors suggested that as a price of her peace-making she would demand bases and the right to maintain garrisons in southern Indo-China and Siam; that the move was in response to direct German pressure and heralded Japan's entry into the European War. The British governor at Singapore issued a public warning that war might be imminent. The Netherlands Government (in exile in London) formally repudiated Mr. Matsuoka's intimation that the Netherlands East Indies must become a part of the "co-prosperity sphere." The British began to mine Singapore harbor, to deploy what troops they had along the Malaya-Siamese frontier, and to redouble their efforts to get something approximating air power into Malaya. On Sunday, February 2, a front-page dispatch from Shanghai to the *New York Times* transmitted something of this alarm; and when the *Times*'s new Tokyo correspondent, Mr. Tolischus, reached his post a few days later he found himself in the midst of what seemed a genuine war crisis.

The reaction among American officialdom appears to have been a good deal less excited. Ambassador Grew felt that while the Japanese were obviously continuing their "nibbling" policy and getting into position for a stroke at Singapore, they were not yet ready to deliver it and probably did not plan to do so until the Germans had made good with their invasion of Britain. Admiral Stark, in an estimate drawn up for the President, saw "no present reason for alarm." His intelligence indicated that the Japanese army forces known to be assembling in Formosa and Hainan (the large Chinese island which closes the Gulf of Tonkin) were still "insufficient for occupying Indo-China and Thailand, for attacking Singapore, and for keeping an expeditionary force ready to use against the Philippines. So far as I can tell, an insufficient number of transports is assembled for a major move."

But London was sounding the tocsin with the utmost urgency. It was known that the Germans were in fact putting heavy pressure on Japan for an attack upon Malaya. On February 11, Lord Halifax, the new British ambassador, was at the State Department with a British staff appreciation urging the basing of American naval forces at Singapore, and he was adding his own earnest hope that the United States would "feel able to take some effective action in the very near future to deter the Japanese." On the 13th there was a sensational public alarm from Sydney. In a joint statement the Acting Prime Minister of Australia and the leader of the Opposition declared that "the war has moved into a new stage involving the utmost gravity"; the Australian War Cabinet was summoned to meet with the military heads and the British commander at Singapore flew in to join the conference. Chinese sources poured in rumors of massing Japanese battle fleets and air forces, and this time the crisis hit even American front pages, with something of a bang.

Two days later, on the 15th, there came a personal message for the President from Prime Minister Churchill, speaking of the "awful weakening" of the British position which would result if Japan moved. "Whatever you can do to instill into the Japanese anxiety as to a double war may succeed in averting this danger. Nevertheless, should we alone be attacked it would be difficult to overstate the grave character of the consequences." Mr. Roosevelt had already shown himself sufficiently adventurous in plans for "deterring" the Japanese. But at a moment when the lend-lease bill was coming under heavy isolationist assault as a device for getting the United States into Britain's war, so careful a politician as the President was unlikely to entertain proposals for putting American men-of-war into a British base. Mr. Roosevelt did revive another idea with which both he and his truculent Secretary of State had been toying. This was to dispatch a small additional cruiser and destroyer force on a "temporary" but admonitory visit to the Philippines. The notion was curiously reminiscent of the elder Roosevelt's gesture with the world cruise of 1908; unfortunately, however, we were a long way from 1908 by that time. Even so, Admiral Stark had to labor earnestly (and with private exasperation) in order to demonstrate to his commander-in-chief the reckless folly of such a move under the dire conditions of 1941; but eventually he succeeded and the plan was laid aside.

As a matter of fact, it is possible that Mr. Churchill was less alarmed over the immediate danger than he seemed to be.

After all, he must have known quite as much as did our own Naval Intelligence about the Japanese dispositions; but he may have discerned here a useful opportunity to mount a "war of nerves." Throughout, the Prime Minister appears to have put a somewhat higher value than the President did upon the possibility of intimidating Japan. A war scare now might impress Tokyo; it might also (and one cannot wholly overlook this possible consideration) impress Washington. It was of the utmost importance to ensure that the United States would fight in case the Japanese moved only against the British or Dutch. In retrospect it is only fair to say that such a commitment was patently necessary in the interests of all, for the great peril to all—to the Americans as well as the Dutch and British—was that Japan would take them in detail, just as the Nazis had taken western Europe. If Mr. Churchill was doing a little missionary work in Washington, he was doing it for our good as well as his own. But it was obviously the British for whom the peril was greatest and who were in most urgent need of a common strategy and a united front.

President Roosevelt, who had already analyzed the situation in much the same terms, could not risk a specific commitment, but he was willing to do whatever could be done by words and gestures. He had already told his press conference (on February 11) that if war should come with Japan it would not diminish the flow of aid to Britain. Secretary Hull was seen significantly in conference with the Australian and Netherlands ministers. The War Department peremptorily ordered home the wives and families of American Army personnel in the Philippines, and on the day of the Australian *demarche*, American consuls throughout the Far East were circularizing all American citizens in their areas, repeating the State Department's urgent advice that all who could should evacuate. MacArthur's embryo Philippine Army announced large-scale "training" maneuvers to be held at an early date. Even the Congress responded to the tensions in the air. Some years before it had refused, in a celebrated episode, to grant the

Navy some five million dollars it had asked for certain dredging work at Guam, requested as a preliminary to the possible conversion of the island into a naval base. The Congress had felt at the time that this would be unduly provocative of the Japanese. Now the House passed, on February 19, with but one dissenting vote, a bill authorizing $245,000,000 for the expansion of naval bases, including authorizations for Guam and Samoa.

More important than any of this perhaps was the closely guarded fact that since January 29 a group of high American and British military, naval, and air officers had been sitting down in Washington to "determine the best methods by which the armed forces of the United States and British Commonwealth, with its present allies, could defeat Germany and the powers allied with her, should the United States be compelled to resort to war." These staff conversations were not to be completed for some weeks more, and they were not primarily concerned with the Far East. But the Far Eastern problem forced itself upon the attention of the conferees; and this was, in fact, the tentative beginning of a common strategy in the East as well as in the West. Presumably, the Japanese knew nothing about these staff conferences. But the other evidences were enough to make it apparent to them that mere bluff would not work. Mr. Matsuoka began to back water.

Indeed, for some time the Foreign Minister had been more and more volubly "explaining" his policy. As early as February 5 he had told the Diet that a rupture between Japan and the United States must be avoided if humanly possible. He made it clear that the Tri-Partite Pact was intended only to help Germany defeat the British; the Germans did not want the United States brought into the war, and the unfortunate American reactions were unforseen and all due to "misunderstandings." Lesser Cabinet ministers were assuring the Dutch that while the Netherlands East Indies must be brought into at least a loose economic federation with "Greater East Asia,"

Japan's aims were not political. Japan was resolved to have equal access to the raw materials of the Netherlands Indies (that meant oil, the one vital strategic material in which Japan was almost totally lacking) and would "leave nothing undone toward this end." But her methods would be peaceable, and the trade negotiations which had been undertaken at Batavia would be resumed.

When Mr. Matsuoka opened the Siam-Indo-China peace conference at Tokyo on the 7th, he seemed satisfied with this first triumph of the "southward" policy. There were no demands for brokerage fees in the form of bases. And a few days later, when the Foreign Minister received Mr. Tolischus and two other American correspondents in a private conference, he startled them, not only by outlining a large, vague proposal for peace in China, but also by stating that there was nothing in the Tri-Partite Pact which would require Japan to go to war in the Pacific. "I told the Germans so and they accepted my interpretation. We'll decide for ourselves what we are going to do."

Next day, when Mr. Tolischus tried to send this very interesting piece of information, he ran into censor trouble. But the Foreign Minister's vanity and volubility led him into a blunder which served much the same purpose as the dispatch might have done. On February 18 his Foreign Office spokesman, Mr. Koh Ishii, emphasizing Japan's peaceful purposes as exemplified in her mediation of the Siam-Indo-China war, intimated that Japan would be glad to act similarly as mediator in the war in Europe. The explosion was immediate; and before Mr. Matsuoka had time to disavow his spokesman, the British Under Secretary of Foreign Affairs blandly announced to the House of Commons that the same suggestion had been conveyed by Mr. Matsuoka himself in a "special message" to Foreign Secretary Eden, couched in "courteous terms." The Germans were naturally thrown into a paroxysm of rage at the idea that their ally was assuming a neutral position in the conflict; while the notion of Japan acting as mediator in the world struggle struck western publics as the acme of the preposterous. Mr. Matsuoka erupted more "explanations," denials, and retractions; but the absurdity had broken the tension. On February 20, only five days after Mr. Churchill's urgent appeal to the President, the Prime Minister sent off another message:

> Have received better news concerning Japan. It seems Jap foreign minister is shortly going to Moscow, Berlin, and Rome for the purpose of covering the failure of action against us. The fear of the United States appears to have postponed attack, which seemed imminent. While completely understanding your situation pending enactment of bill on which our hopes depend, the more their fears can be aroused, the better.

How "imminent" the attack had really been, and how far "fear of the United States" had actually served to postpone it, may today be open to question. But no one can question the shrewdness of the Prime Minister. At all events, the crisis was over, while the lend-lease bill, with the assistance of Mr. Willkie, who had cut short his trip to Britain to hurry home and testify in its behalf, was working slowly toward passage. In Tokyo, in the first days of March, it took a show of the iron fist to force the unhappy French to sign the Siamese peace treaty, but this was accomplished, and on March 11 Mr. Matsuoka presided in a blaze of glory at the final session of the Franco-Siamese peace conference. "The ceremony was staged in the pretentious main hall of the Premier's official residence—a vast, vaulted, and rather bare room in the style of the Imperial Hotel." Mr. Matsuoka, eminently pleased with himself, took the occasion to make official announcement of his forthcoming pilgrimage to Europe.

It was also on March 11 that President Roosevelt affixed his signature to "H.R. 1776" and the lend-lease act was added to the statute books. The battle had been long; it had often been bitter; it had forced a deep searching of many American hearts. But there could be no doubt about the verdict. The bill had passed by 260 to 165 in the House (on the original vote) and by 60 to 31 in the Senate. The House accepted the Senate version by 317 to 71. American policy had been declared, if not unanimously, at any rate by substantial majorities which were supported, from all evidences, by even more substantial majorities among the people. The immense economic, if not the military, power of the United States had been thrown fully into the scales of battle. American neutrality, if it had ever existed, was at an end.

Next day Mr. Matsuoka was taking his departure for the West. He was received by the Emperor and Empress; he prayed to the Sun Goddess for success; at the railway station in the evening Prince Konoye and the whole Cabinet were on hand to shout "Banzai's" after him as the train pulled out. "I am going," he declared, "to explain Hakko Ichiu to the leaders of Germany and Italy and to tighten Axis co-operation toward a lasting peace and a new world order." At any rate, nothing very much could happen until he got back.

So ended the February war scare. Japan had not after all appropriated southern Indo-China or Siam. She had, however, won a prestige victory of serious implications and had established a further diplomatic foothold from which the "southward advance" could later be resumed. What she had lost was less apparent, but perhaps she had lost something. She had thoroughly alarmed the British, the Dutch, and the Americans in the Far East, and she had alarmed official Washington, even if she had not yet aroused the American public. She had awakened many to the appalling deficiencies of the Far Eastern defenses, and had started troops and weapons and planes, even if in wretchedly inadequate numbers, toward the areas she was threatening. And she had helped to promote the first serious moves toward unity of command and strategic direction among the democratic powers. In Washington the Anglo-American staff conferences were progressing. On February 25 "Betty" Stark, writing to "Mustapha" Kimmel at Pearl Harbor, observed:

Our staff conversations (and thank the Good Lord there has been little or no public leak that they are taking place) are nearing their conclusion and we hope will be finished in about ten days.

Actually, it was to take somewhat longer. But if Mr. Churchill had encouraged the war scare, it was not entirely in vain.

II ☞

Mr. Matsuoka's thoughts as he trundled westward over the endless leagues of the Trans-Siberian are not, so far as is known, on record. But it is apparent that the basic patterns had been established beyond possibility of reversal. Out of Japan's political and economic problems, out of years of agitation, out of the subtle interplay of purpose and ambition among the soldiers, sailors, big business magnates, and feudal politicians who ruled the destinies of the Meiji Empire, there had crystallized the fundamental resolve to seize once and for all the hegemony of eastern Asia and the western Pacific. The opportunity afforded by the second World War was unlikely to recur. It must be exploited to eject the western powers from the Far East, to free Japan from their irritatingly superior dominance, to appropriate the enormous riches in raw materials, manpower, and markets with which Japan was surrounded and which would really make her an impregnable military and economic power, beyond challenge in the Far East and actually able, perhaps, to assert her authority throughout the "eight corners of the world."

The patterns had been established; the armies were being massed and trained; the secret military and naval plans were being drawn to meet all contingencies; the people were being mobilized to support the supreme effort. What remained were largely questions of method—and of timing. These were, however, of an anxious character. One of the thorniest of them, to be sure, had apparently been answered by events. That was the issue, over which Japanese Army and Navy strategists had wrangled for years, between the "northward advance" into Siberia or the "southward advance" into the Anglo-American-Dutch tropics. The "Stalinazi pact" of 1939, now confirmed by the Tri-Partite Pact, had settled that one. Japanese spokesmen talked early in 1941 as though the "southward advance" were the accepted policy, assumed by all. It still presented difficult problems, for it was easier to see an opportunity than to know just how it could be successfully exploited. How far could diplomacy carry them, and at what point would they have to rely on war? Could they risk the "southward advance" without a firm guarantee from Russia to secure their rear? Could they risk an attack on Britain's eastern possessions before Hitler had made good his promise to invade Britain? On the other hand, could they risk waiting so long? The Japanese knew well enough that a triumphant Hitler was unlikely to show much respect either for Hakko Ichiu or for the Greater East Asia Co-Prosperity Sphere—unless Japan were firmly entrenched within the latter well ahead of time.

It was the answers for some of these questions which Mr. Matsuoka had set forth to find. But there were others, of a more strictly military nature. Could the Japanese risk singling out British Malaya for the initial spring, or would they have to make it a simultaneous attack upon both Britain and the United States? The advantages of the first were obvious; the perils of the second course were formidable. But in an operation against Malaya alone, they would have the United States Pacific Fleet as a constant threat on their flank and rear. The Philippines stood directly athwart the southward road, affording advance air, submarine, and fleet bases from which this threat might materialize at any moment. Could they leave the United States free to prepare at leisure and then choose the moment which would be most disadvantageous to Japan?

In February and early March the Germans had been urging

them on to Singapore, but making it clear (Matsuoka was quite truthful in this) that they wanted the Americans left out of it. Lieutenant General Hiroshi Oshima, arriving to replace Mr. Kurusu as ambassador to Berlin, was given a thorough indoctrination. There was a memorandum from Grand-Admiral Erich Raeder, commander of the German Navy, demanding that the Japanese get on with the business, with no more haggling about a German invasion of Britain. On February 23 Foreign Minister Von Ribbentrop himself had a long interview with the new ambassador, in which the latter was taken into a high place and deftly shown all the riches of empire—provided that Japan got in on the winning side while the getting was good. Japan need not worry about the British. To be sure, the invasion had been held up by the winter's bad weather, but "the landing is prepared" (in fact, as we now know, it had been abandoned weeks before) and "England's situation would take catastrophic shape overnight." The ambassador was assured that "every eventuality had been provided for; the war has been won today militarily, economically, and politically," and Britain would "soon" be forced to sue for peace. Japan "in its own interest" should get into the war at once.

Von Ribbentrop explained, however, that Germany had "an interest in keeping America out of the war." Japan should confine herself to Singapore. The Foreign Minister dissipated any notion that the Americans might react to such an operation. The United States "could not wage the war militarily at all" across the vast ocean distances; indeed, one of the arguments for a Japanese surprise attack on Malaya was that it was "bound" to keep the United States out of the conflict. "America, which at present is not armed as yet and would hesitate greatly to expose her Navy to any risks west of Hawaii, could do this even less so in such a case." Provided Japan kept her hands off American interests, "it was very unlikely that America would declare war if it would then have to stand by helplessly while Japan takes the Philippines." Even Roosevelt couldn't make war plausible under those conditions; while the American people already "felt instinctively" that they were being drawn toward war "for no reason, by Roosevelt and the Jewish wire-pullers." The isolationist oratory flowing at that moment in the lend-lease debate at Washington may have seemed to substantiate this estimate; and at all events, Ambassador Oshima agreed enthusiastically to everything the Foreign Minister said. A few days later Von Ribbentrop was again arguing the ease of an attack on Singapore, and assuring Oshima that if the Japanese still had any doubts, the Fuehrer himself would be glad to help them plan the operation.

But despite this offer of such eminent assistance, the Japanese evidently did have their doubts. The Americans might not, after all, stay out; and Admiral Yamamoto had concluded that there would be no hope of winning a war with the United States unless the Pacific Fleet could be destroyed. The best chance of doing so was to take it by surprise at the beginning. The Japanese had sound military reason for taking the boldest possible view of their problem. In all the enormous reaches of the Pacific world, the American Fleet was the one really powerful force which they had to fear. To destroy it at the outset; in the respite thus gained to seize the raw materials of Southeast Asia and the Indies; to seize and consolidate the strategic island chains holding the approaches to Japan; in this way to build a military position so impregnable to counterattack that the West, with all its enormous material superiority, would never deliver that counterattack—this was the one plan which made military sense out of the otherwise preposterous ambitions of the Japanese. And it was their own ambition rather than the convenience of the Nazis which they were consulting.

Consequently, it would have to be all or nothing unless—and this was the one alternative—Japan could first reach a diplomatic settlement with the United States sufficiently sweeping to permit the "peaceful" development of "Greater East Asia" without fear of American intervention. If the diplomats could manage that, the soldiers and sailors would be saved the serious risks, which they were otherwise prepared to take, of an American as well as a Chinese, a British, and a Dutch war. An interesting result of this situation, which was seemingly not fully appreciated by the western powers, was that every American gesture toward "deterring" Japan, every added evidence of Anglo-American solidarity in the East, every reinforcement for the Philippines, could only tend to confirm the Japanese military in the conclusion that the United States would have to be included in the initial assault —and that the assault would have to be made soon, before our strength was built up in the western Pacific.

Whatever the Japanese politicians may actually have known about the military and naval war plans (and they seem to have been told nothing about the details), the practical result was the adoption of a dual policy. While the military went ahead developing the Pearl Harbor operation and training for the descent upon the Philippines and Malaya, the diplomats addressed themselves to discovering what chance there was of a basic settlement with the United States. While the bellicose army general, Oshima, replaced Kurusu at Berlin, a very different type of representative was chosen to succeed Horinouchi at Washington. Admiral Kichisaburo Nomura was a "liberal" and a moderate, a man of real statesmanship who was to work with patent sincerity to avert a war. Unusually tall for a Japanese, with a heavy face and frame and a taste for horn-rimmed spectacles, he resembled a slightly harassed American business man much more than a warrior samurai. He had been a naval attaché at Washington during the first World War; he had acquired at that time a good knowledge of the United States, an understanding of the western outlook, and a personal acquaintance with the then Assistant Secretary of the Navy, Mr. Franklin D. Roosevelt. He had close contacts with Stark and other of our higher naval officers. Admiral Nomura landed at San Francisco on Februray 6, just as the war crisis was rising toward its height, "radiating confidence in peace." There was, he told the reporters, "no question whatsoever outstanding between the two countries which cannot be settled in an amicable and satisfactory manner through a timely display of statesmanship by the responsible people of both sides."

Admiral Nomura continued, discreetly, to radiate confidence in peace. On February 19 he received half a hundred newspapermen in the ballroom of the Japanese embassy. He answered questions for three-quarters of an hour; he was "affable and cordial," pacific and evasive. "He was convinced that Japan could expand southward economically without becoming involved in war with the United States." On March 8, as the echoes of the Pacific war scare were already dying away under much more interesting and ominous news from the Balkans, he had his first extended interview with Secretary Hull. A long, a tortuous and exhaustive process of secret negotiation was thus begun.

Secretary Hull later testified that the negotiations with Nomura were undertaken in the light of the "advice of our highest military authorities, who kept emphasizing to us the imperative need of having time to build up preparations for defense." The need was indisputable. We had come within sight of a Pacific war in the preceding weeks; and Mr. Hull, in the light of Japan's declared policies and past record, estimated the chances of ultimately reaching a peaceful settlement at no better than "1 in 50 or even 1 in 100." In this first conversation the essential irreconcilability of the two national policies was to be clearly defined. Mr. Hull bluntly enquired whether Japan could possibly expect the United States "to sit absolutely quiet while two or three nations before our very eyes organized naval and military forces and went out and conquered the balance of the earth." What could the United States gain by remaining complacent before such a process? In answer, the ambassador sought to "minimize" the idea that his government contemplated military conquest; what really troubled Japan were the export embargoes the United States had begun to impose. The ambassador did not "believe" that his government would make any further military moves unless it were forced to do so by American economic pressure. That made matters plain enough. The American position was that Japan must halt or sanctions would be applied against her. The Japanese position was that if sanctions were applied, Japan would be compelled to go forward in self-defense. Under the circumstances it was high time to ask what sanctions this country had available to exert.

In the spring of 1941, the American Army and Navy were bending all of their harrassed energies to preparing for war. Few people realized how completely this disqualified them for fighting one. It was a perhaps natural assumption that the more fiercely the preparations were pushed forward, the more ready we became. The assumption was mistaken. It was equivalent to concluding that because a house was swarming with painters, plumbers, and redecorators it would be so much better prepared for a formal dinner party later in the day. The truth is that throughout 1941 the American military establishment was to a large extent closed for alterations. In the feverish effort to build more ships and provide trained crews for them there was little chance to bring the ships we had to a high pitch of combat efficiency. Amid all the appalling problems of raising, arming, and training an army of millions, it was difficult to provide the few thousands whom we had stationed in the menaced outposts with the strength and weapons which they needed. And much of what did become available had to be drained off through lend-lease to arm those who were doing the actual fighting.

In the latter part of February the Senate Foreign Relations Committee was told that the strength of the Army Air Force amounted to about 4,000 planes; unfortunately, something over half of these were trainers, while the number of the combat types which were obsolete was not explained. Of the production between February 1 and December 1, nearly 2,000 of the various bomber types alone were to go in lend-lease. The Army ground forces had now reached about 867,000 men; but it was not until late summer that the ground forces could be organized into a normal pattern of corps and field armies and large-scale field maneuvers could begin. As for weapons, Secretary Stimson explained to a press conference at the end of February that "we are still in the tooling-up stage." There had been no deliveries at all of the important new 90-mm. and 105-mm. guns, the contracts for which had been let "only" in the preceding summer. A newspaper article, granting that there were as yet no more than some 425 modern tanks in the United States, spoke enthusiastically about the coming production. Light tanks (a type which subsequently turned out to be of little value) would be "rolling off the assembly lines" in another couple of months, while by July or August the great Chrysler tank arsenal should be completing its first mediums.

When Colonel Lindbergh, appearing before the Foreign Relations Committee to oppose the lend-lease bill and to plead for a "negotiated" peace, had gloomily declared that the combined productive capacities of Great Britian and America could not build up an air force in Britain equal to that of the Germans, nobody, fortunately, had believed him. They might have done so had the public known how little had actually been accomplished up to that time. In mid-February a giant bomber of weird appearance and powered by four engines, "the first of 26 built by Consolidated Aircraft Corporation for Great Britain," arrived in New York on its way across the Atlantic. It was "designated merely as B-24." Thus did the Liberator, destined to become the work-horse of global warfare, make its public appearance. The newspapers printed pictures of an odd but powerful-looking little contraption, described as one of the first of the Army's new "midget reconnaissance trucks." The world-famous jeep had been born; but it was to be months before it received its name.

Amid the inordinate problems of rearmament, some efforts were being made to reinforce the Far East, and two squadrons of fighter planes were started toward Manila around the end of February. But admittedly that was only a drop in the bucket. The Philippines would have to wait. The critical need was at Pearl Harbor. That was the key; and that had to come first. "Thank God for Sundays," Admiral Stark exclaimed in a letter to Admiral Kimmel, adopting a phrase that neither man was ever likely to use again after December 7. "It is my only day for quiet study and work, and even then I have to kick somebody out of the office!" There was such an immense amount of work to be done, and so little time and so little means with which to do it. And there was so little certainty about the future. On February 25 the Chief of Naval Operations was again writing to the commander at Pearl:

> The difficulty is that the entire country is in a dozen minds about the war—to stay out altogether, to go in against Germany in the Atlantic, to concentrate against Japan in the Pacific and the Far East—I simply cannot predict the outcome. Gallup polls, editorials, talk on the Hill (and, I might add, all of which is irresponsible) constitutes a rising tide for action in the Far East if the Japanese go into Singapore or the Netherlands East Indies. This cannot be ignored, and we must have in the back of our heads the possibility that we may have to swing to that tide. If it should prevail against Navy Department recommendations, you would have to implement Rainbow III.

The possibility that the tide of war might swing to us, regardless of even Navy Department recommendations, had not as yet fully penetrated the American consciousness. But they were all very much concerned about the theoretic possibilities, at least, of surprise at Pearl Harbor. Admiral Kimmel, in a letter of February 18, was "delighted" to learn that Army fighter planes were on the way, and demanded bombers and anti-aircraft guns as well. "I feel," he declared, "that a surprise attack (submarine, air, or combined) on Pearl Harbor is a possibility." Next day Lieutenant General Short was writing to his own chief that "the following are of great importance . . . (1) Co-operation with the Navy; (2) Dispersion and protection of aircraft and of repair, maintenance and servicing of aircraft; (3) Improvement of anti-aircraft defense. . . ." Short was no less alarmed than his naval colleague over the state of affairs he had found in his new command; the Navy, for its part, found Short "highly co-operative" (Admiral Kimmel had gone so far as to have "a couple of interviews" with him) and fully alive to the situation.

Not all of the difficulties were those of co-operation between the services; there were internal problems as well. In one of Kimmel's letters there was a somewhat plaintive footnote about secret information. He gathered that Naval Intelligence considered it the function of Operations to supply him with secret data, and that Operations considered this responsibility to lie with Intelligence. Kimmel wasn't sure that he had missed anything important, but he would like the matter cleared up. It was, a week or two later, with a lordly note from Intelligence announcing that it was "fully aware" of its responsibility to keep the commander informed of whatever it was good for him to know. That, unfortunately, appears to have ended the matter.

But the main concern on all sides was the peril of surprise air attack. On March 5 the Chief of Staff, General Marshall, followed up his previous warnings with a demand upon Short for an "early review" of the entire air defense position in Hawaii. General Short showed that he was under no misapprehension as to the problem. He had already written that an adequate aircraft warning service was the most urgent need. A radar warning system, capable of detecting hostile planes at something more than the five-mile range of the sound locators, was "vital to the defense of these islands." Protection of the base and fleet was "so dependent upon the early completion of this Aircraft Warning Service that I believe all quibbling over details should be stopped at once." General Marshall understood the pressing nature of the need and applauded Short's "gratifying" energy in trying to get it filled.

But there were difficulties here, too. On March 15 the Chief of Staff explained to Short:

> It will be necessary to comply with certain fixed regulations in those cases where [radar] facilities are to be established on lands pertaining to the Secretary of the Interior. The National Park Service officials are willing to give us the temporary use of their lands when other lands are not suitable for the purpose, but they will not waive the requirements as to submission of preliminary building plans showing the architecture and general appearance. They are also very definitely opposed to permitting structures of any type to be erected at such places as will be open to view and materially alter the natural appearance of the reservation.

When this now almost incredible letter was written, we were less than nine months away from global war in time. In psychology, we were obviously much farther away than that. "Quibbling over details" was not so easily ended. Secretary Stimson had hoped to have the radar warning service installed by June. Actually, the fixed radar sets had not been erected by December; and while some mobile sets of lesser range were in operation, the warning service as a whole was far from complete.

General Short's prophetic anxieties did not stop with the warning system. He was worried by the "vulnerability of both Army and Navy airfields" to sudden air attack. "On all fields the planes had been kept lined up on the field where they would suffer terrific loss. . . . In no case have the arrangements been completed for the dispersion of planes . . . or the precaution of bunkers to protect them." But to provide against such contingencies called for money and manpower, neither of which was readily available. General Short poured in his requests for money; he got very little in return and there were delays and difficulties in using what he did get. To achieve practical results on the ground was a hard, slow problem. To draw the theoretical plans, however, was much simpler; after all, the Army (and to a lesser extent the Navy) had been trained through twenty years of penurious peace to the conduct of paper warfare and the waging of purely "constructive" battle. In March General Short, lacking the actual tools of defense, was active in preparing the paper ramparts against emergency.

A series of Army-Navy agreements were drawn up, over the signatures of all the too numerous high officers involved in the far too complex chains of command to which the key to the Pacific had been entrusted. Admiral Kimmel commanded the Pacific Fleet; General Short commanded the garrison responsible for the defense of its base. That much was simple. But the base itself was commanded by another officer, Rear Admiral Claude C. Bloch, who was responsible in part to Kimmel and in part directly to the Navy Department, and over whom General Short had no control whatever. To make the situation no easier, Bloch, though subordinate to and temporarily outranked by Kimmel in virtue of the latter's command of the Fleet, was actually Kimmel's senior and had formerly commanded the Pacific Fleet himself. But this was only the beginning. One part of what defensive aviation they had was under General Short's air commander, Major General Frederick L. Martin. Another part, including the long-range PBY seaplanes—of vital importance because they were the only thing available capable of distant patrol—belonged to the Navy and was under Rear Admiral P. N. L. Bellinger.

Admiral Bellinger suffered from a really classic case of split official personality. He was the commander of the Naval Base Defense Air Force, which normally "did not exist." He was commander of the PBY's, organized in "Patwings" (Patrol Wings) 1 and 2. In these two capacities Bloch had at least a partial lien over him. But he was also Kimmel's Fleet Air Wing Commander; and though Kimmel had to share him with the base command at San Diego, both Bellinger and his PBY's really belonged to Kimmel. Kimmel had many uses for both other than the pedestrian one of looking after the security of the base, which was really the Army's business, anyway. But though Bellinger (according to the subsequent analysis by the Army Pearl Harbor Board) was actually responsible to no less than five different superior authorities, the Army was not one of them and had no say at all concerning the activities of this officer, who was obviously of key importance to the defense of the base. All the Army could do was to "co-operate"—provided that it could discover, amid the splendid confusion of the naval command system, the point at which to do the co-operating. As the Army Board later observed:

> In this [naval] organization, in which there were two governing heads, Admirals Kimmel and Bloch, with whom General Short had to do business, and their respective staffs with whom Short's staff had to deal, as well as the many-titled Admiral Bellinger with whom General Martin dealt, the problem of co-operation was made somewhat difficult.

Considering that the air danger was recognized on all sides as the most critical, and that none of the various forces involved—neither Fleet, the base, nor the Army—alone possessed anything like sufficient means to meet it, the situation was particularly unfortunate. The theory that a base should be powerfully defended out of its own resources, thus leaving the Fleet free to concentrate on higher things, was no doubt militarily sound. But where the powerful defenses were wanting, it obviously had its perils. The only hope of repelling the surprise attack about which they were so much concerned lay in the closest possible integration and maximum utilization of every available resource, no matter to whom it belonged. The treaties which were now drawn up between the various military and naval powers in Hawaii clearly fell something short of achieving this.

They were numerous and exhaustive. Perhaps the basic document was an agreement reached by Bloch and Short on March 20. This briefly provided that in any attack upon approaching enemy vessels, the Navy would assume tactical command, borrowing bombers as needed from the Army. In the repulse of an enemy air attack over or near Oahu, the

Army would assume tactical command, borrowing a "maximum" of fighter planes from the Navy. On March 31 this simple division of labor was elaborated in a much lengthier "estimate" signed by Bellinger and Martin. The two air commanders quite accurately observed that "in the past Orange [Japan] has never preceded hostile actions by a declaration of war," that "an Orange fast raiding force might arrive in Hawaiian waters with no prior warning from our Intelligence service," and that "the most likely and dangerous form of attack on Oahu would be air attack" probably launched from several carriers approaching within 300 miles of the islands. If made at dawn, there would be "a high probability that it could be delivered as a complete surprise . . . and that it might find us in a condition of readiness under which pursuit would be slow to start." To meet the difficult problem thus presented, the Army would be responsible for an Air Combat Group, which would take in all available fighters and devote itself to interception over the islands; while Bellinger's Base Defense Air Force, collecting whatever it could from the Army, would form a Search and Attack Group to discover or track down the hostile carriers.

On April 11 the whole thing was wrapped up in a really full-dress Joint Coastal Frontier Defense Plan, again signed by Bloch and Short. There were pages of this, going into great detail, and adding the further principle that the Navy would be responsible for "off-shore patrol" and "distant reconnaissance" while the Army would be responsible for an aircraft warning service. The plan as a whole had numerous defects, among them being the fact that at the time it was drawn up the Navy had virtually no means of conducting distant reconnaissance and no fighters to lend to the Army's combat group, while the Army had no aircraft warning system and no bombers that were worth anything to lend to the Navy's attack group. The defensive air forces for which it provided were afterward expressively described by Admiral Bloch as a kind of "volunteer fire department." All the planes involved were normally engaged on their own tasks of training or duty, but were to respond to any alarm:

> You sounded an air-raid alarm, and all these planes, coming off these various forces, with their own duties, their own tasks, their own missions, they came over to Bellinger's, and all the fighters went to Martin; and . . . all of Martin's bombers came over for search and attack.

That the volunteer fire department might have been an uncertain reliance at best seems fairly obvious. But it suffered under the further overwhelming disadvantage that the entire plan under which it was set up was to go into effect only in the event of emergency. This meant that without ample warning it was useless. On various occasions during the ensuing months a theoretical emergency was declared and drills were held to test its intricate command arrangements; but it failed to provide against the possibility that the Japanese might declare the emergency without prior notice.

At the end of March Captain Ellis M. Zacharias, then commanding the heavy cruiser *Salt Lake City*, came in for an interview with Admiral Kimmel. Captain Zacharias spoke Japanese and had a considerable knowledge of intelligence work; he also appears to have possessed one of those quick, original, and unorthodox minds which in all professional services are so justly regarded with suspicion. According to his own recollection, the captain advised the commander-in-chief that if Japan decided for war she "would begin with an air attack on our fleet on a week end and probably on a Sunday morning; that the attack would be for the purpose of disabling four battleships," and that it would be well to institute a daily patrol at least 500 miles out. When the admiral answered that he had no planes for such a patrol, the captain, by his own account, replied: "Well, Admiral, you better get them, because that is what is coming." Others present at the interview hotly deny that any such unseemly words could have been used to the commander-in-chief, and fail to remember any conversation of the kind. But the matter seems immaterial. Whether this warning was actually delivered or not, it was scarcely more prophetic than another Martin-Bellinger estimate, approved by Kimmel, Bloch, and Shore and sent to Washington on April 14. This concluded that the primary job of aviation in Hawaii was the destruction of attacking Japanese carriers; that Japan could "probably employ a maximum of six carriers against Oahu"; that an early morning attack was most favorable for the enemy; and that American plans should consequently be based on such an attack, which would probably call for the fly-off of the planes at dawn from a point about 233 miles from Oahu. Again, one cannot quarrel with the theory, for this was almost exactly what happened, down even to the precise number of carriers which the Japanese employed. The estimate, along with the Joint Coastal Defense Agreement and the ancillary air agreements, was sent off to Washington. Higher authority offered no criticism. The paper ramparts had been built. The real ones were to prove a different matter.

Until April, as General Marshall later testified, the Philippines "had literally nothing," but something was being pumped into Pearl Harbor despite all delays and other insatiable demands. In the search for fighter planes, Marshall "robbed" the combat squadrons in the United States, cutting most of them down to but two planes apiece. The promised 50 P-40B's went off in the *Lexington* in March. Ammunition, guns, other things were beginning to move. Some of the Navy's more clamorous demands were being met, though Kimmel could never escape the paralyzing decimations which swept his trained crews in order to fill the complements of the new ships. With two ground Army divisions in Hawaii there was little anxiety over a possible landing attempt. In those days, when we were still grossly underrating the technical competence of the Japanese and when the actual possibilities, and limitations, of air power were very imperfectly understood by even our own aviators, the air reinforcements did not look as inadequate as they seem today. As the weeks went on, the War Department began to feel somewhat easier about Pearl and even to spare energies for the desperate peril in the far western Pacific.

III ☜

While the clogging wheels revolved and the typewriters clattered in the Munitions Building (that vast, undecorative block of poured concrete run up to provide "temporary" office space for the first World War and destined to survive as no more than a minor unit among the much vaster offices required for the second), events were moving upon the greater stage of world history and politics. Spring was coming, and the grim German armored columns were rolling again across the face of Europe—but this time they were rolling eastward from the Channel coast, much as Napoleon's armies had done before them. On March 1 Bulgaria had joined the Axis and had simultaneously been inundated by a Nazi army of occupation; Yugoslavia was surrounded and Hitler stood upon the frontiers of embattled Greece. The seemingly irresistible process of piecemeal aggrandizement was again under way, and neither the hope nor the means of stopping it had so far appeared.

Nevertheless, along one crucial line it had been brought to a halt. The new movement itself signalized the fact that the Battle of Britain had been won. The British base still stood—few in the United States realized by how narrow a margin—and as long as that was true there was still a chance that one day the gathering strength of the democracies could somehow find a way of launching a counterstroke. Even so, the full significance of the victory above the Channel was not generally understood. But as the German armies continued ebbing from the West to flood into Poland, Hungary, and the Balkans, as the familiar diplomatic pressures were now mounted against Yugoslavia, the hints of it began to accumulate. According to Davis and Lindley, it was in mid-January that Mr. Sumner Welles, Under Secretary of State, had first warned Mr. Constantin Oumansky, the Soviet ambassador, that Hitler planned to attack Russia in June. Now on Thursday, March 20, Mr. Oumansky was at the State Department for a general conference. At the end, Mr. Welles asked him to remain for a moment so that they might speak alone. The ambassador enquired "if I had any further information in confirmation of what I had stated to him secretly in our last interview, namely, that this Government believed that Germany was planning to attack the Soviet Union. I said that I had additional information in confirmation of that report." So the State Department had a good idea of what was coming. Mr. Matsuoka, still trundling westward by way of Moscow to Berlin, apparently did not.

The possession of this information serves to make the Roosevelt policy through that dire spring of 1941 seem less reckless than it might otherwise appear. At all events, during the dramatic and bitterly depressing weeks that were to follow, the Administration was to hold firmly to its positive course. Yugoslavia's hour struck in the latter part of March. The usual combination of bribery and pressure had been applied; the armies had been massed, and on the 25th Yugoslavia, like all the others before her, "peaceably" joined the Axis. But then two days later a world which had come dully to accept the inevitability of Hitlerian expansion was electrified by the news that the Yugoslav army and people had refused. A *coup d'état* ejected the regency of Prince Paul, denounced its signature on the treaty, and flung defiance back at the whole power of Nazi Germany. For the first time a small people had stood up to the might of the German war machine and the poison of the German rot within. Hitler had lost an air battle over Britain; he had now suddenly lost a moral battle, perhaps no less decisive in its ultimate results, at Belgrade. It is difficult to recall today the great upsurge of enthusiasm which that magnificent though foredoomed gesture sent through the anti-Hitler peoples.

Mr. Matsuoka, who had paused long enough in Moscow for a two-hour talk with Stalin and Molotov, arrived in Berlin just as the Yugoslav crisis broke. The Germans gave him everything—a reception at the station, crowd-lined streets, two-and-a-half-hour interview with Hitler, a balcony appearance before the cheering throng in the Koenigsplatz—and Mr. Matsuoka burbled happily: "The Japanese nation is with you in joy or sorrow." Japan "will not lag behind you in fidelity, courage, and firm determination to arrange the world on the basis of the New Order." He pledged Japan's faith in the Fuehrer and said other things in similar vein which by no means went unnoticed in Washington.

In Washington at the same time they were casting up the strategic balances. The Anglo-American staff conferences were completed on March 27, and Admiral Stark transmitted the results to the Fleet commanders in his letters of April 3 and April 4. Written after two long conferences with the President and embodying some of his ideas, they are doubtless an accurate reflection of the Administration's estimate at the time. The admiral summed it up:

> The question as to our entry into the war now seems to be *when* and not *whether*. Public opinion, which is now slowly turning in that direction, may or may not be accelerated. My own personal view is that we may be in the war, (possibly undeclared) against Germany and Italy in about two months, but that there is a reasonable possibility that Japan may remain out altogether. However, we cannot at present act on that possibility.

The Anglo-American war plan was to take effect if the United States entered the war, but involved no commitment to do so. Basically, it provided for drawing on the Pacific Fleet in order to reinforce in the Atlantic, with the British undertaking "if necessary" to transfer naval forces to Singapore "to attempt to hold the Japanese north of the Malay barrier." All British efforts to get the Pacific Fleet into Singapore had been resisted. To the Americans the Atlantic seemed the "decisive theater," from the point of view both of maintaining the British bastion and of protecting our own coasts should that bastion fall. The situation in the Atlantic, Stark wrote, was "much worse than the average person has any idea." Britain was losing merchant tonnage about three times as fast as it could be replaced; the only remedy was a "radical" strengthening of the defenses, and the entire United States Navy would not be too much to employ on that task, if it could be relieved of its other duties. As it was, the Pacific Fleet would remain at Pearl Harbor with its mission of dissuading the Japanese from adventure. Admiral Stark advised his commanders to begin training their forces for the specific tasks assigned them under the new "Rainbow 5," the American part of the joint plan.

Mr. Matsuoka meanwhile had gone on to Rome, where he devoted himself to convincing the Pope that United States policy was simply "prolonging the war" in both Europe and China, whereas Japan in the latter theater was not fighting either the Chinese or China, but merely Bolshevism. On April 4, as Admiral Stark was writing his letters, the Japanese Foreign Minister was back again in Berlin for another long conference with the Fuehrer. Mr. Matsuoka explained that Japan would do her "utmost" to avoid war with the United States, but that if she went into Singapore such a war would probably ensue. The Fuehrer agreed that war with the United States was "undesirable," but that if Japan got involved in one, Germany would "immediately take the consequences" and "strike without delay." Germany had already made all preparations for it, "so that no American could land in Europe"; Germany's "superior experience" in the military arts, to say nothing of the fact that "the German soldier naturally ranks high above the American," could leave no doubt as to the outcome.

Perhaps emboldened by this, Mr. Matsuoka played discreetly with his own opinion that "sooner or later a war with the United States would be unavoidable"; why "should Japan, therefore, not decisively strike at the right moment and take the risk upon herself of a fight against America?" If she could thereby take the South Seas, it might make her impregnable for generations. The Fuehrer well understood and sympathized with such calculations, so like those which he had often made himself. But the matter went no farther; the slippery Matsuoka evaded direct commitment by retiring behind a screen of explanations of his own powerlessness in Japan. The most he would be able to report when he got home would be the fact that "Singapore had been discussed." Mr. Matsuoka presently departed for Moscow on his return journey; doubtless he congratulated himself on the cleverness with which he had got a commitment out of Hitler while giving nothing in return. The Germans may have been amused by the ease with which they had hooked the Japanese without even mentioning the important fact that they were about to assault Soviet Russia.

But the defiant Yugoslavs had to come first. On April 6 Hitler struck back with the full power of his war machine. On the same day Secretary Hull, after a conference with the President, issued a blazing statement:

> The barbaric invasion of Yugoslavia and the attempt to annihilate that country by brute force is but another chapter in the present planned movement of attempted world conquest and domination. Another small nation has been assaulted by the forces of aggression, and is further proof that there are no geographical limitations or bounds of any kind to their movement for world conquest. . . . This Government, with its policy of helping those who are defending themselves against would-be conquerors, is now proceeding as speedily as possible to send military and other supplies to Yugoslavia.

The United States was already deeper in the war, perhaps, than most Americans realized. On April 10 there was another stirring development, as the State Department announced the signature of an agreement with the Danish minister at Washington under which the United States would establish military and air bases on the coast of Greenland. German activity in the area had made the step necessary for defense; and the agreement had been made with the minister since German occupation of Denmark had deprived the home government of its power.

The German propaganda reaction was naturally acrimonious, but there were no signs of any more overt response on Hitler's part. Americans, on the other hand, could see plainly enough that the "defense" in question was not of the American continent directly but of the lend-lease lanes to Britain; yet the popular approval still seemed to be overwhelming. The President moved swiftly to other measures. The Navy had already seized all German and Italian ships interned in our waters. A group of American Coast Guard cutters (two of them were to die gloriously at Oran in the following year, leading our invasion of North Africa) were transferred to the Royal Navy in the wake of the 50 destroyers. And the President declared the Red Sea no longer a "war zone," thus permitting American merchantmen to enter it and deliver their cargoes direct for the British bases in the eastern Mediterranean.

All this was publicly known. The public did not know the extremity of the Atlantic crisis. It did not know that the Navy was studying the establishment of bases in Iceland and in northern Ireland. It knew nothing about the Anglo-American war plan. It did not know that orders would soon be issued (April 21) to our ships on neutrality patrol, directing them to trail all Axis war vessels and broadcast their positions, and to shoot in defense of any American ships that might be attacked. It did not know that further staff conferences were soon to be initiated at Singapore with the Dutch as well as the British, to concert a joint defense of the Far East in case Japan should strike. But that it would have objected if it had known is improbable. As a State Department instruction on April 10 told our representatives with the European neutrals, "it has been made abundantly clear by the people and Government of the United States that we do not intend to stand on the sidelines but that on the contrary we do intend to play our part in resistance against the forces of aggression."

Conviction was necessary in the grim days that were to follow. Hitler knew better than anyone else the dangerous character of the Yugoslav challenge, and when he struck on April 6 he struck to crush it peremptorily and completely. The sudden hopes that he might at last have overreached himself withered at once. The armored columns swept as irresistibly through the mountain passes of the Balkans as they had over the plains of Poland and the highways of France. Belgrade was rubbled within a day or two. The iron tentacles of the panzer divisions, reaching in from Bulgaria behind the Yugoslav flank, had cut organized defense to ribbons within a week, and swung down to overwhelm in turn the Greeks and the small British army which Wavell had sent from North Africa to their assistance.

There was another desperate retreat, down past the flanks of Mount Olympus and through Thermopylae to Athens. There was another desperate evacuation, almost as harried as that from Dunkerque. Nor was that all. To make their gesture to the Greeks, the British had denuded Cyrenaica; Rommel was on the ground there now and his Afrika Korps was soon sweeping the British rear guards out of all the hopeful conquests of the preceding fall and raising again the mortal threat to Suez. And the pursuit of the exhausted remnants out of Greece was not to stop at the water's edge. On May 20 the first wholly air-borne invasion in history leapt the 60-odd miles from the Peloponnesus to Crete, to succeed amazingly after a week or so of weird and bloody fighting in driving British arms from the island, and inflicting calamitous losses upon the naval power whose "command of the sea" was thus arrogantly negated.

The Balkan campaign was paralyzing in its speed, its violence, and in the completeness of its success. It did, however, have two other effects, concealed at the time. The invasion of Crete, though a brilliant victory, had been made at a cost too heavy to encourage a similar attempt across the English Channel. Many believe that it was this operation which finally decided Hitler to forget Britain and go forward with the planned invasion of Russia. If so, the Balkan campaign not only cast the historic die, but insured that it was cast too late. It was testified at Neuremberg that the Yugoslav rebellion forced a postponement of the Russian invasion by about five weeks. As the snows of the ensuing winter closed down around Moscow, those five weeks, bought by the seemingly futile heroism of the Yugoslavs, were to prove a priceless gift to Russia and to the world.

But all that was far in the future. Indeed, as Mr. Matsuoka arrived in Moscow on his return journey, the Balkan campaign itself was only a day old, although no one in Axis circles can have had much doubt about the outcome. The Foreign Minister called again at the Kremlin on April 7, and apparently something he learned there led him to prolong his Moscow visit for a few days. Next day he had a long luncheon conference with the American ambassador, Mr. Laurence Steinhardt, who was an old acquaintance. Quite solemnly he assured Mr. Steinhardt that both Hitler and Von Ribbentrop wanted no war with the United States. On the 9th Mr. Matsuoka was closeted with Molotov for three hours, on the 12th he saw Stalin as well as Molotov. On the 13th he was again at the Kremlin, and that evening he left for home over the Trans-Siberian. Just before he did so it was announced to a startled world that Mr. Matsuoka had signed a nonaggression treaty between Japan and the Soviet Union.

According to his own account at the time, which was at least no more preposterous than several other explanations of this treaty which he was to leave behind him, it had all been a complete surprise to Mr. Matsuoka. "I had not expected a neutrality pact with Russia at all"; he had, indeed, simply called on Stalin and Molotov to make his farewells, and this had led to the conclusion of the pact. "It was negotiated in ten minutes." However that may be, the pact gave an unqualified guarantee that if either nation should "become the object of hostilities" by a third party, the other would "observe neutrality throughout the duration of the conflict." To the delighted Foreign Minister it was a great *coup;* he had insured Japan's rear for the assault on Singapore and for the southward advance—to empire. As he set off again across Siberia, visions of Matsuoka the Master Statesman rose happily in the Foreign Minister's mind. The shrewd opportunist had gone a long way since, as a poor boy, he had become the protégé of an American minister in Oregon; and he would now go farther still. The destinies of Japan were in his grasp, and through Japan perhaps the destinies of the world. Mr. Matsuoka was immensely pleased with himself.

He had, at any rate, left the foreign offices and international experts buzzing. Where the hints and portents of a Russo-German war true after all, and was Stalin moving to cover his own rear in Siberia? Or was the Russian dictator, who had encouraged the Nazi onslaught on Poland in 1939, now cynically egging the Japanese on to fall upon the British and Americans? Mr. Sumner Welles and the Administration may have felt certain of the answer, yet the situation was dangerous. The Navy had completed its plans for the transfer of three battleships, an aircraft carrier, and other vessels from the Pacific Fleet to meet the desperate need in the Atlantic. Mr. Roosevelt now temporarily canceled the movement. The old idea that naval gestures could be used to intimidate, or at least to warn, the Japanese—an idea particularly popular with the State Department and particularly alarming to the Navy—would not down. The Australians had been enthusiastically acclaiming a small naval detachment which had been sent to Sydney and Brisbane as a demonstration of solidarity. The President seemed impressed by the value of the device. "Betty," he exuberantly told his Chief of Naval Operations, "just as soon as those ships come back from Australia and New Zealand or perhaps a little before I want to send some more out. I just want to keep them popping up here and there and keep the Japs guessing." Admiral Stark was plainly without enthusiasm for the strategy of "popping up," which he seemed to think as futile as it was contrary to sound doctrine, but he was loyal to his commander-in-chief. On April 19 he was again writing to Kimmel:

> I had hoped that with the passage of the lend-lease bill we could look forward to some unity on Capitol Hill, but just at present there seems to be very far from that desired unity on vital issues. What will be done about convoy and many other things, and just how much a part of our Democratic way of life will be handled by Mr. Gallup, is a pure guess. From that you might think I am getting a little bit cynical, but believe it or not that is not the case and I am sawing wood as usual and am still cheerful.
>
> The President has on his hands at the present time about as difficult a situation as ever confronted any man anywhere in public life. There are tremendous issues at stake, to which he is giving all he has got. I only wish I could be of more help to him.

President Roosevelt had to listen to many conflicting advisors and weigh many conflicting considerations. At bottom there was the bitter and still unresolved issue between the isolationists and the interventionists. The latter, according to all indices, were in a powerful majority in the country; but the former possessed a strength in Congress and a sounding-board in the Hearst-Patterson-McCormick press disproportionate to their popular support. This basic issue was, moreover, aggravated by partisan politics; it was confused on the one hand by the accumulated animosities of the Roosevelt-haters and on the other by the contradictions inherent in the President's own confidence that he could wage effective war against Nazism and aggression without getting into "shooting" battle. And even among those who shared the President's fundamental view of the world problem, there were many differences and cross-currents of opinion. One policy had been adopted and was in fact to be followed with remarkable consistency to the very end. That was the policy which made the defeat of Germany the primary goal, the question of Japan a secondary one. Should we become involved in the war, we would try to keep Japan out as long as possible; should that fail, we would fight a holding war in the Pacific until the end of the German menace permitted a full concentration on Japan. But how to do it? General Marshall and Admiral Stark, preparing instructions for our representatives at the Anglo-American-Dutch staff conference at Singapore in the latter part of April, were compelled to cast them in a vague and tentative form. The British and Dutch wanted a definite undertaking by all to fight if the Japanese passed a given line. Nothing as concrete and effective as that was possible to the representatives of our still muddle-headed democracy. We have General Marshall's assurance that no commitments to fight unless we were first attacked were ever made at any time. Thus the Singapore agreement, rather like the treaties between our own Army and Navy at Pearl Harbor, could result only in plans to go into effect after hostilities should begin, when it would be too late. As it was, the agreement, signed on April 27, was rejected by Marshall and Stark on the grounds that it involved too many "political" considerations and put too great a burden on American forces. It was never submitted to the President.

American policy that spring was thus scarcely a model of consistency and foresight. But the Japanese leaders, although untroubled by the difficulties of the democratic process, were suffering from their own cross-purposes and conflicts even more acutely. On April 18 Prince Konoye summoned a conference of the political and military heads to consider the first fruits of Ambassador Nomura's efforts in Washington. Secretary Hull had offered to receive any proposals, based on the general principles of nonaggression, peace, and equal opportunity, which Japan might care to make.* Should they take up the offer? The discussion of the problem, as recorded in Prince Konoye's posthumous memoir, is illuminating.

The Japanese wanted three things: The "termination of the China Incident" (which meant completing the conquest of China), the "prevention of the spread of the European War to the Pacific," and "the promotion of economic co-operation" with America. What the latter meant is sufficiently explained in Konoye's words:

> The considerable depletion of Japan's national strength made it desirable to restore and cultivate that strength by disposing of the China Incident as quickly as possible. For the success of Japan's southward advance, which was being advocated in certain quarters, the supreme command itself confessed to having neither the confidence of success nor the necessary preparation. The cultivation of national strength, moreover, necessitated the *temporary* restoration of amicable relations with America and planning for the replenishment of the supply of vital commodities *for the future.* [Italics inserted.]

As for China, they had been making no headway through their puppet regime at Nanking. Obviously, the quickest way

* So Konoye states it in his memoirs. Secretary Hull was always insistent that the initiative came entirely from Japan. The point is somewhat obscure. A correspondence found in the President's papers shows that at the end of January Bishop James E. Walsh, Superior General at Maryknoll, wrote to Mr. Frank C. Walker, the Postmaster General, that "Today we received word by cable that the——Government [Japan] are now ready to send a trusted representative to discuss the terms of a projected agreement." Bishop Walsh had already provided a memorandum outlining a rather elaborate plan of possible agreement. Secretary Hull's comment on these proposals was decidedly skeptical, and he suggested that it would be better to wait and see what Nomura might be bringing rather than get into these "indirect" negotiations. He did add that "we shall of course wish to listen carefully to what he [Nomura] has to say and we can try to convince him that Japan's own best interest [*sic*] lie along lines other than that she is now pursuing."

to "dispose" of the affair would be to enlist the "good offices" of America in bringing direct pressure to bear on Chiang Kai-shek. Such were the bright hopes held out by undertaking negotiations. The difficulty lay in the business about "preventing the spread of the European War." How could the Japanese reach agreement with the United States without violating their commitment under the Tri-Partite Pact to prevent American entry into the war against Hitler? And how could they welsh on the Tri-Partite Pact without losing the claim they had staked under it upon a victorious Germany? Difficult as it was, however, this problem was not too much for the subtle Japanese mind. They would undertake the negotiation, but make it more clear that the object was "world peace" (i. e. not the freeing of the United States to enter the European War) and the building of the "New Order"; meanwhile, although recognizing that "fidelity" might require them to tell the Germans what they were up to, it would be better to keep quiet about the whole business. The Germans might fail to appreciate the astuteness of the Japanese course and raise "opposition" which "might vitiate the success of the desired conversations."

In a memorandum a couple of days later the Army and Navy leaders put the whole thing rather more bluntly:

> Japan must turn the American scheme to good advantage and by embracing the principles embodied in the proposal, attain the objectives of the China Incident, restore the national strength, and thereby attain a powerful voice in the establishment of world peace.

Mr. Matsuoka, meanwhile, had been trundling home across Siberia, happy in his confidences with Hitler and his Soviet nonaggression treaty. The first he heard about the proposed American negotiation was when Konoye got him by telephone at Dairen; and when, on his arrival at Tokyo on April 22, the full plan was exposed to him, he went into a towering rage. "Matsuoka talked endlessly about his European trip," maintained that Mr. Hull's offer was "70 per cent ill-will," and "laid special emphasis upon the question of keeping faith with Germany." In public he was showing himself full of Nazi ideas, talking about the new "Matsuoka diplomacy," seeing himself as a possible dictator of Japan, and exhibiting, as it seemed to Mr. Tolischus, the *New York Times* correspondent, "a head far too large for his old hat." Prince Konoye diplomatically took to his bed with "a cold." Mr. Matsuoka did likewise. The Army and Navy Ministries exerted "their utmost efforts to soothe his feelings" and get the Foreign Minister to consent to taking up the Hull offer, but he was difficult to budge.

The enthusiastic (and of course semi-official) comments of the Japanese press on the Soviet nonaggression pact were not making the situation any simpler. While Admiral Nomura at Washington was patiently expounding the purely economic and pacific character of the "southward advance," the Japanese press had virtually started out on a conquest of the southwest Pacific already. Soviet Russia, it announced, had now joined Japan, Germany, and Italy in the reorganization of world affairs; and the *Japan Times and Advertiser*, the accepted organ of the Foreign Office, described the new position:

> Japan can now undertake either a defensive war or an offensive-defensive one. In the latter, Japan would have to fight first to offset a threatened perilous disadvantage. She is confident that the pact with Soviet Russia assures her rear and right flank against military and naval action.

On April 29, the Emperor's birthday, Tokyo saw its biggest military review in years, while the same newspaper, in an apparently inspired article, explored possible Pacific peace terms in a startling vein. It envisaged as a satisfactory settlement the demilitarization of all American bases in the Far East and the Aleutians, the withdrawal of American influence to the Western Hemisphere, and the grant, even then, of fullest economic equality to the Axis powers in Latin America.

Such emanations of the "Matsuoka diplomacy" may have gone far beyond the policy which the Army, the Navy, and Konoye were following, but the United States had no way of knowing that. And the policy itself involved too many contradictions. They were trying to buy off the United States from opposing them on the path of empire. The trouble was that they had nothing to offer. Their own generals and proconsuls in China were ready to raise a deadly howl at any hint of significant concessions to the American position in regard to "the China Incident"; and quite regardless of the Foreign Minister's pro-Nazi enthusiasms, the others did not dare at bottom to throw off the German connection. They could not pay the one price which might possibly have influenced the State Department—a guarantee of neutrality in the Pacific in the event of American entanglement in Europe. The Germans were suspicious enough as it was of the activities of Admiral Nomura, whom Von Ribbentrop thought to be at heart far too much "inclined toward the Anglo-Saxons"; and with the increasing American intervention in the Atlantic, they were beginning to put pressure on Japan to adopt "a definite anti-American stand."

Under the circumstances the Japanese would have found it difficult at best to play the double game on which they were embarked—convincing Washington that the Tri-Partite Pact was simply a harmless form of words, in no way obligating Japan to join in a German-American war, while convincing Berlin that their American negotiations were simply a shrewd diplomatic maneuver, in no way contravening Japan's fidelity to the Axis. But Mr. Matsuoka was making it impossible. By May 3 he had consented to a proposed note to the United States. He insisted, however, that before sending it in they should first try suggesting a simple neutrality pact, like that he had so masterfully obtained from Russia. He then secretly tipped the Germans off as to what was going on, and asked for Von Ribbentrop's opinions. The futility of the neutrality pact idea was so apparent to Nomura that the latter did not even fully present it to Secretary Hull, but the maneuver wasted another week or so.

It was all very difficult. In an audience on May 10 Prince Konoye found the Emperor "with a very apprehensive expression." * The Son of Heaven had received Matsuoka a day or two before, and had been alarmed by the Foreign Minister's wild talk. If America entered the war against Germany, Japan would have to attack Singapore forthwith; and if the resultant prolongation of the war should produce a German-Soviet collision, Japan would have to attack Siberia and "advance at least as far as Irkutsk." The Prime Minister soothed the august brow with the assurance that the Emperor should not worry too much about Matsuoka; Matsuoka couldn't make war alone, and the high command and the Cabinet would have something to say about "any final decision." Settling the China Incident, the Prime Minister explained, was the most urgent matter at the moment, and for that "making use of America was the only way." Presumably this contented the Emperor; but he was very dubious about Mr. Matsuoka.

Such was the complex conflict of calculations out of which they had managed to distill their proposed note to the United States. Since its adoption on May 3, Matsuoka had been holding it up, waiting for the comments of Berlin. These had not arrived; but because the Foreign Minister wished to forestall a forthcoming address by President Roosevelt, he now ordered the proposals sent in anyway. On the evening of May 11 Admiral Nomura called at Secretary Hull's apartment in the Wardman Park Hotel (where these secret conversations were for the most part carried on) bearing with him a set of documents embodying a proposal for a general settlement between the United States and Japan. They "served," as the State

* This is the phrase as given in the *New York Times*, December 22, 1945, reporting the Konoye memoir as it appeared in *Asahi*. In the translation included in the *Exhibits* of the Pearl Harbor investigation, it is rendered "with the air of great concern."

Department account puts it "to reveal authoritatively for the first time what the Japanese Government had in mind as a basis for agreement."

Secretary Hull accepted the papers, stating "very clearly and slowly" that "I was receiving these documents in a purely unofficial way with a view to examining them and ascertaining whether they . . . would or might afford a basis for a step in negotiations." Thus any rumor or hint that negotiations were in progress could be "truthfully" disavowed. The Secretary also paid his respects to the Japanese Foreign Minister—"there will be real difficulty to persuade even my associates of the absolute dependability of Matsuoka's acts and utterances"—and read the ambassador another of his little lectures on the scourge of Nazism and on the danger of putting one's trust in Hitler. But if Japan really wished to settle the Pacific question on the basis of peace and friendship "there should be no serious difficulty." The ambassador agreed, even to what the Secretary said about Mr. Matsuoka, and declared that war between the two countries would be "an incalculable loss to both Japan and the United States, as well as to civilization." He then withdrew, leaving the Secretary to study Japan's idea of a general settlement.

The Japanese proposals of May 12 (they commonly bear this date, since the corrected translation was not submitted until the following day) were long, elaborately worded, accompanied by an explanatory "annex" and by an explanation of the explanations. They were marked by that elusiveness, that misty ambiguity of implication, that suspicious fuzziness around all the edges which appear to characterize the Japanese official mind in action. The basic sense, however, was scarcely mistakable. They were under six heads, and may be condensed as follows:

1. Each Government to acknowledge the other as an equally sovereign state; to pledge itself to lasting peace and to non-interference with the other's rights, interests, and social order.

2. Japan declares the Tri-Partite Pact to be purely defensive and

"designed to prevent the nations which are not at present directly affected by the European war from engaging in it"; the United States declares that its attitude toward the war will continue to be "directed by no such aggressive measures as to assist any one nation against another" but will be determined solely by the interests of its own defense.

3. The United States will "forthwith" request Chiang Kai-shek to negotiate peace with Japan, at the same time giving secret assurance that American aid to China would be withdrawn if Chiang should refuse.

4. The United States to withdraw the restrictions on trade; the two countries to agree to supply each other with whatever commodities "are, respectively, available or required by either" and to re-establish normal trade relations.

5. Japan's expansion in the Southwest Pacific "is declared to be of peaceful nature" and American co-operation is to be given in Japan's procurement of those raw materials, such as oil, rubber, tin, nickel, which she needs.

6. The two Governments jointly to guarantee the independence of the Philippines, on condition that the islands be permanently neutralized and that Japanese subjects shall not be subject to any discriminatory treatment.

An Addendum specified that the understanding should be kept as "a confidential memorandum" between the two Governments.

So here was something at last upon the table. It was scarcely of a character to appeal either to our plain-spoken Secretary of State or to the Administration and the people whom he represented. Japan offered nothing substantial in regard to China, nothing convincing in regard to her plans for the Southwest Pacific, and nothing whatever in regard to her German alliance. The imprecisions of the paragraph on this latter subject, indeed, would seem to bind us to abandon the British while confirming Japan in her duty to fight us if we did not. But in return the United States was in effect to accept the "Greater East Asia Co-Prosperity Sphere" and not only to acknowledge but actively to promote Japanese hegemony in the western Pacific—forcing the Chinese to come to Japan's terms, reopening our markets to the Japanese war machine, and even assisting it to extract from the Dutch, British, and French the oil and rubber, tin and nickel which it required for further aggressions. Even without the final and insulting suggestion of a joint guarantee of the Philippines, this would have been a complete prescription for insuring to the Japanese military that free hand in Southeast Asia and the Indies which the diplomats had apparently set out to get for them.

IV ☞

On the 14th of May, Major General Jonathan M. Wainwright stood on the pier at Manila, watching the steamship *Washington* pulling slowly out into the placid waters of the great bay into which Admiral Dewey's squadron had steamed just 43 years before. He had been saying good-by—for longer than either of them could know—to Mrs. Wainwright; for the *Washington* was the last ship out of Manila carrying the wives and dependents of Army personnel going home under orders. Under its blanket of tropic heat the old city—capital of our first great imperial experiment, the scene of so many interesting adventures, of so much good work, of so many romantic associations for the Old Army which had conquered and governed it and made careers there —was as pleasantly languorous as ever. The palms waved as idly over the Luneta, the climate was as enervating, the bars and clubs as cheerful, as always. But the "sparkle" had suddenly gone out of Manila. That spring, for the first time, the General had "got the feeling in my bones" that war was inevitable; it was coming "and we all knew it." What they were going to fight it with, or how, was less apparent.

Some months before the first contingents of Australians had landed at Singapore "many thousands strong" (censorship conveniently averted the necessity of saying just how many) and had gone off into the Malayan jungles singing "Roll Out the Barrel" and "Waltzing Matilda." The Dutch in the Indies had long since begun to string barbed wire, to camouflage important buildings, and to organize blackouts. Manila was as yet innocent of even these elementary measures of defense. While General Homma, not 500 miles away in Formosa, was already busy training his invasion force in every detail of amphibious and jungle warfare, the Philippine Department was still making earnest efforts merely to bring Wainwright's skeleton division "up to the full statutory strength of 12,000." Lieutenant Colonel Allison Ind, an Air Corps staff officer from civil life, and an exemplar, as it were, of the new gospel of air power (which had had nothing to do with the conquest or governance of the Philippines), had recently arrived in Manila. He found that his general was the first Air Corps general ever sent to the Philippines. The air chief of staff told him, a trifle bleakly: "There is little here in the way of staff organization. It is up to you to establish our Intelligence Section and a lot of other things which may not be in your line. . . . There is so little time and so very much to do in what there is."

This was, if anything, understatement. Colonel Ind, fresh from the more invigorating air of the United States, severely noted a "flaccidity, a torpidity, and an all-pervading lack of movement or resolution" widespread throughout the Philippine Department. Available air power was confined to some obsolete B-10 bombers and a few almost equally obsolete P-35 fighters which had been diverted from Sweden. When some P-40's finally arrived, it was discovered that the sole access road to our main fighter base, Nichols Field, was too narrow to admit the trucks carrying the knocked-down planes; and when they ultimately got the road widened and the P-40's assembled, it turned out that someone had forgotten to send along the coolant for their engines, without which they were useless. Anti-aircraft defense was confined to some World War I machine guns which were kept packed away in cosmoline. When a Royal Air Force officer came in from Singapore a few weeks later to survey the situation he was compelled to subordinate tact to truthfulness. "You will understand, I am sure," he grimly observed, "if I say that it is my belief that a sudden, determined enemy attack would reduce the effectiveness of your present air force practically to zero." They understood.

In the Far East we had virtually nothing. Pearl Harbor, for all the imposing appearance of its Fleet and fortresses, was still one aching mass of deficiencies. In the latter part of May there was a long memorandum from Kimmel cataloguing his shortages—shortages of everything: trained officers, crews, combat pilots, carriers, modern planes, bombs, air torpedoes, radar, base defense vessels, priorities over Britain and the Army, information, even the support of public opinion. Even in the Atlantic the Navy did not have enough to meet the peril as it was then envisaged, while the true peril was being grossly underestimated, as the terrible year of 1942 was to demonstrate. Nor was the nation which stood behind these slim forces in any sense awake to the real magnitude of the crisis it was confronting. For many reasons, the public was constantly receiving an overoptimistic picture both of the military realities abroad and of the progress of rearmament at home. The idea of "defense," on which the President had harped endlessly in his effort to hold the support of Congress and the public, concealed the necessity for positive exertion; the hope that "short of war" would see us through, again rashly fostered by the President's overconfidence and adroitness, was too widespread. The rearmament effort was being too much hampered by union demands, disputes, and strikes; it was being hampered even more by what some called the "strike of capital"—the reluctance of management to risk profits in costly conversions or accept the grim rule of priorities and allocations regardless of competiitive position. Both difficulties were in fact simply reflections of the inability of the nation and of the Administration to face up to the profound social and economic issues which a major war effort was bound to present. The citizen soldiers of the National Guard, who had been thrust suddenly into active service in the preceding summer, saw themselves approaching the end of a year in uniform; since there had been no fighting, they were beginning to think it time that they should be relieved. The first products of selective service, who had followed them, were not finding Army life especially congenial; since there was no war they could not see why they should undergo its ardors, and there was already worry about their morale. We were waging "defense" with one hand and in our spare time.

The situation was enough to appall the timid. Mr. Hanson W. Baldwin, military critic of the *New York Times* and probably our best-informed civilian military analyst, was distilling caution in the gloomiest terms, and demonstrating in a long and weighty book why, in view of our chaotic preparations and internal disunity, "we must not, cannot now participate in this war." But President Roosevelt was not timid. Bold in his grand strategy, he was perhaps excessively venturesome in some of his tactical inspirations. In the latter part of May, as Hitler completed his Balkan conquest, there seemed a possibility, despite the reports of a coming Russian war, that the Nazis might again turn westward. Between the Pacific, the Atlantic sea lanes, and the garrisoning of the new leased bases, our resources were already stretched thinly enough; but on May 22 the President gave Admiral Stark an "overall limit of thirty days to prepare and have ready an expedition of 25,000 men to sail for and take the Azores." Considering that there were at the moment virtually no transports, no landing craft, no Army troops trained in amphibious operations, and little of anything else required for such an operation, one can understand the note of desperation in Admiral Stark's reaction to this directive.* It is hard to resist the impression that the President suffered from the amateur's ignorance of the real

* Needless to say, it was never put into effect.

difficulties of modern war, and throughout both overrated his own forces and underrated the power of the enemy.

Yet if Mr. Roosevelt was bolder than he always knew, there was a sound reason for boldness. We may have had nothing on the firing line and a confusion of tongues at home. But we did have an enormous latent power, both physical and spiritual; and no one with Mr. Roosevelt's very real and deeply felt faith in the American people could have doubted that it would be mobilized to meet any need. The risks of courage were much less than Mr. Baldwin thought them.* But more important than that were the overwhelmingly greater risks of any other attitude. It was better to force the issue rather than wait until everything was ready and prepared—which, under such a course, it never would be. The history of Europe throughout the '30's was one long, unanswerable demonstration of the perils of timidity.

The President was not timid. On the evening of May 27 there came another "fireside chat" echoing through the radio receivers of the nation. In Tokyo a few hours before they had been celebrating the Japanese Navy Day, and a leading address was by Captain Hideo Hiraide, the official naval spokesman. In an apparent effort to influence what the President was about to say, Captain Hiraide had spoken in terms more belligerent, and more revelatory, than any which the Japanese had used up to that time:

> At the moment that any country challenges our country contrary to justice, the Imperial Navy will arise like lightning and knock out the adversary with blitz action. . . . The Imperial Navy expects to lick even the biggest and strongest navy by employing special strategic operations. The state of preparedness is perfect. . . . Apart from the long-distance bombing strategy, the Imperial

* Admiral Stark, who knew our military deficiencies better than most, nevertheless believed it imperative at this time that we should get into the war at once. Otherwise, he thought, Britain would fall and the situation would be irretrievable.

Naval Air Force is training in such strategy as will deal an unerring blow to the enemy.

Mr. Roosevelt paid no attention. (Nor, it would seem, did our naval authorities at Washington and in Pearl Harbor.) He did not mention Japan or the Far East. The address was a homely but effective call to unity and to action against the menace of Hitlerism. "What we face is cold, hard fact. The first and fundamental fact is that what started as a European war has developed, as the Nazis always intended it should develop, into a world war for world domination." The high-pitched, slightly nasal voice went on. "Your Government knows what terms Hitler, if victorious, would impose. . . . I am not speculating about all this. . . . They plan to treat the Latin American nations as they are now treating the Balkans. They plan then to strangle the United States of America and the Dominion of Canada." The President sketched the consequences of a Hitler peace to labor and agriculture, business and manufacturing—"all would be mangled and crippled under such a system. . . . We do not accept, and will not permit, this Nazi 'shape of things to come.'" Still the voice went on; it was one of the longest of Mr. Roosevelt's wartime radio talks. It raised the Nazi menace to Suez and the Indian Ocean; it raised the menace to Dakar, the Azores, and the Cape Verdes. "The war is approaching the brink of the Western Hemisphere itself. It is coming very close to home."

The President launched into a long exposition of the Battle of the Atlantic and its strategic importance. He revealed that tonnage losses were three times the capacity of British yards to replace and twice the output of American and British yards combined. There were two answers: to increase American shipbuilding and to help "to cut down losses on the high seas." He revealed that our naval patrols were trailing Axis vessels and broadcasting their positions. The national policy was to resist "actively" and "with all our resources every attempt by Hitler to extend his Nazi domination to the Western Hemisphere, or to threaten it," and to "give every possible assistance to Britain" and to all others resisting "Hitlerism or its equivalent." We were already helping to protect lend-lease shipments, and "all additional measures necessary to deliver the goods will be taken." And then there came the call to unity, to the putting aside of fears, of futile hopes for "peace at any price," of industrial conflict, of all lesser ends; and the announcement in the final paragraphs that "I have tonight issued a proclamation that an unlimited national emergency exists and requires the strengthening of our defense to the extreme limit of our national power and authority. . . . I repeat the words of the Signers of the Declaration of Independence: 'With a firm reliance on the protection of Divine Providence, we mutually pledge to each other our lives, our fortunes, and our sacred honor.'"

No one knew exactly what an "unlimited national emergency" might mean in law. But as a means of bringing home the deepening seriousness of the crisis, its impact was unmistakable. Obviously, the President was feeling for a popular mandate for the new warlike measures he had in mind. It was accorded to him. Once more the press and polls were overwhelmingly favorable. Once more the isolationist opposition, while embittered, seemed merely partisan and obstructive rather than calculated to offer any viable alternative to the Administration's course. The President could feel that he had the nation substantially behind him, and the course was maintained.

The address had said nothing about the Far East. The Japanese could have found little in it to encourage them, however, while their own proposals of May 12 remained buried in the silences of the State Department. Meanwhile, the German reaction to their negotiations had arrived—with emphasis. Through frantic cables from Oshima at Berlin, through the "high-handed" representations of the German ambassador, Baron Eugen Ott, at Tokyo, it was born in upon Prince Konoye that the Germans were "harboring extreme antipathy" toward Japan's flirtations with the United States. America's "obligation" not to get into the war in Europe must be "clearly defined"; Germany must be made a full party to the whole negotiation; it was inadmissible for Japan to start talks with the United States without a prior understanding with Berlin. Mr. Matsuoka, with his complete pro-Axis orientation, was making things no easier. Konoye suspected his slippery Foreign Minister of having talked one way in Berlin and having reported in another way at home; it was a problem to know "what was the truth." But the secret talks in Secretary Hull's apartment at the Wardman Park Hotel went on. As May declined into June it was still possible that diplomacy might yield something, while there remained some other avenues to be explored before the Japanese would have to face up to final decisions.

In the interests of the "peaceful" South Seas advance, a Japanese trade delegation in Batavia had been trying to bully the Dutch into providing the assured petroleum supply which was Japan's greatest military need. Dr. Hubertus van Mook, a shrewdly capable Netherlander who had been born in the Indies of a family which had lived there for generations, headed the Dutch representatives. Dr. Van Mook was patient, dilatory, and as evasive as possible. With the fate of Tonkin before his eyes, he was under no illusions as to the peril. But he was firm. The Japanese representative, Mr. Kenkichi Yoshizawa, one of the tougher hatchet men of Imperial diplomacy, was making no progress. A formal demand for oil, rubber, and tin exports, served on June 6, was parried. In Tokyo at the time Ambassador Grew heard that both the Germans and the Japanese extremists were pressing for action against the Indies—the Germans with the argument that the United States would be powerless to protect the Netherlands possessions, the Japanese with the argument that if Japan did not grab them the Germans would. But Konoye's Government finally decided to break off negotiations and bring the trade delegation home, and it was explained that this minatory gesture would not be followed by any "immediate" change in Japanese relations with the Indies. The Dutch did not weaken under the implied threat; instead Dr. Van Mook gave Mr. Yoshizawa a champagne dinner and he was entertained at a lavish farewell fête at the Governor General's beautiful mansion at Batavia. The grounds, in the tropic June, must have been singularly lovely. The mansion was already painted in camouflage.

To observers in the East it meant that one bluff, at least, had been called. But everyone knew the vital importance of oil to the Japanese war economy. The next time, it would not be bluff; and everyone could be reasonably sure that there would be a next time, unless the Japanese militarists could ensure their supply in some other way. But it was not the hour for that; not yet.

June wore on; summer was flooding into the northern world and in the United States the vacation season was getting under way. In the middle of the month there was another sensation, when the news came of the torpedoing and sinking of the American steamship *Robin Moor* in mid-Atlantic, the first American-flag vessel (though not the first American-owned or American-manned) to fall victim to the U-boat. The crew had been hurried into the boats on thirty minutes' notice, and left to spend two weeks or more at sea before they were happily picked up. The President sent a scorching message to Congress on the incident; but perhaps it was all too much an echo from World War I days, or perhaps it was too apparent that episodes of that kind, however lamentable, were minor beside the giant forces with which the nation was involved, and under the circumstances more or less inevitable at best. The editorials were vigorous; but one cannot feel that the sinking of the *Robin Moor* had much influence over events.

Vacations were coming; Washington was growing hot. Secretary Hull, whose health was not of the best, wanted to get away to White Sulphur. Meanwhile, he had at last formulated his next move. On June 21, the longest day of the year,

Ambassador Nomura was summoned and handed what has been aptly called the State Department's "rewrite" of the Japanese proposals of May 12. This document, like the Japanese original, was also lengthy; it was accompanied by annexes and suggested drafts of explanatory letters to be exchanged. It closely followed the Japanese proposals in general form. Only the wording of the six points was deftly changed, by a shift of phraseology here, the insertion of a clarifying adjective there, so as to eliminate virtually everything which the Japanese most wished to include and to substitute virtually all the main points on which American policy was insisting.

Admiral Nomura bore this document away for study and transmission. If he sat that evening by his radio he must have heard, as countless Americans up late in that June midnight heard, the excited voices of the news broadcasters reading the bulletins which announced Adolf Hitler's invasion of Soviet Russia.

THREE

ECONOMIC WAR

I ☞

The German onslaught upon Soviet Russia, delivered in the dawn hours of June 22, 1941, along the whole length of the vast frontier from the Baltic to Rumania, transformed the entire world position at a single gigantic stroke. The possibility had been apparent for years; it had been guessed at for months, prognosticated more and more insistently for weeks. The fact itself still came with a stunning impact. Here was the actuality at last; and it was obvious at once that it would be decisive for human history.

It intensified every hope, and every fear. It suddenly opened to the western democracies the first reasonable possibility of ultimate victory which had appeared since the fall of France; simultaneously, it presented an appalling prospect if Hitler should succeed in this stupendous adventure. It upset every established pattern of thought, gave a violent wrench to all emotional attitudes toward the war, and reversed every political and military calculation. Within twelve hours Mr. Winston Churchill had issued his celebrated declaration, abandoning all his past diatribes against Communist Russia and pledging the resources of the British Empire to the support of the Soviet Union. Within a day Mr .Sumner Welles, Acting Secretary of State, was echoing the Prime Minister, if in more guarded fashion. The "principles and doctrines of communistic dictatorship," Mr. Welles told a press conference, "are as intolerable and as alien [to the beliefs of Americans] as are the principles and doctrines of Nazi dictatorship." But the "immediate issue" was Hitlerism and the repulse of its "plan for universal conquest." Consequently, "any rallying of the forces opposing Hitlerism, from whatever source these forces may spring, will . . . redound to the benefit of our own defense and security. Hitler's armies are today the chief dangers of the Americas."

President Roosevelt had reason to move cautiously. The American people had received no such lesson as had the British in the dire nature of the world crisis, and were far less prepared to sacrifice their preconceptions on the altars of survival. It was not a month since the President himself, in the May 27 address, had linked at least our domestic Communists with the Bundists and Fascists as "enemies of democracy in our midst." Hitler was undoubtedly counting on the Communist issue to drive a deep wedge into the western democratic opposition to him; and our isolationist and anti-Roosevelt spokesmen were instantly vocal in assisting the work. Senator Robert A. Taft of Ohio told a national network audience that "the victory of Communism in the world would be far more dangerous to the United States than a victory of Fascism." Senator Robert M. LaFollette, Jr., was cynical about the "whitewash act" which he foresaw as imminent, in which the American people would be "told to forget the purges in Russia by the OGPU, the persecution of religion, the confiscation of property . . . Finland . . . the vulture role [of] Stalin in . . . Poland" and so on. Senator Bennett Champ Clark of Missouri, appearing at an America First meeting in Brooklyn, felt that this ended any question of entering the war; it would be simply "helping one system of heathenism against another" to do so now. "What profit is it," exclaimed the Senator, "to a God-fearing people to gain dominion over the earth in union with Communism and lose our souls?"

The fact that God was being seriously involved in mundane politics was made evident by another speaker on the same platform, the Rev. Dr. John A. O'Brien, a graduate professor of Notre Dame University, who cried that "the American people cannot be driven by propaganda, trickery, or deceit into fighting to maintain the Christ-hating despot, Stalin, in his tyranny over 100 million enslaved people. The propaganda that we must eventually enter the war in order to save Democracy and Christianity has now received its death blow." The President, who had himself made considerable use of God in the furtherance of policy, was always very sensitive to the political power of the Catholic Church. And there were other arguments. In a long and solemn address Mr. Herbert Hoover advanced the appealing idea that we now need worry no more about Europe's broils; the two totalitarianisms could be left to destroy each other without American intervention. There were many to agree with him.

Our military and naval authorities, however, were not among them. Perhaps because they were misled, in their own way, by the military man's antipathy to Communism, they took a very grim view of the situation. In off-the-record conferences the Washington correspondents were hearing that the very highest Army levels were giving the Russians perhaps six weeks at most; and Hitler might destroy them in a month. Within forty-eight hours after the onslaught Admiral Stark was at the White House to urge upon the President that, "on the assumption that this country's decision is not to let England fall, we should immediately seize the psychological opportunity . . . and announce and start escorting immediately and protecting the western Atlantic on a large scale; that such . . . action on our part would almost certainly involve us in the war and that I considered every day's delay in our getting into the war as dangerous, and that more delay might be fatal to Britain's survival." Amid such varying voices as these there was some hesitation in Washington; the President announced that "of course" we would give our support to the Russians, but he was actually to dispatch Mr. Harry Hopkins, his close friend and confidential agent, to Moscow before definitely determining American policy.

But if there was hesitation at Washington, there was consternation at Tokyo. The ink was scarcely dry on Mr. Matsuoka's neutrality treaty with Russia; the press was still expounding his vision of a Russo-German-Japanese collaboration for the reconstruction of the world; the southward advance was just working up to full power. And at this juncture, the June 22 attack had gone off under the "Matsuoka diplomacy" like a blockbuster bomb. Would all the plans have to be destroyed and remade in reverse? Did the Tri-Partite Pact now require them to go into Siberia instead of Singapore? Treaty engagements aside (and Japan rarely troubled much about the letter of treaty engagements), could they afford to miss this golden opportunity to finish off the northern adversary? Could they afford to seem negligent in their duty to their German ally by pursuing their own interests independently in the south? And what about Mr. Matsuoka, the master diplomat who had landed them in this embarrassing contretemps?

At the first news of the Russo-German war, Mr. Matsuoka, according to the Konoye memoir, had rushed to the Emperor to demand an immediate invasion of Siberia, a postponement of the southward advance, and an avoidance of war with the United States for as long as possible. The Son of Heaven was "much surprised" by all this, and sent the Foreign Minister back for further consultation with his colleagues. Prince Konoye appears to have tried to put on the brakes, to make sense out of his voluble and unreliable Foreign Minister, to "relieve" the Imperial concern, and to concert a policy with the Army and Navy. For ten days the inner circles of the Tokyo Government buzzed like an overturned beehive. There were Cabinet conferences, audiences, consultations. The Germans, who had not even had the courtesy to give them advance notice of the Russian war, were now putting on all the pressure they could bring to bear to get the Japanese into an immediate attack on Siberia. But the Germans were laboring under a certain tactical disadvantage. With their armies slashing daily deeper into Russia, with their propaganda already proclaiming great "annihilation battles" and seeing victory almost at hand, they could not appear to be too eager for help.

They were forced, instead, to use the tactics of enticement. On July 1 there was a telegram from Von Ribbentrop himself: "I have no doubt . . . that perhaps even in only a few weeks Russian resistance over the whole European area of the Soviet Union will be broken." This offered a "unique opportunity" to Japan to free herself once and for all from the Russian threat and thus to secure her subsequent southward expansion at the expense of the British and Americans. The victorious power bloc of "Germany, Italy, and Japan" would be enough "to paralyze any rising tendency in the United States to participate in the war." But Siberia should come first:

> It seems to me, therefore, the requirement of the hour that the Japanese Army should, as quickly as possible, get into possession of Vladivostok and push as far as possible toward the west. The aim of such an operation should be that, before the coming of cold weather, the Japanese Army advancing westward should be able to shake hands at the half-way mark with the German troops advancing toward the east . . . and that finally the whole Russian question should be solved by Germany and Japan in common in a way which would eliminate the Russian threat to both Germany and Japan for all time.

It was an enticing vision. But Von Ribbentrop was too late; it was also on July 1 that the critical decision was taken by the Japanese Cabinet. His colleagues evidently did not share Mr. Matsuoka's confidence in the German ally. Perhaps they were also dubious of Von Ribbentrop's visions of an imminent Russian collapse. Other considerations must have entered into the frenetic conferences. With the United States and the Netherlands Indies between them able at any moment to cut off virtually the whole of Japan's petroleum supply, it may well have seemed too dangerous from a purely military point of view to undertake Siberia until they had first secured the Netherlands Indies oil wells. In the end, according to Davis and Lindley, the best which the Germans could get was a promise to move on Siberia when the German armies reached the Volga; in return, the Germans were to force Pétain to accede "peacefully" to the immediate occupation of southern Indo-China. The Germans could not admit that they would not soon be upon the Volga, and had to let matters go at that.

At its meeting on July 1 the Cabinet reached definitive agreement. In a broadcast after the meeting Konoye emphasized two themes: the "absolute necessity for our country's existence" of "establishing national self-sufficiency," and the fact that "this is no time to be thinking of the fates of other countries." From this much the correspondents shrewdly divined that the decision had been to throw overboard the "Matsuoka diplomacy" and to continue the southward advance. Whatever it had been, the decision was submitted next day, July 2, to formal ratification by a full-dress Imperial Conference. This gathering was surrounded with every apparatus of solemnity and historic significance. There had been only eight previous conferences of the kind since Japan's first tentative entry on the world stage in 1895. The Emperor presided in full naval uniform, and under him there were assembled the Army and Navy chiefs of staff as well as the War and Navy Ministers and the political and economic heads of the Government. A brief statement at the end announced to the Japanese people and to the world that a decision had been arrived at upon the "fundamental national policy to be adopted in meeting the prevailing situations." What it was, of course, was not revealed.

In Prince Konoye's explanation, at once elliptical and touched with naïveté, the "chief aim" of this solemn exercise was "to restrain the Army" and Mr. Matsuoka. The Foreign Minister "vehemently advocated a postitive view. At the moment, the Army had concentrated forces in Manchuria and was in a position to launch a war against the Soviet Union." The Cabinet was against the adventure, but the Army's wishes could not be lightly thwarted:

> In the sense that we had to pay a price for the Army's consent to the decision, the Government recognized the Army's advance in Indo-China. Completely rejecting the Army's demands would have brought a frontal clash with the Army, contributing nothing to the problem of a settlement. Moreover, there was a good prospect that we might use the advance of Japanese troops in Indo-China as the basis of a compromise in the Japanese-American talks then under way. I am confident I will be able to prevent a war.*

Mr. Matsuoka, who was also to leave an apologia behind him, was to advance an even more ingenious explanation. This version admits that he "expressed the view that it would be better for Japan to enter a Soviet-German war on the German side rather than make a southward advance at the risk of a military clash with Britain and the United States. This, however, was not my true intention. It was a trick to restrain the Army and Navy, because I was fully aware that neither . . . had any intention of fighting the Soviet Union." So Mr. Matsuoka was just a "restrainer" like everybody else, only he was trying to stop an advance southward as well as northward!

* The quotations are taken from the report in the *New York Times*, December 23, 1945, of *Asahi's* publication of the memoir. They do not appear textually in the translation included as Exhibit 173 in the record of the Pearl Harbor investigation, though the same ideas are found there in somewhat more discreet language. Thus the Prince states (*Hearings*, Pt. 20, p. 4004) that though the Government leaders "were able to set aside the demands for an immediate war against the Soviets, they were obliged to decide upon the armed occupation of French Indo-China as a sort of consolation prize. At the same time . . . they proceeded with full-scale preparations for a possible war against England and America." And on p. 4019: "The Army and Foreign Minister Matsuoka took a strong attitude toward the Soviet Union. . . . This resolution was drawn up to offset the policies of the Army and the Foreign Minister."

Whatever one prefers to believe, one is left with a fascinating picture of the processes of policy-making in Imperial Japan. And it is hard to know whether to wonder more at the reckless price which the Prime Minister of Japan felt obliged to pay in order to buy off his own Army from the Russian war, or the naïveté of his belief that the new aggression southward would open an avenue to peace with the United States. But at all events the decision had been taken; the die had been cast.

On July 4 President Roosevelt was still uncertain enough of the Japanese intentions to send a message direct to Prince Konoye expressing the hope (in fairly stiff language) that there was no foundation for the reports that Japan was about to enter the war on Russia. All that this slightly gratuitous gesture elicited was a polite disclaimer of any such plan, coupled "incidentally" with a politely acid inquiry as to whether the United States really intended to enter the war against Germany. Clearly Mr. Roosevelt had asked for that one. But the reply at any rate bore out what could already be divined and what was soon to be fully confirmed. On July 8 "magic" came up with the text of the Japanese decision.

"Magic" was the code name for the most closely guarded military secret in Washington—the operations of the Army and Navy cryptanalytic divisions, which had succeeded in breaking various Japanese codes and ciphers, including the top diplomatic code, and were engaged in reading the most confidential communications of our potential enemies. Even the existence of this operation was unknown to all save a few of the very highest Army, Navy, and government officials; the utmost secrecy was essential for the obvious reason that the Japanese would at once change their codes if they got any hint that the codes were being read. The messages, picked up for the most part by three Navy radio monitoring stations on the Atlantic coast, on the Pacific coast, and at Manila, were sent by teletype or air mail to Washington; there the Army and the Navy divided the work of breaking them down into plain Japanese and translating them. Copies of all the important material were distributed by officer couriers to the President, the Secretaries of State, War, and Navy, the Chief of Staff, the Chief of Naval Operations, and the heads of the War Plans and Intelligence sections of the two services. These copies were afterward collected by the couriers and all were destroyed, leaving only two copies in existence, one each for the Army and the Navy files. The field commanders, the ambassadors, even the second and lower echelons of the Intelligence sections in Washington, did not even know that there was such a service.

On the 8th, however, "magic" was providing our high officials with a translation of messages sent by Tokyo to the Washington, Berlin, and Moscow embassies, advising them of the policy which had been adopted at the July 2 conference. It ran:

1. Imperial Japan shall adhere to the policy of contributing to world peace by establishing the Great East Asia Sphere of Co-Prosperity, regardless of how the world situation may change.

2. The Imperial Government shall continue its endeavor to dispose of the China Incident, and shall take measures with a view to advancing southward in order to establish firmly a basis for her self-existence and self-protection.

A supplementary explanation made it clear that disposing of the China Incident meant "bringing the Chiang regime to submission" by both propaganda and fighting; and that "concomitantly, preparations for southward advance shall be re-enforced and the policy already decided upon with reference to French Indo-China and Thailand shall be executed." As for the Russo-German war, "although the spirit of the Three-Power Axis shall be maintained . . . the situation shall be dealt with in our own way." Every means available was to be used "to prevent the United States from joining the war" but "if need be" Japan would "act in accordance with the Three-Power Pact."

Actually, the complete decision, as preserved in the Konoye

memoirs, was considerably more explicit. While the southward advance was to be prosecuted by diplomacy, it was provided that "in case the diplomatic negotiations break down, preparations for a war with England and America will also be carried forward. First of all, the plans which have been laid with reference to French Indo-China and Thai will be prosecuted with a view to consolidating our position in the southern territories. In carrying out the plans outlined in the foregoing article, we will not be deterred by the possibility of being involved in a war with England and America." As a sop to the Army's "Manchuria Gang," it was provided that in case the Russo-German war "should develop to our advantage" they would resort to arms to "settle the Soviet question"; for the present, however, they would stick to watchful waiting, while all plans in regard to Siberia should be carried out "in such a way as to place no serious obstacles in the path of our basic military preparations for a war with England and America."

While the State Department was without the benefit of these interesting details, they could be easily enough inferred from the intercepted message. That made it plain that Japan was going to follow her own policy, not Germany's; that she would mark time on the Siberian border but press the southward advance; that not only southern Indo-China but Siam as well was on the immediate timetable; and that the advance would be pressed with every energy to the point of war. A few days after the conference, a decree announced the general mobilization of the Japanese people; the entire resources of the nation were to be brought to a war footing, and some 2,000,000 more men would be called to the colors to swell the already swollen and ominous ranks of the Imperial armies.

The American newspapers on July 4 were publishing long extracts from General Marshall's biennial report as Chief of Staff. It was able to announce progress in the creation of the new Army; nevertheless, it could still list only 33 formed divisions, of which only four were armored and of which none was yet at full strength. The total establishment had reached 1,400,000 men, but hundreds of thousands of these were still in recruit training or absorbed in the vast "overhead" of a modern army. The whole of our overseas garrisons, including Alaska, Newfoundland, and the Atlantic bases as well as Panama, Hawaii, and the Philippines, numbered as yet only 120,000 men. Equipment, field training, nearly everything else was still lacking, while the Chief of Staff was facing the grim fact that under existing provisions of law what army he had would soon begin to dissolve in his hands, long before it could be completed. The selective service men had been drafted for a year only; moreover, they could not, save in the event of war, be sent beyond the limits of the "Western Hemisphere." With the world on fire and the conflagration spreading, with the peril extreme (as he knew it to be) both from Europe and from Asia, General Marshall saw himself being obliged to discharge his recruits at just about the time they would be turning into reasonably competent soldiers, or unable to send a division overseas without first wrecking it by replacing all its draftees with volunteers. A long section of the biennial report was devoted to a plea, as sober and factual as the general could make it, for the removal of these restrictions and the extension of the term of service. That Congress would accede to the plea seemed at best very doubtful.

One can understand that the Fourth of July celebration at the American Club in Tokyo was not without its sense of strain. The British came as guests. Ambassador Grew made a speech declaring "that America was in there pitching with the rest for a victory of democracy, civilization, and humanity" and the British, presumably, were at least hopeful. Afterward Mr. Tolischus went home to conclude his day's dispatch with the prediction that "Japan has decided to eliminate from East Asia Anglo-American influences, which it holds responsible for resistance by the Indies as well as by Chungking." Elsewhere the shadow was beginning to spread. In Batavia there was a three-day air raid and blackout drill, conducted with all possible realism and with a full appreciation by the participants of the deadly seriousness of the exercise. "Everyone knew it might be the last practice," as in fact it was.

Even Manila was at last awakening to a sense of peril. The first blackout there was held on July 10, with a brilliant tropic moon making everything almost as clear during the blackout as it had been before. Civil defense measures, like the military preparations, were badly tangled in the conflicts between the Philippine and the American authorities over who should foot the bills, but something was being done. And a new, dispiriting phenomenon had begun to appear—the journalistic sightseers and heavy thinkers, passing through on their way to home and safety. In June Mr. Henry R. Luce and his dazzling wife, Clare Boothe, stopped by and lectured them at the High Commissioner's residence. "God help you," Mr. Luce observed succinctly. "Because no one else is going to—and you are in a terrible spot." Frank Gervaisi berated them on their unprepared state. They were to be honored through the succeeding weeks by a procession of eminent observers—Ralph Ingersoll, E. A. Mowrer, Ernest Hemingway, Vincent Sheean—all agreed on two things, "that we were in imminent danger and that we were appallingly unaware of it." For those who had to stay, aware or not, within the fragile defenses which were all the richest nation on earth had been able to provide, these visitors had "a ghoulish quality about them, like the gathering of the vultures before the kill."

But the home public, seven thousand miles away, still inclined to believe that Japanese were congenitally incapable of flying airplanes and grossly uninformed as to the actual and appallingly deficient state of the Far Eastern defenses, had other things to think about. On July 7 there came the White House announcement of the agreement with the Icelandic Government under which the Marines had that day landed in Iceland "to supplement and eventually to replace the British forces which have until now been stationed in Iceland in order to insure the adequate defense of that country." So still another step had been taken, deeper into the British alliance and nearer to actual war, at least upon the lend-lease sea lanes. Even the War Department, posting up General Short at Pearl Harbor on the same day, seemed to take an oddly complacent view of possibilities in the Far East:

> Opinion is that Jap activity in the South will be confined to seizure and development of naval, army, and air bases in Indo-China, although an advance against the British and Dutch cannot be entirely ruled out. . . . They have ordered all Jap vessels in U. S. Atlantic ports to be west of Panama Canal by 1st of August.

It was not long before evidences that Indo-China's hour might be at hand began to appear. And then, on July 16, there came a new and somewhat mystifying maneuver: the Konoye Cabinet suddenly resigned in a body to permit the forming of a government "more capable of coping with the ever-changing international situation."

Next day, while the reshuffling was still going on in Tokyo, an obscure little dispatch from Vichy reported that Admiral Jean Darlan, Pétain's Vice-Premier, had been in conference with the Japanese ambassador, but that "there is no crisis regarding Indo-China." On the evening of the 18th Prince Konoye, summoned to resume the burden, announced his new Cabinet. Changes in some of the lesser posts, extinguishing the remnants of the old political parties and leaving no less than four generals and three admirals in the Cabinet, seemed to confirm the fact that everything would henceforth be in the hands of the military and the non-party big business magnates—the uneasy combination through which Konoye was still trying to control his imitation of a totalitarian state. But there had been only one major change. Mr. Matsuoka had been tossed out.

The new Foreign Minister, Admiral Teijiro Toyoda, though a naval man, was of more "moderate" coloration than the ebullient Matsuoka. But Konoye declared that the new Cabinet would carry out the July 2 policy, and neither the general mobilization under way nor the bellicosity of the official press comment implied a shift toward the courses of peace. Had Matsuoka been dropped, then, simply as a cover to make the imminent stroke in Indo-China more palatable to the United States and Great Britain? There was much reason to think so.

One reason was supplied by "magic." As early as July 15 it had told us that Japan would demand southern Indo-China within the next day or two, and on the 17th it gave us the text of the six-point ultimatum being served on Vichy. Then on the 19th there appeared the translation of a message sent five days before by a Japanese diplomatic official in Canton to his superiors in Tokyo. It read:

> Subsequent information from the military officials to the Attachés is as follows:
>
> 1. The recent general mobilization order expressed the irrevocable resolution of Japan to put an end to Anglo-American assistance in thwarting her natural expansion and her indomitable intention to carry this out, if possible with the backing of the Axis but if necessary alone.
>
> 2. The immediate object of our occupation of French Indo-China will be to achieve our purposes there. Secondly, its purpose is, when the international situation is suitable, to launch therefrom a rapid attack. . . . After the occupation of French Indo-China, next on our schedule is the sending of an ultimatum to the Netherlands Indies. In the seizing of Singapore the Navy will play the principal part. As for the Army, in seizing Singapore it will need only one division, and in seizing the Netherlands Indies, only two. In the main, through the activities of our air arm . . . and our submarine fleet . . . we will once and for all crush Anglo-American military power and their ability to assist in any schemes against us.
>
> 3. The troops soon to occupy French Indo-China will be reorganized as the 25th Army Corps. . . . All preparations have been made. The ship fees have been paid and the expedition will soon proceed from here.

Two days after the translation of this interesting document,

Acting Secretary Welles, in the absence both of Secretary Hull (who was still recovering his health at White Sulphur) and of Ambassador Nomura, requested the Japanese minister, Mr. Wakasugi, to call upon him. The United States, the Acting Secretary informed Mr. Wakasugi, had reliable information "that Japan would take the southern portion of French Indo-China within the next few days. Such an act," Mr. Welles severely explained, "would definitely be in violation of the spirit of the Japanese-U.S. conversations which are being conducted on behalf of maintaining peace on the Pacific." Mr. Wakasugi angled for the source of the report. He was told simply that it "was an accurate one." Suppose, he asked, that Japan did make such a move? Mr. Welles left the clear impression that any further peace negotiations would be useless; but in view of the fact that the new Cabinet had barely taken office, the United States would "patiently await developments" before terminating the discussions.

II ☜

Prince Konoye's somewhat tortured explanations leave the impression that the Cabinet reconstruction was largely a blind. The sole purpose was to get rid of Matsuoka. Berlin, of course, was told that the shift had none but domestic significance; "Japan's policy will not be changed and she will remain faithful to the principles of the Tri-Partite Pact." This message, which was likewise being read almost immediately by "magic," cannot have increased American confidence in Japanese protestations. To be sure, it was not entirely frank. Indeed, one of the troubles about the "magic" material was that it was always so hard to know, at any given time, to whom the Japanese were lying. Matsuoka, continuing to put up a determined rear-guard fight in the German interest, running secretly to Ott, the Nazi ambassador, and interfering with and delaying the American negotiations in every possible way, was rendering it impossible for them to carry on the delicate double game in which they were embarked. His elimination recorded another step in Japan's tendency to free herself from automatic commitments in the German interest without losing the potential benefits of the German connection. It did not in any way affect the "peaceful" rape of southern Indo-China; that decision had been taken, the troops were already on the way, and all that Toyoda could now do was to avert the worst political consequences of a move already determined.

Mr. Matsuoka was no doubt a victim of his own unpopularity, his vanity, his ambition, and his loss of face as a consequence of the German attack on Russia. He had to be dropped because he was paralyzing their diplomacy. But he was also, it would seem, in some measure a propitiatory sacrifice to Washington. Now that "the vague atmosphere" had been dispelled, it was hoped that "negotiations would progress swiftly." Prince Konoye complains that Admiral Nomura failed to "understand" this and to make the most of the gesture in Washington. But one may doubt that the ambassador's understanding was at fault; rather, he understood only too well that gestures of even the most elaborate kind were no longer of much avail against Japanese acts.

Mr. Wakasugi's report of his conversation with Mr. Welles was enough to bring the ambassador back to duty post-haste. But events were moving quickly. On the 22nd Vichy dispatches admitted that important conversations with the Japanese were under way; London heard that the invasion of Indo-China would begin in a day or two; high sources in Washington were intimating that the United States might retaliate by freezing Japanese assets or embargoing the export of oil and cotton. By the time Admiral Nomura reached the State Department, on July 23, the Japanese troops were moving; it was known that Admiral Darlan had agreed to hand over the whole of Indo-China without protest, and Admiral Nomura could only proffer his "explanations."

It was the old argument. Japan had had "no alternative." Mr. Welles listened without interruption as the ambassador contended that the step "was absolutely essential from the standpoint of national security and economic safety." Japan's economic position was "critical"; she was having great difficulty in securing raw materials and in particular food from abroad and must have an uninterrupted supply of rice from Indo-China. But more than that, the Japanese believed that the western powers were bent upon a policy of "encirclement"; this was causing great "uneasiness" in Japan and the need for military security made the new aggression imperative, though purely as "a precautionary measure in the nature of a safeguard." Throughout, however, the ambassador's manner was most conciliatory, and he gave Mr. Welles the impression that he was himself profoundly disturbed by the situation. He assured the Acting Secretary that the new Cabinet was still as anxious to conclude a Japanese-American understanding as the old one had been, and begged the United States not to "jump to hasty conclusions" but to "watch the trend of further developments for a little while yet." In particular, he hoped that the United States would not consider imposing an oil embargo, as that would certainly inflame Japanese opinion "exceedingly."

Mr. Welles was sternly frank in his reply. Since it was obvious that Vichy had agreed to the occupation under German pressure, we must conclude that Japan was still acting in support of Hitler's policy of world conquest. The ambassador's explanations were severely brushed aside. Japan could get all the food, raw materials, and economic security she wanted if she would only follow a peaceful policy in the Pacific, and there was no "possible justification" for the notion that she was threatened with an aggressive encirclement by the United States or Great Britain. The United States, consequently, could only assume that the occupation was notice that Japan "intended to pursue a policy of force and conquest" and was "taking a last step" before proceeding "upon a policy of totalitarian expansion in the South Seas.... This Government could not see that there was any fact or factual theory upon which Japan could possibly fill Indo-China with Japanese military and other forces for the purposes of defending Japan. The only consequent alternative was to regard the occupation ... as being undertaken because of the Japanese realization of its value to Japan for purposes of offense against the South Sea area." Secretary Hull, Mr. Welles concluded, felt that there was now no further basis for the conversations on which they had been engaged. The troubled ambassador withdrew.

His report brought a slightly frantic telegram from his new Foreign Minister next day:

> That the leaders of the United States Government will at this time display a high degree of statesmanship is what I am secretly hoping for the sake of maintaining peace in the Pacific. . . . However, . . . there is the possibility of the United States freezing Japanese funds or of instituting a general embargo on petroleum, thus strongly stimulating public opinion in Japan. Should this plan of freezing Japanese funds be put into effect, it would have an adverse effect on many aspects of our domestic life and might compel us to resort to diverse retaliatory measures.... We cannot be certain that it would not in turn hasten the development of the worst situation.

"Magic" was promptly to make these instructions available to the American leaders. But in face of the preposterously barefaced Japanese excuses for Indo-China, it was evident that the "high degree of statesmanship" could not forever come from one side only. On Thursday, the 24th, Mr. Welles in an official statement told the public virtually what he had told Admiral Nomura the day before. Later on Thursday the President himself tried his hand, and the ambassador was summoned to the White House together with Mr. Welles and Admiral Stark, an old professional friend of Nomura's. Mr. Roosevelt, quite evidently summoning up all of his famous charm, went over the whole ground. But he included the strong hint that, with the gasoline consumption of our own citizens already being curtailed, we could not go on exporting gasoline to power Japanese aggression. For two years, as he put it, we had been permitting the export of oil to Japan because to shut off the supply would give Japan "an incentive or a pretext" for moving on the Netherlands East Indies, and our policy was to do all we could to preserve peace in the Pacific. If Japan attempted to seize the Indies oil by force, the Dutch would resist; the British would immediately come to their aid; "war would then result between Japan, the British, and the Dutch, and in view of our policy of assisting Great Britain, an exceedingly serious situation would immediately result." It was with all this in mind that we had allowed the continued export of oil to Japan. But now the new move into Indo-China "created an exceedingly serious problem for the United States."

It was no use. Ambassador Nomura went so far as to confess that he personally "deplored" the advance into Indo-China, but otherwise he could only repeat what he had said before. President Roosevelt then made a last effort. If Japan would halt the advance and remove whatever troops had already been sent, he would do all in his power to get a firm undertaking from China, Britain, and the Netherlands as well as the United States to neutralize Indo-China and to maintain there the local control of the Vichy officials. Japan would thus be fully assured of both her military security and of her access to Indo-Chinese food and raw materials. The unhappy ambassador could only promise to transmit the proposal immediately; but he seemed in no sense "optimistic as to the result." He muttered something about the necessity for maintaining face and the great difficulty of reversing a policy which had been carried so far. Only a "very great statesman" could do that. The interview terminated. Vichy had that day made formal announcement that Indo-China was to be placed under the armed "protection" of Japan by voluntary agreement. At 8 o'clock the following evening, July 25, a press statement was issued from the "summer White House" at Hyde Park, announcing that an Executive Order (it was actually dated the 26th) had frozen all Japanese assets in the United States, bringing all financial, import and export transactions under the control of the American Government. Within a few hours Britain and the Dominions followed suit; and the Dutch were to do likewise over the week end. If Prince Konoye had really believed that the seizure of Indo-China would afford him a trading "basis of a compromise" in the American negotiation, he had now been abruptly presented with another and very different one in return.

For good or ill, the freezing of Japanese assets—which was to result in a short time in the suspension of virtually all trade between Japan and the United States, Britain, and the Netherlands Indies—was decisive. All our previous sanctions had amounted to little more than irritants. This hit home, as the Roosevelt Administration clearly knew that it would. By strangling the petroleum supply, in particular, it threatened the ultimate paralysis of the Japanese war machine. Japan had to have oil; and this left her but two ways in which to get it: to fight, or else to yield something substantial to the western viewpoint. This was economic war.

The Administration was aware of the danger. An analysis by the Navy's War Plans Division, drafted on the 19th, had definitely recommended against the embargo. It had estimated, on the one hand, that Japan already had oil stocks sufficient for about eighteen months of war operations, and had recognized, on the other, that the embargo would only harden her determination and might easily precipitate war. On the 25th a joint message from General Marshall and Admiral Stark, warning the Pearl Harbor commanders that the embargo order was about to be issued, concluded:

> Chief of Naval Operations and Army Chief of Staff do not anticipate immediate hostile reaction by the Japanese through the

use of military means, but you are furnished this information in order that you may take appropriate precautionary measures against any possible eventualities.

General Short at Hawaii alerted his whole command under the guise of sending it on "maneuvers." A day or two later, Naval Intelligence was advising Admiral Kimmel that "Japan has marshalled its full naval strength and is on a full wartime footing." On the 26th a dramatic order arrived in Manila. Douglas MacArthur, field marshal of the Philippine Commonwealth, had been recalled to active duty as lieutenant general of the United States Army, and appointed to the command of all American Army forces in the Far East. The Philippine Army was to be inducted into the United States service and its mobilization (at last) begun. There were, of course, impressive public statements; General MacArthur proclaimed that the United States "in establishing this command can only mean that it intends to maintain at any cost its full rights in the Far East," while President Quezon pledged the full support of the Philippines to the cause. In Washington they were busy on more than statements. General Marshall felt convinced from this time on that war was coming, and plans began now to go forward in earnest for some real reinforcement for Manila. Such modern equipment as radar sets and self-propelled field artillery was being started on the way; and though the big Flying Fortress bombers were as yet appearing in only a trickle from the factories, a large part of those available was designated for the Philippines.

But if the freezing order seems now to have been the critical step, it is difficult, in retrospect, to see what other course could have been followed. Japan was already undergoing a general mobilization; her excuses for the Indo-China advance were preposterous; we had ample proof from intercepted messages and other sources that she was committed to the southward advance and that her military had prepared a grandiose assault upon Siam, Malaya, Singapore, and the Netherlands Indies;

she was continuing to protest to Berlin her loyalty to the Tri-Partite Pact, and even if her diplomats were sincere in their apparent efforts to "restrain" the military, we had no assurance (and no evidence from past history) that they would succeed. Southern Indo-China was the last possible stop on the road to a general Pacific war. What were the alternatives before the United States?

To do nothing would be to invite the attack to proceed, to acquiesce in the establishment of the military empire of Japan throughout the whole of China and the southwestern Pacific, and to make it reasonably certain that the Philippines would ultimately be swallowed—after the loss of all our potential allies and bases in the area had rendered it impossible for us to defend them. Even if the United States could have accepted such a prospect under other conditions, the desperate crisis in Europe forbade it. We had staked our world policy and our national future on the success of one side in the struggle. The loss to that side of Australia and New Zealand, of all the Far Eastern colonies and resources and very probably of India as well, the sacrifice of China and the doubtless prompt reappearance of an enormously strengthened Japan on Russia's Siberian flank, would have constituted a blow too crushing both materially and morally for our friends to have survived.

Even the blindest isolationism could not really suport a policy of the kind.* With the occupation of southern Indo-

* It seems significant that the minority report of the Pearl Harbor investigation, signed by Senators Brewster and Ferguson, although apparently taking every valid opportunity of criticizing the Administration, finds little or no fault with the basic foreign policy and almost wholly neglects the freezing order. Curiously enough, the investigation itself, while spending a great deal of time over Secretary Hull's miscalled "ultimation" of November 26, which was actually of only minor influence over events, paid hardly any attention to this far more critical decision on July 25. For that reason, the information about it is still scanty, and one has to fall back to some extent on inference in trying to assess the reasoning behind it.

China the United States was forced to do something. Two courses were then open. We could have gambled on the sincerity and effective influence of Konoye and his Government. We could, by letting the Indo-China advance pass without reprisal, have avoided embarrassing them; we could thus, in effect, have backed them in their efforts (assuming that they really were making the effort) to "restrain" the military, to keep the southward advance within peaceful limits, to bring its military phase to a stop in Indo-China, and to secure the militarists' and extremists' consent to an agreement with the United States which this country could sign. To say the least, that would have been a very heavy gamble indeed on the basis of all the information we possessed.

The only remaining alternative was to try to halt the southward advance ourselves while there was till time. For that, gestures were obviously no longer of any avail. We had to use effective weapons or none at all; and freezing was the only real weapon in our hands. We knew how seriously the Japanese regarded it. We knew that it risked precipitating them into war. But nothing less would now serve. If the Japanese of all factions were brought squarely face to face, through the mists of their own evasive thought processes, with the choice between fighting or concessions, they might find that they could make concessions. The President made his compromise proposal to Admiral Nomura, but followed it immediately with the freezing order as if deliberately to lend force to his offer. The chips were down. Both countries were now at the extreme limit "short of war." Both—for it was doubtless as true of our own confused democracy as it was of the romantic samurai and oligarchs of Japan—would now have to face up to realities.

How the Japanese statesmen actually saw them is rather difficult to make out. Through all the documents there nowhere appears any very precise picture of how Prince Konoye and his colleagues envisaged the "peace" for which they were so earnestly, at times almost frantically, to search. Did they really believe that they could bring the southward advance to a peaceful halt in Indo-China? Were they actually contending with their militarists, or were they simply trying to secure by diplomacy the total victory for which the military were simultaneously preparing to strike by arms? It is possible that they did not know themselves. They were trained, most of them, to an opportunistic philosophy of life and politics; they had risen to their power through the intrigues which characterize the political life of any absolutist state, and were representatives of a community which had itself seized a great place on the world stage, with the slimmest of means, by shrewdness, manipulation, the playing of one favorable chance against the next. It is possible that they never did define even to themselves the kind of "peace" which they might achieve. It is hard to doubt that Konoye and Toyoda tried. But what they were really trying to do was not so much to conserve peace in the Pacific as to balance all the dangerous balls with which they were playing—the United States and the Germans, Britain and Russia, Japan's economic needs and political ambitions, their military men, their big business magnates, their Emperor, their own personal power and prestige—into some pattern, any pattern, that would work for the time being and carry them from one crisis to the next.

In Tokyo, at all events, the rupture of the negotiations and the freezing order came as a violent shock. It was on Saturday, July 26, that the Japanese occupation command arrived in Saigon (they were flown in from Hanoi in a French airplane) and at noon the "defense agreement" with Vichy was announced in Tokyo. The news of the freezing order came not long afterward. The stock market collapsed under the impact, while the press thundered with declarations that sanctions, so far from bringing Japan to a halt, could only impel her to go forward to the establishment of the "Co-Prosperity Sphere." But Foreign Minister Toyoda, receiving Ambassador Grew that day, "gave obvious indications of being profoundly concerned at the rupture of the Washington negotiations." Mr.

Grew knew that he had just come from the Emperor, and took this as a reflection of the Imperial dismay. The Foreign Minister inquired "with every indication of concern" whether anything more than freezing was in prospect, and declared that he "had hardly slept at all during recent nights." Mr. Grew received the impression that Toyoda had accepted his office in the belief that Japan could get by with the Indo-China move without American reaction, and that when it came it had shaken them all.

They had not, however, vouchsafed any answer to the President's offer of a neutralization of Indo-China. Washington evidently was waiting, for on Sunday, July 27, it tried again through Mr. Grew, cabling him the proposals which had been made to Admiral Nomura. The ambassador, realizing the critical importance of the proposal, got on the telephone at once and secured an interview with the Foreign Minister at his residence. There he made "the strongest appeal of which I was capable." To his "astonishment," Toyoda replied that he knew nothing about this offer, although it had been made to Nomura three days before. Mr. Grew may have inferred that this was a diplomatic evasion; at any rate, as he came away, he felt no more optimistic than had his Japanese counterpart in Washington. Perhaps the best that could be said for the effort was that at least it had placed the United States "in an unassailable position from the point of view of history."

On Monday, the 28th, there came the action of the Netherlands East Indies, following the American lead. In theory, the Indies oil could still be exported, but as the yen-guilder exchange had been suspended there was in practice no longer any way to pay for it. The Japanese officially took the position that such difficulties were temporary and that the Dutch would soon find a means of resuming shipments, but the press in Tokyo raged more fiercely than before, while a Japanese naval aviator expressed the military reaction to sanctions by releasing a stick of bombs at the American gunboat *Tutuila*, then moored at Chungking. He fortunately failed to kill anyone, however, and his Government was prompt in apology. Matters had not yet reached the shooting stage. But they were serious, on both sides of the Pacific. On July 30 there was a queer telegram ("magic" produced it a few days later) from Nomura to his Foreign Office:

> Today I knew from the hard looks on their faces that they meant business, and I could see that if we do not answer to suit them that they are going to take some drastic steps. [The ambassador recalled the bombing of the *U.S.S. Panay* in 1937, and how seriously that had been taken in the United States.] The latest incident brought all this back to me and I can see just how gravely they are regarding it. Think of it! Popular demand for the freezing of Japanese funds was subsiding, and now this had to happen. I must tell you it certainly occurred at an inopportune moment. Things being as they are, need I point out to you gentlemen that in my opinion it is necessary to take without one moment's hesitation some appeasement measures. Please wire me back at the earliest possible moment.

III ☞

Yet the *Tutuila* incident, as a matter of fact, made no very deep public impression. To the American people, the Far East was still a remote problem. The correspondents might send long, foreboding dispatches; one might read (though usually only on the inside pages) the reckless pronunciamentos of Japanese spokesmen; one might notice Japan's total mobilization for war, but it was still hard to take the Japanese seriously amid the colossal events of the European theater.

As July turned into August the gigantic battles in Russia overshadowed everything. The six weeks which our War Department experts had given the Soviet armies were nearly up. Those armies were fighting now far behind their original lines; the panzer columns were reaching for Leningrad and had taken Smolensk, far up the historic road which had carried Napoleon's hosts to Moscow; in the south they were across the Dniester and deep into the Ukraine. But the Soviet armies, if they were fighting a losing war, were still fighting. Despite all the "encirclements" and "annihilations" they had not been annihilated. The Germans were still a long way from the Volga and a very much longer distance still from that meeting with the Japanese in central Siberia which Von Ribbentrop had so cheerfully predicted. On August 2 an exchange of notes between Mr. Welles and Ambassador Oumansky in Washington assured American economic aid to the Soviet Union.

But we were having trouble enough organizing our own war economy. The nation was surrounded by war, and felt war coming nearer to it. Whole groups of young Americans were fighting in the Eagle Squadrons of the Royal Air Force; others were resigning, mysteriously, from our own Army and Navy air forces and taking passages for the Far East. They were to reappear in the air over Chungking as Chennault's Flying Tigers. There was a kind of war already upon the sea lanes to Iceland. On the last day of July the *Fortune* poll reported that for the first time it had found a majority of its sample (54 per cent of the whole and 58 per cent of those with opinions) convinced that we should back the British until Hitler should be defeated, at the cost of war if need be. Another 22 per cent believed it necessary to support the Administration foreign policy, and only 16.3 per cent of the sample felt that they should resist to the last ditch any move toward war. The isolationists had lost their battle for the public mind. But the nation had not yet translated its opinions into the vigorous action which they demanded. Newspapers like the *Chicago Tribune* and the New York *Daily News* kept up their venomous sniping fire upon an Administration which they pictured as thirsting only to involve us needlessly in "Europe's broils." The giant production effort still seemed to be only stumbling and staggering forward in the midst of administrative confusion and shifts in policy and direction. The Congress was much more timid and obstructive than the people.

Through July General Marshall had been pleading with the House and Senate military committees for action to remove the crippling limitations of the selective service law. He was publicly testifying that for the past two months at least the nation had been in imminent peril of war; and he was going farther than that in secret committee sessions, the gist of which was pretty well reported. Some of the statesmen admitted that they were "impressed"; but many of them still could not overcome either their dread of the political unpopularity of military service, their partisan desire to cripple the Roosevelt Administration, or the old, ingrained idea that the issue of peace or war was one wholly for this country to determine. In the past, in point of fact, we had always started all our wars ourselves. The way to avert war, consequently, was to "stay out of it"; and an adventurous Administration seemed a much greater danger (or at least one more amenable to domestic political pressure) than an adventurous German or Japanese militarism. The Senate brought itself to vote the extension of selective service, but only by 45 to 30, and the prospects in the House were dim. The argument even achieved such grotesqueries as the question of whether Dakar (in 17° West longitude) was not in the "Western Hemisphere," and if not, whether drafted men could legally garrison the eastern end of Iceland, which lies east of the fifteenth meridian; and amid absurdities of the kind the real possibility loomed that Congress might wreck our only half-formed Army at the very moment that the international problem was reaching its most critical and dangerous stage.

The President, however, appeared unworried; and on August 3 he vanished from Washington in order, it was understood, to get a vacation fishing trip off the New England coast. It was not long before rumors began to get about that he might have more than fishing in mind; but they were not published, and as the selective service debate ground on, Washington sank into its heavy blanket of summer heat. In the midst of it, on August 5, a long communication for Admiral Nomura arrived at last from Admiral Toyoda in Tokyo. "The Imperial Government," it began, "is trying to give its attention to the all-important matter of Japanese-U.S. relations. This is not an easy task, for there are numerous obstacles involving domestic politics." The freezing restrictions were taking effect, and many Japanese believed that they were being increased in intensity. "Such reports give the antagonists a strong talking point. This is a situation which causes us no end of anxiety."

Whatever its real source, there can be little doubt about the anxiety. The Konoye Government had been going through another paroxysm of conferences. On July 14, in Mr. Matsuoka's last hours, they had finally agreed upon a reply to the American proposals of June 21; but this had been swept away by the Cabinet shake-up and the Indo-China crisis before Ambassador Nomura had found opportunity to present it. Plainly staggered by the freezing order, the Japanese (including the Army and Navy as well as the civilians) were now in a fever to get the American negotiations restarted. But they had no intention of reversing the course of their war machine by accepting the President's suggested neutralization of Indo-China. Patiently, it was a difficult problem; but in a joint conference on August 4 they achieved a new formula, and it was this which Admiral Toyoda was now transmitting to the ambassador in Washington. The appeal was now to be made on the grounds of the Konoye Government's inability to control its own people. The instructions laid down the flat position that Japan could not be coerced by "encirclement" or economic pressure; such measures were bound to have only the opposite effect, and if there was to be any improvement in Japanese-American relations, everything which could even be construed in Japan as economic pressure "should be abandoned at once." Under cover of this approach the instructions went on:

In form, the proposal which is being forwarded herewith is a reply to the President's plan of the 24th. Our real motive is, however, to incorporate its provisions into the final agreement. With this instrument we hope to resume the Japanese-U.S. negotiations which were suspended because of the delay of the delivery of our revised proposals of July 14 and because of our occupation of French Indo-China which took place in the meantime.

Admiral Nomura was at the State Department next day, August 6. The new proposals inferentially passed over Indo-China as just one of those unfortunate things which had "taken place," and in going on to seek again for a general settlement, lightly sidestepped the whole force of the President's offer. Economic pressure had not been wholly without effect, however, for in one important respect the new proposals differed from the old. Japan was now prepared to undertake not to send her troops any farther into Southeast Asia than Indo-China and to evacute the latter country "on the settlement of the China Incident." Konoye had never got his military to assent to that before, and standing alone it would have represented a very considerable concession. Unfortunately, it did not stand alone. In return, the United States would have to undertake to "suspend its military measures in the Southwest Pacific," to restore normal trade relations, to co-operate with Japan in procuring for her whatever Southwest Pacific raw materials she might require, to bring Chiang Kai-shek to accept Japan's terms for the "settlement" of the "China Incident," and to recognize a special status for Japan in Indo-China even after the promised withdrawal of the troops.

In fact, it was simply the old business all over again: Japan would give slippery promises against resort to war provided she were assured of getting everything she wanted without it. On August 8 Secretary Hull was back again at his desk, and when Ambassador Nomura returned that day for an answer, his reception was a chilly one. The written reply which was handed to him stated merely that the Japanese proposals were "lacking in responsiveness" to the President's July 24 suggestion; as for the general settlement after which the Japanese were angling, the United States felt "that its views . . . have been made abundantly clear." Admiral Nomura absorbed this document. Was there any possibility, he then asked, of the responsible heads of the two states meeting directly, "say in Honolulu," to find a path to agreement? Secretary Hull was not encouraging. Their former discussions, he observed, might have led to understanding; the United States had been "patient" and prepared to move slowly in order to give the Japanese every chance to deal with their own public opinion, but Japan had destroyed the basis for understanding by the rape of Indo-China and was now stimulating the press to inflammatory outcries about "encirclement." Under the circumstances, Mr. Hull intimated, before they could talk of a meeting between the heads of state it was up to the Japanese Government to decide whether "it could find means of shaping its policies" toward agreement and then "to evolve some satisfactory plan."

So another of Tokyo's hopeful inspirations died. The technique of "So sorry; excuse it, please!" appeared to have reached its limits in Washington. It was on the following day, August 9, that the British ambassador, Lord Halifax, was at the State Department to enquire what aid the United States could give if Singapore or the Netherlands East Indies should be attacked. Mr. Hull saw the danger in terms much more alarming than those of Singapore or the N.E.I.; he was envisaging a Japanese advance to the Persian oil fields, to Suez, and to the Cape of Good Hope. Such an advance would deal a more paralyzing blow to the British defense, on which our own policy was staked, than any short of an actual invasion of the British Isles. Mr. Hull left no doubt as to the Administration's desire to resist it; yet all that he could say was that in the event of another Japanese move southward the United States and Britain "should naturally have a conference at once, and this country would then be able to determine more definitely and in detail its situation." Perhaps, however, he felt it unnecessary to say more, for as both men knew, such a conference was at that moment about to begin.

President Roosevelt's fishing trip off the New England coast had brought him by August 10 to Argentia Bay in southern Newfoundland; and his flotilla, led by the heavy cruiser *Augusta*, entered it together with another one led by *H.M.S. Prince of Wales*, newest of Britain's battleships, bearing Mr. Winston Churchill, the First Minister of the British Crown. She also bore Mr. Harry Hopkins, back with his report from Moscow, Mr. Winant, our ambassador to London, and the galaxy of British chiefs of staff and high civil officers who were to meet with their counterparts in Mr. Roosevelt's entourage. The famous Atlantic Conference was under way.

Its main objects were three: to concert a political program of war aims which would recognize the American position in the struggle to which we were increasingly committed; to concert policy in regard to aid to Russia and to secure some undertaking from the Russians in return; and to reach agreement upon the difficult problems of policy and strategy raised by the now acute menace in the Far East. When, something over a week later, the news of the conference broke in torrents of texts, photographs, long "color" stories, and editorial comment, attention was naturally centered on the first two. The third was largely obscured by the unavoidable necessity for secrecy, and not many realized that the Far Eastern problem had also been a major preoccupation of the conference.

Mr. Churchill, still a believer in the efficacy of minatory gestures toward Japan, proposed "parallel action" by the two countries at Tokyo. He wanted a warning that if the Japanese should advance beyond a given line both countries would take countermeasures, that the United States would do so even though war might result; and that if Britain or the Netherlands were attacked the President would ask authority from Congress to aid them. The President was more wary of the implied commitment, more skeptical of the value of threats or more dubious of the support he would get from

Congress. It was not until August 13 that the House at last voted the extension of the selective service act, and it did so then only by the incredibly narrow majority of one. The Senate agreed to the House amendments next day, so that hurdle was safely passed; but it had been an extremely close thing, and the episode cannot have encouraged bold courses at Argentia Bay.

Mr. Churchill wanted a definite undertaking from the President that if either the British or the Dutch were attacked, the United States, Congress permitting, would fight. The President refused. He would make no commitments except as to lend-lease. But he thought that by pressing his neutralization proposal for Indo-China they might hold off any further Japanese aggressions for a month or so. Mr. Churchill agreed, and thought there was a "reasonable chance" of averting war if they could get the Japanese-American negotiations going again on such a basis. Mr. Sumner Welles prepared a draft note for Japan, based on the Churchill idea, carrying the warning that in the event of any further Japanese aggressions the United States would take steps, even though they should result in war. The Under Secretary had departed for Washington two days before the end of the conference. Secretary Hull and the State Department experts rewrote the Welles version, and in the process all reference to war disappeared. The President reached Washington on August 17, and that same day Admiral Nomura was invited to the White House. The statement, as it was finally handed to him, concluded:

> If the Japanese Government takes any further steps in pursuance of a policy or program of military domination by force or threat of force of neighboring countries, the Government of the United States will be compelled to take immediately any and all steps which it may deem necessary toward safeguarding the legitimate rights and interests of the United States and American nationals and toward insuring the safety and security of the United States.

This was, however, but one part of a lengthy interview. Ambassador Nomura had begun by reverting to the suggestion of a direct meeting between the President and the Prime Minister; and he had presented the instructions in which Prince Konoye, expressing his earnest desire of a peaceful solution, offered to meet the President somewhere "midway between our two countries" and sit down to talk the whole matter out. The instructions, incidentally, had already been read by "magic"; and so had the ambassador's own very gloomy comments to Tokyo as to the prospects.

President Roosevelt's answer to the proposal of a meeting was a double one. He first read the warning statement and handed the ambassador a copy. Then, after a break in the conversation to distinguish the two documents, he read a second statement. This sketched the history of the previous negotiations. It alluded to Japan's bad faith in the Indo-China occupation and to the violent press campaigns which the Japanese Government was promoting. In vague, but glowing, terms it advanced the American program for peace in the Pacific, based upon "the application in the entire Pacific area of the principle of equality of commercial opportunity and treatment" and better calculated to assure Japan "satisfaction of its economic needs and legitimate aspirations" than any policy of force. If the Japanese Government felt that Japan could suspend her expansionist activities and embark on a peaceful program for the Pacific along such lines, the United States would resume informal negotiations. But it would be helpful, before resuming the conversations or arranging for a meeting of the chiefs of state, if Japan "would furnish a clearer statement than has yet been furnished as to its present attitudes and plans."

In all essentials, the issue was deadlocked exactly where it had been six months before. The Japanese had been able to offer nothing except the demand, expressed in various ways, that the United States in effect accept their untrammeled military hegemony over eastern Asia and the western Pacific. The United States had been able to offer nothing except a demand for a reversal of Japanese national policy too complete to be easy for any government and certainly impossible to the precariously balanced combination of militarists, magnates, political opportunists, and nationalist fanatics from which Konoye drew his power and over which he presided. Some middle ground might conceivably have been discoverable had the Japanese Government been able to give any trustworthy guarantee that there were limits to its expansionist plans and that it would unquestionably stop somewhere short of the point at which its activities would mortally imperil the anti-Axis coalition on which the security of the United States depended. But that Prince Konoye, entangled as he was both with the Germans and with his own firebrands, was unable to do, even assuming that he really wished to.

For the United States there was little left now, except to spin negotiations out as long as possible, meanwhile clinging to the hope that when the Japanese ultimately came to the point they would not dare go through with it. The hope seemed brighter then, when the world did not yet grasp the complete self-confidence of the Japanese military, the skill and thoroughness of their preparations, or the grim earnestness of their resolve.

FOUR

THE LEADERS' CONFERENCE

I ☞

Washington has long been famous for its oppressive summer heat, and many of those who worked there through that frenzied summer of 1941 remember it as the hottest they ever experienced. No doubt the weather records would bear them out, for heat waves mounting into the high eighties and nineties were sweeping the Northeast all through the late summer and even far into the fall. But there was more than the thermometer to raise the temperatures and tempers of the dripping men who wrestled through these months with all the clamant, unfamiliar, but imperious problems of rearmament, training, industrial mobilization, civilian confusion, domestic politics, and foreign policy.

Around them lay the vast, inert, yet vocal and always potentially invidious mass of the American people—uncertain of its purposes, unwilling to face the sacrifices demanded by its own intuitions, but with an intuitively accurate grasp, at bottom, of the world crisis into which it had been flung. It was reading, according to the best-seller lists, Mr. William L. Shirer's *Berlin Diary;* after that, Mr. Douglas Miller's *You Can't Do Business With Hitler* and Mrs. Alice Duer Miller's moving tributes to the white cliffs of Dover. It was also, when it turned to fiction, reading Mr. A. J. Cronin's *Keys of the Kingdom* and Mr. Eric Knight's *This Above All*, and it had not yet tired of Mr. John P. Marquand's *H. M. Pulham, Esquire.*

In the first week of September Miss Margaret Mitchell was to send the *U.S.S. Atlanta*, a new type of anti-aircraft light cruiser, down the ways at Kearney, N. J. Miss Mitchell was the author of the enormously popular *Gone with the Wind.* Within eighteen months both *Atlanta* and her sister *Juneau*, completing on the next slipway, would be gone upon the great winds of war, lost with hundreds of their men in a furious night battle off the Solomon Islands. But as the summer ended, few in the United States had ever heard of the Solomon Islands. The advertisements were announcing the reopening on Broadway of *Lady in the Dark*, Mr. Moss Hart's and Miss Gertrude Lawrence's brilliant excursion into the more decorative aspects of psychoanalysis; and *Arsenic and Old Lace*, that quaint jest with death and madness in a world much too full of both, was still packing them in. The public, for all its serious interest in the great struggle against Hitlerism, seemed tending to lose itself as well up some odd side alleys of mysticism and make-believe. In early September a new play arrived to establish itself as a smash hit all through that fall and winter. It was a curious piece, *The Wookey*, in which Mr. Edmund Gwenn portrayed the indomitable courage of the Cockney heart under the terror of the bombs through the medium of almost every stock situation and hoary cliché known to the history of the theater. The very fact that its sentimentality made it a huge success, implanting its quoted lines in solemn discussions of war and policy, is in itself perhaps indicative.

Those less intellectually (or financially) equipped could see Mr. Bob Hope in *Caught in the Draft* or such light essays as *Yanks in Tanks*, two of Hollywood's earlier tributes to the new citizen soldiers, whose initial struggles with the art of killing were—and would be for many months—still a subject for comedy. Mr. Hope was to follow his draftees into many a grimmer theater later on; at the time, he was expressing the mood of a nation half in and half out of a desperate war, inclined to take it all in a partly unbelieving, partly nervous, and partly farcical spirit. Everything was daily growing more urgent and more critical; that we were as a nation committed to the defeat of Hitlerism was just as obvious as the ominous fact that Hitlerism was not being defeated, but there was still the faith, or at any rate the hope, that it would never actually come to a "shooting" war. To serve as the mighty "arsenal of democracy" with, perhaps, only some minor battle action in keeping open the sea lanes would surely suffice. If only we poured out the tools of war, the British (in accordance with Mr. Churchill's promise) and the Russians would finish the job for us.

Those responsible, in the steaming vortex of Washington, for pouring out the tools were less confident. Mr. Donald M. Nelson, already high in the command of industrial mobilization and soon to become its head, believes that "1941 will go down in history as the year when we almost lost the war before we got into it." Billions had been spent and many more billions appropriated, but the tools themselves were coming with alarming slowness. In January the amorphous NDAC (National Defense Advisory Commission) had been replaced by OPM (Office of Production Management), a two-headed umpiring and advisory agency under Mr. William S. Knudsen and Mr. Sidney Hillman. From the beginning it had lacked adequate powers either to produce or to manage; and it was now staggering under its accumulated problems in a mood of futility and desperation.

The underlying difficulty was that the nation was neither in the war nor out of it. In our individualistic economic system it was, or it seemed to be, impossible to apply really drastic measures of control and mobilization until the worst came to the worst. Yet if the worst did come to the worst it would then be too late. This was a dilemma with which the President—never strong at best in administration—his New

Deal, and the industrialists and business executives whom it had called in to help wrestled frantically and not too effectively. And by the late summer of 1941 the crisis point was approaching.

The President had started with the idea that it would be possible to superimpose an adequate war effort upon the civilian economy without doing too much damage to the latter; and at the beginning it had worked well enough. Most of the initial billions had to go into the more or less normal activities of construction, plant expansion, and tool building; flooding out through payrolls they were soon creating a seller's market for consumption goods of which big and little manufacturers were naturally eager to take advantage while they still had the chance. In the first half of 1941, while we were supposedly bending all our energies to rearmament, the automotive industry produced and sold more cars for civilian use than in any similar period in history, and by August the nation was cheerfully enjoying what Mr. Walter Lippmann called "this fantastic and disgraceful boom."

But the inevitable squeeze was arriving. The airplane and munitions and shipbuilding plants were reaching the limits of expansion, while their exorbitant demands upon the raw material supply were draining the civilian economy. To continue would demand drastic reductions of manufacture for civilian consumption and massive conversions of the major industries—automobiles in particular—to war production. Yet there was no war to justify the risk in the minds either of the industrial managers or the government officials. A violent internecine battle was raging among the latter, between the "all-outers," strongly New Dealist in tinge, who insisted on the immediate conversion of the entire economy, and the "not quite all-outers," with much support in industrial and even military circles, who were concerned over the danger of crowding business and the consumer too far, who felt that a "shooting war" was improbable, and who were reluctant to tear the whole economic machine apart in order to rebuild it on a war footing.

Much, of course, was being done. We had begun the study of the atomic bomb. Another remarkable invention, the VT or proximity fuse, which many regard as second only to the atomic bomb in military importance, was to be test-fired for the first time in this same late summer of 1941. The groundwork for the subsequent huge expansion had been laid. But such immediate necessities as planes, radar, barrage balloons, artillery of all kinds, were still coming in perilously small quantities. On the 19th of August Senator Harry F. Byrd of Virginia arose on the floor of the Senate to denounce the "failure" of the defense program. In the existing state of preparations, he declared (and he was not far wrong), it would be "an act of utter folly" for the nation to become "a voluntary shooting participant" in the war. The gigantic airplane program, according to the Senator, was actually yielding less than 700 combat planes a month (the Germans were believed to be producing three or four times as many) and of these not more than 60 a month were four-engine bombers, the great pride and basic weapon of the Army Air Force. Production in July had been 200 below schedule. We were far behind in tanks. Only "about a dozen" 90-mm. anti-aircraft guns had been delivered in all; we were behind in both naval and merchant ship construction. The defense agencies were at loggerheads; and Senator Byrd demanded a sweeping reorganization of the entire production system "along sound lines of business efficiency." President Roosevelt pooh-poohed these charges, rather airily assuring the nation that they gave a distorted picture; but he was forced to admit at the same time that the figures as to airplane production were substantially correct. And on the day after the Senator's attack, Mr. Knudsen told his press conference that passenger automobile production would be cut by 26 per cent during the next three months. It was the first real step toward the major conversion of peacetime industry.

There were crises of many kinds. The newspapers were much exercised over what seemed the disgraceful number of strikes in defense industries; and in mid-August the great Federal shipyard at Kearney, where half a billion dollars' worth of ship construction was under way, was closed down by a strike. The President finally brought it to an end by "seizing" the plant. There was troube from the nation's small manufacturers. The giant industries were soaking up all available raw materials under their war contract priorities, making it increasingly impossible for the small plants, which could not get war contracts, to continue. A more and more anguished howl was, of course, going up from the small business men, and they were flocking into Washington to chase through the hopeless maze of bureaus in search of relief. Washington's saga of frustration, of room shortages, of business men sleeping in bathtubs and telephone booths and breaking their hearts in the endless tramp from one office to another was already begun; and when a reporter discovered one man in the Washington Union Station who confessed that he had come not to get something but merely for the trip, it made a news story.

The crucial point was coming at which the nation would have to decide between all or nothing. Yet the House had come within a single vote of defeating the extension of the Army's term of service, and the public was still only dimly aware of what modern war really meant. When a gasoline shortage developed in the Northeast, there was endless wrangle over how to meet the problem (gasoline coupons were still months away); motorists found themselves stranded in the midst of week-end or holiday trips and there was much outcry against the authorities for permitting so dire a situation. The *New York Herald Tribune* ran a series of articles on the probable effects of the defense program. The home construction industry, for example, believed that sacrifices would have to be made; showers would probably have to replace bathtubs in new housing construction and ground-floor heaters might even replace furnaces. In another article Miss Eugenia Sheppard, the fashion writer, found that "this fall, defense limitations are becoming far more serious inconveniences to the fashion industry than the absence of Paris." The limitations were being felt in shortages of metals and plastics for ornament and zipper fasteners, but no one anticipated any lack of wool or dyes.

Such were still the atmospheres in August, 1941, as the crisis of our industrial mobilization approached. There was a barrage of statements from high quarters aimed at arousing the public to a greater appreciation of the danger and a greater effort. On the day that Senator Byrd was making his attack, the President was, elliptically, reading to his press conference a quotation from a paper written by Abraham Lincoln in 1862: "The fact is that the people have not yet made up their minds that we are at war with the South. They have not yet buckled down to a determination to fight this war through." Mr. Knudsen told his own press conference that the country was not showing "the proper spirit." But what good were elliptical quotations from Lincoln if the public could not be shown any specific peril? The President even felt obliged to make an evasive answer when a reporter asked the obvious question of whether his reading of the passage implied that we were "at war" now. In face of isolationist obstruction and opposition, it was considered far too dangerous politically to give any hint that the big new armies, at last beginning to assemble on the southern maneuver grounds, might ever have to be sent abroad.

In the War and Navy Departments, in the civilian agencies, in the training camps, and in the field commands, the endless struggle against shortages went on. They were short of everything. Admiral Kimmel at Pearl Harbor was begging for patrol vessels to eke out his limited facilities for reconnaissance. He was reporting that the entire complement of fighter planes available for the three first-line aircraft carriers and two shore-based Marine fighter squadrons in his command amounted to but fifty-two planes, of which seventeen were obsolescent. In mid-August there came another report from the Army on the air defense problem. General Martin, Short's air commander, repeated in great detail his studies showing that the form of attack most favorable for Japan (and therefore most probable) would be a strike by a maximum of six carriers launched at dawn from a position 233 miles out, and that it would probably come from the north, west, or south rather than from the east. The report asked for 180 B-17 Flying Fortresses as the force required to provide complete reconnaissance and protection against such an attack. But there were only 109 Flying Fortresses in the country at the time, and there were many seemingly more urgent uses for these.*

The top-ranking soldiers and sailors were under few illusions either as to the imminence of the peril or the deficiencies of our preparations. But the nation could hardly be expected to understand how little real content there was yet behind the imposing façade of our "defense effort." Even the international scene seemed a shade or two less ominous. In the latter part of August the colossal German drive into Soviet Russia appeared to be slowing down. It was now in general along the line of the Dnieper—a sufficiently staggering invasion—but very far from the "annihilation" of the Red Army. Certain slight evidences of renewed hesitation at Tokyo could be discerned from the dispatches. Then on Sunday, August 24, Mr. Winston Churchill, in an international broadcast, was making his report on the Atlantic Conference in those same majestic sentences, those same ringing tones of superb con-

* It should be noted, moreover, that even this report, accurate as its estimate was, was still of a somewhat theoretical nature. It specifically noted that Army Air was not at the time "charged with the reconnaissance mission for the defense of Oahu" and it granted that there were not fields available to accommodate 180 B-17's at that period. But "it should be only a matter of time" until projected additional field capacity should be completed.

fidence and courage, which had so often inspired the western peoples. Half-way through his address he turned significantly to the Far East:

> For five long years Japanese military factions, seeking to emulate the style of Hitler and Mussolini . . . have been invading and harrying five hundred million inhabitants of China, . . . carrying with them carnage, ruin, and corruption. . . . Now they stretch a grasping hand into the southern seas of China. They snatch Indo-China from the wretched Vichy French. They menace by this movement Siam. They menace the Singapore British link with Australasia and menace the Philippine Islands, which are under the protection of the United States.
>
> It is certain that this has got to stop. Every effort will be made to secure a peaceful settlement. The United States are laboring with infinite patience to arrive at a fair and amicable settlement which will give Japan the utmost reassurance for her legitimate interests. We earnestly hope these negotiations will succeed. But this I must say, that if these hopes should fail we shall, of course, range ourselves unhesitatingly at the side of the United States.*

The Japanese press raged—"Britain must terminate her anti-Japanese activities immediately"; Japan was resolved to "eliminate all obstacles to her southward advance"—but there were some faint notes of caution, audible to an attentive ear, through the tirades. And with Mr. Churchill's disclosure the public had learned for the first time that there were Japanese-American negotiations of some kind under way. The secret which had been kept so carefully since the spring was out at last; and at his press conference on Monday Secretary Hull confirmed the fact that conversations were being carried on. Careful observers deduced, quite rightly, that as matters stood there was little likelihood that these conversations could come

* This may have represented the British part of the "parallel action" discussed at Argentia Bay, represented on the American side by the President's warning of August 17. But whether there was ever an actual agreement on "parallel action" is a point left in doubt by the Pearl Harbor investigation.

to much; but they served to put a slightly more hopeful face upon the tortuous obscurities of the Far Eastern question.

The Chinese were instantly in a state of alarm, but on Tuesday President Roosevelt moved both to reassure Chungking and to reassert the basic American position by announcing that a military mission was being sent to China to determine how we could best help her with arms and supplies in her war against Japan. It was, of course, fresh fuel for the Japanese extremists. Secretary Hull added more when he made it plain that the United States would insist, despite violent protests in the Japanese press, on free passage for the tankers which we were dispatching to Vladivostok with oil supplies for the Red Army. There were other incidents. The Panama Canal was closed, for "technical" reasons, to transit by Japanese vessels; the Japanese were putting vexatious difficulties in the way of our attempts to evacuate the remaining American nationals in Japan. But the Japanese Government itself seemed to be showing a significant restraint.

Thursday, August 28, was, as it happened, a crowded day. In their morning papers Americans could read reports of all these and other dramatic events; they could also read the embittered comments of an increasingly acid isolationist opposition. In the course of the day the now long overdue upheaval in the war agencies came at last; the Administration trembled, labored, and brought forth another alphabetical board to set on top of the shaky structure. OPACS (Office of Price Administration and Civilian Supply) underwent a process of fission, one fragment being captured by OPM and the other becoming the famous OPA (Office of Price Administration). SPAB (Supplies, Priorities, and Allocations Board) was established over the whole, with Mr. Donald Nelson as its executive director, charged with "bridging the gap between conflicting groups within the Administration" and bringing greater order out of the rising chaos. It did not settle the raging battles between the "all-outers" and "not quite all-outers"; but Mr. Bernard Baruch, the elder statesman, when privately asked for his view, called it "a faltering step forward."

Other events of that day were not reported in the newspapers. The Navy Department issued orders establishing a cruiser patrol against German raiders off the Pacific coast of South America. And it was also on this same Thursday that a squadron of nine B-17 Flying Fortresses took off from San Francisco across the vast Pacific levels. They were on the first leg of the long route which the Army had hastily pioneered by way of Pearl Harbor, Midway, Wake, Rabaul, and Port Moresby to Manila.* The attempt to get something approaching real air power into the Philippines was at last under way. And the four-engine bombers were, presumably, already airborne when, that same morning at Washington, Ambassador Nomura arrived at the White House. He was bringing a personal message from his Prime Minister, Prince Konoye, to President Roosevelt.

II ☞

The scion of the Fujiwaras was making his last tortuous attempt to extricate himself, his Government, and his people from the deadly crisis into which they had drifted. For three anxious weeks Prince Konoye had been pinning everything on the one hope of somehow bringing the President to a personal conference. Precisely what he thought might emerge from it is not easy to divine; but it is clear, at any rate, that it offered a device which might have strengthened his own prestige, restored his failing grip over the war party, and perhaps have entangled the United States into concessions which he could have used to regain the mastery of a situation over which he had now all but lost control.

* Guam, on which Congress had refused to spend money out of deference to Japanese sensibilities, had no airfield capable of receiving the heavy bombers. Consequently, although the Pan-American airliners, which were flying boats, used the direct route through Guam, the B-17's had to go the long way around via New Guinea.

It was on August 4 (just as Mr. Roosevelt was departing for his "fishing trip") that Prince Konoye had laid his project before the War and Navy Ministers. Prince Konoye explained that he was not intending to take "a submissive attitude," that he would "insist, of course, on the firm establishment of the Greater East Asia Co-Prosperity Sphere." But they need not insist on fulfilling that "ideal" all at once. Besides, it already began to look as though the Germans might be involving themselves in a stalemate in Russia. If that happened, the American attitude would "stiffen" and there would be no more chance of getting anything out of the United States by diplomacy. There was not a moment to lose.

The two military ministers listened intently. The Navy by that time was deep in its concrete studies of the Pacific war, which would be primarily the Navy's responsibility, and it was not underestimating the difficulties of the problem. The Navy Minister, Admiral Oikawa, gave a warm assent to the conference idea. But the Minister of War, the tight-lipped little Hideki Tojo, reported in writing that the proposed meeting, which would jeopardize the Tri-Partite Pact and cause serious domestic repercussion, was "not considered a suitable move." Nevertheless, the Army would not withhold its consent if the Prime Minister undertook to attend the meeting only "with determination firmly to support the basic principles embodied in the Empire's Revised Plan to the 'N'-Plan and to carry out a war against America if the President of the United States still fails to comprehend the true intentions of the Empire. . . . You shall not resign your post as a result of the meeting on the grounds that it was a failure; rather, you shall be prepared to assume leadership in the war against America." It was under these grim provisos that the instructions to propose the meeting were sent off to Nomura on August 7.

Washington was of course unaware of General Tojo's stipulations. It did not know that one of Prince Konoye's arguments to the two ministers was that the conference, should it fail, would prove to the Japanese people that the projected war was unavoidable and that this "would aid in consolidating their determination." But this latter aspect of the proposal was easily discerned, and may sufficiently explain the caution with which Mr. Hull received it on August 8 and the reserve with which the President replied to it at his meeting with the ambassador on August 17. Presented both with the warning note of that day and with Nomura's report, Prince Konoye only redoubled his efforts. In Tokyo on the afternoon of the 18th, Ambassador Grew was summoned to a long conference with the Foreign Minister, Admiral Toyoda. The day was oppressively hot, and both men were dripping with perspiration long before the interview was over. The Foreign Minister pressed the "leaders' conference" plan with the utmost urgency. It was the only way of meeting the mounting crisis; already the situation was "extremely strained as a result of misunderstanding between the two countries and sinister designs by third powers." A conference was vitally important. Mr. Grew recognized that the proposal was quite unprecedented in Japanese history; he knew it must have the approval of the Emperor and the other highest authorities; he inferred that Japanese policy had not yet "crystallized completely" and that Konoye, seeing the handwriting now plain upon the wall, was at last genuinely working for peace. Mr. Grew cabled his own earnest recommendation that the proposal should not be rejected without "very prayerful consideration." But what Japan was actually prepared to offer toward a removal of "misunderstanding" or what Prince Konoye could bring to the meeting beyond a repetition of all the old arguments had nowhere appeared.

A week drifted by, enlivened by Mr. Churchill's radio blast on Sunday, the 24th, and by its repercussions. In Washington on that Sunday Ambassador Nomura had been urging upon Mr. Hull that the conference must take place before October 15, but the reasons he gave for setting this fixed date were not wholly convincing. "Magic" was yielding exigent and ominous telegrams. There was one from Tokyo to Nomura, translated on Tuesday, the 26th:

> That message * contains the maximum concessions that we can make, . . . however, whether you can convince the Americans of this is naturally another matter. Now the international situation as well as our internal situation is strained in the extreme and we have reached the point where we will pin our last hopes on an interview between the Premier and the President. Please try to convince Roosevelt and Hull to this effect.

Two days later, on August 28, Ambassador Nomura, as has been said, was at the White House with Prince Konoye's personal message for the President. It was an earnest plea for the maintenance of peace in the Pacific and for the leaders' conference, which would permit "a frank exchange of views" on "all important problems between Japan and America covering the entire Pacific area." Mr. Roosevelt "read it with interest and complimented the tone and spirit of it." The ambassador then produced a second document in the form of an official reply to the President's warning message of August 17. Here at last there should be some indication of what Japan might bring to the proposed meeting. The President "expressed his keen interest to get this reply," took it up, and plunged at once into a reading of it. It was most conciliatory in tone; yet it must have been somewhat disappointing in content. It reiterated Japan's promises to stop with Indo-China and to withdraw from there as soon as "the China Incident is settled"; Japan, it declared, "has no intentions of using, without provocation, military force against any neighboring nation." The rest was unfortunately vague. The President must have noted the phrase "without provocation," and his comments on other passages were somewhat skeptical. He even, according to Nomura's report, "smilingly and cynically" expressed a wonder as to whether, if conversations were re-

* Not identified in the published record of the intercepts. It was, presumably, the message conveying the terms presented on August 28.

sumed, Japan would take the opportunity to appropriate Siam, just as she had seized southern Indo-China during the previous conversations. But he ended by assuring the ambassador that the note seemed "a step forward," that he was very hopeful and much interested in the proposed conference with Prince Konoye.

That same evening the ambassador was at Secretary Hull's apartment at the Wardman Park Hotel, "much encouraged" by the morning's interview and pressing for the conference to be held as soon as possible. He was now talking of the dates between September 21 and 25. But the Secretary dashed these high hopes. Mr. Hull insisted on returning to the basis for agreement, raising in particular the embarrassing question of China as "pivotal" to the whole problem. To this, the ambassador had little to contribute. It is possible that the President and the Secretary between them, aware of the manifest dangers in the conference idea, were already engaged upon a "stall," with the President holding out encouragements that would keep the Japanese interested, while the Secretary made sure that there would be no conference—not, at any rate, unless Japan could be pinned down to something that would make such a conference more than merely a trap for the United States.

Again and again Tokyo had insisted, both to its own representatives and to the United States, upon the imperative need for absolute secrecy in order not to alarm its war party—or, though this was less explicitly put, that "third power" whose ambassador at Tokyo, General Ott, was applying every kind of pressure at his command to hold the Japanese to the Tri-Partite Pact. But the fact that Admiral Nomura had transmitted a message from Prince Konoye to the President leaked out; and though the contents were unknown, it made front-page headlines in the American press. In Tokyo it brought General Ott post-haste to the Foreign Office with a series of stern and peremptory questions, to which he got politely reassuring answers—which would have been of great interest to our own statesmen had they heard them. Whatever they might say to the Germans, the Japanese themselves were thrown into another frenzy of conferences and consultations. There was already a furious "speculation," and Prince Konoye found his maneuvers were growing "difficult." The Army General Staff was reconsidering even the qualified assent it had given earlier in the month; some of its leading members had "swung to the view that the negotiations were useless, and favored war against the United States." The Navy may have been less bellicose; but it was finishing the intensive fleet maneuvers in which it had been putting the final polish on its war training, and it had ordered its top commanders and staff officers to Tokyo to complete the final operation plans.

President Roosevelt knew nothing about all this, of course, but as he journeyed up to Hyde Park for the Labor Day week end, the obvious perils of the whole position—in the Atlantic, in the Pacific, and in our stumbling mobilization—must have been strongly with him. They must have contrasted sharply in his mind with the rich peace of the Hudson Valley hills, teeming and drowsy under the late summer sun. On Saturday, the 30th, there was one of the established Roosevelt rituals, when the President met a small crowd of his country neighbors on the lawn before the farmhouse of Mr. Moses Smith, one of the Hyde Park tenants. It was very possible, he told them, that the dangers of the world "may be even more serious at this moment than they were at the end of August and the beginning of September, 1939." It was merely an informal, "folksy" kind of talk, but the warning it conveyed made big headlines in next day's newspapers.

That Labor Day, September 1, proved a record holiday. There was a bigger jam on the roads and railways, at the resorts and theaters, than any since the last, lush days of the Big Boom in 1929. Even the casualty lists were back to the levels of the opulent past, and some 360 persons were killed in automobile accidents alone. In the evening the nation's radios were tuned to a world-wide broadcast arranged by OPM.

There were talks by the heads of the A.F. of L. and the C.I.O., by Mr. Sidney Hillman and by Mr. Ernest Bevin, British Minister of Labor, speaking from London. All pledged organized unionism to still greater efforts in the defeat of Nazism. But the climax came with President Roosevelt's familiar voice: "We are engaged in a grim and perilous task. . . . Forces of insane violence. . . . Unless we step up the total of our production and more greatly safeguard it on its journey to the battlefields, these enemies will take heart in pushing their attack in old fields and new." Except for that oblique "and new" there was no reference to the danger from Japan. There was no suggestion of a "shooting" war. But there was as bitter an excoriation of Hitlerism as any the President had yet delivered, and there was a "solemn warning" that the task of beating it would be a long one.

The President had made it, perhaps, as explicit as he could. The general public response seemed as firm, as enthusiastic in support of the President's policy, as before. But the isolationist opposition was as persistent and even more bitter. Senator Nye thought the speech "just the usual appeal to the fears of the American people" which would nevertheless "continue to say 'no' to giving any aid other than that short of war." Senator Burton K. Wheeler summoned labor to oppose "a foreign war" but to enlist instead in a "noble war" at home against economic injustice. "America," he proclaimed, "is not dependent upon Mr. Stalin, Mr. Hitler, or Mr. Churchill for its security. We need fear only the reckless adventures of our leaders." The cantankerous Mr. John T. Flynn, heading the New York chapter of America First, announced that the President "most certainly did not speak the will of the American people," while Colonel Lindbergh gave his expert opinion that air power made it impossible for either Germany or the United States to attack the other across the ocean distances. The Colonel added the thought that before the war was over Great Briain would probably "turn upon the United States" as "she has turned on France and Finland."

Few doubted that the great majority of the country was in fact behind Mr. Roosevelt, but through this constant sniping-fire warnings tended to lose their effect. "It has taken a long time," as "Betty" Stark philosophized in another letter to "Mustapha" Kimmel, "to get the psychology started. . . . The country still is, to a considerable extent, asleep to the effort required." The Chief of Naval Operations was "perfectly delighted" when someone told him that, on trying to buy an electric refrigerator, it had appeared that there were no more available. And it was still impossible for anyone really to take the Japanese seriously. When Lieutenant-Colonel Itsuo Mabuchi, important because he was official spokesman for the Japanese Army, announced that "Japan is now compelled to smash the anti-Japanese encirclement. . . . Breaking through this anti-Japanese encirclement means entry into a long-term war against Anglo-America," nobody paid much attention. Representative Melvin J. Maas, returning from a six weeks' tour of Pacific duty as a colonel in the Marine Corps Reserve, confidently told the reporters that the Japanese were "deathly afraid" of the Pacific Fleet. Despite withdrawals to the Atlantic and some lingering deficiencies of equipment, he declared, the Fleet was adequate to its task, while "the Hawaiian Islands are more powerful than Gibraltar ever was because their defenses are geared to modern warfare." Even as Mr. Maas spoke, Admiral Yamamoto was assembling his officers in the Navy Ministry at Tokyo, to begin a ten-day war game, devoted to refining the last details of the plan for going into those defenses and scuppering the Fleet behind them. The grand design for Pacific mastery was coming to completion. But nobody knew anything at all about that.

In Washington on the Tuesday after Labor Day one secret, however, did come out. Mr. Wilfrid Fleisher of the *New York Herald Tribune* had penetrated the mystery of the Konoye message; and next morning his paper announced in a front-page dispatch that it had been "authoritatively learned" that Prince Konoye had proposed a personal meeting with the

President, presumably to be held on board a warship somewhere in the Pacific. The fat was fairly in the fire. Before the day was out there was an anguished cable from Tokyo ("magic" soon had it decoded) for Ambassador Nomura:

> Since the existence of the Premier's message was inadvertently made known to the public, that gang that has been suspecting that unofficial talks were taking place has really begun to yell and wave the Tri-Partite banner. In the midst of this confusion at home Fleisher's story in the *Herald Tribune* relating the rumor of a proposed conference between the Premier and the President, which was unfortunate, to say the least, as you can well imagine. . . .
>
> Because of the circumstances being what they are, we would like to make all arrangements for the meeting around the middle of September, with all possible speed, and issue a very simple statement to that effect as soon as possible. (If the middle of September is not convenient, any early date will meet with our approval.) . . .

In Tokyo at the same time Prince Konoye, breaking a silence of some weeks, issued a public statement conveying another of those cryptic warnings that Japan was facing "the gravest crisis in her history." The White House, loyal to its undertakings with the Japanese, gave out a flat denial of the Fleisher story, but it was not hard to guess that this was of a "diplomatic" character. And as the President's secretary was telling the correspondents that there had been no invitation to a conference, the President himself was receiving Ambassador Nomura (on Wednesday afternoon, September 3) to hand him the reply.

The gist of it was that the President was very favorable to the conference idea, but that in view both of Prince Konoye's difficulties with his own war party and of the relations of the United States with the other Pacific powers, it would be essential first to arrive at some firm basis for the meeting. Prince Konoye had somewhat vaguely declared himself in agreement with the basic principles of peace on which the

United States had been insisting from the beginning. The President noted this with gratification and restated those principles:

1. Respect for the territorial integrity and sovereignty of each and all nations.
2. Support of the principle of noninterference in the internal affairs of other countries.
3. Support of the principle of equality, including equality of commercial opportunity.
4. Nondisturbance of the *status quo* in the Pacific except as the *status quo* may be altered by peaceful means.

To avoid any mistake, the note added that the United States understood that Japan's assurances "exclude any policy which would seek political expansion or the acquisition of economic rights, advantages, or preferences by force." The United States could enter no agreement not in harmony with these principles. In their conversation with the ambassador the President and Mr. Hull "repeatedly emphasized" the necessity for Japan to clarify her position as to abandoning a policy of force; it was suggested that the Japanese should take some days to think it over, to consider their course in China and the possibility of taking some positive steps toward educating their own public to a less bellicose attitude. The ambassador, who "seemed to appreciate" the point of view, took his leave.

But fresh excitements were immediately to supervene. On the day after this interview there was dramatic news from the Atlantic; and on Friday morning, September 5, eight-column banner headlines were proclaiming that an American destroyer had been fired on with torpedoes in the waters southwest of Iceland and had fought back with depth charges. The *U. S. S. Greer*, an old World War I "four-piper," had been undamaged in the exchange; otherwise, all details were obscure and conflicting statements from Washington and Berlin did little to clarify them. What was plain, however, was that the United States had traded the first shots "fired in anger" with the forces of Nazi Germany. In the days that followed few had many thoughts for the odd little yellow men in Tokyo. Indeed, the newspaper announcing the *Greer* episode also reported the safe arrival at Vladivostok of the first American tanker with aviation gasoline for the Red Army. Despite the public threats of the Japanese militarists, their Government was doing nothing to hinder the shipments. It seemed further evidence that the Pacific could be left to the diplomats; and all eyes turned to the Atlantic.

Mr. Wendell Willkie issued a stirring appeal to the President to "meet the challenge with determination and force. I hope, and I know you hope, that the President of the United States serves notice on Nazi Germany that the United States expects its ships to go unmolested across the North Altantic." The editorial pages and the news commentators boiled. Mr. Roosevelt, for his part, scarcely needed urging. The *Greer* affair afforded the opportunity for his next careful advance upon a course which was becoming increasingly imperative. The British were in a much worse case on the Atlantic than the public knew. As early as June Admiral Stark had thought it essential for the United States to enter the war in order to avert a British collapse, and through subsequent weeks our naval high command had continued to take a gloomy view of the British difficulties at sea. The President had much reason to believe that unless they could get massive and "shooting" help from the American Navy, the lend-lease program, and with it the one hope of winning the war with our materials rather than with our men, would fail. The torpedoes which lashed past the *Greer* afforded an opportunity to notch up that help to a new level.*

* It must be admitted that it was a somewhat disingenuous opportunity. To present the affair as an unprovoked attack was less than accurate. The *Greer*, advised of the U-boat's presence by a British seaplane, had gone in search of her, picked her up on the sound gear, and thereafter tracked her, broadcasting her position in accordance with orders. The U-boat was also operating on sound; her periscope

On Thursday, September 11, there was another nationwide broadcast from the White House. "This was piracy, legally and morally," the President told his millions of listeners. He listed the many attacks and threats of attack on American and American-owned vessels (the latter, thanks to the neutrality act, sailing for the most part under the gaudy flag of the Republic of Panama). "There has now come a time when you and I must see the cold, inexorable necessity of saying to these inhuman, unrestrained seekers of world conquest and permanent world domination by the sword—'You seek to throw our children and our children's children into your form of terrorism and slavery. You have now attacked our own safety. You shall go no farther.' . . . These Nazi submarines and raiders are the rattlesnakes of the Atlantic. . . . From now on, if German or Italian vessels of war enter the waters the protection of which is necessary for American defense, they do so at their own peril."

The exact implication was still a little obscure, but the address was short-waved throughout the world in eighteen languages and its seriousness was sufficiently apparent. The isolationist leaders were bitterly caustic. Robert E. Wood, the Chicago business man who had been enlisted to head America First, called it "an undeclared war in plain violation of the Constitution" and a "betrayal of the most solemn promise a candidate ever made to his people"; the aging Senator David I. Walsh of Massachusetts deplored "the President's provocative utterances," while Colonel Lindbergh

was never seen and there appears no reason to doubt the German statement that she was unaware of the nationality of the pursuing destroyer. The chase had gone on for some hours (during which the U-boat received one pattern of bombs from the British plane) before the quarry turned and discharged the first torpedo at the unseen tracker. This forced Greer to reply. After further exchanges of torpedoes and depth bombs, all without result, the U-boat dove deep and made off. Greer continued to search for her through some six hours more before resuming the voyage to Iceland.

concluded that "the three most important groups which have been pressing this country toward war are the British, the Jewish, and the Roosevelt Administration." But on the other hand a telegram signed by 1,100 persons from 26 states called on the President to ask for a declaration of war on Germany; while the opinion polls continued to show heavier majorities than ever for all aid to Britain, even at the risk of war. The Nazi propaganda machine naturally raged from Berlin; but Hitler was deep in Russia and there was still no sign of a German declaration of war upon us. Four days later Mr. Frank Knox, the Secretary of the Navy, made matters plain by announcing in an address that "beginning tomorrow" American naval vessels on the route to Iceland would be under orders "to capture or destroy . . . Axis-controlled submarines or surface raiders encountered in those waters." On the Atlantic, the "shooting orders" were a fact at last.

If we had been paying little attention to the Japanese during all this, the Japanese had been paying a great deal to us. At just about the time that Mr. Roosevelt and Mr. Hull, on the afternoon of September 3, were spelling out their prescription for Pacific peace and politely advising Ambassador Nomura that Japan should make some positive contribution to it, Prince Konoye in numerous conferences with the Army and Navy was writing out Japan's own prescription, which was of a somewhat different tenor. These "new proposals" were completed by September 4, before the receipt of the American reply. But the "new proposals," for American consumption, were only a part of the basic decisions which the Japanese realized that they would have to face.

On September 5 Prince Konoye laid before Emperor Hirohito the "Plans for the Prosecution of the Policy of the Imperial Government" which were to be formally submitted to an Imperial Conference on the following day. In striking contrast to the Four Principles of Mr. Roosevelt and Mr. Hull, they provided:

1. Determined not to be deterred by the possibility of being involved in a war with America (and England and Holland) in order to secure our national existence, we will proceed with war preparations so that they be completed approximately toward the end of October.

2. At the same time, we will endeavor by every possible diplomatic means to have our demands agreed to by America and England. Japan's minimum demands . . . together with the Empire's maximum concessions are embodied in the attached document.

3. If by the early part of October there is no reasonable hope of having our demands agreed to . . ., we will immediately make up our minds to get ready for war against America (and England and Holland). . . . Special effort will be made to prevent America and Soviet Russia from forming a united front against Japan.

The minimum demands were sterner, if anything, than those on which Japan had been insisting. The United States and Great Britain must agree not to interfere in or obstruct the settlement of the "China Incident," and must close the Burma Road and cease all aid to China; the two democracies must agree not to increase their Far Eastern military forces nor to establish bases in Siam, the Netherlands Indies, China, or Siberia, while no demands for the liquidation of Japan's "special relations" with Indo-China would be considered; America and Britain must agree to restore normal trade relations, to provide Japan with needed raw materials from their own possessions, and to assist Japan in establishing "close economic relations" with Siam and the Netherlands Indies. Only, it was specified, after all this had been agreed to, would Japan make her maximum concessions. They were confined to undertaking not to use Indo-China as a base for operations against any country save China, to withdraw troops from Indo-China "as soon as a just peace is established in the Far East," and to guarantee the neutrality of the Philippines.

Confronted with this adventurous program, the Imperial Presence appears to have manifested considerable concern.

The Emperor observed that the "Plans" seemed "to give precedence to war over diplomatic activities." When Prince Konoye sought to reassure him he was not impressed; and Konoye sent for the Army and Navy chiefs of staff, Field Marshal Gen Sugiyama and Admiral Osami Nagano. When these officers arrived, the August One attacked the field marshal with some spirit. How long did he think it was going to take to end an American war, once it should be started? Sugiyama gave his confident (and, as it turned out, quite accurate) estimate that South Pacific operations could be "disposed of in about three months." The Emperor was not satisfied. "When the China Incident started," he remarked, "you were War Minister. I seem to remember at the time you said the Incident could be disposed of in about one month. The Incident has lasted for four years and is not settled even now."

The field marshal, in "trepidation," began to make excuses about the immense size of the Chinese hinterland; the Emperor, raising his voice, cut him off: "If the Chinese hinterland is extensive, the Pacific is boundless." What was the basis for the three-month estimate? The chief of staff "hung his head, unable to answer." Admiral Nagano can hardly have improved matters by contributing the thought that Japan was like an invalid in a long decline, for whom a drastic operation might be necessary. "Just now we are deciding whether an operation is needed." But at least it gave Hirohito an opportunity to come back to his original point. Was he right in assuming that the High Command put emphasis primarily on diplomacy? The two chiefs of staff answered in the affirmative. Apparently, this was the best that Imperial Majesty could do.

Next morning, Saturday, September 6, the formal Imperial Conference convened. The Emperor was still dissatisfied about that business of whether they were putting war or diplomacy first; and this time only the Navy Minister answered up while the staff chiefs kept silent. The Emperor reprimanded the High Command with evident asperity, at the same time drawing from his pocket a slip of paper containing a poem written by the Emperor Meiji:

Since all are brothers in this world, why is there such constant turmoil?

"Everyone present was struck with awe, and there was silence throughout the hall." Finally Nagano rose, and expressing his "trepidation at the prospect of the Emperor's displeasure," committed the High Command to the principle of diplomacy first, with resort to war "only when there seemed no other way out." The Conference adjourned in an atmosphere "of unprecedented tenseness." But meanwhile they had adopted the "Plans for the Prosecution of the Policy." What Konoye had achieved, apparently, was some temporary postponement of the war to give him a little more time for his diplomatic activities. But what possible chance there was that he could secure Anglo-American assent to the minimum demands seems not even to have been discussed.

Yet the supple and aristocratic scion of the Fujiwaras appears to have hoped that he could still somehow manage it. That same Saturday evening he took the unusual step of inviting Ambassador Grew to dinner (in a private house and in the utmost secrecy) so that he might personally press the "leaders' conference." Prince Konoye was persuasive in his evidences of good faith and of his earnest desire for peace. The ambassador understood, to his delight and not a little to his surprise, that the Prime Minister "subscribed fully" and wholeheartedly to the President's four principles of peace. Mr. Grew, who naturally knew nothing of the very different principles to which the Prime Minister had also subscribed at the conference only a few hours before, was impressed. Konoye assured Grew that he had the warmest support of the military in his effort for peace; that the Army would commit itself to the "leaders' conference" by sending along a full general and the Navy by sending a full admiral. He would himself spare no means to success, but the conference must come "with the least possible delay." The ambassador hastened to put all this upon the cables. He may have had his reservations, but it seemed most promising.

Saturday evening in Tokyo is still only Saturday morning in Washington. Mr. Grew's report was in the State Department in the course of the day; but so, unfortunately, was Admiral Nomura, bearing the Japanese "new proposals" which Konoye had completed on September 4.* The private assurances reported by Mr. Grew scarcely seemed to square with the unhelpful tone of this official answer. The new proposals (on which we had urged Japan to spend some time and constructive thought) did not even square very well with the fair words of the original Konoye invitation. Secretary Hull was disagreeably impressed. The Japanese seemed to be up to their old tricks again, advancing alluring general promises, only to "narrow" them down drastically as soon as it came to cases. These new proposals, in which we had hoped to find some real basis for the meeting of the leaders, were simply the old demands wrapped in different phraseology. The pledge against further military adventure in the Southwest Pacific was still qualified; there would be none "without justifiable reason." There was no commitment as to the terms which Japan expected, with our assistance, to exact from China; we were still required to suspend our own military measures, and there was even a strong hint that we must accept Japanese control over our trade relations with China. Contrasting all this with Mr. Grew's hopeful report, the Secretary reflected upon the past duplicities of Prince Konoye and his Governments. The United States took both the new proposals and the whole question of a leaders' conference under further advisement.

* Nomura explained that this document had been drafted before receipt of the President's communication as to the leaders' conference, but that his Government felt that it would suffice as a reply. This offhand treatment of our earnest representations was not in itself calculated to inspire confidence.

In the ensuing days, however, there seemed to be some relaxation of the tensions in the Pacific. It was noticed that anti-American editorials had disappeared from the Japanese press. On the 11th of September Tokyo announced a reorganization of the Army command, under which the Emperor would assume personal command of a new Defense Headquarters controlling all troops except the expeditionary forces already in China and Indo-China. Some military observers thought this ominous, but the correspondents read it as an assertion of a restraining Imperial hand over the Army gunmen. There were hints of a coolness between Tokyo and Berlin, and other scraps of evidence, such as the continued free passage of our tankers to Vladivostok, seemed reassuring. The evidences which would not have seemed reassuring were, naturally, concealed from the world. On September 13 there was another joint conference in which the basic peace terms to be imposed on China were elaborated and adopted. At the Naval Ministry the war game had been concluded. It was also on September 13 that the naval command completed the preliminary draft of "Combined Fleet Top Secret Operation Order No. 1." This embodied the detailed planning for the grand assault, which would be opened with a surprise attack at Pearl Harbor and would simultaneously strike for Malaya and Singapore, for the Philippines and the Indies.

But outwardly, the pressures in the Far East seemed to be sinking into abeyance.

III ☞

Another fortnight slipped away. In the latter half of September it seemed clear that the gigantic offensive in Russia, which had made such terrifying gains all through July and August, was slowing down. Leningrad held out; so did Odessa. The Germans announced the capture of Kiev on September 19, and it was a disheartening blow. But they had had a hard fight for the city; the war which some experts said would be over in three weeks had lasted now through three months, and the Russian powers of resistance seemed if anything only to grow under defeat. The Red Army had even achieved one limited counterattack in the Smolensk region. It had retaken no great area, but it had been successful enough for the Russians to escort the western correspondents over the battlefield—giving them their first even distant glimpse of the struggle—and their dispatches naturally reflected a certain optimism. Prophecy was still guarded; but memories of the first Napoleon began to revive and cartoonists began to depict Russia's famous "General Winter," whose icy reinforcements were now not so many weeks away.

This did not help the harried men who were struggling in Washington with the "defense" program and the advancing production crisis. They were still desperately behind the real need; nevertheless, the country could sense that something like a corner was being turned. Confronting a steel shortage when large amounts of steel were still going into non-defense construction, SPAB finally took the plunge and issued orders looking toward the total mobilization of all strategic metals. Mr. Nelson remembers this as marking "the first time that . . . an official government agency had decided to undertake an all-out program. . . . *All* of America's tremendous strength was to be applied to the job at hand." The cost of living was on its way up. There were new cutbacks in the production of heavy consumers' goods. A new tax bill was to take effect on October 1, levying on railway tickets, jewelry, furs, and other luxuries, raising the taxes on liquor and theater tickets, and putting five-dollar Federal tax stamps on automobile windshields. The Army was organizing a volunteer aircraft warning system, and portly veterans of the first World War were beginning to spend chilly nights on windswept rooftops. "Civilian defense" had begun its patriotic, if generally rather unhappy, history. And in Washington the top conferences were growing more tense, more numerous, and more suggestive of war.

Irregularly but with increasing frequency as the summer

dwindled, the President was summoning meetings of the Secretaries of State, War, and Navy with the military chiefs, Marshall, Stark, and sometimes General Arnold, commander of the Army Air Force. They referred to these gatherings among themselves as the "War Cabinet" or the "War Council." Every Tuesday morning at 9:30 the three civilian Secretaries also met in Mr. Hull's office behind the late-Victorian Renaissance splendors of the State Department. This informal but established conference constituted perhaps our chief working organ of co-ordination between the arms of policy and of war. As crisis developed, it was often to have extra meetings.

In mid-September, in the hot fields and chigger-infested woods of Louisiana, some 450,000 men, divided into field armies with all supporting echelons fully organized, were engaged in a great maneuver battle. It was the first full-scale and effective peacetime war exercise in American history. The newspapers gave it columns of photographs and description. The troops still wore the washbasin-like "tin hats," the uncomfortable breeches and leggings of the World War I uniform, and their equipment had a sketchy look beside what one saw in photographs from the European fronts. The published critiques of the commanders, moreover, were frank. While the spirit was admirable, the errors were many and the troops were clearly "not yet ready to take the field under modern conditions of warfare." Exen so, one may doubt whether the public had any real idea of the enormous deficiencies—in equipment, experience, tactical leadership, and command coordination—which remained to be corrected.

But if there were deficiencies on the maneuver ground, they were nothing compared to those which still reigned, only half appreciated, in the imperiled outposts. The nine B-17 bombers which had set out from San Francisco on August 28 were at Port Darwin in North Australia—that grim and torrid pearl fishery on the farther shore of the Arafura Sea—early in September, and on the 12th they were arriving safely on Luzon. For that time, it was a considerable feat; and 26 more of the big planes were to take off after them, beginning on September 30. In October, the 19th Bombardment Group would be formed complete at Clark Field, in the hill country north of Manila. But the air commanders in the Philippines wanted Flying Fortresses by the hundred. These 35 were all they were ever to get. Even for them there were no adequate facilities. In the whole of the islands there were only two fields which could receive them—totally insufficient for proper operation and dispersal—and covering fighter forces were woefully weak. There were no spare parts, communications were unreliable, intelligence almost nonexistent, while there was a dangerous want of any considered and co-ordinated strategic plan for the employment of the air power which they represented.

Other reinforcements were straggling in. An anti-aircraft regiment and two tank battalions, with 100 light tanks, were sent off in September. Along with them went 50 of the new self-propelled field guns, all that the United States possessed at the time. Enough of the precious radar equipment was found to provide for three coastal stations. The Navy was sending young Lieutenant Bulkley and his later famous "expendables," with their matchwood flotilla of six motor torpedo boats loaded on the deck of a tanker. In the latter part of September, General MacArthur was observed in a two-day series of conferences with President Quezon. They were at last really getting down to the business of mobilizing MacArthur's Philippine Army. Some 20,000 Filipinos had already been called up, and it was explained that "during the remainder of 1941" another 100,000 or so would be incorporated into the United States service, filling up by stages the paper organization of ten divisions. Anonymous high officers were telling the correspondents that "vast increases" in the men and munitions available were already making any Japanese invasion an "extremely hazardous" undertaking. What General Homma, waiting on Formosa with his highly trained invasion forces, may have thought of this is not on record. But the correspondents can scarcely be blamed if they began cabling home suggestions that Japan had "missed the boat," nor can the home public be blamed if it believed them.

The Philippines lay directly athwart Japan's course of empire, and no one there was under any illusions as to the nature of the threat. But Pearl Harbor saw its problem in a less clear perspective. They were of course all working on the supposition that war with Japan was imminent. Admiral Kimmel intimated in one of his letters that he would be only too glad if he could be guaranteed as much as six months before the war would be on them. But they felt themselves far behind the front lines. They were immersed in the clamant tasks of training and staging to the forward areas; and those theoretic studies of possible air-borne attack on their own base tended to fade from the mind under the day-to-day pressure. General Short was absorbed in the problems of completing his defenses, not in those of fighting them; the Navy was full of its offensive role under "Rainbow 5"—the raiding operations into the Mandates with which, when war came, it was to pin down or harass Japanese sea power. Its immediate concern was not for Pearl Harbor but for the outlying atolls, Johnston, Midway, and Wake, which would serve to cover such raids and which were the indispensable island "aircraft carriers" by which the big bombers for the Philippines had to pass.

In August Admiral Kimmel had got off a first detachment of 165 Marines, with a battery of six 5-inch fixed guns and some anti-aircraft, to Wake Island's barren sand bars. The first flight of B-17's to Manila emphasized the importance of that scrap of coral; reinforcements for the Marines and a large force of civilian construction workers were being sent on, and in mid-September Admiral Kimmel, in a letter to "Betty" Stark, commented on the situation in terms which seem to illustrate the general state of mind in the Pacific Fleet command:

I feel better now that we have gotten something at Wake. . . . While by no means "impregnable," its present defensive strength is considerable and will require the exposure of quite a force to capture it. It is even possible that should its capture be an early objective of Japan, such an effort might be supported by a substantial portion of their Combined Fleet, which would create, for us, a golden opportunity *if we have the strength to meet it.*

Thus were Major James P. S. Devereux, the men of his Marine Defense Battalion, and some thousand civilian workers sentenced unwittingly to four years in Japanese prison camps. The idea that Japan's "early objective" might be something much bigger than Wake Island had evidently not occurred to Admiral Kimmel. Of course, precautions were being taken. They were very alert against submarine attack. Since June they had been holding weekly drills with the Army in the problems of air-raid defense. The drills had developed "many weaknesses" in the "volunteer fire department" system, but inter-service co-operation seemed "very satisfactory" and it was felt that they were making steady improvement. The Fleet was too busy with its own training to pay much attention to the Army's progress with its radar warning system. There were still no barrage balloons, though Secretary Stimson had hoped to have them long before. Nor were there any anti-torpedo baffles, to guard against a raid like that which the British had driven home so successfully against the Italians at Taranto. They would have been awkward things at best, and letters from the Navy Department conveyed the impression that Pearl Harbor was too shallow to permit the use of air-borne torpedoes. That was as far as the torpedo nets ever got. Unlike Admiral Yamamoto's staff, our own people never really studied this question with a careful eye.

The irreverent Captain Zacharias, of the *U.S.S. Salt Lake City*, was "amazed" in these weeks at the "unrealistic attitudes" he observed around him. He was later to recall that he needled his acquaintances on the staff with embarrassing questions: "When are you going to stop these surprise inspections and prepare for surprise attacks?" It cannot have increased his popularity with the higher brass. There were some other officers who, disgusted by what seemed to them the ponderous inertia and incompetence of the vast Pearl Harbor machinery, were glad to get orders for the Philippines.

So a golden September declined into fall. On the 23rd, the White House correspondents trooped into the Presidential press conference to find Mr. Roosevelt in a "stern" mood. His words were "tinged with bitterness" as he announced that American merchant ships would have to be armed against the U-boats, and that the neutrality act, which had so far prevented this, would have to be modified or repealed. He was bitter also because the Seafarers' International Union had tied up 22 vessels with a strike for bigger war bonuses. But it was equally front-page news, two or three days later, when the Brooklyn Dodgers won the pennant for the first time in twenty-one years and "Dem Bums" entered the national legend. Fall was coming, and with it war upon the sea lanes seemed to be coming fast. Yet a sea war, except for those comparatively few who might be directly concerned, would be a remote affair, almost a "spectator war," with its box scores of tonnage sunk or saved rather like the box scores of a football game or a baseball season. The larger horizons looked distinctly less threatening, on the whole, than they had for weeks. Nevertheless, on September 22 Admiral Stark was writing again, this time to "Tommy" Hart, commanding the Asiatic Fleet at Manila, with a copy to Kimmel:

> As to conditions in your part of the world, Mr. Hull has not yet given hope of a satisfactory settlement of our differences with Japan. Chances of such a settlement are, in my judgment, very slight. . . . The press is making much at the moment of the way the Far Eastern situation has apparently quieted down. One cannot help being impressed with the optimistic note of the editorial writers and columnists in this regard. For my own part, I feel that false hopes are being raised.

The feeling was soon to be confirmed. Unknown to the editorial writers, the diplomatic wires and the airwaves were sizzling all through the middle and latter part of September, as Prince Konoye continued to press for the leaders' conference and Secretary Hull continued to stave it off with demands for some solid foundation on which it might be held. Mr. Hull had begun by asking for a more precise statement of Japan's terms to China. As definitively formulated by the Japanese joint conference on September 13, they were of a formidable character. While providing for "neighborly friendship," "respect for sovereignty and territorial integrity," "no annexation," "no idemnities," and the "fusion" of the Chiang Kai-shek Government with the Japanese puppet regime at Nanking, they also called for other things. One was "co-operation between Japan and China for the purposes of preventing Communistic and other subversive activities . . . and of maintaining public order in China." To this end, Japanese troops and naval forces would be stationed in "certain areas" of China for as long as might be necessary. "Except" for such forces, Japan would withdraw her military. Another provision declared that "there shall be economic co-operation between Japan and China," particularly in the development of Chinese resources for "national defense." This, it was added, would not restrict economic activities of third powers in China "so long as they are pursued on an equitable basis." Apparently it would be for Japan to decide what constituted an equitable basis.

Such was the peace in China which the United States was expected to underwrite. The terms were handed to Mr. Grew on September 22 and were brought to Mr. Hull's apartment at the Wardman Park by Admiral Nomura on the evening of the 23rd. The ambassador explained that with this communication Japan had said her say; all that she wished to say was now before us and any further clarification of detail could be left to the leaders' conference. It is hardly surprising that the Secretary of State should have taken a serious view of the situation. That same day he had a very secret talk with Admiral Stark; the gist of it, as Stark summed it up in a letter to

Kimmel, was that "conversations with the Japs have practically reached an impasse." And the following day the well-informed Mr. Fleisher was hearing much the same thing; the Pacific negotiations, he reported to the *Herald Tribune*, had reached "a critical stage."

President Roosevelt was leaving for Hyde Park and Secretary Hull jotted a pencil memorandum for him to take with him: "My suggestion on Jap situation—for you to read *later*." It was brief and was, in effect, that they should make one more try for something better, recalling the seemingly fair promise of the original Konoye proposal, pointing out how Japan had thereafter "narrowed" it down, and asking the Japanese to go back to their original ground. On Sunday, the 28th, the President gave his assent from Hyde Park: "I wholly agree with your penciled note." There seems to have been a good deal of consultation in these final days of September, with more thought than before for the purely military aspects of the problem. Admiral Stark recalled that he neither supported nor opposed the leaders' conference, but gave his personal opinion that the President and Mr. Hull "were right in not just going out to discuss something" with Prince Konoye in the absence of "some preliminary agreement." The War Department sent up a staff appreciation, signed by the Acting Assistant Chief of Staff, G-2 (Intelligence): "This division is of the opinion that neither a conference of leaders nor economic concessions at this point would be of any material advantage" unless it were first possible to get a definite Japanese commitment to withdraw from the Axis. G-2 thought, rashly, that "forceful diplomacy" with "ever increasing military and economic pressure" still offered the best chance of gaining the time we so badly needed. Independently the Secretary of War, Mr. Stimson, had come to a similar view . He was impressed by the necessity for "great care" to avoid "an explosion by the Japanese Army" during the next three months, while we were getting the Philippines rearmed. But "this means," he added, "that while I approve of stringing out negotiations during that period, they should not be allowed to ripen into a personal conference between the President and P[rime] M[inister]. I greatly fear that such a conference if actually held would produce concessions which would be highly dangerous to our vitally important relations with China."

The Secretary of State, pondering his very delicate and difficult problem, was also alert to the "critically discouraging effect" which the conference would have upon the Chinese. From every point of view there was dynamite in it. If it failed, it would give the Japanese military the opportunity of blaming the failure on the United States (just as Konoye had argued in gaining the military's assent to the proposal) thus weakening our "moral position" and facilitating their aggression. Mr. Hull reflected upon Prince Konoye's extreme anxiety to keep the proposed conference secret from his own war party and from the Germans—a hint either of intended duplicity or of a weakness in Japan's political arm which, even if it made commitments in good faith, would again prevent it from imposing them on the military. The Secretary reviewed all the tortuous negotiations of the past months, and they left him "thoroughly satisfied" that without some convincing prior evidence that Japan was ready to turn to a more peaceful course, "a meeting with Konoye could only result either in another Munich or in nothing at all. . . . I was opposed to the first Munich and still more opposed to a second Munich."

Our government, of course, knew nothing about the deadly time limit which the war party had imposed on Prince Konoye's efforts, but it was plain that the frantic—and very suggestive—pressure for haste was rising. On the 25th of September a Foreign Office official told Mr. Grew that Japan was waiting "from moment to moment." The 27th brought the first anniversary of Japan's signing of the Tri-Partite Pact. On that day, amidst ominous public celebrations of the anniversary, Foreign Minister Toyoda summoned Mr. Grew and urged immediate action in the most pressing possible terms. Japan could start at any moment. They had a ship ready. "Any further delays would place the Government in an exceedingly difficult position from the point of view of the Tri-Partite Pact. . . . Time is of paramount importance. . . . It is essential that the meeting should be decided on with all possible speed." Japan would be pleased if it could be scheduled for October 10 to 15. As Mr. Grew privately put it to his diary, they were "rarin' to go."

At the same time, Ambassador Nomura was at the State Department. Although he had stated only a few days before that Japan's case was complete, he now had another long document to hand in, rewriting all that had gone before in still smoother language. It did not add much. On Monday, the 29th, he appeared once more, this time at the Wardman Park, to ask again "with an apparent touch of embarrassment" for the American reply to the leaders' conference proposal. Under questioning, Admiral Nomura gave it as his personal opinion that if there were no meeting the Konoye Government would probably fall, to be replaced by "a less moderate leader." Ambassador Grew had come to the same conclusion. He was convinced that if the United States continued to insist on prior agreement the conversations would only drag out to nothing. His report went on:

> This will result in the Konoye Government's being discredited and in a revulsion of anti-American feeling, and this may and probably will lead to unbridled acts. The eventual cost of these will not be reckoned, and their nature is likely to inflame Americans, while reprisal and counterreprisal measures will bring about a situation in which it will be difficult to avoid war. The logical outcome of this will be the downfall of the Konoye Cabinet and the formation of a military dictatorship which will lack either the disposition or the temperament to avoid colliding head-on with the United States.

Even Mr. Grew's informed imagination could not encompass the fact that the Japanese were at that moment deliberately planning the head-on collision. But he understood much better than the War Department's G-2 that further military threat and economic sanctions would neither in fact undermine Japanese strength nor deter her militarists. His position, it would seem, was that the "strong" policy we had adopted had done its work; that while it could not convert the military it had converted Konoye; that the leaders' conference was the Prince's last chance of committing Japan to a peaceful course and consequently our last opportunity to reap the fruits of our firm stand. The net of his advice was that we should take the opportunity and agree to the leaders' conference even without a prior commitment.

It was advice not lightly to be rejected. Yet Ambassador Grew was without benefit of "magic"; he probably knew less than Washington did about the continued intimacy between Tokyo and Berlin; his view of the Chinese attitude was necessarily foreshortened. And it all sounded too much like the old, old Japanese trick of extorting diplomatic concessions on behalf of the military by pleas that otherwise the military would overthrow the diplomats. The Grew telegram, moreover, still seemed to imply that there was time for maneuver; it scarcely suggested that Konoye's collapse would be immediate. Secretary Hull stood by the decision which he had outlined in his memorandum to the President and which the President had endorsed. A day or two more was consumed in preparing the American reply along these lines. On Thursday morning, October 2 (it was Mr. Hull's seventieth birthday), Admiral Nomura was invited to the Wardman Park and handed a strictly confidential "oral" statement of our position. He read it through, and his face fell.

IV ☞

With the American statement of October 2 the great project of a leaders' conference, on which Prince Konoye had pinned all his hopes and efforts though the past two months, fell to the ground.* The wording was, of course, most tactful, but the sense was plain. The

* It may be useful to recapitulate at this point the course of these rather involved negotiations.

They began with the Japanese proposals of May 12 [p. 82]

To this, the United States replied on June 21 [p. 93] rewriting the Japanese proposals in a contrary sense.

The Japanese answer was completed on July 14 [p. 122] but never delivered, because the United States broke off the negotiations as a result of the occupation of Indo-China. At the same time, however, the President, on July 24, proposed the neutralization of Indo-China [p. 112] as a possible basis for agreement. Immediately thereafter the United States froze Japanese assets and put an end to commercial relations.

The Japanese evaded replying to the proposal for the neutralization of Indo-China. Instead, in their note of August 6 [p. 123] they endeavored to reopen the previous discussions for a general settlement. Their proposals, however, differed from their former ones only in offering to evacuate Indo-China after peace had been imposed on China. The United States rejected the note as "unresponsive."

On August 8 Nomura transmitted Konoye's first suggestion for a personal meeting with the President [p. 124]. On August 17 President Roosevelt issued his warning against further aggression, but at the same time showed himself not unfavorable to the conference idea [p. 126-7]. On August 28 Nomura delivered Konoye's personal message urging the conference and at the same time a "reply" to the August 17 warning which proved vague in its implication [p. 142].

The President answered Konoye's message on September 3 [p. 147-8], again showing himself favorable to the meeting but asking for the establishment of some prior agreement. He outlined his four principles of peace. He urged Japan to reconsider her whole policy very carefully.

Instead, the Japanese answered on September 6 with their "new proposals" which had already been drawn up. These simply repeated the previous Japanese position [p. 155]. On September 22 they transmitted the terms which they wished to impose on China [p. 163], which went far beyond anything the United States could support. The American response was the "oral" statement of October 2 which put an end to the conference idea because (although the Americans did not know this) Konoye was operating under a time limit from his own military.

document rehearsed the promising assurances of Prince Konoye's original proposal; it noted the Prince's statement to Ambassador Grew that he "subscribed fully" to the Hull-Roosevelt four basic principles of peace. It then expressed the "disappointment" of the United States at the way these assurances had subsequently seemed to dissolve in the imprecisions of Japan's specific proposals. It intimated that on three points in particular a more "clear-cut manifestation of Japan's intention" would be welcome: on economic opportunity in China, on withdrawal of troops from China and Indo-China, and on Japan's relations with the Axis. We had received the impression that Japan was qualifying the principles which she professed to accept. "If this impression is correct, can the Japanese Government feel that a meeting between the responsible heads of government under such circumstances would be likely to contribute to the high purposes which we have mutually had in mind?" We suggested renewed efforts to establish a firmer foundation for the proposed meeting.

Or in other words it was no soap. The ambassador expressed the fear that his government would be "disappointed," as it had so earnestly desired the meeting. There was some further conversation, in which Admiral Nomura developed the idea that the one real sticking-point would be the question of withdrawing troops from China. The two other matters should be susceptible to adjustment. Presently, after receiving another little lecture on the virtues of peace and liberal economic principles, he withdrew. Secretary Hull departed for his office at the State Department. There he found that the State Department Correspondents' Association had prepared a little surprise for him—a cake in honor of his birthday. It glowed with twenty-one candles, one for each of the American Republics which Mr. Hull had brought into the "Good Neighbor" policy of peace.

The American reply was the end of Prince Konoye. He had reached "the early part of October"—the deadline which the Army had given him—without result; it was now time "to make up our minds to get ready for war against America (and England and Holland)." It is not to be supposed, however, that there was anything instantaneous about this latter process. It was, in fact, to take them another two weeks of frantic trans-Pacific telegraphing, tortuous expedient, and almost continuous conference and consultation before they could bring themselves to the inevitable. There is an elusiveness about the Japanese mind in action, a kind of fuzzy inability to face alternatives or frame clear statements, which seems to go far beyond the similar qualities observable in Western statesmen. It appears to reflect something deep in the very structure of Japanese language and experience; and the phrasing of the supposedly definitive Imperial Conference directive —"immediately to make up our minds to get ready"—is itself a striking example. This quality is what makes it difficult today to put one's finger on the precise moment (if, indeed, there can be said to have been one) at which Japan went to war. Like Prince Konoye, the others who adopted that directive must have done so with a thought somewhere in the back of their minds that it need not really mean quite what it said, that something would turn up, that the catastrophe they were clearly preparing would somehow be averted, and that ultimate, absolutely final decision could somehow be postponed. But nothing had turned up. The final decision was before them, stark and inescapable. They were to have a bad two weeks over it.

The diplomats labored with the Americans while the politicians and soldiers debated amongst themselves. Nomura cabled on the 3rd his impression that things were not "absolutely hopeless," that the United States had worded its statement "in such a way as to permit a ray of hope to penetrate through." The Foreign Minister, Toyoda, plunged into a frantic effort through both Grew and Nomura to get a bill of particulars as to just what would satisfy the United States. Various interesting items flitted through the tense dispatches. At one interview it was gravely explained to Mr. Grew that he had been mistaken in reporting that Prince Konoye "subscribed fully" to President Roosevelt's four principles of peace; what the Prime Minister had done was to subscribe "in principle" only. It seems grimly humorous now, but at the time it could not have increased Washington's confidence in Konoye. Again on October 10 Toyoda told Grew that it was impossible to get adequate information out of Nomura; the Foreign Minister feared that his ambassador was "very fatigued" and broached the idea of sending another high diplomat to Washington to assist him. This seems to have been the first suggestion of the Kurusu mission, which thus cannot be wholly ascribed to the subsequent Tojo Government.

Though the American reply was still a secret, it was outwardly evident that the tensions were rising again. The Japanese press was once more breaking out with belligerent pronouncements. On October 5 there was a nationwide broadcast from Tokyo by three high Cabinet members. All spoke in the most formidable terms, while the Navy Minister, expressing his "bitterness" over the dark prospect, added that nevertheless "as far as the Imperial Navy is concerned, you may rest assured that everything has been done to meet any untoward happening." After the war a Japanese naval aviator told American interrogators that on this same day, October 5, a group of about one hundred of Japan's crack naval pilots were assembled on board the carrier *Akagi* in Shibushi Bay, Kyushu. They were told in the utmost secrecy that on December 8 (Japan time) the war would begin with a carrier strike against the American fleet in Pearl Harbor. It appears to be the earliest actual mention of the famous date which has been discovered.

We had, of course, no means of knowing what went on aboard the *Akagi*. But a few days later (on October 9) a translated intercept was emerging from "magic." It was a message which had been sent on September 24 from the Foreign Office in Toyko to the Japanese consul in Hawaii, and appeared at first glance to be simply another item in the already considerable traffic in which Tokyo had been demanding reports of our ship movements from its consulates. Perhaps that was the reason for the delay of over two weeks in making the translation. But the complete text had an unusual look. It ran:

> Strictly secret.
>
> Henceforth, we would like to have you make reports concerning vessels along the following lines in so far as possible:
>
> 1. The waters (of Pearl Harbor) are to be divided roughly into five sub-areas. . . . [The five areas were then lettered and described.]
>
> 2. With regard to warships and aircraft carriers, we would like to have you report on those at anchor (these are not so important), tied up at wharves, buoys, and in the docks . . . (If possible we would like to have you make mention of the fact when there are two or more vessels alongside the same wharf.)

Lieutenant Commander Alwyn D. Kramer, in charge of the Navy section responsible for the translation and distribution of the intercepts, tagged this with the notation "interesting message" and it was sent along to the Army and Navy high commands. None of Tokyo's previous orders had called for information in such detail. None had divided or "plotted" a harbor in such a way that the relative positions of the ships within it could be reported. None had been interested in whether two or more vessels were at one dock. Colonel Rufus S. Bratton, chief of the Far Eastern section of Military Intelligence, thought that the Japanese were displaying an unusual interest in Pearl Harbor, and has declared that he discussed the matter with his naval colleagues "on several occasions." The kind of information for which this message called was patently unnecessary to the ordinary check on American ship movements which the Japanese were making elsewhere. It suggested a plan for a submarine or air attack upon the Fleet while it was in port. The possibility was considered; but Naval Intelligence (according to Colonel Bratton) observed that if this was the explanation the Japanese were only wasting their time, since the Fleet would not be in port if war came.

The evaluation went no farther; and although additional intercepts were to come in from time to time, indicating that the consul was obeying his orders and that Tokyo was putting considerable emphasis on them, the final step to the correct deduction was never made. The hint which had come through the Peruvian Legation in Tokyo far back in January, the Navy's own fears that war might open with a surprise air attack on Pearl, General Marshall's estimate that the first six hours would be the most dangerous, the studies of the Oahu commanders—all alike seem to have been forgotten. It was not thought necessary to advise either Kimmel or Short of these so-called "bomb plot" messages. Whether the field commanders would have been more alert to their significance than Naval Intelligence in Washington can, of course, never be known. The two commanders naturally believe that they would have been; others, examining the whole record, may at least entertain a doubt.*

Another suggestion of these days was to take on later importance. On October 9 Washington dispatches reported that the United States and Japan were working on "a limited agreement . . . a temporary *modus vivendi*" in which the United States would offer some partial relaxation of the trade restrictions in return for a Japanese undertaking to renounce "any further aggression in Asia" for the time being. This idea was

* A mere belief on the part of Kimmel and Short that the Japanese were planning an air attack *when war came* would not, it must be observed, have materially changed the history of Pearl Harbor. The one clue which would have been of consequence was a clue that Japan intended to *start the war* in that way. (This point appears very clearly in Admiral Bellinger's testimony, in the *Hearings*, Pt. 8, p. 3484). Today the clue may be found in these messages, but at best it is a rather faint one. In missing it, Naval Intelligence made a tragic error. In the circumstances of the time, however, others might easily have made it, too.

to recur; but if it was seriously advanced in early October it appears to have had no effect upon the anguished death struggles of the Konoye Government.

Behind the closed doors and secret screens in Tokyo the consultations were rising to an ever more furious tempo. Out of the whole mass of conference and diplomatic activity, the question of the withdrawal of Japanese troops from China was emerging (just as Admiral Nomura had intimated that it would) as the critical issue. Without some yielding on that point it appeared hopeless to look for an agreement with the United States. But as early as October 7 the tight-lipped Minister of War, Tojo the "Razor Brain," told his Prime Minister that there the Army would not yield. The conferences went on, in a crisis atmosphere which the Germans were not making any easier.

Alarming dispatches had been coming in from the Japanese embassies at Berlin and Rome, reflecting the growing disgust of the Axis partners with the Japanese-American negotiations. General Ott in Tokyo had been putting on all the heat at his command, trying to pin the Japanese down to a positive commitment to declare war on the United States in the event of war between the United States and Germany. The Germans were beginning to feel our pressure on the Atlantic. We had issued and publicized our "shooting" orders. The President had called for the modification or repeal of the last vestiges of the neutrality act in order to permit the arming of American merchant ships. But as this American threat grew more formidable on the Atlantic, the Germans were seeing their prospects brightening again in Russia. On October 3 Hitler, breaking a silence that had begun to be noticeable, appeared in the Berlin Sportspalast to tell his cheering henchmen that the Russian enemy had been "hit so hard that he will never rise again" and that a "gigantic new development" was even then under way. This was the great drive aimed at the capture of Moscow before the closing in of winter. The Germans thought that they had the end of the Russian war in sight and were in consequence no longer much interested in promoting a Japanese attack on Siberia. But Japanese help in checkmating the United States, thus preventing us from intervening to break the stranglehold which the German submarines and air forces were trying to clamp on Britain and the Empire, would still be most useful. In Tokyo the German pressure mounted; and so did the formidable possibility that Germany was about to prove the winner after all.

On the 9th of October Dr. Otto Dietrich, Hitler's personal press chief, made his famous appearance before the corps of correspondents in Berlin to tell them that "the last great battle of this year" (as Hitler had called it) had been crushingly won. The Red Army had suffered a disaster of such magnitude that an effective Russian military leadership no longer existed. Total collapse was "imminent." Even if Stalin could raise new armies, they could not last for two weeks; and if Moscow was still refusing to admit the situation it was, perhaps, because the disorganization was so great that Moscow itself did not know what had happened. Next day the newspapers of the world were blazing with the tidings. The war in Russia was virtually over—or so the Germans said.

The effect of all this on the crisis conferences in Tokyo is not difficult to imagine. Prince Konoye saw the Foreign Minister twice on October 10; there was a joint conference of the political and military heads on October 11, and on Sunday, October 12 (it was Prince Konoye's fiftieth birthday), the Prime Minister assembled at his home the Ministers of War and Navy, the Foreign Minister, and the President of the Cabinet Planning Board. The inevitable was fairly before them. Even then the Navy, with its tradition of noninterference in political matters, was trying to play it both ways. However complete its preparations and whatever it may have told its young pilots, it was disinclined to take the responsibility. The Navy Minister, Admiral Oikawa, opened the deliberations:

> We have now indeed come to the crossroads where we must determine either upon peace or war. I should like to leave this decision entirely up to the Premier. And, if we are to seek peace, we shall go all the way for peace. Thus, even if we make a few concessions, we ought to proceed all the way with the policy of bringing the negotiations to fruition. . . . If we are to have war, we must determine upon war here and now.

The scion of the Fujiwaras was likewise squirming under the inevitable, but he did achieve an at least conditional decision: "If we were to say that we must determine on war or peace here, today, I myself would decide on continuing the negotiations." But the grim little Minister of War would have none of that. General Tojo pinned his Prime Minister down:

> This decision of the Premier's is too hasty. Properly speaking, ought we not to determine here whether or not there is any possibility of bringing the negotiations to fruition? To carry on negotiations for which there is no possibility of fruition, and in the end to let slip the time for fighting, would be a matter of the greatest consequence.

Was there, he asked the Foreign Minister (a question which might better have been asked when they adopted their policy on September 6), any chance of "bringing negotiations to fruition?" Toyoda was compelled to confess that without some concession in regard to the "stationing of troops in China" there was no chance. As he put it:

> If in this regard the Army says that it will not retreat one step from its former assertions, then there is no hope in the negotiations. But if on this point the Army states that it would be all right to make concessions, however small they may be, then we cannot say that there is not hope of bringing the negotiations to fruition.

But General Tojo would not retreat even by a single step. "The problem of the stationing of troops," he said, "in itself means the life of the Army, and we shall not be able to make any concessions at all." Prince Konoye tried to move him. Why not, he suggested, "forget about the glory, . . . perform the formalities as America wants, and achieve a result that will in actuality be the same as 'stationing troops'?" But Tojo would not budge, and after four hours of it they broke up without decision. Yet the decision had been made, nevertheless. Next day, the 13th, Prince Konoye had a two-hour audience with the Emperor and later consulted Marquis Kido, the reigning Elder Statesman—in itself a virtual announcement that his Cabinet was through. On Tuesday he made a last try with the tough little general. He observed that he, the Prince, already bore a heavy responsibility for the initiation of the "China Incident," not yet concluded after four years of warfare, and was unwilling to enter upon a greater war "the future of which I cannot at all foresee." He repeated his argument about granting the formalities in return for the substance; but General Tojo brushed aside such weakness:

> If at this time we yield to the United States, she will take steps that are more and more high-handed, and will probably find no place to stop. The problem of withdrawing troops is one, you say, of forgetting the honor and of seizing the fruits, but to this I find it difficult to agree from the point of view of maintaining the fighting spirit of the Army.*

Again the talk ended nowhere, and the two went into the meeting of the Cabinet. The Cabinet did not even take up the crucial issue, for Tojo opened by "strongly and excitedly" stating why the negotiations should be terminated and none wished to raise a voice against him. The handwriting on the wall was now unmistakable. Tojo knew that he had won, and that evening he forced the issue with a message to Prince Konoye, informing the Prime Minister that he and his Cabi-

* It was not only a question of morale. With every week of delay the United States was growing stronger in the Far East. Obviously, Tojo, like the Navy, realized that if they were going to fight they would have to fight at once.

net should resign. As the general rather cogently put it, if the Navy, in leaving the whole decision up to Konoye, meant that it was unwilling to fight, then that in turn must mean that the policy of September 6 had been "fundamentally overturned" and that it would be necessary to form a new Government and start all over again from the beginning. Prince Konoye's rope had run out. Next day, the 15th, was spent on the question of a successor, while the press began to thunder and the Navy spokesman, Captain Hiraide, issued a stream of statements more belligerent than anything which had yet come from the more "moderate" service: "Final parting of the ways. . . . The fate of our Empire depends on how we act. . . . It is certainly at such a moment as this that our Navy should set about its final mission. . . . Japanese-American relations are extremely critical. . . . The Japanese Navy is itching for action." It was the first time that the Navy had publicly intimated that a Japanese-American war might be imminent.

Tojo's nominee was Prince Higashikuni, a cousin of the Emperor and Chief of the Imperial General Staff. But Hirohito did not want a prince of the blood involved so directly in the coming adventure, and there was no time to argue about it. On the morning of Thursday, October 16, Konoye gathered the resignations of the Cabinet members, and Prince Higashikuni was thus preserved from responsibility. He was preserved, ironically enough, only to become Prime Minister four years later, when he would take the post as the first Japanese chief of state in two thousand years of history to serve under a conquering foreign power. But that could not be foreseen. On Friday, October 17, the new Prime Minister was announced—General Hideki Tojo, the "Razor Brain" of the "Manchuria Gang."

Appropriately, as it seemed, it was the beginning of the ancient two-day autumn festival, when the Emperor's emissary laid the first grains of the new rice crop upon the shrine at Ise and when the descendant of the Sun Goddess himself honored the spirits of the soldier dead at the Yasukuni shrine in Tokyo. But as the Emperor took his way to the shrine, a foggy mist was enveloping the streets, and by the time the new Cabinet was sworn in later that day, it had turned to a steady drizzle.

FIVE

THE RAZOR BRAIN

I ☞

On Friday morning, October 17, Americans throughout the country were picking up their newspapers to find them blazing with dramatic and foreboding headlines. The *New York Herald Tribune*, for example, summed up the tumultuous events of the past twenty-four hours under a five-column combined head:

SOVIET CABINET REPORTED FLEEING MOSCOW;
JAPAN'S GOVERNMENT QUITS IN U.S. CRISIS;
ROOSEVELT CALLS CHIEFS OF ARMY AND NAVY

The subheads on the Russian war were given first emphasis:

Soviet Government Said
To Be Moving to Kazan
450 Miles Farther East

Moscow Battle Rages Fiercely
Axis Armies in Blazing Odessa

But the dispatches from Tokyo and Washington received almost equal prominence:

Tokyo Pro-Axis Regime
Forecast in Failure of
Talks with Washington

White House Conference
Lasting Two Hours Linked
To Tokyo, Soviet Crises

The stories poured out the details. In Washington it was the "general impression" that the fall of the Konoye Cabinet announced the final breakdown of the already deadlocked Japanese-American negotiations; a "clash" with Japan was already upon the horizons of the possible. The Secretaries of State, War, and Navy, General Marshall, and Admiral Stark had spent an hour and fifty minutes at the White House with the President and Mr. Harry Hopkins, and afterward they had been grimly uncommunicative. Mr. Hull and Mr. Knox found only a few meaningless words for the reporters; Mr. Stimson, General Marshall, and Admiral Stark "had absolutely nothing to say when they came out. Mr. Hopkins, who lives at the White House, didn't even come out."

Less official commentators were quick to fill these silences. The crisis on the Russian fronts tended somewhat to overshadow the developments in Tokyo, but the menacing character of the latter was by no means overlooked. The *Herald Tribune* editorially summed up the situation with a prophetic accuracy:

> [The Japanese war machine] is about to seize control of national policy and start something that will evoke a counter-something that will cost the wretched Japanese people plenty. We do not pretend to know what it will be. But we do know that it will be in line with Hitler's plans; that it will therefore fail, and that it will therefore reduce Japan eventually to innocuous desuetude.*

Yet few seemed to worry much over what that "something" might be. There was still that persistent tendency to underrate the Japanese, and some were even advancing the idea that it might be just as well if Japan did precipitate the long-threat-

* The anonymous author of this prophecy was Mr. Rodney Gilbert, a long-experienced student of Far Eastern affairs.

ened Far Eastern war, thus allowing Britain and the United States to crush the menace once and for all and turn their full energies to Europe. The truth is that during those first two weeks of October, while the Japanese had been involved in their complex indecisions, the war atmospheres had been rising in the United States. No one had been particularly startled when the Budget Bureau had published its revised estimates on October 4, indicating that total expenditures for the current fiscal year would mount to $24.5 billions and that the over-all cost of the "defense" program, adopted or projected, would run to $60 billions or more. Another big Army maneuver was getting under way, this time in the Carolinas, where some 350,000 men of Lieutenant General Hugh A. Drum's 1st Army were to spend two months in large-scale field exercises. "Civilian defense" was beginning to assume some attributes of reality. The Army had established an aircraft warning net, manned by civilian volunteers and complete with information and operation centers like those with which the motion-picture "documentaries" on the Battle of Britain had made everyone familiar. The system was given its first major test in the second week of October, when 40,000 volunteer spotters scattered from Boston to Cape Hatteras tracked the movements of 400 "attacking" aircraft in an extended exercise.

On the Atlantic sea lanes (though this was not generally known) the "shooting orders" had developed into what amounted to full naval war. Our naval vessels were already serving, on occasion, under British command and British men-of-war under American command. British troop convoys being hurried out to the reinforcement of Singapore were escorted through long reaches of the Atlantic by American squadrons, protecting them against German submarine attack. Though the public did not know this, it was made aware that the pressure was rising. On October 9 the President sent in his message to Congress calling for the removal of the neutrality act prohibitions against the arming of American merchant ships, and describing the Nazis in passing as "madmen" and "modern pirates." The modifying resolution was introduced the same day. Then on October 11 there was a more dramatic development, when the Navy announced the "capture and disposition" by American forces of a German-controlled weather reporting station which had been discovered operating on the remote coasts of Greenland. A small vessel, ostensibly belonging to the Norwegian puppet government, her crew, and three German agents had been taken. In the *Greer* affair we had exchanged our first shots with the Germans; here we had taken our first prize of war. The sands were running faster.

Such were the immediate backgrounds against which there came the news of Prince Konoye's fall. Whatever the commentators might guess about it, the military and diplomatic staffs had to evaluate it for possible action. At the State Department on Thursday, the 16th, they were running up drafts of a proposed direct appeal from the President to the Japanese Emperor, suggesting a leaders' conference, but one which would include Chiang Kai-shek. The notion, however, was laid aside. At the Navy Department they were preparing a warning telegram for the Pacific outposts. It went off that day to Hart at Manila and Kimmel at Pearl Harbor, over Admiral Stark's signature as Chief of Naval Operations:

> The resignation of the Japanese Cabinet has created a grave situation. If a new Cabinet is formed it will probably be strongly nationalistic and anti-American. If the Konoye Cabinet remains, the effect will be that it will operate under a new mandate which will not include rapprochement with the United States. In either case hostilities between Japan and Russia are a strong possibility. Since the United States and Britain are held responsible by Japan for her present desperate situation there is also a possibility that Japan may attack these two powers. In view of these possibilities you will take due precautions, including such preparatory deployments as will not disclose strategic intention nor constitute provocative actions against Japan. . . . Inform appropriate Army and Naval District authorities. Acknowledge.

In the Philippines this estimate may not have added greatly

to the tensions they were already feeling. In Hawaii it should have come with a greater impact. Admiral Kimmel, at any rate, showed it to General Short in accordance with the instruction; and thus Pearl Harbor had its first formal and official, if still rather tentative, warning.

Next day, Friday the 17th, the news came in that Tojo, the Army general, had been chosen as Konoye's successor. But again this was over-shadowed by more thrilling news from the Atlantic. The *U.S.S. Kearny*, one of our best and newest destroyers, had been torpedoed in those same perilous seas southwest of Iceland; she was being brought into port; the casualties, if any, were unknown, but the Navy was hunting her assailant. This was worse than the *Greer*. This really was war. In Washington that afternoon the House passed the merchant ship arming bill with a rush—though not, it had to be admitted, with the unanimity that might have been hoped. The vote was 259 to 138, and the Republican minority, bitterly hostile as most of them were to the Roosevelt leadership, had voted nearly three to one against.

"Things have been popping here for the last twenty-four hours," Admiral Stark wrote that day in another of his personal letters to "Mustapha" Kimmel; and then he went on to elaborate a little on the official warning of the day before:

> Personally I do not believe the Japs are going to sail into us and the message I sent you merely stated the "possibility"; in fact I tempered the message handed to me considerably. Perhaps I am wrong, but I hope not. In any case after long powwows in the White House it was felt we should be on guard, at least until something indicates the trend.

By Saturday they had the composition of the new Cabinet, with Tojo retaining the War Ministry and assuming that of Home Affairs as well as the premiership; with Shigenori Togo, a former ambassador to both Berlin and Moscow and believed to be an advocate of a strong policy toward the United States, as Foreign Minister, and with little that was reassuring about the other names. They also had the new Prime Minister's one-minute radio broadcast announcing his policy:

> I am fully convinced that speedy action and iron will under the aegis of the august virtues of His Majesty the Emperor are the only ways in which to overcome the present difficulties.

In a brief press conference Prime Minister Tojo made it clear that the three bases of his policy would be the settlement of the China Incident, the establishment of Greater East Asia, and the maintenance of the pro-Axis alignment. But our people had heard that sort of thing too many times before. Now that the crisis had come at last, there was a tendency to feel that perhaps it was not as bad as had been expected. At the Tokyo embassy Mr. E. H. Dooman, the counseller, was seeing a silver lining. After all, the Japanese Army in taking full power had also assumed full responsibility, and Tojo was a strict disciplinarian who could keep his fire-eaters in order. Ambassador Grew was inclined to a similar view. Prince Konoye had sent private word of how he had labored "successfully" to secure a successor who would continue the American conversations; and the Ambassador, perhaps a little guilelessly, thought it a reasonable guess that with the Army openly in command the negotiations might actually have a better chance than before. In Washington, a naval appreciation prepared for Admiral Stark held that "we are inclined to overestimate the importance" of Japanese Cabinet changes; peace or war would still, as in the past, turn purely on Japanese calculations of military expediency.

In the War Department they were also having some second thoughts over the week end. Brigadier General Leonard T. Gerow, chief of War Plans, thought the Navy's warning message had been, perhaps, a trifle precipitate. Brigadier General Sherman Miles, the tall, soldierly, and not overly brilliant G-2 (chief of Intelligence),* agreed with him that whatever the

* General Miles was the son of General Nelson A. Miles, Commanding General of the Army at the time of the Spanish-American

Navy's dispositions might require, it was unnecessary for the Army to begin as yet on such things as "preparatory deployments." Between them they prepared a modifying message which went off on Monday, the 20th, to Short and MacArthur over the signature of the Adjutant General:

> Following War Department estimate of Japanese situation for your information. Tension between United States and Japan remains strained but no repeat no abrupt change in Japanese foreign policy appears imminent.

A couple of days later "magic" was providing what must have seemed strong confirmation for this judgment, in the form of the first instructions from the new government to their ambassador in Washington:

> The new Cabinet differs in no way from the former one in its sincere desire to adjust Japanese-United States relations on a fair basis. Our country has said practically all she can say. . . . We feel that we have now reached a point where no further positive action can be taken by us except to urge the United States to reconsider her views. . . . Choosing an opportune moment . . . let it be known to the United States by indirection that our country is not in a position to spend much more time discussing this matter. Please continue the talks. . . .

So there was to be more talk. That phrase about there not being "much more time" may have had an ominous ring, but at any rate it appeared that there would be no immediate change in the situation. The Army, the Navy, and the State Department relaxed to await clearer indications of the "trend," while the public, with its newspapers and radio broadcasts filled with other things, rather lost sight of the quaint little Japanese.

The last half of October brought enough developments in

War and hero of the all but bloodless conquest of Puerto Rico. The son had received his first experience of war as a youth, when his father took him on an inspection of the celebrated, and lamentable, embarkation camp at Tampa in 1898.

other fields. The *Kearny* made port, with an enormous torpedo wound in her side and with eleven men lost as well as ten more wounded. These were the first service casualties of the war. Few supposed that they would be the last; but it was still hard to picture the country as actually at war. The terrible Russian fronts, on the other hand, gripped the mind. On October 20 it was announced that the Germans were within 62 miles of Moscow, closing in from both the northwest and the south. Premier Stalin had proclaimed a state of siege, and the citizens of the capital were pouring out to dig defenses and man the strong points. Next day the news was definite that the government had withdrawn, not to Kazan but to Kuybyshev, the ancient Samara, lying 500 miles to the eastward on the Volga. Yet nearly a fortnight had gone by since the Germans had confidently announced the final liquidation of the war in Russia, and it was obvious that the "annihilated" Red armies were still fighting stubbornly. Other significant items began to appear in the news. Berlin admitted on October 23 that the great southern drive through the Donets Basin was slowing down, and spoke of the driving snowstorms and freezing nights that were impeding the operations of the panzer divisions on the Moscow front. General Winter was arriving; and it seemed not only possible but probable that the great war in Europe was not over after all.

On the Atlantic sea lanes there were more sinkings of American-owned merchantmen, with a lengthening death roll. In Washington on October 25, the Senate Foreign Relations Committee, amid some rather obscure political maneuvering, voted by 13 to 10 to report a considerably broadened version of the House ship arming bill. But on that same day Mr. John L. Lewis—choosing a moment of national crisis, as he had done before and was to do again—called out the 53,000 workers in the "captive" coal mines which supplied our major steel plants. Rejecting an urgent appeal from the President to continue work pending mediation of the dispute, the dictatorial chieftain of the United Mine Workers closed the captive mines and thus shut off a vital source of supply for the whole defense industry. For many days thereafter this dispute in the coal mines, coming on top of other serious labor troubles, was a cause of greater anxiety, almost, than the war. It certainly claimed much more attention than the doings of the Japanese. The Japanese, for their part, probably did not overlook the doings of Mr. Lewis.

In Washington the diplomatic conversations went on, but with a sense of marking time until the Tojo Cabinet should have made up its mind. At Pearl Harbor General Short, perhaps lulled by the War Department estimate, continued his training schedules. Admiral Kimmel, on the other hand, was under orders to effect "preparatory deployments." He dispatched a dozen of his long-range Catalina patrol planes to Midway and readied six more for Wake Island; he established a patrol of two submarines off Wake and ordered six others to keep themselves prepared to "depart for Japan on short notice"; he tightened up some of his security regulations in the maneuver areas off Pearl, but otherwise maintained much the usual routines. At the same time the Navy Department, in a more dramatic precautionary move, advised all American merchantmen in the Pacific that "there is a possibility of hostile action by Japan against U. S. shipping" and ordered all vessels in the western Pacific into friendly ports. The transports with reinforcements for the Philippines were required to proceed thereafter only in convoy and under naval escort.

The Navy also felt a fresh anxiety about the island steppingstones on the trans-Pacific route of the heavy bombers, and ordered Kimmel "to take all precautions for the safety of the airfields at Wake and Midway." He had a comprehensive study of the problem worked up by his staff, and the movements to which this eventually gave rise were to have an important effect upon later events. In Washington Secretary Knox, speaking informally but publicly to a group of high naval officers and industrialists, told them that war with Japan was "inevitable" if the Japanese insisted on carrying forward their plans for expansion, and he believed they had no idea of renouncing them. This made impressive headlines. For the time, however, the military and civil officials were largely waiting on developments.

Defiant of warnings, the isolationists were rising to make what they knew would be their last stand, over the ship arming bill. The debate opened in the Senate on October 27, with Senator Tom Connally, the florid chairman of the Foreign Relations Committee, making an impassioned appeal for action and with Senator Vandenberg of Michigan—the Republican expert on foreign policy, as yet unaware that he was destined to become a pillar of Republican internationalism and a close colleague of Senator Connally in the peacemaking—leading the opposition. The bill, he proclaimed, was a "prelude to inevitable war" and to a new American expeditionary force in Europe. That evening the President at a Navy Day dinner in Washington was using the attack upon the *Kearny* as a text for another fighting address: "The shooting has started. . . . 'Damn the torpedoes; full speed ahead.' . . . I say that we do not propose to take this lying down." It did not still the thunders of Middle Western isolationism and of Republican hostility to "that man" in the White House. Next day Senator Taft of Ohio was charging that Franklin D. Roosevelt had tricked the people into war; Senators La Follette and Nye were to follow him, prophesying Communism, Fascism, and war if the bill were passed. On the evening of October 30 the New York chapter of America First organized a monster mass meeting at Madison Square Garden, with Colonel Lindbergh and Senator Wheeler as featured speakers. They poured out their envenomed attacks upon the Administration. The Colonel, who had already been prophesying the abolition of elections and a seizure of dictatorial power by the New Deal, shouted that the United States no longer enjoyed representative government. "There is no danger to this nation from without. Our only danger lies from within."

It was a supreme effort. But it is doubtful that the effect

was what had been anticipated. The Colonel had previously managed to tar America First with the brush of anti-Semitism, while the enthusiastic influx of pro-Fascists and proto-Nazis was too clearly pinning the swastika on the whole movement. In face of these tendencies, in face of the now obvious national peril, and in face of the fact that the country as a whole still clearly supported the President's foreign policy, America First had been suffering serious defections. The character of the angry crowd that filled the Garden could only encourage them:

> Throughout the evening, most mentions of the President's name were booed and hissed. At times, voices from the crowd yelled "Hang Roosevelt!" or "He's a traitor!" or "Impeach the President!" . . . One prediction of quick death for Hitler drew only weak applause.

These dubious patriots were still streaming home from the Garden when, in a black and stormy midnight sea on the Iceland passage, the *U.S.S. Reuben James*, another of the old "four-piper" destroyers, suddenly and with no warning whatever took a torpedo full amidships on the port side. She lacked the ruggedness of the newer ships; the one explosion ripped her in two and the bow sank immediately. As the stern went under a few minutes later there was another violent explosion, apparently of her own depth charges, which killed many of those in the water or swept them from the liferafts to drown in the darkness and the clogging fuel oil. The rescuing ships could save only 45 men (only eight of these were unwounded) and an even 100 lives were lost.

It was a shock. In the Senate next day Mr. Connally was thundering for instant vengeance on this "dastardly act of aggression"; but others, even in the Administration ranks, were arguing for calm. It was already known that the Administration had enough sure votes to pass the ship arming bill. However, a motion for an immediate vote was lost; too many statesmen still had undelivered speeches which they wished to commit to posterity. The debate ground on. Meanwhile Mr. John L. Lewis allowed his miners to go back, temporarily, to work. But he still held the knife suspended over the war economy, while the even graver threat of a national railway strike was now developing. Through the ensuing few weeks the confused, disordered, irresponsible workings of our democracy at home in this crisis time were a constant source of anxiety. But at the White House and the State Department, as October turned into November, the Far East was again claiming first attention. The "trend" was beginning to appear.

The first alarm had come from Chungking. On the 28th of October there was a long telegram from Brigadier-General John A. Magruder, head of the American military mission which had just arrived in the Chinese capital. Magruder was reporting his first interview with the Generalissimo, Chiang Kai-shek. The Generalissimo, "intently earnest," declared that he needed immediate, emergency assistance. The Japanese, he knew, were planning to strike from Indo-China through Yunnan against the Burma Road "by the end of November." If the Burma Road were cut China would fall and the Japanese would thereupon sweep all of Southeast Asia. And the Chinese could defend the road only if they had powerful air support from Britain and America. The Generalissimo pleaded for the President to use his influence with the British to induce them to send air power from Singapore and to support a joint warning to Japan that any advance through Yunnan would be considered inimical to the interests of Britain and the United States.

It was the first of a spate of urgent appeals from Chungking. On Thursday, October 30, Mr. Roosevelt was handed a message in similar terms which the Generalissimo had sent to him through Mr. T. V. Soong, at that time in Washington. The President scribbled a note upon it for Mr. Hull:

> C. H. Can we do anything along these lines? How about telling Japan a move to close Burma Road would be inimical? F. D. R.

That morning the American newspapers had carried brief dispatches quoting "military sources" in Shanghai as reporting that the Japanese were moving 1000 men a day into Indo-China and that a Japanese attack upon either Yunnan or Siam seemed imminent. Military sources in Shanghai were not particularly reliable; but matters were again beginning to look serious. On Saturday, November 1, Secretary Hull assembled in his office a conference of his own advisers together with Gerow for the War Department and Captain "Pinkie" Schuirmann, liaison man for the Navy, to consider Chiang's cry for help. It was no longer much use issuing warnings, the Secretary was inclined to feel, unless the military could "back them up." How about it? The military retired with this suddenly formidable problem.

By Monday, November 3, the trend in Tokyo was becoming much clearer and more ominous. Ambassador Grew had taken two cautious weeks to estimate the real meaning of the Japanese Cabinet shift. Various informants had come to him; some had emphasized the pacific intentions of the Emperor, at least one had told him that a "blitz" attack on Siam was already prepared. That Monday the ambassador summed up and sent in his conclusions. The report was cautious and somewhat too wordy, but two points emerged quite clearly: Mr. Grew thought it a dangerous illusion to imagine that mere threats or economic sanctions would restrain Japan; and he thought that this time the Japanese meant business. The ambassador explained that he was no appeaser, but he did not want the United States to underrate Japan's capacity "to rush headlong into suicidal conflict" and he did not want us to blunder into a war without knowing what we were doing. If the negotiations which the Tojo Cabinet was continuing should come to nothing, "Japan's resort to measures which might war with the United States inevitably [*sic*] may come with dramatic and dangerous suddenness."

The same afternoon the Army-Navy Joint Board met to contemplate the poser which the State Department and the

Generalissimo had handed them. They were all there—Stark, Marshall, Rear-Admiral R. E. Ingersoll (Stark's Assistant Chief of Naval Operations), Major General H. H. Arnold (commander and expert press agent of the Army Air Forces), Towers for Naval Aeronautics, Gerow, Schuirmann and others. Faced with the slimness of our own available resources, there was definitely no enthusiasm for rushing to Chiang Kai-shek's defense. The Navy "felt that the present moment was not the opportune time to get brash." General Marshall felt that what air forces we had in the Far East would be more effective where they were. "It was his belief that by the middle of December the Army forces in the Philippines would be of impressive strength, and this in itself would have a deterrent effect on Japanese operations." The concensus was to go slow; to try to string things out as long as possible with the Japanese, even at the cost of some "minor concessions" which "the Japanese could use in saving face." It was decided to prepare a report for the President along those lines. It was also, incidentally, decided to study an alternate route to Manila for the heavy bombers—"less vulnerable to hostile interference" than the road by Midway and Wake.

And then on Tuesday, November 4, "magic" placed the answer in our hands, in a sheaf of telegrams sent that day by Foreign Minister Togo to Ambassador Nomura. The Japanese, after two more weeks of conferences, had again decided their policy; and here it was, available to our own high officials almost, if not quite, as quickly as it was to Admiral Nomura:

> Well, relations between Japan and the United States have reached the edge, and our people are losing confidence in the possibility of ever adjusting them. In order to lucubrate on fundamental national policy, the Cabinet has been meeting with the Imperial Headquarters for some days in succession. Conference has followed conference, and now we are at length able to bring forth a counterproposal for the resumption of Japanese-American negotiations. . . . This and other basic policies of our Empire await

the sanction of the [Imperial] Conference to be held on the morning of the 5th.

Conditions both within and without our Empire are so tense that no longer is procrastination possible, yet in our sincerity to maintain pacific relationships . . . we have decided . . . to gamble once more on the continuance of the parleys, but this is our last effort. Both in name and spirit this counterproposal of ours is, indeed, the last. I want you to know that. If through it we do not reach a quick accord, I am sorry to say the talks will certainly be ruptured. . . . I mean that the success or failure of the pending discussions will have an immense effect on the destiny of the Empire of Japan. In fact, we gambled the fate of our land on the throw of this die. . . .

There seem to be some Americans who think we would make a one-sided deal, but our temperance, I can tell you, has not come from weakness, and naturally there is an end to our long-suffering. Nay, when it comes to a question of our existence and our honor, when the time comes we will defend them without recking the cost. . . .

It is to be hoped earnestly that looking forward to what may come at the end—at the last day of Japanese-American negotiations—the Government of the United States will think ever so soberly how much better it would be to make peace with us; how much better this would be for the whole world situation.

Your Honor will see from the considerations above how important is your mission. . . . Now, just as soon as the Conference is over, I will let you know immediately, and I want you to go and talk with President Roosevelt and Secretary Hull. I want you to tell them how determined we are and try to get them to foster a speedy understanding. . . . I want you to follow my instructions to the letter. In my instructions, I want you to know there will be no room for personal interpretation.

"Magic" also yielded the texts of the "counterproposals" which were sent in separate telegrams. There were two. "Proposal A" was "our revised ultimatum." In case that did not work, Nomura was supplied with "Proposal B." In the event of deadlock over the first, he was told, it would be necessary, "since the situation does not permit of delays," to "put forward some substitute plan. Therefore, our second formula is advanced with the idea of making a last effort to prevent something happening."

As a matter of fact, there was no very essential difference between the two, or between either and the proposals on which Japan had been standing for months. Under "B," the final, rock-bottom offer, Japan would undertake to make no military invasions "in southeast Asia and the South Seas with the exception of French Indo-China." In return the United States would co-operate in securing for Japan the raw materials she required from the Netherlands East Indies, would cancel the freezing order and "furnish Japan with the petroleum she needs," and put no obstacle in the way of Japan's "efforts to make peace with China." Nomura could also say, "if necessary," that as soon as peace was established in China "Japan has no objection to promising to evacuate her troops."

The whole of these texts was available on November 4. The Imperial Conference was to take place on the following day; consequently, the American government actually knew what Japan was going to decide before she had taken the formal decision herself! No doubt the fogginess of the Japanese language and thought processes made sound evaluation difficult, yet it seems strange that these messages made no greater impact than they did. They would appear plainly to have answered the three major riddles of the moment: (1) The Tojo Cabinet was continuing negotiations only in the hope of getting a complete surrender from the United States; (2) the time was very short before "something" would happen; (3) this "something" would involve the United States and could hardly be anything less than war. The last was the really crucial revelation. All through those final weeks there was an idea that while Japan was presumably about to burst out somewhere she would probably by-pass the Philippines in order to start with Yunnan or Siam or perhaps even the British in Malaya, leaving us alone. The fear was that if she did it would be very difficult to arouse American opinion to intervene in time. But here was the plain evidence that on "the last day of Japanese-American negotiations" something dreadful was going to happen—to the United States. Here was very nearly the full key to what was coming.

But its significance was not fully grasped. Perhaps one reason was that the Japanese had already begun an elaborate campaign of camouflage. It was also on November 4 that Foreign Minister Togo, having sent off his messages to Nomura, dispatched an emissary to Ambassador Grew with the word that the Foreign Office wished to send a special envoy to Washington to assist Ambassador Nomura. The mission was being entrusted to Mr. Saburu Kurusu, (the career diplomat whose lot it had been to sign the Tri-Partite Pact a year before), and "for technical reasons" it was urgently desired that he reach Washington by November 13. Would it be possible to hold the Pan-American clipper, then about to take off from Hong Kong, long enough for Mr. Kurusu to make it? Mr. Grew remembered that the idea of a mission of this kind had first been broached in the last days of the Konoye Cabinet. It looked hopeful, and at worst seemed to assure us more time. Mr. Grew got upon the wires at once; the clipper was held, and Mr. Kurusu took off for Hong Kong next morning. When Tokyo publicly announced the mission a few hours after his departure, the hopes which throughout the Far East had sunk almost to the vanishing point suddenly rebounded.

Wednesday, November 5, was a long * and critical day. As Mr. Kurusu, that ambiguous dove of peace, was winging his way southward over the China Sea, the Imperial Conference was assembling behind him in Tokyo to take a final decision

* In this narrative, it must be remembered, all the days are "long." From the time a day began at Tokyo at midnight until it ended at Washington with the ensuing midnight was a period not of twenty-four but of thirty-eight hours. It is helpful to remember that of the events of any given date, those at Tokyo occurred first and that as the working day ended in Japan it was just beginning in Washington.

which this time was really to be a final one. At this conference the policies and diplomatic proposals which had been transmitted to Nomura were formally ratified. It was also on this day, at about the time the Japanese government was making its encouraging announcement of the Kurusu mission, that the Japanese Navy issued to its task force and naval base commanders the complete text of "Combined Fleet Top Secret Operation Order No. 1," embodying the detailed plans for Admiral Yamamoto's grand design. It provided that on the outbreak of war "in the East, the American Fleet will be destroyed and American lines of operation and supply lines to the Orient will be cut; in the West, British Malaya will be occupied and British lines of operation and supply lines to the Orient, as well as the Burma Road, will be cut." There followed the bulky orders, schedules, and tables laying out the whole giant operation.

Though Washington had no inkling of this, there was enough that Wednesday to absorb its attention. There was a long telegram for the President from Mr. Winston Churchill. Chiang Kai-shek's frantic appeals had been reverberating in Whitehall. The Prime Minister was almost as wary about sending planes from Singapore as General Marshall had been about sending them from the Philippines. But Mr. Churchill was impressed by the thought that the collapse of Chiang "would not only be a world tragedy in itself, but it would leave the Japanese with large forces to attack north or south." Thinking that the Japanese had as yet made no "final decision," he suggested that the President might remind Japan that an attack on Yunnan "would be in open disregard of the clearly indicated attitude of the United States." Britain would, of course, second such a move, but the Prime Minister felt that a warning by Britain alone would be ineffective, "because we are so much tied up elsewhere."

On the other hand, there was also a joint memorandum for the President from General Marshall and Admiral Stark, embodying the answer of the American military for the problem the State Department had set them. The Army's G-2 thought that Chiang was crying before he had been hurt. They doubted that Japan was mounting an offensive across the 300 miles of almost unknown and highly impassable mountain terrain that separated Indo-China from the Burma Road, and they thought that even if the Japanese were contemplating such an operation it would take them at least two months more merely to get it started. The joint memorandum observed that the United States, on the other hand, was in no position to initiate the full-scale Pacific war that would certainly result from an intervention of our air forces in China. "At the present time the United States Pacific Fleet is inferior to the Japanese Fleet and cannot undertake an unlimited strategic offensive in the western Pacific." Our only plans for the Pacific were purely defensive, since basic Anglo-American strategy called for the defeat of Germany first. Even for the defense, there were still grave deficiencies in the Philippines, but by mid-December our air and submarine strength there should have become "a positive threat to any Japanese operations south of Formosa" and by February or March the threat would reach a "potency" that might well be a deciding factor in deterring Japan. Rather than making adventurous gestures now, it was much better to avoid war as long as possible, meanwhile building this threat to effective size. Military action should be undertaken only in case of a direct Japanese attack on American, British, or Netherlands territory, or in case the Japanese should move into the Kra Isthmus, far western Siam,* Portuguese Timor, or New Caledonia and the Loyalties.

Specifically, Marshall and Stark recommended:

> That the dispatch of United States armed forces for intervention against Japan in China be disapproved.

* The memorandum expressed it as a move into Siam "west of 100° E. or south of 10° N." This defines the Siamese-Burman border and the Siamese section of the Kra Isthmus between Burma and Malaya. Central Siam and Bangkok were excluded.

That material aid to China be accelerated. . . .

That aid to the American Volunteer Group * be continued and accelerated. . . .

That no ultimatum be delivered to Japan.

This recognized the necessity of our fighting if the British or Dutch were attacked, or even directly threatened, but for the moment was not encouraging. And there was still more to come. Before the day was out "magic" was yielding a fresh batch of telegrams in which Togo advised his ambassador and (unwittingly) our top officials of the results of the Imperial Conference. As it had adopted the program, Nomura was instructed to go ahead with "Proposal A." The American officials read on:

If the United States expresses too many points of disapproval to Proposal A . . . we intend to submit our absolutely final proposal, Proposal B. . . . Be sure to advise this office before Proposal B is submitted to the United States.

As stated in my previous message, this is the Imperial Government's final step. Time is becoming exceedingly short and the situation very critical. Absolutely no delays can be permitted. . . . I wish to stress this point over and over.

We wish to avoid giving them the impression that there is a time limit or that this proposal is to be taken as an ultimatum. In a friendly manner, show them that we are very anxious to have them accept our proposal.

And then, as if this were not enough, there came another telegram (likewise translated on this same Wednesday, November 5), not only proving that it was an ultimatum which confronted us but even giving the time limit:

(Of utmost secrecy)

Because of various circumstances it is absolutely necessary that all arrangements for the signing of this agreement be completed by the 25th of this month. . . . Please understand this thoroughly and

* These were Chennault's Flying Tigers, who were just getting organized and who were still a deep official secret.

tackle the problem of saving the Japanese-U. S. relations from falling into a chaotic condition. Do so with great determination and with unstinted effort, I beg of you.

This information is to be kept strictly to yourself only.

Secretary Hull may have given a grim smile to the final sentence. Literally as well as metaphorically Japan was "telegraphing her punches"; we now had the complete diplomatic plan and the approximate end date. Why the Army and Navy did not give the commands at Manila and Pearl Harbor at least some intimation of this date and of the crisis to which it pointed is admittedly rather hard to understand. But Secretary Hull, at any rate, knew how black was the horizon. When the reporters assailed him that day for comment on the Kurusu mission he was "non-committal." The United States, he intimated, had had nothing to do with it beyond providing the travel facilities, and he left the impression that there was little chance now that any eleventh-hour scheme could break the deadlock.

It was to take a couple of days to digest all these developments and to determine the next course of policy. On Thursday, the 6th, Mr. Stimson, the Secretary of War, had a long private conference with the President. Mr. Roosevelt was full of the Far Eastern problem and of what to say to Kurusu when he should arrive. "The President," Mr. Stimson told his diary, "outlined what he thought he might say. He was trying to think of something which would give us further time" and was playing with that idea of a temporary *modus vivendi*. Mr. Stimson was skeptical of it; he feared the effect on the Chinese and the possibility that it might commit us to halting our reinforcements for the Philippines, which we so desperately needed. They left the matter in the air. By Friday, November 7, however, the President had at least made up his mind on the question of aid for Chiang Kai-shek; and he answered Mr. Churchill that day, in general along the lines of the Marshall-Stark memorandum. In Japan's bellicose mood, he suggested, a formal warning might have an effect opposite to that intended; he preferred to stick to lend-lease for China and to building up the Manila and Singapore defenses.

Admiral Nomura was at the State Department that Friday morning, dutifully presenting what Secretary Hull could recognize as "Proposal A." The conversation went round in much the same circles as before, adding nothing of consequence. Mr. Hull knew that he had at least another eighteen days or so, and that nothing, in any event, was likely to happen until Mr. Kurusu should arrive. But the gravity if the situation was obvious. Admiral Nomura departed. There was a regular meeting of the Cabinet that Friday afternoon, and Mr. Hull went to it with his mind full of foreboding.

According to Mr. Stimson's diary, the President "started to have what he said was the first general poll of his Cabinet and it was on the question of the Far East—whether the people would back us up in case we struck at Japan down there." Secretary Hull, according to his own account, talked for about fifteen minutes, pointing out the dangers of the situation:

> I went over fully developments in the conversations with Japan and emphasized that in my opinion relations were extremely critical and that we should be on the lookout for a military attack anywhere by Japan at any time. When I finished, the President went around the Cabinet. All concurred in my estimate of the dangers.

They were unanimous also that the country would support them in a war. The showing would have been even stronger, Mr. Stimson thought, "if the Cabinet had known—and they did not know except in the case of Hull and the President—what the Army is doing with the big bombers and how ready we are to pitch in." It might have been stronger still had anyone known that a few hours before, Admiral Yamamoto, from his flagship in Hiroshima Bay, had issued his Operations Order No. 2, tentatively setting the day for the great attack as December 8, Japanese time.

II ☜

In the Senate the oratorical wells which had been flowing for eleven days were drying up at last, and on Friday evening a vote was reached on the ship arming bill. The result was not too encouraging. The bill passed, but by only 50 to 37, and the Republican Senators were three-and-a-half to one against it. Since this was an amended version, moreover, it now had to go back to the House, and more time would be lost. The nation, for its part, turned to the pleasures of another week end. In the New York theaters one could see Maurice Evans in a fine *Macbeth;* Leonora Corbett in Noel Coward's ghostly confection, *Blithe Spirit,* or Mr. Danny Kaye in *Let's Face It,* a somewhat earthy burlesque of training-camp warfare, which was still so much more amusing than the real variety. The newspapers and broadcasts were full of a number of matters. Another naval vessel, the tanker *Salinas,* had been torpedoed on the Iceland passage, but happily without casualties. The defenses of Leningrad and Moscow were still holding and there were indications that the German onslaught might be spent. The State Department had announced a billion-dollar lend-lease loan for Russia, and the Kremlin was sending Mr. Maxim Litvinoff, its western-minded diplomat, as ambassador to Washington.

At home, the major worry was the threatened coal strike. One other item did not appear in the news. A secret committee of the National Academy of Sciences had just completed a report which for the first time emphasized the potential military importance of "an explosive fission reaction with U-235." The report, dated November 6, found that "a fission bomb of superlatively destructive power will result from bringing quickly together a sufficient mass of element U-235. This seems as sure as any untried prediction based upon theory and experiment can be." Unfortunately for themselves, the

Japanese people and Admiral Yamamoto (lying at anchor in Hiroshima Bay) were as ignorant of this as we were of Japan's explosive preparations.

The news scarcely conveyed the real tensions felt in Washington; but it reported the Japanese press still talking in the most truculent and arrogant fashion, and when Mr. Fiorello LaGuardia, just re-elected Mayor of New York and also serving as the national Director of Civilian Defense, returned from a two-day visit in the capital, the reporters found him unusually grave. The Far Eastern situation, he told them, was "really alarming, and any move now on the part of Japan concerns us very vitally. That is something which makes everything else seem rather unimportant." But the interview did not seem particularly important to the editors, who buried it in the deeper recesses of the Sunday papers.

At the Friday Cabinet meeting it had been agreed that the situation was so critical that the country ought to be warned in a series of speeches; and Armistice Day, on the ensuing Tuesday, offered an obvious occasion. The first stirring address, however, was to come not from Washington but from London. On Monday, November 10, Mr. Winston Churchill appeared at a luncheon at the Mansion House—the celebrated rostrum which had so often been used for major pronouncements by British statesmen—and the central portion of his speech was given to the Far East. It carried a startling disclosure:

> Now a large part of the United States Navy, as Colonel Knox has told us, is constantly in action against the common foe. . . . Now we have an air force which is at least equal in size and number . . . to German air power. . . . Owing to the effective help we are getting from the United States in the Atlantic, owing to the sinking of the *Bismarck* . . . we now feel ourselves strong enough to provide a powerful naval force of heavy ships, with its necessary and ancillary vessels, for service if needed in the Indian and Pacific Oceans. . . .

> The United States . . . are doing their utmost to find ways of preserving peace in the Pacific. . . . Should they fail . . . —and it is my duty to say it—that should the United States become involved in war with Japan, a British declaration will follow within the hour.

The "within the hour" pledge was sufficiently impressive. But a British battle fleet at Singapore would mean a wholly new factor in the equation. The military commentator, Major George Fielding Eliot, was inspired to an ecstatic article. This was the "golden moment"; if Japan should fight now, her case would be "hopeless" and "the prompt elimination of Japan in her role of nuisance ally to the Axis must follow." Throughout Tuesday, Armistice Day, those with a taste for radio oratory could listen to a succession of speeches in somewhat grimmer, but also somewhat less concrete, terms. The President laid a wreath on the tomb of the Unknown Soldier at Arlington; the United States, he said, was again as in 1917 facing "a terrible danger." Under Secretary Welles spoke at a memorial service to Woodrow Wilson in the Washington Cathedral; "the tides," he said, "are running fast; at any moment war may be forced upon us." Mayor LaGuardia, at the Eternal Light in Madison Square, warned of "real danger" not only in the Atlantic but in the Pacific as well. General Marshall warned against Axis propaganda and the insidious menace of sabotage. But Secretary Knox, dedicating the new naval air base at Quonset, Rhode Island, was perhaps more specific than any. "Our people must understand that grave questions are about to be decided—that the hour of decision is here." It was "impossible to overemphasize or exaggerate" the perils in both oceans. The Pacific held "grim possibilities."

The Secretary did not know that in fact it held at that moment some ten or more long-range Japanese submarines, which sailed on November 11 from Yokosuka (the great naval base near Yokohama) for Oahu. This was the first actual offensive movement in the unfolding of the Yamamoto plan, for they were sailing on war service, with the mission of mopping up any American vessels which might escape from Pearl Harbor under the planned assault. Mr. Knox continued: "Just what the morrow may hold for us in that quarter of the globe no one may say with certainty. The only thing we can be sure of is that the Pacific, no less than the Atlantic, calls for instant readiness for defense."

These speeches seem plain enough today. Yet their impact was less than had been hoped. The big headlines next morning went to Mr. Lewis's coal strike, again reaching a dangerous crisis, while the condensed versions of the warning addresses may have sounded like only so much Armistice Day oratory. After all, the nation had so often heard administration spokesmen trying to "rouse the public" to unstated perils that the verbal currency had perhaps lost its value. Whether the Army and Navy commanders put any greater weight on these statements by their chiefs does not appear. Routine still lay heavy over our preparations. At the Cabinet meeting Mr. Stimson had felt secretly proud of "what the Army is doing with the big bombers and how ready we are to pitch in." Major General Lewis H. Brereton, one of the abler of our Army air officers, was not sharing that emotion. He was getting a first-hand view of what the Army was doing with the big bombers.

On November 3 General Brereton had stepped ashore from the clipper at Manila, to take over command of MacArthur's Far Eastern Air Force from the ponderous and ailing officer to whom it had previously been entrusted. MacArthur received him with literally open arms, and was delighted with Brereton's news concerning the reinforcements under way. Indeed, they would be considerable, assuming that they all got there in time, and MacArthur told Brereton that "it seemed likely that nothing would happen before 1 April 1942." The "mobilization and training schedule of the Philippine Department and of the Philippine Army was based on that assumption." Brereton left almost immediately for a five-day inspection of his new command. In his memoirs he describes what he found as "disappointing." It seems a striking instance of understatement.

General Brereton from the first had opposed the idea of sending out the four-engine bombers until they could be covered and supported by a fully-organized air force with all its appurtenances for defense, information, operations, supply, and repair. He now found himself with the 35 B-17's which seemed so impressive to Mr. Stimson and the War Department, with about 100 modern fighters, and with virtually nothing else.

> The idea of an imminent war seemed far removed from the minds of most. Work hours, training schedules, and operating procedure were still based on the good old days of peace conditions in the tropics. There was a comprehensive project on paper for the construction of additional airfields, but unfortunately little money had been provided prior to my arrival.

There were still only two fields in the entire archipelago which could take the four-engine bombers: Clark, in central Luzon, north of Manila, with adequate facilities, and Del Monte, in northern Mindanao, which had excellent runways but as yet no facilities whatever. (Del Monte, it was later to appear, did possess one priceless advantage—the Japanese were unaware of its existence.) Nichols Field, at Manila, was being somewhat languidly improved so that it could also receive the B-17's, but the project was not scheduled for completion until January 1. Another project for expanding its wholly inadequate depot facilities had just been returned from Washington "for modification and revised estimate of funds." There were still no spare parts for either bombers or fighters. There were no anti-aircraft defenses on any of the fields. The aircraft warning service was "pitifully inadequate." The installation of one radar set was being completed at Iba, on the west coast of Luzon; the two other sets which had been provided were never to get into operation. The unpaid Filipino volunteers who made up the spotting force were poorly organized and the communications net, relying on the commercial telephone lines, was unreliable. In his own headquarters, General Brereton found himself without officers for a number of important staff positions, and what staff he did have was inexperienced. Money and manpower for construction, which the Army still had to get through the Commonwealth Government, were difficult to secure.

General Brereton managed to infuse a somewhat more martial energy into this decidedly peaceful scene. "On November 6 I issued a new training schedule which caused some dissatisfaction because it increased work hours to a maximum." One bomber and one fighter squadron were ordered on three-hours' notice. The air warning service was put on a twenty-four-hour basis and pay was found for the Filipino volunteers. A base detail with gasoline and ammunition was sent to Del Monte. Despite protests from Civil Service, the air force depots went on a sixteen-hour day. One week after his arrival, General Brereton took off for Australia to inspect his long and of course absolutely vital line of communications from the United States. This was on the day that the Japanese submarines sailed from Yokosuka.

Not long before, Mr. Kurusu had passed through Manila. To the Americans he seemed "sprightly and affable," even if not particularly optimistic, and civilian Manila concluded like many others that nothing could happen at least while he was still talking in Washington. MacArthur's ground forces continued the measured pace of their induction and training activities. But the Navy was preparing to move its few heavy ships southward out of range of surprise; and on November 15 all fighter planes of the Far East Air Force were ordered to be kept fully gassed and armed around the clock, with pilots on thirty minutes' notice. Despite the shortage of technicians, the one completed radar set, at Iba, was put into twenty-four-hour operation. An Interceptor Center was established at Manila to receive and collate the reports from the native spotters, and an Operations Center with a plotting board set up at

Clark, to which Interceptor reports were relayed by teletype. Even so (if General Wainwright's memory has not deceived him), MacArthur was still thinking as late as November 25 that he would have at least until the following April.

At Pearl Harbor they were feeling an even less desperate sense of urgency. Admiral Kimmel and General Short both seem to have been energetic, bureaucratically efficient types; and they struggled persistently and plaintively, though more or less unsuccessfully, to extract from Washington the men, the money, the equipment, and the construction which they felt that they would need—when war came. But that very effort perhaps diverted the mind from war itself. Both were bedeviled by the problems of training. They were deluged with inexperienced reserve officers and with raw troops and crews. They were simultaneously assailed by all the problems of the new weapons, new tactics, new gadgets which (two years after the outbreak of war in Europe) our services had imperfectly assimilated.

Up to the end of October Kimmel had hardly more than a handful of the long-range Catalina flying boats, the only naval aircraft capable of distant patrol. When 54 new ones at last came in during November, they were not yet "shaken down," and few spare parts came with them. As Short gradually began to accumulate modern fighter-plane types, he also accumulated green pilots to fly them, and these had to be trained. And his Hawaiian Air Force was carrying another burden—that of staging the B-17's on to the Philippines. The big bombers were being flown from San Francisco without ammunition and with only skeleton crews, in order to give them a safe gas capacity for the long jump; and Short's people had to train the men to fill up their crews as well as put the bombers themselves in condition to go on. Short had twelve B-17's of his own, but by the end of November six of these, stripped of parts in order to supply the Philippine planes, were no longer operable, while the remaining six were fully employed in crew training.

Washington, which felt that it had given Hawaii more of nearly everything than had gone to any other base, probably did not realize what heavy loads it was imposing in this way, or how far the base itself still was from what might be called a war footing. The established week-end tradition held undisputed sway in fleet and garrison. The training schedules for the naval task forces favored the week end in port. Sunday was the Army's "day off"; nearly every other Sunday Admiral Kimmel and General Short played golf together, and many officers emulated them on the links or tennis courts. As crisis deepened over the Pacific there were other evidences that it was deepening less rapidly in the minds of the Pearl Harbor command. When Major General Henry T. Burgin, Short's chief of artillery, sought to keep his 3-inch mobile anti-aircraft batteries (the principal ground defense against air attack) supplied with ready ammunition, he was firmly rebuffed. As he testified afterward:

> You may recollect yourself the great difficulty in prying loose ammunition from our storehouses and from Ordnance during peacetime. It was almost a matter of impossibility to get your ammunition out because in the minds of everyone who has the preservation of ammunition at heart it goes out, gets damaged, comes back in, and has to be renovated. . . . I asked for ammunition for the anti-aircraft. We were put off. . . . Same old reason, that they didn't want to issue any of the clean ammunition, let it get out and get dirty, have to take it back later on and renovate it; and besides, we would get our ammunition in plenty of time should any occasion arise.

Unfortunately, it was not to work out that way. The one means they had of guarding against surprise was the new-fangled radar business,* which no one but a handful of Signal

* Radar, this is to say, was the only protection against surprise which could be employed without interfering with other activities. A complete off-shore patrol was doubtless impossible with the means available, but submarines, destroyers, flying boats, perhaps some of the obsolete Army bombers, could have been used to cover the more

Corps and Air Force people knew much about. The Navy's ship-borne radars were useless when the Fleet was in port, because of the high surrounding hills. The Army's three fixed radar sets had suffered many delays, and never got installed. Six mobile sets, however, had begun to arrive toward the end of summer. One had been put into operation, purely for training purposes, at Schofield Barracks; but it took time to produce competent technicians, and it was not until the middle of November (about the time Mr. Kurusu was passing through Honolulu) that the other five sets, still in a training status, were at last moved out to their field positions.

In an above-ground "shack" down near Fort Shafter a handful of younger officers—a kind of beachhead, as it were, of more modern military technology upon the continent of tradition—were struggling manfully to get the radars working and to establish a makeshift Interceptor Center, without which the instruments themselves would be useless. Higher headquarters were unco-operative, as Major Kenneth P. Bergquist of the Air Corps testified, perhaps because of "a lack of education as to what air defense was and what it could do." When he was asked if he had tried to work through his own immediate superiors, he was clearly apologetic:

> I tried to do most of this work of getting this up by verbal contacts and plugging along by myself, which was perhaps a lack of knowledge on my part; experience, rather.

They borrowed a lieutenant from the Navy who had trained in this kind of business with the R.A.F. in England. He threw himself with helpful eagerness into the task, but the Navy seems to have paid even less attention to their representative and what he was up to than the Army paid to its own officers. At a conference of this band of brothers, held as late as November 24, they decided that they might by an all-out effort

---

dangerous sectors, at least, had anyone appreciated the necessity and been willing to break the inertia of the training routines.

be able to get a working radar warning system of a kind into operation in another two weeks.

Above the whole of this rather tranquil scene there still reigned the sovereign principle of "co-operation"—the ingenious gift of the ancient and jealous rivalry between Army and Navy to our system of high command. Since the completion

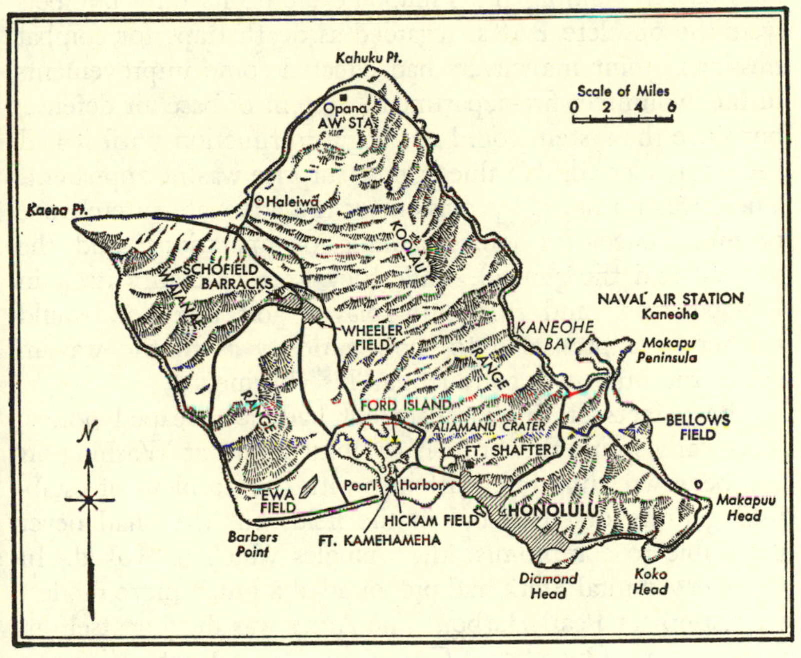

OAHU

of its master work, the paper battlements of the Joint Coastal Defense Plan, little more had been done to unravel the dangerous confusions between the Pacific Fleet (Kimmel), the Hawaiian Department (Short), the 14th Naval District (Bloch), the Hawaiian Air Force (Martin), and Admiral Bellinger, who, it will be remembered, suffered under no less than five different official personalities. The Navy was still charged with distant reconnaissance, but Admiral Bloch, who seems to have come as near as anyone to bearing this responsibility, still had no planes whatever with which to meet it. The 81 PBY Catalinas finally assembled by the end of November all belonged in the first instance to the Fleet. The Army was still obligated to lend its long-range bombers for the repulse of an approaching enemy; but aside from the six B-17's absorbed in training the Philippine crews, its only bombers were the obsolete B-18's, regarded as death traps for combat missions. Joint maneuvers had effected some improvements in the "volunteer fire-department" system of base air defense; but since the system could not begin to function until it had been duly alerted, its value against surprise was not apparent. There was no normal provision for the adequate interchange of intelligence, for joint planning or operations; and the admiral and the general, while they were cordiality itself in "co-operating" and frequently played golf together, would neither have presumed to show curiosity as to the way in which the other was conducting "his" business.

The defects of this arrangement had not escaped notice. Since early spring the Army-Navy Joint Board at Washington had been wrestling intermittently with the problem of establishing unity of command in the field, but they had never been able to compromise the wrangles which it evoked. In October Admiral Stark had propounded a much more modest suggestion for Pearl Harbor. The Army was digging itself an underground Operations Center in the extinct Aliamanu Crater near the port. Might it not be a good idea for the Navy to combine with them and put a center of its own in alongside, so that the operations officers for the parallel military and naval activities would at least be in physical proximity? Short took Kimmel and Bloch up to the crater a week or so afterwards, but the admirals were unimpressed. Bloch recommended against the idea. Kimmel concluded that conditions on Oahu in the event of war would be "definitely different" from those which in Great Britain had necessitated the establishment of joint operations centers. What would be required would be "strategic rather than tactical co-operation" and "therefore . . . rapid receipt and exchange of information and arrival at quick decisions is of less importance." At least one lower-echelon naval officer in Washington was not entirely satisfied with this, but it ended the matter for the time being. Again, in Washington on November 17 General Gerow was reporting to General Marshall the impossibility of breaking the deadlock over unity of field command, and rather regretfully recommending that they would have to continue under "co-operation." In less than two weeks after December 7 both unity of command and the joint operating center had been peremptorily established at Pearl Harbor, with no back talk about either.

Meanwhile General Short had been constructing, in the interests of efficiency, a subtle pitfall for himself. On November 5 he issued a revised "SOP" (Standing Operating Procedure) to his command. This prescribed, among other things, the various conditions of alert which might be ordered according to circumstances. In the year before, his predecessor, General Herron, had gone on the theory that an alert was an alert—you had to be ready for all or nothing—and had provided for but one state of readiness, which put everybody in battle stations with full equipment. But Short, in the eyes of some of his colleagues, was primarily a "training" man. The wastefulness of needlessly disrupting all training and preparatory activities in order to put the troops out into the canefields on guard against non-existent dangers strongly impressed him. He had already broken up his alert into three phases, and he now renumbered them.* Perhaps because the

* While the event would seem to prove General Herron right, it must be remembered that Herron in 1940 had no such urgent training and expansion problems as Short was compelled to cope with. Herron had a more or less stable, Regular Army force; Short was caught in the dilemma, suggested on an earlier page, that in 1941 our services were "closed for alteration." Whether in any given case it

country was not actually at war, sabotage was everywhere in 1941 a major preoccupation. To the military on Oahu, surrounded by an inscrutable mass of 160,000 Japanese-Americans, and with almost every military activity exposed by the topography of the island to the inspection of any passer-by, sabotage was inevitably almost an obsession. That was the first, indeed the only obvious, danger. The former No. 3 alert against sabotage alone now became No. 1; it called mainly for the posting of guards over bridges and utilities, and for the close bunching of the planes on the airfields so that they might better be protected from prowlers. Alert No. 2 was against both sabotage and air attack; this not only required the posting of the anti-aircraft batteries and the issue of their ammunition but also called for the dispersal of the planes. No. 3 was the all-out alert for repelling sea-borne invasion as well as air attack; it put everybody in the field and kept them there, and, of course, disrupted all normal routines. In itself not illogical, this arrangement fatally promoted a psychology in which, at any hint of danger, one would pull lever No. 1, and then wait for further warning before thinking about No. 2 or No. 3.

If Short was preparing a trap for himself, Kimmel quite as unwittingly, was preparing a move which perhaps alone saved the nation from total disaster. In addition to his other cares, there was that directive, received at the time of the Japanese Cabinet crisis, to take all precautions for the safety of the Wake and Midway airfields. The plan which had now been evolved provided mainly for reinforcing those atolls with Marine fighter planes. On November 10 the preparatory order was issued. The plan was to put a dozen Marine fighters on Wake and eighteen on Midway and to prepare facilities for basing PBY patrol planes at each. Tenders with the necessary stores and ammunition would be sent out at once; when the bases were ready the aircraft carriers would ferry out the short-

---

was better to hurry on the basic improvements or to stop and rig some temporary makeshift was never an easy decision. Short's alerts were by no means unreasonable in themselves.

range fighters. It was as a result of this plan that the Japanese failed to find the carriers present in Pearl Harbor on December 7, and thus missed the one element of the Pacific Fleet whose loss might have been decisive.

For the rest, the Fleet, like the Army, went upon its appointed rounds. They were all quite aware that war might be imminent. The Army's anti-sabotage precautions were very complete, and the Navy was intent upon the danger of a surprise submarine attack. Vice Admiral W. S. Pye, commander of the battleships and Kimmel's second-in-command, afterward explained that the fleet never went to sea for maneuvers without having a PBY patrol fly ahead to scout the practice grounds, and without having all submarine precautions in force in the ships. Then, as the Army Board rather brusquely asked him, "it would appear . . . that the Army was sabotage minded and the Navy was submarine minded?" For the Navy, Admiral Pye readily agreed.

Such, in general, was the situation in our major bastion of Pacific defense when the affable if somewhat uncommunicative Mr. Kurusu passed through on his mission of peace. He made, as a local Japanese agent reported, a very good impression. The clipper bore him onward. It was on Friday, November 14—four days after Kimmel's orders initiating the Wake and Midway operation, three days after the Japanese submarines had sailed from Yokosuka for Oahu, three days after the blasts of Armistice Day oratory had sought to put the nation on its guard, and one day before the fighter pilots in the Philippines were ordered on thirty minutes' notice—that the clipper swept Mr. Kurusu in over the Golden Gate and deposited him at San Francisco. "I hope," he told the waiting reporters, "to break through the line and make a touchdown. . . . If I didn't have a hope, why do you think I came such a long way?" The Saturday morning newspapers, which reported these words, carried a number of other interesting items. The President had announced his decision to withdraw from their imperiled posts the thousand-odd Marines who had been guarding the Peiping Legation and upholding the flag at Shanghai. Before Leningrad and Moscow the Russian armies were apparently making some further desperate headway against the invaders. The Japanese Diet would open its ominous special session that day. And Mr. John L. Lewis, after the President's declaration that the government would neither tolerate a stoppage in the "captive" mines nor compel the managements to accept the union demand for a closed shop, had consented to postpone until Monday the strike which had been set for that evening.

III ☞

The week which had elapsed since Mr. Hull had secretly warned the Cabinet to look out for a Japanese attack "anywhere, at any time" had witnessed a tragi-comedy in the House of Representatives, where for a few hours it had seemed that the ship arming bill might fall victim after all to our complicated confusions. A group of Southern Democrats, led by Representative Howard W. Smith of Virginia, had seen in it an opportunity to deliver a flank attack against union labor in general and Mr. Lewis in particular. Mr. Smith, observing that he had voted for the original ship arming bill as well as all other defense measures, announced that the Senate's broadened version would amount to a "declaration of war" and that he could not vote for that "until we are prepared. . . . This will not happen until the President is moved to protect the rights of American workers to work and puts a stop to labor racketeering." Simultaneously, as it happened, the heads of the five great railway unions, who were demanding a 30 per cent increase of pay, sent out their orders for a general railway strike to begin on December 7. The isolationists in the House joyfully received Mr. Smith's unexpected reinforcement; and it seemed possible that America's whole foreign policy might go to wreck in this crisis of civilization on the rocks of the labor problem. The administration, turning on all its pressure, managed to save the ship arming bill, which passed the House on November 13. But the vote, 212 to 194, was a close thing. The Democrats were only three-and-a-half to one in favor; the Republicans were more than six to one against.

Other things had been happening as Mr. Kurusu winged his way eastward. News was beginning to come in, fragmentarily, of increasing Japanese concentrations in Indo-China, apparently aimed not at Yunnan but at the Siamese border. It was announced that in the western Mediterranean, early on the morning of November 14, the British aircraft carrier *Ark Royal*, repeatedly claimed by German propaganda, had at last actually been torpedoed and sunk. The U-boat commander who got home the fatal shots could not have known, any more than anyone else, that as a result of his exploit the British battle fleet en route to Singapore would have to meet its crisis hour without benefit of air cover. In Washington, diplomatic activity had been grinding on. Admiral Nomura, in a long interview with the President and others with Secretary Hull, had continued to press "Proposal A" in various revisions. Through Nomura, through Grew, and through the British ambassador in Tokyo the Japanese were more and more insistently demanding haste. And "magic" was even more to the point than these official representations. On the day after Armistice Day it yielded a telegram from Togo to Nomura:

> The United States is still not fully aware of the exceedingly criticalness of the situation here. The fact remains that the date [November 25] set forth in my message #736 is absolutely immovable under present conditions. It is a definite deadline and therefore it is essential that a settlement be reached. . . . You can see, therefore, that the situation is nearing a climax. . . . When talking to the Secretary of State and others, drive the points home to them. . . . Do everything in your power to have them give their speedy approval to our final proposal.

On November 14 "magic" produced another telegram from Togo, transmitting an expanded version of "Proposal B," although this was still to be held pending instructions. Apparently, the idea behind "Proposal B," which was more curt and drastic in tone than "A," was that when all else failed it might serve to shock the Americans into compliance. It was next day, the 15th, that Mr. Hull felt impelled to observe to Ambassador Nomura that Japan's representations were becoming "suggestive of ultimatums," of a kind which the United States ought not to receive.

But that same Saturday afternoon, November 15, Mr. Kurusu was landing at last at the Washington airport. The newsreel men thrust a microphone before him and asked for his message to the American people. "I greet you," he said, "with all my heart." He thought he had a "fighting chance for peace." With whatever secret he may have brought, Mr. Kurusu was whisked away to the Japanese embassy, and an appointment was made for him at the White House for the ensuing Monday.

Ambassador Nomura appears to have realized very clearly both the hopelessness of the deadlock which he was ordered to resolve and the recklessness of the military gamble into which his government was rushing. In a long, deferential, and very cautiously worded telegram to Foreign Minister Togo, "for your information only," he emphasized the firmness of the American determination, the certainty that if Japan plunged into the "southward venture" she would have to fight the United States as well as Britain, and the fact that in spite of American involvements in the Atlantic the United States could still throw its "main strength" into a Pacific war He gave his estimate that in Russia "the apex of German victories has been passed." And he ventured to suggest, though he knew he would be "harshly criticized for it," that his government use "patience for one or two months in order to get a clear view of the world situation." On Sunday he got his answer (the correspondence was available in "magic" next day), prompt and peremptory:

> In your opinion we ought to wait and see what turn the war takes and remain patient. However, I am awfully sorry to say that the situation renders this out of the question. I set the deadline for the solution of these negotiations in my #736 and there will be no change. . . . Press them for a solution on the basis of our proposals. . . .

The Yokosuka submarines were already well out to sea by that time. In Indo-China, Formosa, the home bases, the wheels of the great machinery of invasion were beginning to turn. A few hours after Togo sent this dispatch, the aircraft carrier *Kaga,* one of Japan's two largest, weighed and stood out of Saheki Bay, Kyushu. She set her course for Hitokappu Bay, a bleak, obscure anchorage on Etorofu Island in the southern Kuriles, and the designated assembly point from which the Pearl Harbor task force was to sail. It was also at about this time that the naval Communications Intelligence unit at Pearl Harbor, which had been tracking Japanese ship movements by intercepting and analyzing the latter's radio traffic, "lost" most of the Japanese aircraft carriers and some of the battleships. But as that not infrequently happened, they thought nothing in particular of it.

On Monday morning, November 17, the American press was giving considerable prominence to the opening of the Japanese Diet and to the fiery speeches which had accompanied it. Foreign Minister Togo declared that "there is naturally a limit to our conciliatory attitude"; and Prime Minister Tojo, appearing before the Diet in his full general's uniform, spoke "forcefully" for some ten minutes in an address broadcast to the nation. He demanded an end to the Anglo-American economic "blockade" and military "encirclement" of Japan; he demanded that third powers keep their hands off Japan's settlement of the China Incident, and he made it plain that time was short. Mr. Tolischus of the *New York*

Times thought that the showdown must be at hand, but our embassy people were still inclined to feel that the fireworks might be mainly for home consumption. Nevertheless, Ambassador Grew put a strictly confidential cable on the wires that day for Mr. Hull, emphasizing the necessity for guarding against "sudden military or naval actions." His consuls were reporting Japanese troop concentrations in both Formosa and Manchuria, indicating that Japan was getting ready to move either north or south. And if the Japanese moved, they would exploit every advantage, "including those of initiative and surprise." Mr. Grew realized that his most important duty was to give warning, but he had to advise the Secretary that his opportunities for observation were "negligible" and that he would probably be unable to do so.

For most, the really big event that Monday was John L. Lewis's coal strike, as the Senate received a bill for seizing the affected mines and as Administration leaders declared that they were acting to see "who is running the United States." But press and public also followed the slim figure of Mr. Kurusu as he and Admiral Nomura took their way to the State Department for a preliminary conference with Mr. Hull and as all then went on to the President's study in the White House. They remained there for about an hour; and there were few in Washington that afternoon to predict success for the new mission.

Secretary Hull afterwards testified that it was soon apparent that Mr. Kurusu had brought "nothing new to talk about. He had no new ideas, no new information. He was simply pleading that we must agree on the diplomatic side of this, or something awful would happen. About the first words he said to me were that the Pacific Ocean was like a powder keg. Then he went on and pretty soon made the statement that Japan had reached the explosive stage." This, however, was telescoping matters a little. The Monday conferences were largely given to rehearsing all the old ground in general terms, and they broke up with the understanding that the two ambassadors would return to the State Department on Tuesday to get down to cases with Mr. Hull. There were no further official contacts that day, but in the evening the two ambassadors went to call on a member of the Roosevelt Cabinet. There are indications that this was Postmaster General Frank C. Walker and that the call had been pre-arranged. (Mr. Walker had no new ideas, no new information. He was simply plead- the White House switchboard shows that he telephoned Mr. Hull both at 6:25 that evening and again at 9:22 next morning.) At all events, the Cabinet member unofficially stressed the President's desire for an understanding and threw out the suggestion that "if Japan would now do something real, such as evacuating French Indo-China, showing her peaceful intentions, the way would be open for us to furnish you with oil and it would probably lead to the re-establishment of normal trade relations."

This accorded with the one thing which Mr. Kurusu does appear to have brought with him; and armed with this hint the two presented themselves at the State Department at 10:30 Tuesday morning. The conference lasted nearly three hours, traversing again the three main points at issue—Japan's adherence to the Tri-Partite Pact, the trade embargo, and China—but making no progress on any. As the talk went on, however, the Japanese became more and more urgent as to the necessity of doing something to arrest the dangerous trend of the situation, until, near the end, Ambassador Nomura came out with it. He suggested that "to ease the exceedingly critical situation, the first step would be to mutually return to the situation which existed prior to the date on which the freezing of assets order was put into effect, (in other words, Japan would withdraw from south French Indo-China and the United States would rescind her order to freeze the assets). Talks should then be continued in a more congenial atmosphere." * Sec-

* This is the version as the ambassadors reported it to Tokyo. In an interview in Tokyo in June of 1946, Mr. Joseph B. Keenan, chief prosecutor in the Japanese war criminal trials, stated that Kurusu had

retary Hull was clearly not too enthusiastic about this idea, and even observed rather bluntly that if we should unfreeze the assets on those terms we would have no assurance that the troops withdrawn from southern Indo-China would not be "diverted to some equally objectionable movement elsewhere." But he did say that he would consult with the British and Dutch. The ambassadors finally withdrew, to write up long and anxious reports to Tokyo which, as usual, Mr. Hull would soon be reading.

In the long telegrams which the two ambassadors drafted that Tuesday afternoon, they seem to have been trying equally to give a fair report of what the President and Mr. Hull had said to them, to get home the idea that the United States could no longer be put off by "mere promises," and to induce their government to support their Indo-China proposal as a temporary expedient. Kurusu urged it as a "stopgap." Nomura advised that the presentation of "Proposal B"—the bludgeon designed in the last resort to bring the Americans to their senses—would only make "an understanding more difficult to

---

left Japan empowered to offer a withdrawal from the whole of Indo-China in return for the end of freezing, resumption of oil shipments, and end of aid to China; but *en route* the Tojo government "changed the rules" on him and limited him to a withdrawal from southern Indo-China only. But the matter is obscure. Nomura, it is to be noted, said nothing about ending aid to China. Moreover, the Keenan statement is apparently disputed by Togo's telegram of Wednesday (*infra:* p. 223) which seems to prove that the suggested stop-gap compromise was Nomura's and Kurusu's own inspiration, and that Kurusu brought no new authorization with him. If that is true, one is led to the further inference that the idea of this compromise was actually "planted" by Mr. Walker in the minds of the two ambassadors and was part of a subtle "stall" on the part of Mr. Hull and the President, who were trying by every means in their power to spin matters out. Yet one hesitates to take the Togo telegram too literally; the Japanese, even among themselves, were rarely literal, and it seems quite possible that the wording of the telegram represented simply a polite disavowal of instructions which had actually been given. I have assumed here that Kurusu did bring something with him, but it is questionable.

realize than if we went on with our discussion of 'Proposal A'." All this was in Tokyo by Wednesday morning.

Foreign Minister Togo presumably knew, as the two ambassadors almost certainly did not, how far the military preparations had already gone. The ships were at sea; the troops were assembling; the vast operation was under way. And while it is possible, within limits, to postpone such an operation, it is not possible—especially in the case of a plan as far-flung and as closely co-ordinated as was this one—to suspend it indefinitely. The one thing the Tojo Government had been angling for was a complete American surrender—"please make the United States see the light" as one telegram put it. They were willing to take the domestic risk of calling off the war even at this late hour, but only if the United States would give them a really substantial victory without it. These reports of the 18th can only have convinced them that the Americans did not "see the light." Kurusu and Nomura had even offered a withdrawal from southern Indo-China, and the Americans were continuing to boggle over the Tri-Partite Pact and China. The one recourse was to shoot the works. In a somewhat involved telegram on Wednesday, November 19, Togo did so. The proposed trade of southern Indo-China for an end of freezing, he suggested, would still leave the way open for the United States "to bring up rather complicated terms." He went on:

> The ambassador [Kurusu] did not arrange this with us beforehand, but made the proposal . . . for the purpose of meeting the tense situation existing within the nation, but this can only result in delay and failure in the negotiations. The ambassador, therefore, . . . will please present our B Proposal of the Imperial Government, and no further concessions can be made. If the United States' consent to this cannot be secured, the negotiations will have to be broken off; therefore, with the above well in mind, put forth your very best efforts.

The ambassadors made one more desperate appeal, asking that it be taken up to the Prime Minister himself. It was a question, they argued, between an imminent "armed clash" or "finding some provisional arrangement." The message went on: "The displeasure felt by the Government is beyond my power of comprehension, but as I view it, the present, after exhausting our strength by four years of the China Incident following right upon the Manchuria Incident, is hardly an opportune time for venturing upon another long drawn out warfare on a large scale." It was no use; Togo told them to get on with it, adding that Prime Minister Tojo "also is absolutely in accord with this opinion." The ambassadors bowed to the inevitable. Thursday, the 20th, was Thanksgiving ("America's biggest holiday" as Nomura explained in his report) but they asked for and received an appointment with Secretary Hull. They presented to him, in its latest revision, "Proposal B."

It had undergone a considerable amount of editing in the flying telegrams between Tokyo and Washington. As it was finally presented on Thanksgiving Day, it read:

1. Both the Governments of Japan and the United States undertake not to make any armed advancement into any of the regions in the southeastern Asia and the southern Pacific area excepting the part of French Indo-China where the Japanese troops are stationed at present.

2. The Japanese Government undertakes to withdraw its troops now stationed in French Indo-China upon either the restoration of peace between Japan and China or the establishment of an equitable peace in the Pacific area.

In the meantime the Government of Japan declares that it is prepared to remove its troops now stationed in the southern part of French Indo-China to the northern part of the said territory upon the conclusion of the present arrangement which shall later be embodied in the final agreement.

3. The Government of Japan and the United States shall cooperate with a view to securing the acquisition of those goods and commodities which the two countries need in Netherlands East Indies.

4. The Governments of Japan and the United States mutually

undertake to restore their commercial relations to those prevailing prior to the freezing of assets.

The Government of the United States shall supply Japan a required quantity of oil.

5. The Government of the United States undertakes to refrain from such measures and actions as will be prejudicial to the endeavors for the restoration of general peace between Japan and China.

On that day, November 20, General Homma in Formosa had received his final orders for the invasion of the Philippines, and at about the same time Admiral Yamamoto was instructed to complete the assembly of "forces necessary for war operations" in their stand-by areas. Incidentally, it was likewise on November 20 that the pilots and ground personnel of our 27th Bombardment Group arrived at Manila. Unfortunately, all of their planes, which were A-24 dive bombers, constituting our major weapon against a sea-borne invasion, were in a later convoy which never reached the islands.

Though Secretary Hull knew nothing of the Japanese operations orders, he did know from "magic" that the document before him was Japan's ultimatum. Togo himself had so described it. It was "our last effort," "our absolutely final proposal," his Government's "final step"; if American assent could not be obtained "negotiations will have to be broken off," and it was presented under a time limit. Nomura had been given an imperative deadline now but five days away. It was an ultimatum and one "which on its face was extreme." As Mr. Hull later testified:

The plan thus offered called for the supplying by the United States of as much oil as Japan might require, for suspension of freezing measures, for discontinuance by the United States of aid to China, and for withdrawal of moral and material support from the recognized Chinese government. It contained a provision that Japan would shift her forces from southern Indo-China to northern Indo-China but placed no limit on the number of armed forces which Japan might send into Indo-China. . . . There were no provisions which would have prevented continued or fresh Japanese aggressive activities in . . . for example, China and the Soviet Union.

To have accepted, as Mr. Hull put it, was "clearly unthinkable. It would have made the United States an ally of Japan in Japan's program of conquest and aggression and of collaboration with Hitler. It would have meant yielding to the Japanese demand that the United States abandon its principles and policies. It would have meant abject surrender of our position under intimidation. The situation was critical and virtually hopeless."

For the moment, the Secretary said that he would take the proposal under advisement. There was some further general argument. The two ambassadors bowed themselves out; and as they left it seems at last to have begun to dawn upon our officials that these curious little yellow people would have to be taken with deadly seriousness. The State Department, the White House, the War and Navy Departments buzzed into a furious activity.

Mr. Kurusu was at the Secretary's apartment at the Wardman Park early next morning (Friday, November 21), talking about the Tri-Partite Pact and trying to minimize Japan's obligations under it. Thinking of the ultimatum, Mr. Hull "suddenly inquired of him if his Government had anything more to offer on the general peace situation, and he quickly said 'No.' So there we had nailed down what he said was the last proposal, and what their interceptions had informed us was very final in the matter." It was the beginning of an excited day. At the State Department they had been working over a sweeping project for a Pacific settlement which had emanated, oddly enough, from the staff of Mr. Henry Morgenthau, Jr., the Secretary of the Treasury. Since the draft involved various important military undertakings, a conference had been called on it with the service authorities; and Mr. Hull reached his office in time to sit down at 9:45 with Admiral Stark, General Gerow, and his own advisers. The officers had some reservations, and they presently retired to submit their written comments later that day. The episode is chiefly of interest because General Gerow's memorandum observed:

> The adoption [of the Morgenthau proposals] would attain one of our present major objectives—the avoidance of war with Japan. Even a temporary peace in the Pacific would permit us to complete defensive preparations in the Philippines and at the same time ensure continuance of material assistance to the British—both of which are highly important. . . . War Plans Division wishes to emphasize it is of grave importance to the success of our war effort in Europe that we reach a *modus vivendi* with Japan.

"*Modus vivendi*" were magic words. The idea had occurred while Konoye was still in office. At least a fortnight before the President had been playing with it, "trying to think of something which would give us further time." The suggestion had been implicit in the hints given by, apparently, Postmaster General Walker in his interview with the two ambassadors on Monday evening, and the ambassadors themselves had made it explicit on Tuesday. There is a memorandum in Mr. Roosevelt's handwriting, undated but seemingly of about this time, sketching possible terms: "U.S. to resume economic relations—some oil and rice now—more later. Japan to send no more troops . . . U.S. to *introduce* Japs to Chinese . . . but . . . to take no part in their conversations," and so on. With Thursday's ultimatum, the idea of a stopgap arrangement suddenly became desperately attractive.

It was made no less so in the course of the day by a report from the Dutch that the Japanese were reinforcing the Palaus. Reports of increasing troop movements into Indo-China were a commonplace by this time; but reinforcements there might still mean only an intimidation of Siam. The Palaus were another matter. The extreme southwestern outpost of Japan's Pacific Mandates, the Palaus were at once the nearest Japanese territory to the Netherlands East Indies and a flanking position off Mindanao threatening a pincer attack * on the Philippines. The gravity of this development was unmistakable. What to do?

Acceptance of the ultimatum was "unthinkable"—for once, perhaps, in the literal sense, as no one seems even to have thought of doing that. The alternatives, as Mr. Hull afterward put it, were to make no reply, which would enable the Japanese Government to justify an attack to its own people; to give a flat rejection, which would have much the same effect; or to "try to present a reasonable counterproposal." For the latter purpose there were various drafts available. On Armistice Day the State Department's Far Eastern Division had completed a proposal along broad lines as a possible shot in the locker in the battle to keep conversations going. There was the elaborate Morgenthau scheme. But none of this was of much use in this critical emergency. We were, as Mr. Hull said afterward, "clutching at straws." The *modus vivendi* idea, coming from many quarters, was the biggest straw in sight. The slaves of the State Department's lamps were put to work; and by next morning (Saturday, November 22) they came up with the first draft of a counterproposal compounded equally out of an offer of a *modus vivendi*, or temporary truce, and out of the general principles for settlement elucidated by the Armistice Day and Morgenthau drafts.†

For most Americans the big event of that Saturday was Mr. Lewis's order in the late afternoon, finally calling off the strike in the "captive" coal mines (his demands were subsequently granted in arbitral proceedings) after the urgent appeal which

* Which the Japanese were in fact preparing to deliver, with a force including two aircraft carriers.

† The genesis of the *modus vivendi* is so represented by the testimony. Yet a study of the intercepts already available at this time should have shown that there was no possibility of Japan's accepting it. This leaves a question as to whether Mr. Hull ever really thought that it might work, or whether from the beginning it was simply a device to gain a few days more time, to bring in the British and Dutch, and to make the American record clear.

the President had addressed to him that morning. But it is doubtful if they had much thought for the coal strike in the State Department. "Magic" this day produced a new and startling datum in the form of a dispatch of the same date from Togo to Washington:

> (Urgent)
>
> To both you ambassadors:
>
> It is awfully hard for us to consider changing the date we set in my #736. You should know this, however, I know you are working hard. Stick to our fixed policy and do your very best. Spare no efforts and try to bring about the solution we desire. There are reasons beyond your ability to guess why we wanted to settle Japanese-American relations by the 25th, but if within the next three or four days you can finish your conversations with the Americans; if the signing can be completed by the 29th (let me write it out for you—twenty-ninth); if the pertinent notes can be exchanged; if we can get an understanding with Great Britain and the Netherlands; and in short if everything can be finished, we have decided to wait until that date. This time we mean it, that the deadline absolutely cannot be changed. After that things are automatically going to happen. Please take this into your careful consideration and work harder than you ever have before. This, for the present, is for the information of you two ambassadors alone.

"Things are automatically going to happen!" Today, it is difficult to see how this message could possibly be interpreted as meaning anything other than war—and a war directly involving the United States—to be launched shortly after the 29th of November, which was then exactly a week away. And, if it was so interpreted, it is equally difficult to understand why another two days were allowed to slip past before the first war warning was dispatched to the Pacific commanders. Perhaps it was only that it was hard to think of everything in this altogether unprecedented moment. For what was happening was that for the first time in the entire history of the United States a foreign power (and one which we looked down upon as a mere shoestring upstart) was deliberately making an aggressive attack upon us. Nothing like that had ever happened to us before; always we had started our wars ourselves. The whole situation was so totally alien to our experience that even when we had it in black and white in Japan's own ultra-secret telegrams we still could not adjust our minds to the fact.

In the light of what is now known, these Japanese deadlines are more understandable. The Pearl Harbor task force actually sailed from the Kuriles early on November 26 (mid-afternoon of the 25th by Washington time) which perhaps sufficiently suggests the reason why the ambassadors had originally been given the 25th as the outside date. But some time on this Friday or Saturday an order was issued to the task force informing it that it would be recalled in case agreement should be reached with America after it had gone to sea. Togo's four-day extension of the deadline followed. If we could not bring ourselves to believe that Japan would really attack us, the Japanese on their part, perhaps, could not believe that the United States would have the arrogance to go on into war once Japan's determination had been made clear. Even after the task force had sailed, there would still be some ten days before it arrived at the attack position; there would still be an off-chance of bringing the United States to its senses.

Ignorant though they were of the Japanese military plans, the Americans at least knew that the crisis was extreme. On Saturday morning (the 22nd) Mr. Hull, armed with the *modus vivendi* draft which had been worked up the evening before, summoned the British and Chinese ambassadors and the Netherlands and Australian ministers to the State Department. The Secretary summarized for them the history of his long negotiations with the Japanese. He showed them the Japanese ultimatum and outlined his suggested reply. In brief, it offered a three months' truce, under which Japan would undertake to make no military advances either north or south, to evacuate southern Indo-China, and to reduce her forces in the northern part of that country; in return, the United States would relax her freezing and export restrictions to the extent necessary to permit the export of food, some raw cotton, medical supplies, and enough petroleum to meet "civilian" requirements. The problem of China would be left open. Dr. Hu Shih, the Chinese ambassador, was "somewhat disturbed" at this last, but was mollified by the fact that the truce would at least safeguard the Burma Road. The others seemed "well pleased" with the plan, although the Secretary was forced to point out that there was probably not one chance in three that Japan would accept. As he later put it, we were really offering her only "a little chicken feed." The diplomats broke up, to report to their governments. As they came out, Lord Halifax, speaking for all, told the reporters that his government had "complete confidence in Mr. Hull's handling of the discussions, and is in complete agreement with the line he has taken." The reporters' news stories tended to reflect this confidence; at last Japan was evidently facing a real united front of the "ABCD" powers.

Since the delivery of their ultimatum, the Japanese, as the Secretary later recalled it, had "worried me almost sick about getting a quick reply." The two ambassadors were back again to see him at 8 o'clock that Saturday evening. The Secretary told them of his consultation with the representatives of the other ABCD powers and hinted at a relaxation of freezing if it were only possible to get some evidence of "peaceful intent" out of Japan. The Secretary thought the Japanese were expecting the United States to make all the concessions; Mr. Kurusu answered that we seemed to expect all the concessions to be made by Japan. But that was byplay. What the two Japanese wanted was an immediate answer to the Thursday proposal, and Admiral Nomura pressed for it with the utmost urgency, until in the end the Secretary, with a touch of his well-known irascibility, told them that if they couldn't wait until Monday "there was nothing he could do about it," as he had to get the views of the other governments. Nomura apologetically granted that Japan "would be quite ready to wait until Monday."

For the moment, nothing more could be done. The two ambassadors went home. Around them, in the city and the nation, the Saturday evening theater and night-club crowds, flush with defense money, were sitting late. Washington's hard-working bureaucrats, officers, and officials were turning in, most of them, for a long Sunday morning's sleep and the usual day of rest. In our great mid-Pacific bastion they were knocking off work; the week-end passes were being issued; the customary Sunday golf and tennis dates were being arranged. Pearl Harbor was exactly two weeks away.

IV ☛

Those who sat over their Sunday newspapers next morning found them filled chiefly with Mr. Lewis's sudden ending of the coal strike. There was also encouraging, though still unclear, news from North Africa, where the British had launched what was declared to be a massive armored counter-attack designed to drive Rommel and his Afrika Korps once and for all out of Libya. The reports from Russia, on the other hand, were again very grave. The Germans had mounted one more tremendous drive for Moscow; they were claiming to be in the city's outer defenses, and the Russians admitted that some of their spearheads were a bare 30 miles away. But in Washington, although the diplomatic wires hummed, there were no conferences scheduled for the day. In the rapidly developing Far Eastern crisis, Sunday brought a momentary pause. There was, however, no pause in Japan's military preparations. The Japanese 2nd Fleet sailed on this day from the Inland Sea, setting its course southward for Formosa, whence it was to support the invasion of the Philippines, while the Pearl Harbor task force (designated as the 1st Air Fleet), having completed its assembly in Hitokappu Bay, was fueling for its great adventure.

The Sunday passed; with Monday morning, November 24, the diplomatic activity revived with a rush. In Tokyo, Foreign Minister Togo summoned Ambassador Grew to impress upon him the finality of the Japanese proposal, the impossibility of any further concessions, and the expectation that in return for those offered the United States would drop Chiang Kai-shek forthwith. Mr. Grew rushed his report upon the cables. Perhaps he also noticed a magazine article out that day in which a Japanese business man, considered an expert on the United States because of his American business connections, discoursed upon our weaknesses. They included a high standard of living "and therefore a lack of spiritual power to endure hardships," and a "low national morale; at the first American defeat Senators Taft and Nye and Charles Lindbergh would lead a revolt that would expel Roosevelt and install Republicans with a peaceful policy."

In the State Department over the week end they had been making "a desperate effort" to reword the *modus vivendi* proposal into some form that might stay the Japanese; and a second draft was ready by Monday morning. The telephone wires between the State, War, and Navy Departments were busy. Early in the afternoon General Marshall and Admiral Stark were in conference with Secretary Hull over the terms; and immediately afterwards the ABCD representatives—Lord Halifax, Dr. Hu Shih, Dr. Loudon for the Netherlands, and Mr. Casey for Australia—were back again at the Department. It was a long conference, and a somewhat unsatisfactory one.

The Chinese ambassador was alarmed over the clause which would have limited Japan to 25,000 troops in Indo-China. He thought it should be no more than 5,000. Mr. Hull tried to explain that this was a stopgap measure to buy peace for three months, and that to get it the powers would have to pay something. Without such a temporary arrangement an outbreak might come "any day after this week." The others seemed not to have looked at the matter from that point of view. According to Mr. Hull's notes:

I remarked that each of their governments was more interested in the defense of that area of the world than this country, and at the same time they expected this country, in case of a Japanese outbreak, to be ready to move in a military way and take the lead in defending the entire area. And yet I said their governments . . . do not seem to know anything about these phases of the questions under discussion. I made it clear that I was definitely disappointed at these unexpected developments, at the lack of interest and lack of a disposition to co-operate.

Only the Netherlands minister was prepared to pledge his Government to the support of the *modus vivendi*. Secretary Hull ended by indicating that unless he got more from the others, he was not sure that he would present the proposal at all. The meeting broke up; and as the diplomats came out the reporters noticed that they looked a good deal more grim than they had on Saturday.

While this was going on, Mr. Grew's report of his conference with Togo that morning was coming in, making quite clear what the Japanese were expecting of us. There also arrived fresh intercepts from "magic" which underlined the situation beyond possibility of mistake. One was a message of that day from Tokyo to Washington, "very urgent," which said flatly:

Our expectations . . . go beyond the restoration of Japanese-American trade and a return to the situation prior to the exercise of the freezing legislation and require the realization of all points of Proposal B. . . . Therefore, our demand for a cessation of aid to Chiang (the acquisition of Netherlands Indies goods and at the same time the supply of American petroleum to Japan as well) is a most essential condition. In view of the fact that this is a just demand, the fact that the Government of the United States finds it hard to accept makes us here in Japan suffer inordinately.

After that there cannot have seemed much hope at best for

the *modus vivendi* and its "chicken feed." But Mr. Hull was under the heaviest pressure from the War and Navy Departments to buy a little more time, and he was not quite prepared to give up. A message, to be sent by the President to "the former naval person" (Mr. Churchill's somewhat antic code name for himself), was drafted at the State Department and sent over to the White House. It sketched the situation and the *modus vivendi* proposal. Mr. Roosevelt scribbled a concluding sentence or two on it: "I am not very hopeful and we must all be prepared for real trouble, possibly soon"; added his "O.K." and shot it back. It went off from the State Department at 11 o'clock Monday night.

Others were awakening to the fact that we might be in "real trouble" soon. With this day's developments it was becoming apparent to both Admiral Stark and General Marshall that their own departments might be critically involved before long. That Monday afternoon after the staff chiefs' conference with Mr. Hull, Admiral Stark dispatched a message for Hart at Manila and Kimmel at Pearl Harbor. It was the first specific "alert":

> Top secret.
>
> Chances of favorable outcome of negotiations with Japan very doubtful. This situation coupled with statements of Japanese Government and movements of their naval and military forces indicate in our opinion that a surprise aggressive movement in any direction including attack on Philippines or Guam is a possibility. Chief of staff [Marshall] has seen this dispatch concurs and requests action addressees to inform senior Army officers their areas. Utmost secrecy necessary in order not to complicate an already tense situation or precipitate Japanese action. Guam will be informed separately.

Peremptory orders had already gone out to route all trans-Pacific convoys through Torres Strait—that is, by the long road east of the Japanese Mandates and south of the Netherlands Indies barrier—and when Pearl Harbor protested in the case of a ship bound for Guam it was told to comply with the order and send her around by this route to Manila, whence the cargo would be transshipped back to the island. The alarm bells were beginning to ring.

With Tuesday morning the State Department came up with still a third draft of the *modus vivendi.* At 9:30 Secretaries Stimson and Knox arrived for their usual Tuesday meeting with the Secretary of State. Mr. Hull, according to Mr. Stimson's contemporary diary notes, "showed us the proposal for a three months' truce which he was going to lay before the Japanese today or tomorrow. It adequately safeguarded all our interests, I thought as we read it, but I don't think there is any chance of the Japanese accepting it because it was so drastic [i.e., offered Japan so little]. . . . We had a long talk over the general situation." Returning to the War Department, Mr. Stimson presently collected General Marshall, and the two went on to the White House for the meeting of the President's "War Council" at noon. Hull, Stimson, Knox, Marshall, and Stark were all present. Mr. Roosevelt plunged at once into the Far Eastern crisis. Again, according to Mr. Stimson's diary, "he brought up the event that we were likely to be attacked perhaps (as soon as) next Monday, for the Japanese are notorious for making an attack without warning, and the question was what should we do. The question was how we should maneuver them into the position of firing the first shot without allowing too much danger to ourselves. It was a difficult proposition." At the moment it seemed so, at any rate; considering our own confusions and the danger, or what they thought was the danger, that Japan would make a decisive move into the Kra Isthmus but without striking at American territory.

Mr. Hull recalled that at this meeting he "gave the estimate which I then had that the Japanese military were already poised for attack. The Japanese leaders were determined and desperate. They were likely to break out anywhere, at any time, at any place, and I emphasized the probable element of surprise in their plans. I felt that virtually the last stage had been reached and that the safeguarding of our national security was in the hands of the Army and Navy." General Marshall had a recollection of the Secretary's saying: "These fellows mean to fight; you will have to be prepared." * They argued the matter for an hour and a half. But the evidence of Mr. Stimson's diary suggests that what worried them chiefly was how to explain matters to the country in case they should have to go into war suddenly to counter a Japanese move not ostensibly directed against the United States. Mr. Stimson recalled the President's warning to Japan after the Atlantic Conference in August; this, he suggested, had served notice on the Japanese that if they invaded Siam they would be "violating our safety." The President had only to announce that a move into Siam now would put the warning into effect. "So Hull," his diary noted, "is to go to work on preparing that."

But history was moving even faster than Mr. Stimson's statesmanship. At the State Department there was a dispatch from the American consul at Hanoi, transmitting a report that the Japanese intended to launch an attack on the Kra about December 1, and recording more landings of troops and equipment in Indo-China. When Mr. Stimson got back to the War Department he found further dramatic intelligence awaiting him. There was a G-2 report that a large Japanese expeditionary force, having assembled in the mouth of the Yangtse with heavy equipment and even landing craft, had already sailed. "Five divisions," he noted in his diary, "have come down from Shantung and Shansi to Shanghai and there they had embarked on ships—30, 40, or 50 ships—and have been sighted south of Formosa. I at once called up Hull and told him about it and sent copies to him and to the President of the message from G-2."

* It was some time on this day, the 25th, that "magic" translated the ambassadors' last appeal to Tojo (p. 224) with its references to an "armed clash" and "venturing upon another long drawn out warfare on a large scale." This was perhaps the most explicit reference to war contained in the intercepts up to that time.

The records indicate that Mr. Stimson's call to Mr. Hull was made at 4:30 that Tuesday afternoon, the 25th. On the other side of the world at that moment, Wednesday's winter dawn was coming up over the southern Kuriles. In bleak Hitokappu Bay on Etorofu, a place which Secretary Hull had never heard of, the massive anchor winches were rumbling home, the engines were being rung ahead, the light ships were taking station, and Vice Admiral Chuichi Nagumo's 1st Air Fleet, with screening and supporting forces, was sailing under strict radio silence for Oahu. If Secretary Hull could have known that, his problem, obviously, would have been much easier than it was as he now sat among the dispatches pouring in.

There was a long one from the British Foreign Office. The Foreign Secretary, Mr. Anthony Eden, was glad to confide the whole business to Mr. Hull, but he intimated that the demands of the *modus vivendi* proposal should be made a lot stiffer; they should "stipulate for the total withdrawal from Indo-China not merely of the Japanese 'troops' . . . but of Japanese naval, military, and air forces with their equipment and for the suspension of further military advances in China" as well as everywhere else. Mr. Eden seemed not to have grasped the idea at all; he apparently had no realization that this was an extreme emergency measure to gain time. Nor did the Chinese. They were reacting with an explosive violence going far beyond Dr. Hu Shih's original doubts, and burning up the wires with their protests. There was a cable from Mr. Owen Lattimore, at that time adviser to Chiang Kai-shek, direct to Mr. Lauchlin Currie, one of President Roosevelt's administrative assistants:

> I feel you should urgently advise the President of the Generalissimo's very strong reaction. I have never seen him really agitated before. . . . Any "*modus vivendi*" now arrived at with Japan would be disastrous to Chinese belief in America. . . . Japan and Chinese defeatists would instantly exploit the resulting disillusionment and urge oriental solidarity against occidental treach-

ery. . . . Even the Generalissimo questions his ability to hold the situation together if the Chinese national trust in America is undermined by reports of Japan's escaping military defeat by diplomatic victory.

The Generalissimo himself cabled through Mr. T. V. Soong:

> The morale of the entire people will collapse. . . . The Chinese Army will collapse, . . . so that even if in the future America would come to our rescue the situation would be already hopeless. . . . The certain collapse of our resistance will be an unparalleled catastrophe to the world, and I do not indeed know how history in the future will record this episode.

Ambassador Hu Shih appeared that evening in person with a cable from his Foreign Minister:

> The Generalissimo showed strong reaction. . . . We are . . . firmly opposed to any measure which may have the effect of increasing China's difficulty in her war of resistance, or of strengthening Japan's power.

The Ambassador himself was somewhat less excited in his approach. But though Mr. Hull lectured him at some length, endeavoring to get home the idea that this was a purely stopgap device, designed to gain the time our military needed for more effective resistance, and one which would not in fact leave China any worse off than she was, Dr. Hu Shih permitted no doubt about the Chinese alarm.

For Secretary Hull a long, tumultuous day was ending, and he could not delay his answer to the Japanese much longer. The morning had begun with Stimson's telling him that Japan would never accept the *modus vivendi,* and further "magic" intercepts during the day amply confirmed the estimate. From his own side he had got support for the plan only from the Dutch. Eden was either uncomprehending or lukewarm (or, perhaps, convinced that it was all over and astutely maneuvering to commit the United States). The Chinese were both outraged and frightened. Meanwhile, he now knew that the Japanese were already on the move southward with massive force. As Mr. Hull went to bed, the *modus vivendi* idea can no longer have seemed of much use.

With the dawn of Wednesday, November 26, it seemed no more so. Shortly after midnight there had come a telegram from London: "Most secret for the President from the Former Naval Person":

> Of course, it is for you to handle this business and we certainly do not want an additional war. There is only one point that disquiets us. What about Chiang Kai-shek? Is he not having a very thin diet? Our anxiety is about China. If they collapse our joint dangers would enormously increase. We are sure that the regard of the United States for the Chinese cause will govern your action. We feel that the Japanese are most unsure of themselves.

So Mr. Churchill was against it, too. Meanwhile, Mr. T. V. Soong had delivered the Generalissimo's cable through Knox and Stimson. A little after 9 the Secretary of War was on the wire. According to Mr. Stimson's diary:

> Hull told me over the telephone this morning that he had about made up his mind not to give (make) the proposition that Knox and I passed on the other day to the Japanese but to kick the whole thing over—to tell them he has no other proposition at all. . . . Chiang Kai-shek had sent a special message to the effect that that would make a terrifically bad impression in China; that it would destroy all their courage. . . . T. V. Soong had sent me this letter and has asked to see me and I called Hull up this morning to tell him so and ask him what he wanted me to do about it. He replied as I have said above—that he had about made up his mind to give up the whole thing in respect to a truce. . . .

A few minutes later Mr. Stimson was on the telephone to the White House, to ask the President if he had received the memorandum on G-2's report of a Japanese expedition sailing from Shanghai:

[The President] fairly blew up—jumped into the air, so to speak, and said he hadn't seen it and that that changed the whole situation because it was an evidence of bad faith on the part of the Japanese that while they were negotiating for an entire truce—an entire withdrawal (from China)—they should be sending this expedition down there to Indo-China.

The President would seem to have been still laboring under an optimistic idea of what it was that the Japanese were really negotiating for. But they were all much influenced still by the experience of July, when, in the midst of what they had thought were general peace negotiations, Japan had suddenly moved into southern Indo-China. It looked like another trick of that kind.

At the same time the atmospheres of crisis were deepening in the War and Navy Departments. The Army-Navy Joint Board met that morning, and Marshall and Stark directed the immediate preparation of a memorandum for the President on the military steps to be taken should the negotiations be ruptured. Unfortunately, however, General Marshall had an engagement to inspect the 1st Army's big maneuver battle—the concluding stage of the exercises that had been under way for the past month—which was then reaching its climax along the Peedee River in the Carolinas. The general took his departure; with the result that through the next thirty-six critical hours the military head of the Army was to be unavailable. Secretary Hull telephoned early in the afternoon to Admiral Stark, but when Stark tried in turn to reach Marshall the latter had already gone. The diplomatic arm was thus deprived temporarily of the help of what was probably our ablest military brain.

During all this the two Japanese ambassadors had been waiting in their embassy, whiling away the time as best they could. They had wanted a reply by Monday, and Wednesday was already wearing away. That was in itself almost reply enough, and they messaged Togo:

There is hardly any possibility of having them consider our "B" proposal in toto. On the other hand, if we let the situation remain tense as it is now, sorry as we are to say so, the negotiations will inevitably be ruptured, if indeed they may not already be called so. Our failure and humiliation are complete.

They must have been unaware of the extent to which the war machine was already in motion, for, supposing "that the rupture of the present negotiations does not necessarily mean war," they ventured to throw out one last suggestion for a possible truce offer. But after the instructions they had been getting they couldn't have had much hope for it.

At 2:30 Ambassador Hu Shih and Mr. T. V. Soong were at the White House, presumably to repeat the agitated cries from Chungking. Shortly after they left, the Secretary of State arrived. He had reached his decision; and he laid before the President a memorandum embodying it. The State Department's draft proposals, it will be remembered, were in two parts. The one, based on the Armistice Day and Morgenthau drafts, restated our broad principles and outlined the kind of general Pacific settlement we wished to achieve; the other advanced the temporary *modus vivendi* proposal. Pointing this out, Mr. Hull's memorandum continued:

In view of the opposition of the Chinese Government and either the half-hearted support or the actual opposition of the British, the Netherlands, and the Australian Governments, and in view of the wide publicity of the opposition and of the additional opposition that will naturally follow through utter lack of an understanding of the vast importance and value otherwise of the *modus vivendi*, without in any way departing from my views . . . I desire very earnestly to recommend that at this time I call in the Japanese ambassadors and hand them a copy of the comprehensive basic proposal for a general peaceful settlement, and at the same time withhold the *modus vivendi* proposal.

What else, if anything, he may have said about the indicated improbability of Japan's accepting the *modus vivendi* in any event, or about the critical military problem before our half-formed military forces in the Philippines, is not recorded. With no direct consultation, so far as is known, by either man with the heads of the Army and Navy, the Presidential assent was given. Mr. Hull returned to his office and immediately summoned the two ambassadors; they reached the State Department at a quarter to 5 that Wednesday afternoon, November 26. Admiral Nagumo's 1st Air Fleet was a day's run out at sea by that time. The ambassadors were ushered in:

> The Secretary handed each of the Japanese copies of an outline of a proposed basis of agreement between the United States and Japan and an explanatory oral statement. After the Japanese had read the documents, Mr. Kurusu asked whether this was our reply to their proposal for a *modus vivendi*. The Secretary replied that we had to treat the proposal as we did as there was so much turmoil and confusion among the public both in the United States and Japan.

The Secretary went on with a good many more tergiversations. The ambassadors probably paid little attention. They were stunned by the "proposed basis of an agreement" which they had just read. This, the so-called "Ten Point note," was, in fact, an unvarnished statement of what the United States really wanted in the Far East. As Mr. Stimson understood it, it was "not a reopening of the thing but a statement of our constant and regular position." To Mr. Hull, it was, apparently, a kind of return to first base—an honest redeclaration of our principles and our maximum demands, from which, perhaps, a new process of barter might begin. To the two Japanese, conceiving of themselves as practical men trying desperately to find some practical means of staving off a catastrophe which they knew to be imminent, it must have come as sheer, grotesque fantasy. There was a lot of introductory matter about Mr. Roosevelt's and Mr. Hull's famous "four principles" which the Japanese brushed aside. But the suggested terms of settlement included such concrete proposals as:

(3) The Government of Japan will withdraw all military, naval, air, and police forces from China and Indo-China.

(4) The Government of the United States and the Government of Japan will not support—militarily, politically, economically—any government or regime in China other than the National Government of the Republic of China with capital temporarily at Chungking.

It was unbelievable; the two ambassadors were "dumbfounded." Mr. Kurusu said "that when they reported our answer to their Government it would be likely to throw up its hands." Mr. Hull reprovingly suggested that they might wish to study our proposals further before discussing them. In despair the ambassadors asked for an interview next day with the President; the Secretary intimated that this could be arranged. The ambassadors retired, to cable desperately to Tokyo. Succinctly summarizing the American proposals, they added:

> We were both dumbfounded and said that we could not even cooperate to the extent of reporting this to Tokyo. We argued back furiously, but Hull remained solid as a rock. Why did the United States have to propose such hard terms as these? Well, England, the Netherlands, and China doubtless put her up to it. Then, too, we have been urging them to quit helping Chiang, and lately a number of important Japanese have been urging in speeches that we strike at England and the United States. Moreover, there have been rumors that we are demanding of Thai that she give us complete control over her national defense. All this is reflected in these two hard proposals, or we think so. . . . Unfortunately, there are no hopes of acceptance of our demands within the time limits you set.

It is clear today that, with the wheels of the Japanese war machine already turning up to full power, none of this had the importance which the harried actors believed it to have at the time. As far as Tokyo was concerned, our reply simply underlined what had been obvious earlier in the day—that the United States was not going to give the Far East to the Rising

Sun without a war. In Washington, however, it did serve to set the alarm bells ringing louder. At 1:54 that afternoon a message had been dispatched from the President to Mr. Francis B. Sayre, High Commissioner of the Philippines:

> Preparations are becoming apparent . . . for an early aggressive movement of some character although as yet there are no clear indications as to its strength or whether it will be directed against the Burma Road, Thailand, Malay Peninsula, Netherlands East Indies, or the Philippines. Advance against Thailand seems the most probable. I consider it possible that this next Japanese aggression might cause an outbreak of hostilities between the U.S. and Japan. . . .

Sayre was told to advise President Manuel Quezon of the Commonwealth, and tell him that Mr. Roosevelt was counting on him. In Washington that night there was a guarded press release from the State Department, and next morning big headlines were informing the American public that the United States, apparently abandoning the *modus vivendi*, had presented its "final terms" to the Japanese. Peace or war, the correspondents recognized, might hang upon the Japanese response. The terms themselves were not made public.

Secretary Stimson presumably read these headlines, and he was on the wire early Thursday morning, the 27th, to find out what had happened—whether Mr. Hull had presented the *modus vivendi* or whether he had "kicked the whole thing over" as he had indicated on the preceding morning that he might do.

> [Hull] told me now that he had broken the whole matter off. As he put it, "I have washed my hands of it and it is now in the hands of you and Knox—the Army and the Navy."

If that were the case, it clearly behoved the Army and the Navy to get busy. Mr. Stimson telephoned the President, who in general confirmed the gravity of the situation. General Arnold came in to talk about orders for a photographic reconnaissance of the Marshalls and Carolines, which the Navy wanted and to which the Army had agreed to assign two of the long-range B-24 Liberator bombers. This in itself was moving closer to war. But it was not the chief preoccupation of the moment. From the Navy Department, Knox and Stark came over to confer. Marshall was away at the maneuvers—"I feel his absence very much," Mr. Stimson told his diary—but Gerow of War Plans was there as a substitute, and between them they got to work. "The main question has been over the message that we shall send to MacArthur. We have already sent him a quasi alert, . . . and now, on talking with the President this morning over the telephone, I suggested and he approved the idea that we should send the final alert. So Gerow and Stark and I went over the proposed message to him from Marshall very carefully."

The alarm bells were ringing in earnest—in Washington. While they were thus engaged at the War Department, Secretary Hull was holding an "off-the-record" press conference for the more trusted Washington correspondents in an obvious—if necessarily somewhat awkward—effort to alert the nation without at the same time saying too much. Mr. Hull told them that dispatches which had come in that morning reported the landing of 20,000 Japanese troops at Saigon and the transfer of another 10,000 from northern to southern Indo-China in the course of the past five days. The Secretary believed there were not less than 70,000 men in southern Indo-China (other estimates were much higher) and thought an attack upon Siam might soon begin. Mr. Hull was perhaps too guarded, but he did make it clear that negotiations had reached a point of rupture which might not be repaired; and his final word was that the advance on Siam might come "in the next two or three days." He failed to suggest that Japan might attack anywhere else.

At 2 o'clock the Japanese ambassadors were at the White House for the interview they had requested with the President, but it added little except more lofty argument to a situation which was now obviously desperate. The significant events of that Thursday were taking place in the War and Navy Departments. At their conference in the morning Stimson, Knox, Stark, and Gerow had not only discussed the messages to be sent the field commanders, but had also had before them the memorandum for the President, which the Army-Navy Joint Broad had directed to be drawn up, analyzing the military problem. "If the current negotiations end without agreement," it began, "Japan may attack: the Burma Road; Thailand; Malaya; the Netherlands East Indies; the Philippines; the Russian Maritime Provinces."

These were the over-all possibilities; this was the initial statement, required by established military doctrine, of "the worst" to be foreseen. But even this statement was innocent of any suggestion that Japan might attack several of these objectives simultaneously, still less that the assault might reach as far as Pearl Harbor. Having laid down the possibilities, the memorandum went on to analyze the probabilities. Siberia was ruled out as highly unlikely. It was felt that "the magnitude of the effort" required "militated against" an attempt on Malaya or the Indies until "the threat exercised by United States forces in Luzon" should first have been removed. That left Burma, Siam, or, possibly, the Philippines. The memorandum did not try to guess between them. The "most essential thing," it urgently emphasized, was "to gain time." The Philippines were still far from ready. There was great concern for the safety of an Army convoy near Guam and for the 4th Marines, then in process of sailing from Shanghai for Manila. "Precipitancy of military action" must be avoided as long as possible. The memorandum recalled the "deadline" covering the Burmese border and the Kra Isthmus which had been adopted on November 5. Until the Philippine reinforcements were complete, any advance into Siam short of these limits should be met only with a warning. But the inference was plain that an advance beyond them would have to be met by war.

Mr. Stimson was as acutely aware of the need for time as

were Stark and Gerow, but he told them "that I didn't want it at any cost of humility on the part of the United States or of reopening the thing which would show a weakness on our part." The military men "reassured" him on that score, however, and he suggested only some minor changes. So much for the memorandum. The urgent problem was what to tell MacArthur and Hart. (It seems plain that Pearl Harbor and the other Pacific commands were only an incidental consideration.) This was really none of the civilian Secretary's business; it was Marshall's, but Marshall was away and they all knew something had to be done at once. It was an anxious problem. In face of actual crisis at last, the services, of course, wanted time—as always. The President was insistent that whatever happened the Japanese must strike the first blow. The State Department had left them, they felt, in some uncertainty as to the exact diplomatic position. Gerow came up with a draft message, and Stimson had to do the best he could, trying with his legal mind to take all considerations into account. He called back Secretary Hull to get a precise picture of the situation, and with this briefing largely rewrote the opening sentences of the message. It was finally put together among them; and that afternoon, Thursday, November 27, it went off to MacArthur:

> Negotiations with Japan appear to be terminated to all practical purposes with only barest possibilities that Japanese Government might come back and offer to continue. Japanese future action unpredictable but hostile action possible at any moment. If hostilities cannot, repeat cannot, be avoided the United States desires that Japan commit the first overt act. This policy should not, repeat not, be construed as restricting you to a course of action that might jeopardize the successful defense of the Philippines. Prior to hostile Japanese action you are directed to take such reconnaissance and other measures as you deem necessary. Report measures taken. Should hostilities occur you will carry out the tasks assigned in revised Rainbow 5 which was delivered to you by General Brereton. Chief of Naval Operations concurs and requests you to notify Hart.

MacArthur and Hart had their alert. But there remained the other Pacific commands. Obviously, with a few changes the same message would do for them. The references to the Philippines would have to come out; in Hawaii and on the West Coast, moreover, the dangers of sabotage and of alarming the civil population seemed relatively much greater than those of military attack. General Miles, who as G-2 was responsible in such matters, had wanted to put in a specific warning against sabotage, but Gerow barred that as tending to weaken the "main point." Nevertheless, certain modifications in this sense were introduced into the second message, No. 472, which was dispatched to Short at Oahu and to Andrews at Panama. In this, the first three sentences were identical with those in the telegram to MacArthur. It then continued:

> This policy should not, repeat not, be construed as restricting you to a course of action that might jeopardize your defense. Prior to hostile Japanese action you are directed to undertake such reconnaissance and other measures as you deem necessary but these measures should be carried out so as not, repeat not, to alarm civil population or disclose intent. Report measures taken. Should hostilities occur you will carry out the tasks assigned in Rainbow 5 so far as they pertain to Japan. Limit dissemination of this highly secret information to minimum essential officers.

This went at about 6 in the evening. General Miles, having lost his point about sabotage but still worrying over it, contented himself with a brief message to Short's G-2 in Hawaii: "Hostilities may ensue. Subversive activities may be expected."

In the War Department they felt that they had done their part. But the Navy had its own responsibilities. Admiral Stark had concurred in the MacArthur message and had asked that it be shown to Hart, but the Navy could not leave it all to Mr. Stimson. About 6:30 a dispatch went out from the Chief of Naval Operations to both Hart and Kimmel, at once more terse and more informative than the Army message:

Top secret

This dispatch is to be considered a war warning. Negotiations with Japan looking toward stabilization of conditions in the Pacific have ceased and an aggressive move by Japan is expected in the next few days. The number and equipment of Japanese troops and the organization of naval task forces indicates an amphibious expedition against either the Philippines, Thai, or Kra Peninsula or possibly Borneo. Execute an appropriate defensive deployment preparatory to carrying out the tasks assigned in WPL 46 [Rainbow 5]. Inform district and Army authorities. A similar warning is being sent by War Department. SPENAVO [the naval mission in London] inform British. Continental districts, Guam, Samoa directed take appropriate measures against sabotage.

So the alert was sounded; so the warnings were sent. In Washington that evening the correspondents, informed by the Hull press conference, were busy on their big stories. "U.S.-Japanese Parleys Near Breakdown; Crisis Grows; Attack on Thailand Feared" the headlines would shout next morning. America and Japan, the stories would say, had been brought "closer to war than at any previous time in history." This crisis Thursday—"a very tense, long day," as Mr. Stimson called it—drew finally to its close. In the far western Pacific at the same moment a new dawn was breaking over the navigating bridges and broad flight decks of Admiral Nagumo's squadron. The weather was not bad; again nothing was in sight. Not a single prying ship or plane or patrol boat of any kind had been encountered. In the engine rooms below, the turbines were humming steadily. Down the long, dim shaft-alleys, far beneath the level of the gray Pacific seas, machinist's mates were feeling the massive bearings and watching the great propeller shafts turning without cease. Every turn was taking them nearer to Pearl Harbor, nearer to their greatest hour.

SIX

WAR WARNING

I ☞

As the corps of White House correspondents flocked into the President's regular Friday press conference on the morning of November 28, their minds were of course full of the deepening Far Eastern crisis. Mr. Roosevelt began with at least one note of reassurance. For days he had been hoping to get down to Warm Springs, in the North Georgia hills, where it was his custom to take Thanksgiving dinner with the staff and patients of his foundation for combatting infantile paralysis. This year the dinner had had to be postponed; but now he felt that he could afford a short holiday. He would leave that afternoon, to be away, he hoped, until the following Tuesday, although he could not say definitely as to that because of the Japanese situation. For the rest, the President made no effort to minimize the seriousness of the Far Eastern problem.

The press conference ended, to be followed immediately by the noon meeting of the "War Council," with Hull, the two service secretaries, Marshall (now back from the maneuvers), and Stark. The torrential developments of the past two or three days were evidently taking clearer shape in their minds. After all, the one salient fact was that at that moment a Japanese expeditionary force estimated at some 25,000 men was at sea, heading somewhere—perhaps the Philippines, perhaps the Kra Isthmus, perhaps the Netherlands Indies. It was already reported south of Formosa. If it were merely going to Saigon as further reinforcement for southern Indo-China it would not be an immediate menace. But if it should round Cape Cambodia and pass into the Gulf of Siam it would become a direct and dire threat to all the ABCD powers. "It was agreed," according to Mr. Stimson's diary, "that if the Japanese got into the Isthmus of Kra the British would fight. It was also agreed that if the British fought we would have to fight. And it now seems clear that if this expedition was allowed to round the southern point of Indo-China, this whole chain of disastrous events would be set on foot of going." It was "the concensus of everybody that this must not be allowed."

Harsh facts were catching up with our still temporizing statesmanship. The deadline, which only a day or two before had been comfortably re-established over western Siam, was now suddenly being moved up to Cape Cambodia. The Japanese must be prevented from passing into the Gulf. But how? They agreed (for what would seem many obvious reasons) that the United States could not simply strike at the expeditionary force as it went by. But what else could we do? The only alternative was still another "warning." The President played with the idea of a message from himself to Hirohito. Mr. Stimson objected. You couldn't warn an Emperor; particularly they couldn't do so in language both public and forceful enough to rouse the American people to the necessity for warlike measures. In the upshot it was decided to draft a secret message to the Emperor and at the same time a Message to Congress which the President could hold ready for use if necessary. On that, the "War Council" broke up; President Roosevelt departed by rail for Warm Springs and the State, War, and Navy Departments got to work on the drafts. It would still take some time for the Japanese convoy to traverse the South China Sea, and there was every prospect of a quiet, if busy, week end.

It was probably not until after the President had left that "magic" produced a message, dated that same day, the 28th, which provided Japan's answer to our note of the 26th. It was from Togo:

> Well, you two ambassadors have exerted superhuman efforts, but in spite of this the United States has gone ahead and presented this humiliating proposal. This was quite unexpected and extremely regrettable. The Imperial Government can by no means use it as a basis for negotiations. Therefore, with a report of the views of the Imperial Government on this American proposal which I will send you in two or three days the negotiations will be *de facto* ruptured. This is inevitable. However, I do not wish you to give the impression that the negotiations are broken off. Merely say to them that you are awaiting instructions and that, although the opinions of your government are not yet clear to you, to your own way of thinking the Imperial Government has always made just claims and has borne great sacrifices for the sake of peace in the Pacific. Say that we have always demonstrated a long-suffering and conciliatory attitude but that, on the other hand, the United States has been unbending, making it impossible for Japan to establish negotiations. . . . From now on, do the best you can.

Surely, this was all the answer we should have needed. We already knew that next day, the 29th, was the day after which things were "automatically going to happen." Here we were told that the negotiations were "ruptured" and that there was no possibility of renewing them. We were even told, moreover, that for some reason Japan was anxious to conceal this fact from us, and that whatever the ambassadors might produce henceforth would be in the nature of a blind.

There was still further evidence from "magic" that day. A message of a week before, translated that day, set up a special code for use in case of "emergency." The Washington embassy was advised that in case of a rupture of normal communications channels—something which could hardly happen except in the event of war—a warning would be inserted "in the middle of the daily Japanese-language short-wave broadcast." The words "Higashi no kazeame" ("East wind, rain") would mean "Japan-U.S. relations in danger," and so on with similar code words for Russian and British relations. "When this is heard, please destroy all code papers, etc." * Why all this did not more immediately energize our loose-jointed systems of military and diplomatic command or inspire a closer liaison with our now imminently prospective allies is another thing which is very hard to understand. But the Togo message at least indicated that there would be another "two or three days" more before the final crisis. The President was allowed to continue his journey to Warm Springs.

It was obvious that from this point on the only function of the Kurusu mission was to serve as camouflage. Originally, Premier Tojo seems to have had a double motive in dispatching the second ambassador. The Japanese were at no time anxious to take on the great gamble of a three-front war if they could get what they wanted without one. The Kurusu mission might possibly bring the United States to yield; and up until the Hull note of the 26th the Japanese actually seem to have hoped that we would do so. If not, the mission would meanwhile lull suspicion, help gain the time necessary to mount the gigantic assault and to insure the complete surprise upon which its success wholly depended. For that purpose, the less Mr. Kurusu knew the better a blind he would be. It seems clear that neither Nomura nor Kurusu knew anything at all about the Pearl Harbor plan;† and while both men must have had a general idea of what was coming, they were quite evidently ignorant of the timing and the details. From the

* Pearl Harbor, as well as Washington, was aware of this message and listened intently thereafter for the code words. The question of whether they were ever, in fact, sent or heard was exhaustively investigated by the various inquiries. The weight of evidence seems to indicate that no "winds execute" message was ever received. In view of what was received, it appears to be a very minor point at best.

† The Japanese declared after the war that the Pearl Harbor plan was disclosed to no one outside of a very few top naval officers.

beginning, Mr. Kurusu was probably more of a blind than he himself knew.

As November ran out, various other carefully planned devices of "deception" were put into effect—unfortunately with all too much success. The Japanese knew that they could not conceal their movement against Malaya, and doubtless were at pains not to do so; for by focusing all attention on the Gulf of Siam, this movement was in itself admirable "deceptive" cover for the operations elsewhere. Toward the end of November a program of false radio traffic was begun, to mislead our radio trackers into placing the various Japanese ships and squadrons where they were not. It was announced that one of Japan's crack liners, the *Tatsuta Maru,* would sail for the Americas on December 2 to pick up Japanese nationals. This seemed to imply that the war must still be at least some weeks away. She actually did sail on schedule, carrying among others a score of Americans who were taking this last chance to get home—in happy ignorance of the fact that she was under orders to run out to the International Date Line and then return.

But the basic elements of surprise and deception were built into the great scheme itself. The Japanese saw clearly that the three keys to the mastery of the western Pacific were Singapore, the American offensive air and sea strength in the Philippines, and the United States Pacific Fleet. The plan was to strike for all three simultaneously. Singapore, which had to be approached by way of the Kra Isthmus, could not well be surprised and would presumably take some time. But given surprise the other two could be knocked out in the first hour of the war.

The "publicized" attack on Malaya was based on Camranh Bay, the magnificent anchorage on the east coast of southern Indo-China; it was supported with cruiser and destroyer forces and provided with powerful land-based air cover. For the more secret blow at the Philippines, the archipelago was ringed from three sides. The main body of the Japanese 2nd Fleet, built around two battleships, was to move down from Formosa into the South China Sea where it could lend support if needed. A striking force including two aircraft carriers was ready in the Palaus, whence it was to move in from the eastward. But the main attack was to be delivered from Formosa, where there were not only General Homma with his invasion army but where two land-based naval air flotillas, with a total of 360 planes, were poised for the initial and, it was hoped, the lethal blow.

The cornerstone of the whole conception, however, was the Pearl Harbor strike. To this was devoted the bulk of Japan's carrier-borne air power and the best pilots of the Empire; for this the training had been most intensive and the secrecy most complete. Pearl Harbor determined the starting date and hour for the entire scheme. H-hour everywhere else—far away in the Gulf of Siam or on the Formosan airfields—had to coincide with dawn at Oahu. The ideal day would have been December 10, when the moon's phase would have given the maximum of darkness for the approach, but the Americans' notorious week-end habit together with the routine which usually brought our ships into harbor on Sunday made it imperative that a Sunday be chosen. For that reason the date was moved up to December 8, Japan time.

The primary targets were the battleships and carriers; the knocking out of our aviation was a secondary objective, to prevent interception or pursuit. An attempt to land and capture the islands was considered but rejected; the logistic problem seemed insuperable and the requisite convoys of slow transports would almost certainly have been detected. For the destruction of the ships the best weapon, as Taranto had demonstrated, was the air-borne automobile torpedo. But the Japanese knew as well as our own people that the restricted and shallow waters of the harbor made the successful launching of such torpedoes very difficult. Unlike our people, they set themselves to overcoming the difficulties. They fitted the torpedoes with short vanes or "wings" to prevent their diving to the bottom when dropped, and planned to send the planes in very close to the water, which should be practicable if the defense were not alerted against them.

The American heavy ships, however, were customarily moored in pairs against the shore, which meant that the inner ships could not be reached by torpedoes, while the presence of protective nets or baffles would render the torpedoes useless against any of them. To provide for these contingencies and to take care of the airfields, powerful forces of both level and dive bombers were added to the attack, with, of course, fighter cover over all. Various approach routes were weighed. The ships would have to be refueled on the way, and the disadvantage of the far northerly course was that its wintry seas would make the operation difficult. But on more southerly routes the chances of detection would be much greater. The Japanese decided that they would have to trust to luck and to intensive training for the refueling. The course adopted took them half-way between the Aleutians and Midway Island, beyond range of patrol aircraft from either and far from all regular steamer tracks.

The movement had begun on November 11 with the departure of ten or more long-range "I"-type submarines from Yokosuka. Three of these set their course to the northward to place themselves as an advance screen ahead of the main body. The remainder appear to have assembled at Kwajalein in the Marshalls, sailing thence for Hawaii. They were to be off Pearl Harbor not later than the evening before the attack. Each of five of them carried a two-man midget submarine on her back, to be launched off the entrance. The midgets were to try to work their way into the harbor and do what damage they could; but this was regarded as a suicidal exploit of the young officers, on which the higher command put no great reliance. The big submarines were to lie off the entrance in order to catch surviving American ships, which might be expected to come pouring out.

Vice Admiral Nagumo's main body had sailed from Hitokappu, as has been said, at 6:00 A.M. on November 26 (Japan time). It included a screening and supporting force of nine destroyers, a light cruiser, two heavy cruisers, and two battleships, *Hiei* and *Kirishima.* The striking force numbered no less than six carriers—*Akagi* (flag), *Kaga, Shokaku, Zuikaku, Soryu,* and *Hiryu.* (There were but seven carriers at that time in the whole American Navy and only three of these were in the Pacific.) On their flight decks and in their hangars the Japanese carried a total of over 360 aircraft—which would have been powerful by the standards of the time even for a land-based air force—manned by the cream of Japanese pilots and aircrews, all trained to the minute for the specific task ahead. The fleet was now shaping its course at reduced speed for 42° N. 170° E., a point far to the northwest of Midway, where it was to refuel on the afternoon of December 3. The pilots believed that theirs was a near-suicidal mission; and in their staff studies the high command had allowed for the loss of two out of the six carriers. If discovered more than two days before the attack, the force was to return at once to Japan; while Nagumo was told that if the Washington negotiations should "succeed" at any moment up to the actual launching of the strike, he would be recalled.

Of all this lethal and grandiose plan, the Americans knew certainly only that an expedition estimated at 25,000 men was on its way toward Indo-China, Malaya, or the Indies. They were aware that the Philippines were menaced, though they had little realization of how dire the menace was. Of the Pearl Harbor strike they had not the slightest inkling. They knew the base was vulnerable to air attack. They had discussed the possibility that Japan would begin a war by launching a surprise raid. Their own studies had shown just how such a raid could be successfully delivered. But all our staffs, our planners, our analysts of information, our whole apparatus of military foresight and direction were simply incapable, amid those atmospheres of peace and superior self-esteem, of the imaginative effort which would have divined the truth. The hints from "magic" went unnoticed. Marshall and Stark, Gerow and Richmond Kelly Turner (the two chiefs of War Plans), Miles and Wilkinson (the two chiefs of Intelligence) were absorbed in the innumerable preoccupations of Europe, of the Atlantic, of raising and training the new forces. Nowhere was there an agency which could sit down, review the whole Japanese problem in its every aspect, and arrive unhurriedly at valid estimates of what was to be anticipated and of what could be done about it. When the war warnings were dispatched on the afternoon of the 27th, Washington knew that war was imminent; it had no conception of the kind of war which was actually impending.

II ☜

There remained the field commanders, the men immediately responsible for the security and the effective use of the forces which had been entrusted to them. They did not have Washington's sources of information, but neither did they have Washington's distractions. Because their view was more limited, it should have been more intensive. For months their one task had been to prepare for a Pacific war, to foresee its possible problems and to put themselves in position to meet them to the best of their ability and to the fullest extent of the resources with which they had been provided.* There cannot be the slightest doubt that they all

* Kimmel, despite his own numerous complaints about inadequate resources, had recognized this from the beginning. In a letter to his top officers, dated February 4, just after his assumption of command, he had stated the principle with admirable clarity: "Many matters of Fleet material readiness are susceptible of improvement. . . . Current readiness plans, however, cannot be based on any recommendation for, or expectation of, improved conditions or facilities. Such plans must be based only on hard fact. They must be so developed as to provide for *immediate* action, based on facilities and materials that are *now* available." The italics are Kimmel's.

knew war to be an imminent probability—their letters and dispatches, the actions and precautions which they did take make no sense on any other assumption—and they had only to read their newspapers to understand how rapidly the crisis was deepening. It was their first business to estimate and be ready for whatever was coming, and the dispatches of November 27 told them that, whatever it might be, it was close at hand. "Hostile action," said the Army dispatch, "possible at any moment." The Navy dispatch said flatly that this "is to be considered a war warning."

In the Philippines this was enough to galvanize the commands into all the action of which, at that late date, they were capable. The Philippines were standing in the direct line of the expected Japanese advance; there the tensions were already heavy by the latter part of November. Indeed, a couple of days earlier, on the 25th, MacArthur had rung up Major General Wainwright. Wainwright commanded the Philippine Division of the United States Army, and was busy preparing the divisional maneuvers which had been scheduled for December. But he was also the commander-designate for the whole northern Luzon defense (to be made up of Philippine Army divisions as well as United States troops) in the event of war. "Jonathan," said the MacArthur voice over the telephone, "you'd better get up north and take command of that North Luzon Force now. Forget the maneuvers. How soon can you go?" * Wainwright answered that he could start as soon as he could get downstairs to his car, but MacArthur deprecated such haste; he still seemed "less eager and tense than I was" and was still saying that they would have until April. With the definite warnings two days later that hope was to evaporate; but in the meantime General Wainwright got up to his new headquarters at Fort Stotsenburg, next to Clark Field in central Luzon.

* The date suggests that MacArthur may have been moved by the Navy's first warning, sent on the afternoon of Monday, the 24th.

His headquarters, he found, was "just about nil." For staff, to direct the four mobilizing Filipino divisions under his command, he had three officers—an adjutant, "a supply man and a surgeon." The four divisions were in an embryonic state, undermanned, short of artillery, short of ammunition, short of supplies and transport. The infantry was without combat training. The artillery of one division had never fired even a practice shot, and was actually to loose off against an advancing enemy the first rounds it ever discharged. The Filipino officers were "extremely inexperienced." This, it must be remembered, was ten days before Pearl Harbor. General Wainwright flung himself into the task of assembling a staff and scrounging supplies. By that time "the tension could be cut with a knife."

General Brereton, returning from his hasty swing around the Australian lines of communication, had landed at Clark Field in the middle of the week. Coming in, he had been disagreeably impressed by the inadequate dispersal of the B-17 bombers on the field, and had given emphatic expression to his views on the subject. Reaching Manila, he had recommended that the Air Force should go immediately on a war footing; General MacArthur had concurred, and Brereton put half his forces on a round-the-clock alert, established blackouts at the fields and depots, and ordered all Air Force personnel to remain on station except for the 15 per cent allowed weekend passes. The one radar at Iba was operating twenty-four hours a day. When Brereton was told of the War Department warning (it was not shown to him), there was not much more that he could do. "We are on the alert and as ready as we'll ever be with what we've got."

For Admiral Hart the first sentence of the Navy message—"This dispatch is to be considered a war warning"—was enough. The rest of it, as he testified, didn't matter "from where I sat." Hart had 30 PBY patrol planes, six PT motorboats (the "expendables"), thirteen old four-piper destroyers, 29 submarines of which six were modern, and three cruisers

—*Houston*, a heavy cruiser, *Boise*, a powerful light cruiser,* and *Marblehead*, a light cruiser of World War I design. The cruisers and a majority of the destroyers were sent southward to Netherlands Indies ports, where they would be dispersed against air attacks. The PT boats and submarines were readied for action. The PBY patrol planes were put on intensive reconnaissance—toward Formosa, across the South China Sea, and over the entrances to the Celebes Sea.

They had been tragically slow in starting in the Philippines. But the November 27 messages put them on the alert with everything they had. Early on the 28th MacArthur, responding to the instruction to "report measures taken," messaged the Chief of Staff:

> Reconnnaissance has been extended and intensified in conjunction with the Navy. Ground security measures have been taken. Within the limitations imposed by present state of development of this theater of operations everything is in readiness for the conduct of a successful defense. Intimate liaison and co-operation and cordial relations exist between Army and Navy.

Ten thousand miles away in the Panama Canal Zone, the warning bells had also rung loud. Panama, admittedly, had little to distract its mind from its one great mission of defending the Canal. It was not busy on offensive plans or on training and staging for other areas. General Andrews' detailed report seems to make it clear that Panama was fully alerted. The local naval forces (although Andrews believed them wholly inadequate) were conducting "continuous surface patrol" supplemented by as intensive an air patrol as their limited number of planes permitted. The Army had its two completed radar installations on a twenty-four-hour watch; the Air Force had its bomber headquarters and half its fighter planes on a round-the-clock alert; the anti-aircraft artillery

* *Boise* did not join until December 4. She had not been regularly attached to the Asiatic Fleet.

was in position and in continuous readiness. As in Manila, they were as ready as they could be with what they had.

At the great mid-Pacific base at Oahu, unfortunately, the warnings came with a somewhat different impact. General Short could not afterward remember whether he ever saw the naval warning sent on November 24. On the morning of the 27th he had been in conference with Admiral Kimmel and members of both staffs. They had not, however, been discussing the possibilities of attack; on the contrary, the question was still over that business of reinforcing Wake and Midway. Could the Army help out the Navy?

Washington had advised Admiral Kimmel that the Army would be willing to supply 25 of its fighter planes for each of the two islands and would undertake to relieve the Marine garrisons with infantry. But it had no anti-aircraft artillery to spare, while the planes would have to be ferried out in naval carriers. Here was one of those complicated problems in separately trained services and divided command which the organization of that time was ideally designed to produce, and for which the best brains of the two top commanders were required. Kimmel would have been glad to have Army help, but could not relinquish command over these naval outposts; Short would not send his own planes and men unless he retained complete command over them and unless the Navy would cede him both the islands and the Marine artillery that would have to remain to provide anti-aircraft protection. There was an added difficulty. Since there were no docks at the atolls, the only way to handle fighter planes in or out was to fly them from or to the decks of carriers. The Army pilots could take off from a flight deck but were not trained or equipped to land on one; consequently, once they were put on Wake and Midway they would be permanently immured there. Thus to dispose of 50 fighter planes would eliminate almost half of Short's force of modern fighters for the defense of Oahu. As he later testified: "The question came up as to how serious was the need for pursuit [fighter aviation] for the immediate protection of Honolulu. Admiral Kimmel asked Captain McMorris, his operations officer, what he thought the chances of a surprise attack on Honolulu were, and Captain McMorris replied, none. . . . Admiral Kimmel took no exception to the statement of Captain McMorris. As I remember, Admiral Bloch was there, and there seemed to be no difference of opinion at all."

With this—perhaps somewhat propagandistic—verdict fresh in his mind, General Short went back to his headquarters at Fort Shafter. Within a few minutes the Army warning—"Hostile action possible at any moment. . . . Take such reconnaissance and other measures as you deem necessary," with its accompanying admonitions about leaving the first overt act to Japan and not alarming the civil population—was laid before him. With no more suspicion than the Navy had of Admiral Nagumo's ships, at that moment pounding steadily nearer, General Short called in his chief of staff, Colonel Walter C. Phillips. Colonel Phillips was scarcely one of the most brilliant brains in the Army; indeed, it seemed to a number of witnesses in the later investigations that one of General Short's weaknesses was his inability to get top-flight men around him. The two considered the orders.

Before them lay their three efficiently prepared levers of action: No. 1, the alert against sabotage; No. 2, the alert against air attack; No. 3, the all-out alert. The war that was coming was thousands of miles away in the Southwest Pacific; if it struck American territory at all in the beginning it would strike the Philippines or, conceivably, Guam. In Hawaii, the overriding danger was sabotage. If anything worse should be coming, it would be the Navy's job to warn them in time—Short had neither means nor responsibility for distant reconnaissance or for tracking Japanese ship movements—and the Navy had told him only a few minutes before that there was no danger of surprise air attack. But sabotage was Short's pigeon, and it would be Short's funeral if anything went wrong in that respect. Meanwhile, to go into the No. 2 or No. 3

alert would disrupt all his training schedules, including the training of the B-17 crews who were so badly needed in the Philippines. Making no attempt to consult the Navy or his own air general, Martin (who was so much concerned over the danger of surprise air attack), or anyone save his chief of staff, General Short fell squarely into the trap he had built for himself. In less than thirty minutes he had reached his decision. Displaying those powers of prompt action and ability to take responsibility which are so much applauded by military textbooks, General Short ordered Alert No. 1 into effect, and dispatched his report to General Marshall:

> Reurad [*in re* your radio] 472 twenty-seventh report Department alerted to prevent sabotage. Liaison with Navy.

All over Oahu that afternoon the guards were being posted or doubled at bridges and utilities. And on the Army airfields the planes were being lined up on the aprons, in accordance with Short's SOP, as closely bunched as possible to protect them against saboteurs. Colonel William J. Flood, commander at Wheeler Field, the main fighter-plane base in the center of the island, disliked the idea of concentrating the planes and appealed to General Martin. "Well, Flood," said the latter, "the orders are to concentrate"; and presently they were specifically confirmed from Short's headquarters.*

* Short's defense was afterward to make much of the alleged vagueness and "do-don't" character of the War Department warning. But there is an interesting bit of evidence to indicate how the order sounded at the time it was received. Word of it was brought to General Maxwell Murray, commanding the 25th Division, by his liaison officer. Phillips, the chief of staff, read the order over twice to this liaison officer, but did not permit him to take any notes. Returning to Murray's headquarters, he gave the message orally; Murray then directed him to write down the message as he had just delivered it, and file the paper in the safe. This paper survived. It read:

"Negotiations have come to a standstill at this time. No diplomatic breaking of relations and we will let them make the first overt act.

The Army command at Pearl Harbor was thus alerted against sabotage, and against virtually nothing else. The antiaircraft artillery remained in barracks and its ammunition in the magazines. Five of the mobile radar sets had been established in their field positions, and Short ordered them put into operation from 4 to 7 each morning (the most dangerous period) and thereafter from 7 to 11 on weekdays for training. The rest of the time they were shut down—when even Panama had its two sets operating around the clock. And even the 4-to-7 watch, as a matter of fact, represented purely a training procedure.

In the shack at Fort Shafter young Major Bergquist had put together an Information Center where enlisted operators were learning to receive and plot the reports from the radars. But the vital apparatus of liaison and control—the human mechanism which could evaluate the plots, collate the information, and dispatch the requisite orders to the fighter forces and antiaircraft batteries—was wholly wanting. The Navy had not been asked or had not troubled to detail an officer for the purpose. The brigadier general in command of Army interception was in the United States, attending a school in these new-fangled mysteries. It occurred to Major Bergquist that since he had operating radar sets and the rudiments of an Information Center, he might as well start training officers in the essential executive functions without which the system would be useless. "When," as he later testified, "I was informed that they had received orders to operate the stations from 4 to 7, I took it upon myself to have an officer down there, because I could see no reason why they should just operate the station and not do anything with the information

---

You will take such precautions as you deem necessary to carry out the Rainbow plan. Do not excite the civil population. This will be held to minimum people." There seems nothing particularly equivocal about this version, which presumably represents the essence of the message as it impressed itself on those at Short's headquarters on November 27.

they got. So I did have an officer there each morning. . . . My only instructions to them . . . were to . . . to go down there and learn as much as they could about the setup during the time they were on." Bergquist, an Air Force officer, could do nothing about the Navy or the artillery. But during the ensuing ten days various unhappy Air Force lieutenants were being told off to report at the Information Center at the dim hour of 4:00 A.M. and there learn as much as they could about the setup.

The newspapers noticed the extra guards and there were brief dispatches in the American press: "The Hawaiian Department of the United States Army was placed on 'alert' today—equivalent to war footing. . . . A similar order was issued last July soon after Japanese credits were frozen. . . . Officials said the Army has been virtually on a war footing since."

The Navy "war warning" arrived at Admiral Kimmel's headquarters soon after the Army message had reached General Short. The Navy was no less efficient than the Army. The battleships were at sea at the moment, under Kimmel's second-in-command, Vice Admiral W. S. Pye. Kimmel immediately radioed him that there was danger of war and instructed him to take all precautions. This principally meant redoubling the measures which had long been in effect against submarine attack. But that was about the extent of the Navy's specific preparations. In most respects they, like the Army, felt themselves already on a war footing. The ships were normally kept in "Condition 3" of readiness, which meant, among other things, that about one-quarter of their anti-aircraft batteries were manned at all times, with ready ammunition at hand for the remainder. Intelligence was working at high pressure and Operations was busy on the projected raid into the Marshall Islands, which was to be their first war move under Rainbow 5. The security of the base itself was the business of the Army and, "in so far as the Navy had a responsibility," of Admiral Bloch. Admiral Kimmel, moreover, was preoccupied at the moment with that matter of reinforcing Wake and Midway. In that connection, the argument with the Army would have to be settled in due course; but meanwhile Vice Admiral William F. Halsey in *Enterprise* was sailing on the following morning with the twelve Marine fighter planes which had already been ordered to Wake, and the eighteen others for Midway were to go a week later in *Lexington.*

At this juncture there turned up their liaison officer with the Army, bearing a copy of the War Department warning which Short was sending over. This reserve lieutenant, Harold S. Burr, was the only naval officer at Short's headquarters; it was upon his lowly shoulders that there rested the main weight of official responsibility for contacts between the Navy and its Army protectors. Short was afterward to argue that the Navy ought to have learned through him anything it needed to know about Short's dispositions. He was, as Phillips, the chief of staff, put it, "an officer of a very high type, specially selected, an outstanding naval officer." Lieutenant Burr's own estimate was more modest; he himself testified that he was "a sort of leg man" for the 14th Naval District. With the opportune arrival of this messenger in Kimmel's office, the admiral handed him a copy of the Navy warning to take back to Short. But when he returned to Shafter, neither Short nor Phillips was there. Lieutenant Burr, who had read both messages, was "very much upset" that he couldn't find the general, but finally turned the Navy dispatch over to Short's G-3, the senior officer present, who said he would take responsibility for delivery. Nervously, Burr hoped that it would be all right. "I was," as he later explained, "a very young reserve officer, only being on duty a short time, and tremendously impressed with the importance of that message."

But the Wake operation was the principal concern at Kimmel's headquarters that Thursday. Admiral Halsey had attended the morning's conference with the Army and he remained with Kimmel all day, putting the finishing touches on the rather complicated details of his expedition. Halsey saw the war warning as it came in; unquestionably, it added to the gravity of a mission which was to take his task force nearly 2,500 miles due west toward Japanese territory. Suppose Japanese forces should be encountered? He turned to Kimmel: "How far do you want me to go in this business?" "Well," Kimmel replied, "all I can tell you is to use your common sense." To Halsey, they were "the finest orders that were ever given to a man." Halsey sailed on Friday morning, November 28, with *Enterprise* (flag), three heavy cruisers, *Chester, Northampton,* and *Salt Lake City,* and a destroyer squadron. Halsey's idea of what constituted common sense under the crisis conditions to which they had come was to put "all ships in readiness for instant combat," put war heads on the air torpedoes, fully load all planes with machine-gun ammunition, bring up bombs to ready positions, impose radio silence, maintain a daily air patrol 200 miles ahead of his squadron, and issue verbal orders to sink any Japanese ship they encountered. Halsey's common sense may have run a bit ahead of the orders from Washington, but seems sufficiently to prove that there were no illusions at Pearl Harbor as to the imminence of war. Kimmel himself was careful to cover the movement by ordering the squadron of twelve PBY patrol planes at Midway to proceed to Wake, to fly patrol along the route and then to search 500 miles out from Wake during the time that Halsey's task force would be in the vicinity. Another PBY squadron was ordered at the same time to replace the first at Midway, flying by way of Johnston Island and searching as it went. Small submarine patrols were also posted off Wake and Midway. The whole sector west from Oahu was thus very thoroughly covered. Unfortunately, it was because of that very possibility that Admiral Nagumo was pursuing a course some thousand miles to the north of Halsey's.

On Friday morning, as Halsey sailed, there was another naval conference to review the position. The net of it appears to have been much on the order of Short's conclusions the day before. A day or two previously the Navy's Combat Intelligence unit, engaged in analyzing Japanese radio traffic, had got what looked like evidence of two aircraft carriers and a strong submarine concentration at Jaluit in the Marshalls. Admiral Kimmel himself ordered that this be checked with the similar unit at Cavite, in the Philippines. Cavite agreed as to the submarines but disagreed (correctly, as the event was to prove) about the carriers. So it looked as though the Japanese carrier forces were still in home waters. There was nothing specific before Admiral Kimmel to warn him. Like Short, he had his own clamant training problems. He concluded that, aside from the Wake and Midway operations, normal schedules might be maintained.

Such was Pearl Harbor's reaction to the November 27 warning messages. They had been told that Japan was probably about to strike. They had been told that the United States might be involved with the first blow (in the Philippines or at Guam). They were trained to the idea that Japan always started her wars without warning. They knew that the Pacific Fleet was the one most valuable Allied piece upon the whole great board of Pacific strategy. But the possibility that Japan might strike for it at the outset simply did not occur to any of them. The Knox estimate in January had considered it "easily possible" that a war "would be initiated by a surprise attack" on Pearl; Marshall's instructions to Short had held that "the first six hours of known hostilities" would be the danger period at Hawaii; through the spring and summer the studies of Martin and Bellinger had shown exactly how the surprise would be effected, even to predicting the precise number of carriers that would be employed.* Kimmel himself, in a revision of his Confidential Letter to the Fleet on security measures, issued as recently as October 14, had taken as one of his assumptions "that a declaration of war *may be preceded* by: (1) a surprise attack on ships in Pearl Harbor, (2) a surprise attack on ships in operating area, (3) a combination of

* See pp. 36, 39, 58, 63, 65, 136.

these two." (Italics inserted.) They were now officially informed that the war was imminent. But their minds were simply not adjusted to receive the concept of an initial surprise attack. Japan was the weak, ineffectual power which had not been able to defeat even the Chinese in four years of war. She was economically feeble. Our staff studies had shown that the most which would be logistically possible to us at the beginning would be a mere raid into the nearby Marshalls; how could Japan mount an attack across much greater distances against Oahu?

The Army was waiting for the Navy to give it warning of any such possibility. The Navy, though it had claimed the responsibility, never thought of advising the Army of its inability to discharge it. No one suggested putting the Joint Coastal Frontier Defense Plan into effect. That, as General Short rather naïvely testified, was to become operative only in "emergency," and until the morning of December 7 there was no emergency. A joke had been going around Oahu that summer to the effect that if Japan was going to start a war it was earnestly to be hoped that she would not do so on a Sunday. Indeed, in April a circular dispatch from Stark's office had specifically reminded the naval districts of the Axis propensity for launching attacks on weekends or holidays and had directed that Intelligence personnel "should take steps on such days to see that proper watches and precautions are in effect." But it never occurred to either Kimmel or Short to change their week-end schedules.

Short made no particular effort to drive his radar warning system to completion. Kimmel made no effort whatever to enlarge or extend his routine air patrols. Bellinger, the immediate commander of the PBY patrol planes and the Navy's key man in the air defense of the base, was never even told of the war warning messages, and remained in complete ignorance of them until some days after the disaster. Admittedly, a completely effective patrol would have been impossible with the available resources. Nevertheless, many considerations pointed to the north and northwest as the most dangerous sectors; Bellinger testified that he so regarded them; it seems certain that if any effort had been made these sectors both would and could have been covered and that the Japanese would very probably have been detected in time. But no effort was made; and Kimmel neglected to tell the Army of this serious gap in the defensive armor. Kimmel had "every confidence" in Short and Marshall. Short, on the other hand, though he was to be in several lengthy conferences with Kimmel over the Wake-Midway business during the next few days, neglected to ask the admiral what the latter was doing about reconnaissance. "Neither of us," as the general later explained, in what would seem a classic exposition of the beauties of divided command, "would have wanted the other to be prying into matters that *didn't concern him*." *

After receipt of the November 27 warnings, Kimmel's chief of staff never met with Short's, and Short's chief of staff didn't think it was his "function" to tell the Navy that the Army was alerted only against sabotage. Fielder, the Army Intelligence head, had no conferences with Layton, his Navy opposite number. Raley, the Army Air Force Intelligence head (A-2) under Martin, was in fairly close touch with Layton and received in guarded form a certain amount of the information which the Navy was distilling from its radio traffic analysis. But this only had the unfortunate effect of lulling Army Air into a belief that the Navy knew where all the Japanese ships were. "If that statement was made once to me," as Martin's chief of staff testified, "it was made half a dozen times." The net result was that from November 27 onward the Navy did not know that the Army was totally unprepared for an air attack and the Army did not know that the Navy was quite unable to warn them should one be coming. They each had so much confidence in the other and were co-operating so earnestly that it never occurred to any of them to sit

* Italics inserted.

down, analyze the total situation, and ask what they were really doing.

Saturday, November 29, was the day of the Army-Navy football game, when American ships, shore stations, and Army posts throughout the world tuned their radios to the Philadelphia Stadium. To some in the imperiled Philippines, at least, the thought occurred that this might be Japan's chosen moment for attack. But it was not. Navy won, 14 to 6. Nothing happened.

III ☞

"Report measures taken." That fatal sentence in the War Department warning was, as it turned out, the trap which General Gerow had dug for himself and Marshall. By Friday, the 28th MacArthur's and Short's reports were back. MacArthur's was brisk, complete: "Everything in readiness," and so on. Short's said: "Department alerted to prevent sabotage. Liaison with Navy." Gerow, chief of War Plans, ought to have weighed this carefully. Having required a report, he had made himself responsible for the adequacy of the measures reported. He should have considered just what the message meant; had he done so he might, by checking it against Short's SOP, have realized what the actual status of the Hawaiian Department was.* Appar-

* Complete fairness perhaps demands some elucidation here. Short's new SOP had not at this time been received in the Department. But even the old one, which was on file, might have indicated the limited nature of the alert against sabotage. "Liaison with Navy," on the other hand, was misleading. Against the background of the summer's joint defense plans it could easily have suggested a far greater degree of readiness than existed. Actually, there was no liaison that amounted to anything. Gerow was, moreover, like Marshall, dependent on subordinates for the receipt and checking of the replies in the first instance; but he never sought to pass the responsibility down to any under him.

ently, he did not; the Philippines were what they were all worrying about and no one was thinking much of Hawaii. Admiral Turner, chief of Naval War Plans, also saw Short's reply; he testified afterward that he thought it inadequate but it "didn't occur" to him to interfere in this Army business.

Short's message was clipped under MacArthur's and the two sent on to General Marshall. Marshall's initials on the MacArthur message show that it passed under his eyes, but whether he also looked at the brief telegram from Short underneath it he could not afterward remember. At any rate, it passed unnoticed. The primary responsibility was Gerow's, but General Marshall cannot escape the fact that papers given him for initialing put him under the responsibility of reading and judging them. In this case, he either did not judge or else judged wrongly. It was another in the long series of tragic lapses which seem almost to have been designed, as if strung upon a deliberate thread of Fate, to insure the inevitability of the Pearl Harbor disaster.

On the day before, not long after Short had ordered his sabotage alert, he had received General Miles's supplementary message to the Hawaiian G-2 ordering precautions against "subversive activities." This was of no help. It tended to confirm Short in the correctness of his alert; it also tended to mislead Gerow. The latter, at least, testified that when Short's report came back he confused it with a response to this G-2 message, although address and number reference should have warned him that it was not. With confusion already thus compounded, General H. H. Arnold, chief of the Air Force, now put in his oar. On Friday he appeared with a message prepared by his own Intelligence, A-2. The Air Force was full of the sabotage menace. As General Arnold testified:

> We had been having a lot of trouble with our airplanes all over the United States. . . . We had had many accidents that we could not explain. . . . In certain cases the finger pointed right directly at sabotage; in certain other cases, looking back on it now, I know it was inexperienced workmen. . . . But at that time we were so

convinced that it was sabotage that we had sent sabotage messages all over the United States.

Arnold's A-2 now wanted to broadcast another sabotage warning to all air stations. General Miles "very strongly objected." The horrid head of Army-Navy jealousy is frequently apparent in the record; here one seems to detect the almost equally horrid head of Air Force-ground Army jealousy. At the cost of much patient bureaucratic effort, Miles had got it "definitely established that counter-subversive activity of all kinds was G-2's responsibility and solely G-2's responsibility." He had already sent his own sabotage message. This wasn't A-2's business; the A-2 message was rashly worded so that it might incite to all kinds of illegal measures and public alarm, and besides, if there were to be any more warnings they should go properly through ground Army channels and not simply to the Air Force's own commanders, as if the Air Force were an independent service. There was a long argument that afternoon, which ended in a disastrous "compromise." *Two* messages would be sent. One, signed by the Adjutant General, would go direct to the commanding generals, including, of course, General Short:

> Critical situation demands that all precautions be taken immediately against subversive activities. . . . Also desired that you initiate forthwith all additional measures necessary to provide for protection of your establishments, property, and equipment against sabotage, protection of your personnel against subversive propaganda, and protection of all activities against espionage.

Under the seemingly innocuous pretext of ensuring "speed of transmission," the second message would go out at the same time through the commanding generals to their respective Air Force commanders. It was in the main a paraphrase of the first but was signed by Arnold. Thus were the amenities preserved and the balance in the ground-air war kept even. The effect upon the real war so soon about to begin was insufficiently considered.

For the result was lamentable. General Short, on receipt of the November 27 warning, had ordered his sabotage alert; shortly thereafter he had received the first sabotage warning, which seemed to confirm his action. He had reported what he had done; the only response was another warning re-emphasizing the importance of protecting "establishments, property, and equipment against sabotage." But that was not all. Washington considered the matter so urgent that to secure "speed" these orders were repeated direct to Martin, his Air Force general. Obviously, his planes were the most vital "property and equipment" which he had. General Short must have reflected with satisfaction upon his promptness and efficiency in getting the planes bunched under guard; he sat down, at any rate, to send a long report cataloguing all the admirable measures he had instituted against subversive activities. This report elicited no sign from Washington that it had met with anything but approval. Actually, it had got lost somewhere in the secretariat of the General Staff (under Colonel Walter Bedell Smith) and none of the high officers ever saw it; but Short, naturally, could not know that. After the two anti-sabotage messages of November 28, Short received no further warning, no special instructions, and no questions as to the correctness of his course of any kind.

While A-2 and G-2 were achieving this triumph between them, the Air Force's powerful publicity machinery was, as it happened, releasing to the press extracts from a confidential speech which General Arnold had recently delivered at West Point. This gave a glowing picture of the state of Army Air, with "2,500 or more modern combat type warplanes," with 800 of these ready for action in advanced bases outside the United States, and with the planes themselves of the most advanced design. The British, General Arnold explained, considered our P-40 fighter superior to their Hurricane "although we no longer rate the P-40 better than a good pursuit trainer." (He did not add that this "good pursuit trainer" was, and for a long time would be, the best the Army had in all the great reaches of the Pacific and East Asia.) The B-17 bombers had for some time been executing, in British hands, "day and night raids over Germany at 34,000 feet with virtual immunity from enemy fighters and ground fire." The new Bell P-39 fighter, now in mass production, had proved itself "a match for the Spitfire and Messerschmidt up to 16,000 feet," and so on. However textually exact, there was hardly an implication in these statements which was not to be tragically disproved in the ensuing weeks and months. The speech was published at a moment when, as General Arnold himself was to put it long afterward, Army Air was "equipped with plans but not with planes" and when the total of Army aircraft which were even considered to be "actually suited to combat service" amounted to no more than 1,157. The incident is of interest now as showing that, if our public, our diplomats, and our prospective allies were grievously overconfident on the eve of the Pacific war, it was not entirely their fault.

That Friday evening, the 28th, as the President's train bore him southward, the tensions in Washington were growing no less. The few who were parties to "magic" had Togo's message in effect announcing that in another day or two it would be all over. But the public indications as well were growing sufficiently ominous. There were prominent dispatches from Shanghai reporting that the Japanese had seventy transports on the way south, with great quantities of men and material, and that there were increasing naval concentrations in Indo-Chinese waters; while even the Vichy radio contributed similar reports from its officials at Saigon and Hanoi. Japanese broadcasts monitored in the United States were reacting to our Ten-Point note with the utmost violence: "The United States has broken the peace. . . . The United States in presenting its terms practically as an ultimatum has spoken the last word. . . . The United States alone is responsible for what seems almost inevitable now." Washington correspondents that evening found high sources grim and resolute; there would be no compromise with aggression.

In the State, War, and Navy Departments they were hard at work on the draft declarations which had been decided on at the morning's "War Council." By noon next day, Saturday, Hull, Stimson, and Knox had thrown together a short appeal to Hirohito and a much longer message to Congress and the American people. Mr. Hull was dubious as to the wisdom or value of the first; the second, in any event, was not to be used until matters were on the verge of war, but both were sent along to Warm Springs. Secretaries Stimson and Knox went to the Army-Navy game at Philadelphia, along with scores of high officers and officials.

That day, too, Lord Halifax was back at the State Department. The British, who had been so confident and so little interested when the question of the *modus vivendi* had been up, were now having some second thoughts as actual crisis loomed before them. Secretary Hull read the ambassador a politely tart lecture on the loose and disjointed way in which Allied diplomacy was being conducted. Besides, it was too late for diplomacy now.

> I expressed the view that the diplomatic part of our relations with Japan were virtually over and that the matter will now have to go to the officials of the Army and Navy. . . . I said that it would be a serious mistake . . . to make plans of resistance without including the possibility that Japan may move suddenly and with every possible element of surprise and spread out over considerable areas and capture certain positions and posts before the peaceful countries interested in the Pacific would have time to confer and formulate plans.

The ambassador, though seemingly still a little skeptical of this last, agreed as to the "badly confused mechanics" of inter-Allied relations. Yet not even the Secretary could propose anything specific to do about it, and Lord Halifax, in his turn, departed for Philadephia and the Army-Navy game. Mr. Hull did not. He was now clearly alive to the deadly seriousness of the military situation, and news dispatches coming in that day from Tokyo appeared to confirm the worst fears. The Japanese Cabinet had met for the second day in succession to consider the American note, and Premier Tojo had broadcast a message to the peoples of Japan, China, and Manchuria:

> The fact that Chiang Kai-shek is dancing to the tune of Britain, America, and Communism at the expense of able-bodied and promising young men in his resistance to Japan is only due to the desire of Britain and the United States to fish in troubled waters in East Asia by pitting East Asiatic peoples against one another and to grasp hegemony in East Asia. . . . For the honor and pride of mankind we must purge this sort of practice from East Asia with a vengeance.

On top of everything else, this seemed critical. Late Saturday evening Secretary Hull resorted to the telephone. The President had reached Warm Springs in the morning and had at least been able to have his belated Thanksgiving dinner. Mr. Hull now advised him that he would probably have to cut short his vacation, brief as it was to have been. Before the evening was over it was announced that the President had ordered his train in readiness for the next day, and would be back in Washington on Monday morning.

At about the time that this announcement was being given to the reporters at Warm Springs, the dawn of Sunday, November 30—the last Sunday of peace—was coming up over Tokyo. Admiral Nagumo's powerful task force was well out into the empty North Pacific by that time. The other troops and squadrons and air flotillas were taking their H-hour stations. There was to be a big mass meeting in Tokyo that day, and others throughout the Empire, at which Premier Tojo's belligerent pronunciamento was to be repeated and embellished. In Manila there was no relaxation of the oppressive tension; in Oahu, on the other hand, they were taking their day off (their last for many months) and presumably getting in their golf and tennis. The American public at its Sunday breakfast tables again had exciting headlines before it: Tojo's broadcast under banner heads; the President hurrying home from Warm Springs; Washington sources pessimistically sure that peace or war was hanging on Japan's decision. The Russian news that day was better; Rostov, at the mouth of the Don, had been retaken from the invader, and the Red Army was claiming advances even on the outskirts of Moscow. There was fresh reason to hope that Hitler's "last great battle of the year," which in spite of tremendous gains had never quite come off since October, might never come off at all. From North Africa, on the other hand, the news was dubious; Rommel was still being described as in a "trap," but the trap was looking more and more like another deadlock and the substantial failure of the great British effort at annihilation.

At the State Department they were to have a busy and anxious Sunday. "Magic" yielded another message, in which Togo urged his ambassadors "to make one more attempt verbally along the following lines. . . . The Imperial government is at a loss to understand why [the United States] has taken the attitude that the new proposals we have made cannot be made the basis of discussion . . ." and so on. But it bore the suggestive addendum: "In carrying out this instruction please be careful that this does not lead to anything like a breaking off of negotiations." The blind was growing almost painfully obvious.

Then shortly after noon there came a direct message from Prime Minister Churchill for the President:

> It seems to me that one important method remains unused in averting war between Japan and our two countries, namely, a plain declaration, secret or public, . . . that any further act of aggression by Japan will lead to the gravest consequence. I realize your Constitutional difficulties but it would be tragic if Japan drifted into war by encroachment without having before her fairly and squarely the dire character of a further aggressive step.

The moment for such a *démarche*, Mr. Churchill thought, might "be very near."

We now know that "drifting" was hardly the word for it, at a moment when Japan was heading for war with every turn of Nagumo's propellers; we know that the Japanese appreciated the "dire character" of what they were about more clearly than did Mr. Churchill or anyone else on the occidental side. But the Prime Minister's telegram at least records the extremity of the British desire to have us with them. "Forgive me, my dear friend," it ended, "for presuming to press such a course upon you, but I am convinced that it might make all the difference and prevent a melancholy extension of the war."

Lord Halifax and Mr. Casey, the Australian minister, were also back at the State Department, anxiously pressing now for delay, for more time for military preparations, and so on. By this time little could be done about that, however, and rather more to the point was a memorandum which Lord Halifax left with the Secretary:

> There are important indications that Japan is about to attack Thailand and that this attack will include a sea-borne expedition to seize strategic points in the Kra Isthmus. . . . R.A.F. are reconnoitering on an arc of 180 miles from Tedta Bharu for three days commencing November 29 and our Commander-in-Chief, Far East, has requested Commander-in-Chief, Asiatic Fleet at Manila to undertake air reconnaissance on line Manila-Camranh Bay on the same days. Commander-in-Chief, Far East, has asked for permission to move into Kra Isthmus, if air reconnaissance establishes the fact that escorted Japanese ships are approaching the coast of Thailand, and he asks for an immediate decision on this point. . . .

The nub of it was that the British felt it vital to invade Thailand before they were themselves attacked, in order to forestall the Japanese. They wanted to make their case for this conventionally immoral, but under the circumstances desperately necessary and fully justified, action; and they wanted to know what the United States would do about it. Even at that eleventh hour, all Mr. Hull could say was that he would put it up to the President on the latter's return next morning. We were still paralyzed, in a moment which every informed official knew to be one of extreme crisis, by the ghosts of neutrality and isolationism. Admiral Stark did immediately wire Admiral Hart at Manila to comply with the request of the British commander at Singapore (Air Chief Marshal Brooke-Popham) for an air patrol to Camranh Bay. This relatively innocuous action, taken just one week before Pearl Harbor, seems to have been the first instance of actual military co-operation before the breaking of a storm which everyone knew could only be weathered, if at all, by the closest kind of military unity among the British, Dutch, Australians, and Americans.*

So the last Sunday of peace wore inconclusively away. The President that evening was rolling northward through the darkness. The correspondents were writing up their dispatches. And Mr. Kurusu was talking with some sense of injury over the trans-Pacific telephone to the Tokyo Foreign Office (with "magic" listening in). The President, he explained, was returning to Washington reportedly because of Tojo's speech. "Unless greater caution is exercised in speeches by the Premier and others, it puts us in a very difficult position. All of you over there must watch out about these ill-advised statements. Please tell Mr. Tani." Tokyo, the ambassador complained, had been "very urgent" previously about the negotiations, but "now you want them to stretch out. We will need your help. Both the Premier and the Foreign Minister will need to change the tone of their speeches! ! ! Do you understand?

* According to Admiral Hart's testimony he had already instituted the patrol before the orders were received, perhaps exceeding his authority in doing so. He had also stretched a point when he started his cruisers south to Dutch ports two or three days before. Admirals were not supposed to send men-of-war into foreign ports without arranging the matter through the State Department before hand. But Hart had explained to the Dutch that they would simply put in for fuel, adding with a figurative wink that the refueling might take a long time. Needless to say, the Dutch understood.

Please all use more discretion." Tokyo said that it understood. Kurusu said that he and Nomura were to see Hull again in the morning. There was one other interchange. "We received a short one from you," said Kurusu. "There is a longer one coming, isn't there?" Tokyo left the inference that there was.

IV ☞

In Tokyo early on Monday morning, December 1, the Japanese Cabinet met at the official residence of Premier Tojo to take what would seem to have been the final, the definitive, the irrevocable decision. It gave its formal approval of the commencement of hostilities against the whole allied forces of the West; and shortly thereafter the orders were issuing from the Chief of the Naval General Staff to the Commander-in-Chief of the Combined Fleet (Yamamoto) and the Commander-in-Chief of the China Area Fleet:

> 1. It has been decided to enter into a state of war between the Imperial Government on one side and the United States, Great Britain, and the Netherlands on the other during the first part of December.
>
> 2. The C-in-C Combined Fleet will destroy the enemy forces and air strength in the eastern seas [and] at the same time will meet any attack by the enemy fleet and destroy it.
>
> 3. The C-in-C Combined Fleet will, in co-operation with the Commander of the Southern Army, speedily capture and hold important American and British bases in eastern Asia and then Dutch bases. Important strategic points will then be occupied and held. . . .

There was another order to Yamamoto alone:

> Japan under the necessity of self-preservation has reached a decision to declare war on the United States of America, British Empire, and the Netherlands. The C-in-C Combined Fleet shall at the start of the war direct an attack on the enemy fleet in the

Hawaiian area and reduce it to impotency using the 1st Air Fleet as the nucleus of the attack force.

Domei, the Japanese news agency, in reporting that the Cabinet meeting had been held, said that the decision had been to continue negotiations at Washington. Ambassador Grew and the American correspondents, with no means of learning better, could only report, as they did, that while there was no sign of Japan's backing down, Tokyo was anxious to carry on the talks for the time being.

But Washington cannot have been seriously misled. In the course of that Monday "magic" came up with a great spate of illuminating intercepts. There was one dated November 29 from the Japanese consulate in Bangkok to Tokyo, reporting that even the pro-Japanese faction among the Siamese were clinging to neutrality and that either side, whether Japan or Britain, which first invaded Siam would be regarded as an enemy. The telegram went on:

> Therefore, for Japan to be looked upon as Thai's helper, she should put Britain in a position to be the first aggressor. For the purpose of accomplishing this, Japan should carefully avoid Thai territory, and instead land troops in the neighborhood of Kotaparu [Kota Bharu] in British territory, which would almost certainly force Britain to invade Thailand from Patanbessa [Padang Besar]. . . . Apparently this plan has the approval of [the Siamese] Chief of Staff Bijitto.

Another message, also of the 29th, was from Berlin. This gave a long and interesting report of an interview between Ambassador Oshima and Von Ribbentrop. "It is essential," the Foreign Minister had urged, "that Japan effect the New Order in East Asia without losing this opportuntiy." He was most pressing. The United States probably wouldn't fight. Oshima wanted to know about the Russian war? Von Ribbentrop was voluble. The Fuehrer himself had just declared that "he is now bent on completely wiping out that state" and had announced that "practically all the main military objectives had been obtained and that a greater part of the German troops would shortly be brought back to Germany. Following up these campaigns the Caucasus campaign will be launched in earnest. Next spring Germany will advance to and cross the Ural Mountains and chase Stalin deep into Siberia." When? "In about May of next year according to present schedules."

In this, the Foreign Minister was rather more cautious than he had been in July,* but when Oshima expressed the hope that air connections might ultimately be established between Germany and Manchukuo he was prompt to say that they had been considering that matter "for some time." By next summer, he believed, air connections from the Urals to Japanese territory might not be "an impossibility." More than that, he heard that Britain was tottering; the Conservatives were split; Churchill's influence was on the wane. In any event, Germany would never make peace with Britain; she would never abandon Japan, and if the latter got into war with the United States, "Germany, of course, would join the war immediately. There is absolutely no possibility of Germany's entering into a separate peace with the United States under such circumstances. The Fuehrer is determined on that point."

But even more significant was a series of messages from Tokyo to Berlin, dated the 30th:

> Conversations begun between Tokyo and Washington last April . . . now stand ruptured—broken. . . . In the face of this our Empire faces a grave situation and must act with determination. Will your Honor therefore immediately interview Chancellor Hitler and Foreign Minister Ribbentrop and confidentially communicate to them a summary of the developments. . . . Say very secretly to them that there is extreme danger that war may suddenly break out between the Anglo-Saxon nations and Japan through some clash of arms and add that the time of the breaking out of this war may come quicker than anyone dreams.

Again, referring to our Ten-Point note of the 26th:

* Page 98.

In it there is one insulting clause which says that no matter what treaty either party enters into with a third power it will not be interpreted as having any bearing upon . . . the maintenance of peace in the Pacific. This means specifically the Three-Power Pact. . . . It is clearly a trick. This clause alone, let alone others, makes it impossible to find any basis in the American proposal for negotiations. . . . The United States . . . has decided to regard Japan, along with Germany and Italy, as an enemy.

But still more to the point was a message of that Monday, December 1, from Tokyo to Washington:

The date * set in my message #812 has come and gone, and the situation continues to be increasingly critical. However, to prevent the United States from becoming unduly suspicious we have been advising the press and others that though there are some wide differences between Japan and the United States, the negotiations are continuing. (The above is for only your information.)

And finally, as if to leave no possible doubt about it, there were two more messages from Tokyo to Washington, also of December 1:

When you are faced with the necessity of destroying codes, get in touch with the Naval Attache's office there and make use of chemicals they have on hand for this purpose. . . .

And:

The four offices in London, Hong Kong, Singapore, and Manila have been instructed to abandon the use of the code machines and to dispose of them. The machine in Batavia has been returned to Japan. Regardless . . . of my circular message . . . the U.S. (office) retains the machines and the machine codes.

Destruction of codes could mean but one thing—war, and war so sudden that it would give no time for a preliminary withdrawal of the diplomats, carrying the codes with them.

* November 29, after which things were "automatically going to happen."

These messages meant imminent war with Britain and the Netherlands. The concluding instructions to the Washington embassy to retain its codes might have been misleading, save for the fact that Manila was included in the order to destroy, while the whole tenor of the Japanese correspondence could leave no doubt that the United States was expected to be in the conflict from the outset.

All of these messages were translated and available in Washington on December 1. The records fail to show the times at which they were distributed and one cannot, consequently, trace the exact order and timing of their impact upon the events of the day. But they were building a pattern entirely consistent with those events in the minds of the President, the three Secretaries, and the high Army and Navy officers who were in the secret.

The nation, of course, could not be in the secret; and in Chicago that day the America First Committee was issuing its formal announcement that it had abandoned its "non-political" policy and in the coming year would go directly into the primary and general elections in order to try to elect Congressmen pledged to isolation. In so doing, it explained, it was seeking to resist a "trend toward Fascism in America" which was apparent when "the legislative branch of the government surrenders to one man its power to make decisions for the people." The "one man" at that moment must have been only too acutely aware that the decisions which were about to determine history were beyond his power, of that of anyone else in the United States.

The two ambassadors arrived at the State Department on Monday morning to find a "highly dramatic" scene (as they reported it), with newspaper men and even Department officials thronging the corridors, thinking that they had brought with them Japan's answer to the November 26 note. But they had not; they had, in fact, brought nothing new. Mr. Hull, wearing "a deeply pained expression," read them a severer lecture than he had yet given on the "bluster and bloodcurdling threats" emanating from Tokyo and on the heavy southward troop movements that were now filling the newspaper as well as the diplomatic reports. We "could not sit still" under such developments; and we did not propose to be driven from the Pacific. The ambassadors deprecated all this as best they could, and urged the United States to "deep reflection."

President Roosevelt was back in the White House by midday, and went immediately into conference with Secretary Hull and Admiral Stark. Mr. Harry Hopkins came for a luncheon session, being driven up from the Naval Hospital, where he was a patient. Mr. Sumner Welles was briefly summoned thereafter, and later in the day saw Lord Halifax. There are no minutes of any of these conferences, but their tenor is not hard to guess. While they went on the "magic" intercepts were appearing. The naval and military intelligence estimates were plumping more strongly than ever for an early Japanese descent on the Kra. Captain A. H. McCollum, head of the Far Eastern Section of Naval Intelligence, prepared a summary that day for a conference in Admiral Stark's office; and his own conclusions alarmed him so much that he asked whether the field commanders had been adequately warned. He received "categoric assurance" from both Stark and Richmond Kelly Turner that this had been done. The newspaper reports alone would have been almost enough. Domei came up—very ominously—with a report from Bangkok alleging that 50,000 Australian troops were on the point of invading Siam. It seemed obvious preparation for an imminent Japanese invasion. Manila had a rumor of a huge Japanese fleet off Borneo. Hong Kong and Singapore were canceling leaves; throughout the Far East everyone was standing to the alert.

President Roosevelt through that afternoon had much to weigh. "Magic" made certain conclusions inescapable. Whatever the Japanese Cabinet had in fact decided a few hours before, the statement that it had decided to continue negotiations was purely camouflage. The Berlin messages showed clearly that Japan had finally thrown her hand in on the side of the Germans, and that the war might "come quicker than anyone dreams." The message from Bangkok proved that an assault on Singapore was to be a leading feature of it when it came (and, incidentally, sufficiently exculpated the British from any queasiness about Siamese neutrality). Although Manila was specifically mentioned only in the message about destroying the code messages, virtually every reference the Japanese had made among themselves showed that the United States was to be included in the coming war. There was but one missing piece in the pattern—the answer to our November 26 note, which Togo had said would come in "two or three days"; the "longer one," as Kurusu had called it. Of that, as yet, there was no sign. When it appeared, crisis would be upon us.

This was the background. In the foreground of the immediate problem was Mr. Churchill's pressing request for a new warning that the United States would fight if Japan struck at Singapore. There was the urgent appeal of Brooke-Popham at Singapore that he be authorized to invade Siam first. There were Halifax's and Casey's belated appeals for delay, accompanied, however, by their anxious desire for assurance that when war came the United States would enter it. In the light of "magic" this final point must already have begun to seem rather academic. But what to do to stave off the war itself? And what to do about the actual fighting of it when it came?

The last question the President left, understandably, to the fighting men whom he had appointed, in whom he had confidence, and on whose abilities he had every reason to rely. What he failed to do—understandably or not—was to forge the powerful united front of the ABCD powers which the military men needed to back them up. Uncertainty as to what the United States would do was tending to paralyze them all, including the Americans. The President had conducted the diplomatic negotiations with Japan on behalf, to a large extent, of all the rest. "Magic" leaves the presumption that he knew fully as much about the Japanese plans and thoughts as did any of the others. The moment had come, if it were ever likely to, for building a really effective military-diplomatic alliance, and the one person who possessed the knowledge and the power to have formed it was the President of the United States. But America First was announcing that it would enter next year's elections on behalf of isolationism. Such eminent, and very influential, figures as former President Hoover, as Mr. Alfred H. Landon, Republican Presidential nominee in 1936, as Senator Robert H. Taft of Ohio, son of a President and himself a leader of the Republican opposition, as Mr. Joseph W. Martin, Republican Minority Leader of the House, as well as numerous others, were doing their best to convince the nation that the only threat of war lay in the irresponsible and dictatorial leadership of the "one man," Franklin D. Roosevelt. The "Hearst-Patterson-McCormick Axis" was thundering to the same effect. Again, it was only on that very Monday that the great railway unions, after a thirty-five-hour argument, finally agreed to the settlement which averted the complete paralysis of the nation's rail transport system that had been set for December 7. For good or ill, the President eschewed the urgent problem of trying to establish a solid coalition of the Western powers in the Pacific against the Japanese attack.

The President could not, or at any rate did not, do the one thing which at that late hour might have buttressed the defense. He could not engage the United States in a firm alliance. He evidently felt that he could not accept Mr. Churchill's suggestion for a categoric warning. There were not many weapons left in his armory. But as Monday waned, he was still playing with one which, however feeble it may have been, had attracted him for some time—an appeal direct to Emperor Hirohito. It was about all that was available, and the President evidently realized that war was virtually upon him. That evening there went off a somewhat bizarre order to Admiral Hart, explicitly at the President's direction, requiring the admiral to charter "three small vessels" with Filipino crews and with them to establish a "defensive information patrol" close along the Indo-Chinese coast, in the heart of Japanese-controlled waters. The admiral was also ordered to report on all reconnaissance efforts being carried out by both Navy and Army. The President clearly felt himself close to war that Monday night, and the message to Hirohito was the last resort.

It was already Tuesday's dawn in Tokyo, and Hirohito was soon to find himself closer to war, perhaps, than he wished to be. The real decision had been taken at the Cabinet the day before, but there was still the business of submitting it to the Emperor. According to the circumstantial reconstruction by Richard E. Lauterbach,* the Chief of the Naval General Staff, Nagano, summoned Yamamoto to the Imperial Palace that morning. Admiral Yamamoto "emphasized that the American Pacific Fleet at Pearl Harbor . . . must be neutralized. With colored maps he went over the battle order. . . . The attack, he said, might last three hours, begining at 3:00 A.M. on December 8." The August Presence "seemed glum, but asked a few technical questions." Yamamoto explained about the fins on the torpedoes and the supporting level and dive bombers, and the Son of Heaven seemed satisfied. The two admirals returned to the Naval Ministry where the first issued to the second the almost absolutely final final orders—apparently the first in the record which definitely named the date on which they must all have been calculating for weeks:

From: The Chief of the Naval General Staff
To: C-in-C Combined Fleet

The hostile action against the United States of America, the British Empire, and the Netherlands shall be commenced on 8 December. Bear in mind that, should it appear certain that Japanese-American negotiations will reach an amicable settlement prior to the commencement of hostile action, all forces of the Combined Fleet are to be ordered to reassemble and return to their bases.

* In *Life* magazine, March 4, 1946.

Thus armed, Yamamoto radioed his own order:

From: C-in-C Combined Fleet
To: Pearl Harbor Task Force (1st Air Fleet)
Execute attack. 8 December designated as X day.

In Manila that Tuesday Mr. Maxim Litvinoff, the new Soviet ambassador to the United States, who had just flown in from Singapore, got off across the Pacific on his way to Washington. He had seemed "calm" enough. Brereton's B-17's had taken up the patrol toward Formosa (MacArthur, mindful of his orders about overt acts, wouldn't let them reconnoiter over Formosa itself, but limited them to the international boundary through Luzon Strait) and Hart's PBY's were able to concentrate on the South China Sea. In midmorning they spotted nine Japanese submarines heading south along the Indo-China coast; later they sighted three more, off the mouth of Camranh Bay, also heading south, and in the bay itself they counted twenty-one transports at anchor, "mostly large." But at Singapore, about 2:30 that afternoon, a sudden report had run. Those who could look to seaward had made out, looming reassuringly over the horizon, the massive bulk of *H.M.S. Prince of Wales*, with *H.M.S. Repulse* in her wake and the attendant destroyers around them. The promised battle fleet had arrived at last. The two great ships passed majestically up the channel to the naval base. Nothing as big or as impressive had been seen there for years, and the British were at pains to let the whole world know of their arrival.

Tuesday afternoon at Singapore was still early on Tuesday morning at Washington. That day Secretary Hull found himself laid up with a cold, and it was Under Secretary Welles who summoned the two Japanese to the State Department in the course of the morning. He handed them a communication from the President, adverting to the Japanese troop movements and brusquely demanding an explanation:

The stationing of these increased Japanese forces in Indo-China would seem to imply the utilization of these forces by Japan for purposes of further aggression. . . . Please be good enough to request the Japanese ambassador and Ambassador Kurusu to inquire at once of the Japanese Government what the actual reasons may be for the steps already taken and what I am to consider is the policy of the Japanese Government. . . .

The ambassadors said that they would inquire. In the course of the conversation Mr. Welles took the opportunity to angle after the expected reply to our note of November 26. Ambassador Nomura assured him that one was coming, but that it might take a few more days.

Mr. Welles crossed over to the White House to represent his chief at the President's noon "War Council." Mr. Donald M. Nelson recalls that he was at the moment with the President, talking over something about priorities, and was interrupted by the announcement of the conference. "All right, Mr. President," he said as he rose to go. "How does it look?" The President shook his head gravely. "Don," he said, "I wouldn't be a bit surprised if we were at war with Japan by Thursday." Mr. Nelson was the chief of our whole industrial mobilization, yet this was the first intimation he had received that war might be so imminent!

At the council there were only the President, Stimson, Knox, and Welles. Mr. Roosevelt traversed the whole ground once more, and Mr. Stimson sensed that he had "made up his mind to go ahead." According to the Stimson diary, he was "still deliberating the possibility of a message to the Emperor, although all the rest of us are rather against it." He was apparently decided on the message to Congress and to the people. Mr. Roosevelt told them that "he was going to take the matters right up when he left us."

First, however, there was his Tuesday afternoon press conference. The throng of reporters, fishing insistently for some hint of what the United States was going to do, got no satisfaction. But the President did tell them about the demand served that morning on the Japanese for an explanation of the troop movement. He made it plain that we were expecting a reply, but he also made it plain that there was no time limit and that the demand was in no sense an ultimatum. The radio broadcasts and the next morning's news had to be built around that somewhat insubstantial basis. But the reporters got considerably more fiery quotations from lesser officials; and at least one Congressman, the redoubtable Andrew Jackson May, Chairman of the House Military Affairs Committee, went so far as to tell them that "Congress will support a declaration of war now if Japan moves southward." None of his colleagues, however, were willing to stick their necks out so far as that. And the day declined with a touch of what was almost comic relief as both the Japanese embassy and the Tokyo news dispatches tried belatedly, and unconvincingly, to demonstrate that Tojo had never made that speech about "purging" East Asia, or that if he had, he had not meant it or had meant it in some other way.

Around midnight that evening, as the newspaper presses in the eastern United States were beginning to roll with this grist of news for the morning, the morning in the Far East was already far gone. And just west of the International Date Line, in the cold and empty North Pacific seas at 42° N., 170° E., it was already mid-afternoon of Wednesday, December 3. Vice Admiral Nagumo's task force was assembling there to refuel from the accompanying tankers. Luck and training were with them. The weather interposed no important difficulties. In the week they had been at sea they had neither sighted nor been sighted by anyone. There was no hint that their mission had been suspected anywhere. Everything had gone perfectly according to plan, and they now had their final attack orders. Refueling completed, the task force resumed its course at increased speed. In Tokyo at about the same time Ambassador Grew was attending the state funeral of one of the dowager princesses. Foreign Minister Togo expressed his "disappointment" at the turn affairs were taking, but the Navy Minister, Shimada, greeted Mr. Grew most "cordially."

The young pilots of Admiral Hart's "Patwing 10," searching westward again on Wednesday, found observation difficult through the clouds of the monsoon season, and the report that afternoon was: "No results." But during the preceding night the operators at the Army's radar station at Iba had seen unexpected "blips" on their oscilloscope, they had tracked strange planes off the Luzon coast, and in the dawn light a single stranger had appeared, visually observable high over Clark Field, as if on reconnaissance. Some of the ground people even then could not believe that he was really a Japanese, but MacArthur acceded to the Air Force view and issued orders that if the plane reappeared it was to be intercepted and forced down or destroyed. He still did not feel authorized to permit American reconnaissance over the Formosan airfields, about which we knew next to nothing.

As Nagumo was completing his refueling, Halsey was already nearing Wake. The twelve Marine fighter planes were to be flown off next morning. Back at Pearl, Admiral Kimmel and General Short were still deep in their argument over an Army garrison for Wake and Midway.* On Oahu during that final week there was a general feeling of unconcern, though

* This was Tuesday afternoon at Pearl. It is not always easy to keep the correct time relations in mind. As explained in an earlier footnote, Washington was fourteen hours behind Tokyo. But Pearl Harbor was five and one-half hours behind Washington and consequently nineteen and one-half hours behind Tokyo. This can be understood by recalling that Pearl Harbor lay close to the International Date Line, where the time difference beween one side and the other is twenty-four hours. Nagumo refueled in 170° E. on the afternoon of December 3, east longitude time. It was thus the afternoon of December 2 at Pearl. It was late in the evening of December 2 at Washington and still forenoon of December 3 at Tokyo. Halsey flew off his planes early on the morning of December 4, east longitude time, which was Wednesday morning, December 3, at Pearl and Wednesday evening at Washington.

it was tempered for some by an underlying uneasiness. A few of the higher Army officers, like Major General Henry T. Burgin, commander of the coast and anti-aircraft artillery, felt that the anti-sabotage alert was scarcely sufficient, but their opinions were not asked. The headlines in the Honolulu newspapers were proclaiming crisis and impending war in the southwest Pacific more loudly, if anything, than the press in the States. Many of the younger officers acquired a sense that things were getting dangerous from reading, as one testified, *Time* magazine. In the married officers' quarters there were doubtless some rather anxious conversations over the highballs. But no one in high authority suggested to them that Hawaii might be attacked; they were not on combat alert, and there was no effort to infuse a combat mentality. They were a rear base.

The one thing approaching a warlike act with which the Army was concerned was the photo-reconnaissance mission over the Japanese mandates, on which they were preparing to dispatch two B-24 Liberators as soon as they should be received from the mainland. The War Department had authorized this a few days before, about the time that the Navy's Combat Intelligence at Pearl believed that it had discovered a carrier division in the Marshalls. Cavite, it will be remembered, had disagreed with the estimate, but the mission was to go anyway.

Combat Intelligence, for its part, as well as Captain Edwin T. Layton, the Fleet Intelligence officer, were fully alive to their responsibility for keeping track of Japanese ship movements. Unfortunately, however, radio traffic analysis was far from an exact science; at best there was a large element of shrewd guesswork in it, and Combat Intelligence had been having its troubles. About the first of November the Japanese had changed all their call signs, and it had taken time to identify the new ones. Then on December 1 the call signs were changed again. This in itself strongly suggested that something was impending, and the intelligence summary of

December 1 noted it as an indication of "an additional progressive step in preparing for active operations on a large scale." Admiral Kimmel, scanning the summary, underlined this passage; and then directed Layton to make up for him a consolidated "location sheet" showing the whereabouts, so far as known, of all Japanese vessels. In doing so, Layton realized that they knew almost nothing about the Japanese carriers. The intelligence summary of November 14 had placed the bulk of them as probably in Japanese home waters, and in the intervening two weeks there had been only a few dubious hints and scraps—most of which, as is now evident, we actually owed to the Japanese campaign of radio deception. The summary of December 2 had to confess "almost a complete blank of information on the carriers today"; and Layton's accompanying location sheet, while guessing at some of them, was unable to list any of the four first-line ships in Carrier Divisions 1 and 2. Admiral Kimmel pounced on that: "What, you don't know where Carrier Division 1 and Carrier Division 2 are?" Layton confessed that he did not, although he thought them probably still in home waters.

> Then Admiral Kimmel looked at me, as sometimes he would, with somewhat a stern countenance and yet partially with a twinkle in his eye and said, "Do you mean to say that they could be rounding Diamond Head and you wouldn't know it?" or words to that effect. My reply was that "I hope they would be sighted before now."

Yet the possibility that they actually might be rounding Diamond Head (and at that moment they were only five days' steaming away) and the necessity for taking steps to insure that if so they would be sighted simply did not come home to either mind. Another of those fatal lapses had sunk forever into the pool of time. Perhaps it was partly because Admiral Kimmel was so deeply absorbed at the time in the problem of Wake and Midway. On Monday both Kimmel and Short received telegrams from their respective departments in Washington about the projected Army relief of the Marine garrisons. On Monday afternoon the two commanders held a "long conference" on the subject. Kimmel would have liked to get back his Marines, but Short wouldn't garrison the atolls unless he was given command over them. Kimmel replied with asperity: "Over my dead body. The Army should exercise no command over Navy bases," or words to that effect. On Tuesday, the 2nd, Kimmel came to Short's headquarters bearing a long letter he had drafted to "Dear Betty" Stark on the matter, and the two went all over it again. As a matter of fact they were both, for one reason or another, taking an increasingly dim view of the project, and Short agreed to much in the letter. Nevertheless, they had another extended conference on Wednesday, the 3rd, when Short brought his own telegram for the War Department to Kimmel's headquarters. Though they had their differences, it was "a perfectly cordial personal relation." Indeed, this lengthy series of conferences was afterward to be adduced as proof of the harmony of "co-ordinate" command at Pearl Harbor. No doubt it was harmonious enough. Yet in all these long and intimate consultations on three successive days it never occurred to either man to discuss the command at Pearl itself. It never occurred to Kimmel to tell Short that the Navy had lost the Japanese carriers and had no means of warning him against surprise; it never occurred to Short to tell Kimmel that the Army was relying wholly on the Navy for such warning and was itself helpless against a surprise; Kimmel did not even pass on the supposed information about carriers in the Marshalls. The last wasn't the Army's business.

Both men, together with their higher staff officers, were afterward to feel deeply aggrieved over the fact that Washington, with its passion for "security," withheld from them the information from "magic" and other sources. But the degree of secrecy and "security" which obtained within Pearl Harbor itself would seem to offer Washington at least a plea in mitigation.

Sweeping across the turning globe, Wednesday morning's sun reached Washington. It brought with it the headlines about the President's demand of the day before for an explanation of the Japanese troop movements. It also brought into the Japanese embassy a curt, and on the face of it preposterous, answer for the ambassadors to submit. This, at least, was too much for Nomura; withholding the reply, he messaged back a protest to Togo in which a touch of western irony would seem to struggle with eastern politeness:

> I presume, of course, that this reply was a result of consultations and profound consideration. The United States Government is attaching a great deal of importance on this reply. . . . If it is really the intention of our Government to arrive at a settlement, the explanation you give, I am afraid, would neither satisfy them nor prevent them taking [a] bold step. . . . I would like to get a reply which gives a clearer impression of our peaceful intentions. Will you, therefore, reconsider . . . and wire me at once.

It left diplomacy during the day more or less up in the air. The position was that we were now waiting for the explanation of the troop movements and waiting also for the answer to the November 26 note, which would be the critical document. Secretary Hull, recovered from his cold, held a press conference on Wednesday, but there was not much to add to what he had said before. Some began to think that the whole fracas in the Pacific was simply a "war of nerves" which might be indefinitely prolonged. Others, commenting on the arrival of the British battle squadron at Singapore, felt that there was now real strength upon the ground which might deter the southward advance, but that if Japan did attempt a challenge it was vital that the United States should enter the war from the first moment. On Capitol Hill that day the House, outraged by Mr. Lewis and his coal miners, by the narrowly averted rail strike, and by the continuing strikes in defense industries, staged a sudden "rebellion" and passed the drastic Smith anti-strike bill, the most extreme of a number of measures of the kind before it, by 252 to 136. Its terms are of no consequence, as it was soon to be swept away by torrential events; but it suggests the attitudes of those last days.

For those with access to "magic" the day brought one further significant development. On Monday there had appeared those two messages about destroying the code machines, but specifically exempting those in the Washington embassy. Now there came another message from Togo to Washington:

> Among the telegraphic codes with which your office is equipped burn all but those now used with the machine and one copy each of "O" code and abbreviating code (L). (Burn also the various other codes which you have in your custody.) Stop at once using one code machine unit and destroy it completely. When you have finished this, wire me back the one word "haruna."

It evidently began to sink into the minds of the Naval Intelligence people that this code business was getting serious. The great difficulty about "magic" throughout was, of course, that if the Japanese knew we possessed it, its value would be at an end; and if the Japanese (who had their own means for breaking some of our codes) should learn that we were disseminating information that could only have come through reading their messages, the secret would be out. "Distribution" is one of the worst headaches of all military intelligence, for it is obviously pointless to get information unless it is utilized, yet to utilize it is always to risk destroying the source through which alone one can get more. In this case, the matter seemed so important that the risk was taken. Early Wednesday afternoon the telegrams went out to Hart and Kimmel over Admiral Stark's signature:

> Highly reliable information has been received that categoric and urgent instructions were sent yesterday to Japanese diplomatic and consular posts at Hong Kong, Singapore, Batavia, Manila, Washington, and London to destroy most of their codes and ciphers at once and to burn all other important confidential and secret documents.

A second message to the same effect added that the British Admiralty reported that the Japanese embassy in London had already carried out the order. Yet Admiral Kimmel was later to testify that as the days went by after November 27 he was inclined less and less to believe that Japan was going to attack the United States. The small impression which this vital piece of information appears to have made upon him at least encourages a doubt as to whether he would have interpreted other "magic" messages any more successfully than did Washington. But that Washington also failed is indisputable. Another "magic" message translated on Wednesday was already over two weeks old. It was one from Tokyo to the consul at Honolulu about that business of ship reports: "Make your 'ships in harbor' report irregular, but at a rate of twice a week. Although you are already no doubt aware, please take extra care to maintain secrecy." It suggested nothing to those who read it. Several other intercepts of the same kind were accumulating; most of them were not even translated until after December 7. Then they took on a terrible and only too obvious significance.

Mr. Donald Nelson gave a dinner on Wednesday evening at the Carlton Hotel for Vice-President Wallace and the members of SPAB (Supplies, Priorities, and Allocations Board). Mr. Nelson had seated Mr. Frank Knox at his left. Remembering what the President had said the day before, he tried "guardedly" to pump the Secretary of the Navy. The latter was not reticent. "Don," he said, "we may be at war with Japan before the month is over."

"Is it that bad?" Mr. Nelson asked him. "You bet your life it's that bad," was Mr. Knox's response. Even so, Mr. Nelson did not, really, believe it.

SEVEN

THIS IS PEARL

I ☞

Manila:

It was the morning of Thursday, December 4, East longitude time. An even week had gone by since the coming of the war warnings, and nothing that they had heard from Washington, seen for themselves, or learned from their newspapers and news broadcasts had done anything to diminish the tensions they were under. Again during the night the Iba radar had picked up the tracks of unidentified planes, and before dawn there had been a stranger over Clark Field for a second time. But the monsoon clouds were heavy; the searchlights could not reach him and it was useless to send up fighter planes. The visitant departed. It was decided that if he came back next morning they would wait no longer on protocol but open up with the anti-aircraft artillery.

Hart's PBY's ranged again on Thursday over the South China Sea, but did not venture as far as Camranh Bay, where they had already been observed for three days in succession by the Japanese. What had happened to the concentration of transports which had been seen there on Tuesday, no one knew; "negative results" was the report on Thursday's reconnaissance. They could all feel the hot breath of the crouching tiger on their necks, but they could make no first move themselves. Hart had already done what he could by dispersing his ships and getting his submarines to sea. At Camp Stotsenburg, Wainwright was throwing a staff together and doing what little was possible toward turning his raw Filipino recruits into an army of defense. Across from his headquarters, on the adjacent Clark Field, there rested the big, graceful shapes of the B-17's. They were a reassuring sight; but they belonged to Brereton and the air people and Wainwright had nothing to do with them.

Brereton's own position was anything but a happy one. Though the pilots for the vital dive bomber group had arrived, their planes were still somewhere on the Pacific.* A second group of B-17's on which they had been counting—the 7th Bombardment Group—was still held up by weather on the American west coast, though it was hoped they might be taking off at any moment. Until they came, the 35 B-17's of the 19th Bombardment Group, now resting on Clark Field, would represent the sum total of American striking power in the western Pacific, as well as the principal defensive strength of the Philippines. To cover them, Brereton had five squadrons of fighters with 90 planes in all, most of them P-40's or P-40E's—the latter the best fighter type we then had in service, even though General Arnold rated it as only a "good pursuit trainer." These were distributed at various fields, one squadron being at Clark and two at Nichols Field near Manila. In addition there were some odds and ends. A single fighter squadron of the Philippine Army, under Captain Jesus A. Villamour, was to prove its skill and heroism, but its twelve planes were obsolete. There were some observation planes and a dozen obsolete B-18 bombers. But for practical purposes the Far Eastern Air Force consisted of the 33 four-engine bombers and ninety approximately modern fighters. Against them, though they were not fully aware of it, were poised the

* According to Colonel Ind this was just as well, as they had been shipped without the firing mechanism for their guns and would have been useless had they been received.

360 aircraft of the two crack Japanese naval air flotillas in Formosa.

But the situation was much worse than the discrepancy in numbers would suggest. There were still too few fields for satisfactory dispersal; anti-aircraft at the fields they had was still inadequate or nonexistent; communications were still unreliable, and the command organization deficient. Not having been allowed to reconnoiter Formosa, their target data was of the sketchiest kind. And although the big bombers had been rushed out as the major reliance in the Far East, there was as yet no real plan for their utilization in the event of emergency. Brereton was subordinate to MacArthur, and at that time MacArthur had not received the extensive education in the potentialities and management of air power which the Japanese were so soon to administer. Neither the commanding general nor his chief of staff, Sutherland, appears to have understood the requirements of air warfare very well, and Brereton had his troubles with them. On Thursday Brereton, after canvassing the whole situation with his own staff, came to the conclusion that he would have to get some, at least, of the precious B-17's off the exposed and overcrowded field at Clark. That meant sending them far southward to Del Monte, in Mindanao, the only other field that could receive them. Sutherland was reluctant to permit this retreat, even though he seems to have had no particular plans of his own for the employment of the bombers in a crisis; but on the promise that they would be brought back again as soon as more fields were ready he finally authorized the move.

That night they waited tensely for the strange reconnaissance planes. Nothing showed. In a way, no doubt, it was worse than if the strangers had returned. The Japanese were all around them, but invisible. On Friday, the 5th, twelve of the B-17's flew down to Del Monte. The monsoon weather made search difficult for both the Army patrols over Luzon Strait and the Navy PBY's over the China Sea, and nothing was observed. But that afternoon a plane came in from Singapore, bearing Admiral Sir Tom Phillips, commander of the British battle squadron and British naval commander-in-chief in the Far East. Admiral Hart welcomed him, and the two went into earnest conference.

Phillips needed help. He was supposed to have arrived in Singapore with a balanced fleet, including an aircraft carrier, four battleships, and adequate light vessels. He actually had two battleships and four destroyers. The carrier *Ark Royal*, originally assigned to him, had been sunk in the Mediterranean; *Indomitable*, which was to have replaced her, had gone aground in the West Indies. Of his four battleships, two—*Revenge* and *Royal Sovereign*—had not arrived. Hart could do nothing to fill such deficiencies as these, but he could help out with destroyers. Unfortunately, the United States was still neutral and Hart had no authority to place United States ships under British command, even though that kind of thing had been going on for some weeks in the Atlantic. But he could get ready. Admiral Phillips stayed overnight, and on Saturday, December 6, the two worked out an agreement. A division of four American destroyers was then at Balikpapan, the oil port on the east coast of Borneo. Hart started them for Batavia, whence they could reach Singapore within forty-eight hours if need be. Admiral Phillips took off late in the afternoon. By that time, all the higher Army and Navy officers in Manila were feeling that it was a question of days, perhaps only of hours.*

* Late that Saturday night the American naval attache in Singapore, Creighton, messaged Hart that Brooke-Popham, the British commander-in-chief, had received a telegram from the British War Office, which Creighton quoted as saying: "We have now received assurance of American armed support in cases as follows: (a) we are obliged execute our plans to forestall Japs landing on Isthmus of Kra . . . (b) if Dutch Indies are attacked . . . (c) if Japs attack us. . . . Therefore without reference to London put plan in action if first you have good info [that the Japanese were making any of these movements]." This message of Creighton's has been adduced as "proof" that the Roosevelt Administration had entered into an offensive alliance with the

There had, however, been no news since Tuesday of the big Japanese force which Hart's PBY's had spotted that day at anchor in Camranh Bay. And then, as Saturday evening fell, the news suddenly arrived. Hart's pilots on Saturday found 30 transports and a cruiser in Camranh. But around noon British search planes from Malaya had sighted two large Japanese convoys—35 transports in all escorted by cruisers and destroyers—off Cape Cambodia, heading west into the Gulf of Siam. Their destination might be Bangkok; or it might be the Kra Isthmus and the assault on Singapore.

Shortly before 9 o'clock Saturday evening, Hart's message conveying the news went off to the Navy Department, as well as to Kimmel and Bloch for information. It was then shortly before 8 o'clock, Saturday morning, by Washington time.

Washington:

Washington had awakened on Thursday morning to a juicily scandalous sensation. "Colonel" Robert R. McCormick's *Chicago Tribune*, the bitterly anti-Roosevelt voice of Middle Western isolationism in its most extreme form, had published to the world what it declared to be a secret report of

---

British before the Japanese attack. Yet Creighton afterwards could not remember where he had got the text which his message quoted and thought that it might have been "nothing more than rumor." More to the point, it was all news to Hart at the time, and the admiral queried Washington about it; which, considering that Hart was the commander who would have to give the "armed support," hardly indicates that there was any matured plan for going to Britain's assistance.

The inference is that this was an echo of the appeal made to Washington on the preceding Sunday (see p. 281) to authorize a British advance into Siam. The record does not show any official answer to this appeal. If, in that eleventh hour, the British were unofficially told to go ahead, it would seem that the worst one could allege against whoever told them was that he was suffering from a rare attack of common sense. There is some reason to think that the assurance may have been transmitted through Mr. Welles in his meeting with Lord Halifax on Monday (p. 288) though Mr. Welles afterward could not recall this.

the Army-Navy Joint Board, laying down plans for a total military establishment of over 10,000,000 men, of whom 5,000,000 were to be formed into an expeditionary force for the invasion of Germany by July 1, 1943.

It was intended, of course, to convict the Roosevelt Administration of deliberately plotting the great foreign war which the Administration had repeatedly claimed it was doing all in its power to avoid. In pursuit of this patriotic purpose, Colonel McCormick had not hesitated to reveal top secret military plans in an hour of urgent crisis; he had also used the hoary political stratagem of giving to what was patently no more than precautionary planning the color of a decision already taken. Washington buzzed with fury; the War Department declared that the matter would be investigated, and Secretary Knox, calling it a disclosure of "the most highly secret paper in the possession of the Government," said the same for the Navy. In the conferences of that day there was probably almost as much excitement over this episode as over the Far Eastern crisis itself, and the affair survives today as still another illustration of the difficulties inherent in the conduct of a democracy's foreign relations in the moment of extreme emergency.

But the Far Eastern emergency was much too extreme to be denied even for a day. If the Japanese were burning their codes, it was incumbent on our people to begin doing the same. General Miles had already messaged preliminary instructions to the military attaché in Tokyo, adding the warning that "early rupture of diplomatic relations with Japan has been indicated." Captain John R. Beardall, the President's naval aide, who customarily brought him the "magic" material, was to recall pointing out the Japanese code-burning message (presumably on this Thursday) as "a very significent dispatch." The President studied it carefully and looked up: "Well, when do you think it will happen?" Beardall thought that "it" might happen "most any time."

The Navy had started its telegrams to the naval attachés

at Tokyo, Bangkok, Peiping, and Shanghai: "Destroy this system at discretion and send word 'Jabberwock' when done. All registered publications except this system must be destroyed immediately." This was followed up on Thursday afternoon by similar but even stronger instructions to the Naval Station at Guam, ending: "Be prepared to destroy instantly in the event of emergency all classified matter you retain." A copy of the Guam message went to Kimmel and Bloch; once again, it made no deep impression on them. It was also on Thursday that "magic," working through its backlog of ship report messages, translated one a fortnight old to the Japanese consul at Honolulu: "Strictly secret. Please investigate comprehensively the Fleet — bases in the neighborhood of the Hawaiian military reservation." Once again, this made no deep impression on Washington. Oahu was not advised.

The President had a two-hour session on Thursday with the majority and minority leaders of Congress, in which he went over the whole Far Eastern situation. Afterward he saw Knox and then Hull. That afternoon there were news dispatches from Tokyo. Domei was proclaiming the American terms to be "utterly impossible to accept" and the crisis seemed to be growing no less acute. But we were still waiting for Japan's move. In their embassy that afternoon the two Japanese ambassadors were—no doubt ruefully—regarding one indication of what that move would be. To Nomura's protest over the "explanation" he had been told to give for the troop movements, Togo had wired back peremptorily:

> What you say in your telegram is, of course, true, but at present it would be a very delicate matter to give any more explanations than set forth in my #875. I would advise against it, because unfortunate results might follow, so please reply in accordance with my afore-mentioned message.

There was no help for it; but at least they could delay making the reply for some hours longer. They asked for an appointment at the State Department for the following day, Friday, the 5th.

On Friday morning the newspaper headlines were announcing, though without undue excitement, that the Japanese answer was expected that day; that it would probably reject the Hull terms and that a breakdown of the long negotiations seemed imminent. At the White House the President was dictating a letter to Mr. Wendell Willkie. The Australians had suggested that it would be helpful if Mr. Willkie could pay them a visit, and the President was passing the suggestion along to "Dear Wendell" with his cordial assent. But, he added at the end, "there is always the Japanese matter to consider. The situation is definitely serious and there might be an armed clash at any moment if the Japanese continued their forward progress against the Philippines, Dutch Indies, or Malaya or Burma. Perhaps the next four or five days will decide the matter." * At the State Department Mr. Hull must have been thinking the same thing, as the two ambassadors appeared with Foreign Minister Togo's "explanation" for the southward troop movements:

> As Chinese troops have recently shown frequent signs of movements along the northern frontier of French Indo-China bordering on China, Japanese troops, with the object of mainly taking precautionary measures, have been reinforced to a certain extent in the northern part of French Indo-China. As a natural sequence of this step, certain movements have been made among the troops stationed in the southern part of the said territory. It seems that an exaggerated report has been made of these movements. It should be added that no measure has been taken on the part of the Japanese Government that may transgress the stipulations of the Protocol of Joint Defense between Japan and France.

Confronted with this barefaced absurdity (explicitly dictated, as we knew from "magic," by Tokyo itself), Mr. Hull

* The copy bears a notation in Mr. Roosevelt's hand: "This was dictated Friday morning—long before this vile attack started. F.D.R."

acidly remarked that it was the first he had heard of the Japanese having been reduced to the defensive in northern Indo-China. He had understood that their troops had been sent there in order to attack the Chinese. If they were now themselves in danger of attack it was, he suggested, an added reason why they should get out of Indo-China altogether. Nomura, trying to make it sound a little less grotesque, exceeded his instructions to the extent of mentioning Japanese alarm over the "increasing naval and military preparations of the ABCD powers in the Southwest Pacific." The Secretary could only observe that he would be glad to hear anything further which Japan might wish to communicate on the matter; and the conversation wandered off down the old and futile beaten paths. There was still no sign of an answer to the November 26 note.

Secretary Hull crossed over to the White House for luncheon with the President, and there was a full Cabinet meeting afterward. In the course of the afternoon Tokyo sources began to emit a rather belated smokescreen. A Japanese Foreign Office spokesman explained to the press that Japan's position was being "misunderstood"; in spite of the seeming deadlock in negotiations, Japan still hoped that they would "continue with sincerity." At the War Department at Washington (where Secretary Stimson had given his press conference to an excoriation of the *Chicago Tribune*) plans were being announced for Christmas leaves. Of the 1,500,000 men then in the Army, it was hoped that almost half could be granted ten- or fifteen-day furloughs. But that, of course, was routine; in the higher offices in the Munitions Building few were putting any faith in Tokyo's "sincerity."

Admiral Richmond Kelly Turner, the Navy's Chief of War Plans, was alarmed by the change in the Japanese radio calls, by the lack of information on Japanese fleet movements, by the destruction of codes, and all the other omens of the past few days. He dropped in to the office of Rear Admiral Royal E. Ingersoll, Stark's Assistant Chief of Naval Operations, and for an hour the two men talked over the whole position, considering in particular what more they might or ought to do toward warning the Fleet commands. They reviewed the November 27 warning; it seemed to have everything in it, including the specific instructions to effect a "defensive deployment." They finally went in to consult with Stark himself, who agreed with them. "It was the unanimous decision that the orders . . . were sufficient."

That Friday there were two more "magic" messages from Tokyo to Honolulu about ship reports. One, nearly three weeks old, asked explicitly for reports on ships anchored in "Area N, Pearl Harbor"; a second, dated November 29, said significantly: "We have been receiving reports from you on ship movements, but in the future will you also report even when there are no movements." It apparently occurred to no one to ask why the Japanese should want reports on movements even when there were no movements to report.

Military and Naval Intelligence were, however, busy on another task. The Secretary of State had rung up and demanded a complete accounting of Japanese forces in Indo-China, so far as they could be estimated, for the use of the President. The Navy's tabulation was ready by Friday afternoon—105,000 men, 250 planes, and a large assortment of naval vessels. The War Department did not send up its estimate until Saturday, but it was somewhat more complete. Counting troops in transports, it allotted 125,000 men to Indo-China, with 450 planes, most of them in the south; it also estimated that there were 400 planes and 40,000 men in Formosa and 200 planes with 50,000 men on Hainan Island, off the south China coast. Neither estimate had a word about the carrier force in the Palaus, nor, of course, about Nagumo's squadron, now rapidly running down far to the northward of the Hawaiian chain. General Miles was also engaged on Friday in polishing up the latest of his periodic forecasts of the global war situation, covering, at length and with admirable thoroughness, the developments to be anticipated between

December 1 and March, 1942. The section devoted to the Far East recognized that the forces of all other powers concerned "are on the defensive against Japan," but it took what was to prove a grossly optimistic view of their defensive capabilities. It concluded that "the most probable line of action for Japan is the occupation of Thailand." Perhaps it would be only Thailand; and the widest possibilities considered failed to embrace Pearl Harbor.

That evening the State Department followed the example of the Army and Navy and ordered the embassies in Tokyo and Chungking and the consulates in Hong Kong, Saigon, Hanoi, and Bangkok to prepare to destroy their confidential papers. "The sending of this instruction is in the nature of a precautionary measure. . . . The concerned officers should quietly formulate plans to deal with an emergency if and when it arises." There was nothing impetuous about the State Department.

Friday evening fell, and again the Washington correspondents were getting off their stories for the morning. Some of them, influenced by Tokyo's outgivings, felt that there had been a lessening of the tension during the day. But all eyes and thoughts were riveted (as the Japanese presumably intended that they should be) on the military movements in the far southwest Pacific. So Friday passed, and Saturday, December 6, came up over Washington. And with it there came the first news. Admiral Hart's message, reporting the British discovery of the two convoys off the tip of Cape Cambodia, was filed at 8:55 P.M., Saturday, Manila time, which was 7:55 Saturday morning in Washington. The message was available in Washington before 11 o'clock; while a notation shows that it was 10:40 A.M. when a message came in to the State Department from Ambassador Winant in London, reporting the same news. Singapore had intimated that the convoys might be headed for Bangkok; but this London message said flatly that they were "sailing slowly westward toward Kra, fourteen hours distant in time."

Here was the alarm in earnest. Mr. Sumner Welles, who had been putting the chance for peace at one in a thousand, reduced it that day to one in a million.

Pearl Harbor:

Thursday, December 4, at Pearl Harbor was much like the days that had gone before and like the next two which were to succeed it. There have been no similar days in Hawaii since. They were getting along with their manifold preparations as rapidly as their funds, their orders, the peacetime conditions and work schedules, and the distaste of the big Hawaiian landowners for undue disturbance of their pineapple and cane fields would permit. The Army was assiduously on guard against sabotage. The Navy was busy with its preparations for getting the carrier *Lexington* off next day with the eighteen Marine fighter planes for Midway. Halsey had already flown off the fighters for Wake, and was now on his way back to Oahu. The PBY squadron which had covered the Wake operation would be coming in on the morrow for rest and refit. The newspapers were full of the war clouds over Indo-China; but when the Navy Department's message instructing Guam to prepare to destroy its codes came through, Admiral Kimmel did not consider the information "vital" and did not trouble to tell General Short about it. It accorded with the assumption of a southwest Pacific war, and for that they were all ready.

With *Lexington's* departure there would be virtually no Navy fighter planes at Oahu, and only a small number of Marine fighters and light bombers on the Ewa field, just west of Pearl. When the twelve PBY's from Wake got in, Admiral Bellinger would have a total of 69 of these long-range patrol aircraft (nine of them temporarily out of commission) at Oahu, plus twelve more still at Midway to cover the *Lexington* task force. Of those at Oahu, 36 were based on Ford Island, in the middle of Pearl Harbor itself; 33 were at the Kaneohe base on Oahu's opposite (eastern) coast. The great majority were new planes which had arrived during November; they were not properly "shaken down" and there was a paucity of spare parts—a standard situation in the Pacific in those perilous days—with which to cure the inevitable "bugs." These planes had been flying regular patrols to the northward of Oahu, though these were primarily of a training nature. Such "daily scouts" were flown outward as far as 400 miles from Monday through Thursday, but Thursday's was the last. The planes then went to base for maintenance and for the week end. The first business of the PBY's was to conserve and prepare themselves for the planned raid into the Marshalls, and Admiral Kimmel saw no reason to use up in unnecessary defensive patrols the only flying boats which he had for offensive operations.

General Martin, General Short's air commander, had no planes at all capable of long-range patrol except the six operable B-17's which were being used to train the air crews for the Philippines. He had a considerable collection of antiques, including some 30 B-18 bombers, most of them at Hickam Field, just east of Pearl Harbor. But no one regarded them as combat types. There was an observation squadron at Bellows Field, next to Kaneohe on the east coast, which flew anti-submarine reconnaissance over inshore waters but which, like most Army elements in Hawaii, did not work on Sundays. The Army's main contribution to the air-borne defense of Hawaii was "105 pursuit planes that were modern enough to fight." * Many of these, however, were in the hands of very green pilots. That week one squadron of them was at Bellows, engaging in target practice, and another was at Haleiwa, an obscure airstrip on the northwest coast of Oahu, practising landings and take-offs. The bulk of the fighters was at Wheeler Field, next to Schofield Barracks in the center of the island, where they were parked wing-to-wing in accordance with the

* Short's testimony before the Army Board (Pt. 27 p. 243). The tabulation given in Exhibit 4 (Pt. 12 p. 323) shows a total of 99 P-40's, of which only 64 are listed as "in commission" at the time of the attack. In addition it shows twenty P-36's "in commission."

SOP for the anti-sabotage alert. It would have taken about four hours to get them gassed, armed, and into the air.

The training routines continued. The heightening tensions at Washington were only vaguely communicated to Pearl Harbor. There had been a rather curious fracas earlier that week between Naval Intelligence and the Federal Bureau of Investigation, both of whom had been putting illegal taps on the telephone lines of the Japanese consulate. The telephone company had discovered this and made trouble; Naval Intelligence, under the impression that the F.B.I.'s bungling had given away the business, was "incensed" at the civilian investigators. Remembering its orders to avoid international complications, it had summarily ordered all the taps removed, and its own were taken off. But the F.B.I., apparently unknown to the Navy, retained one tap on the telephone line of the consulate's cook.

On Thursday Vice Admiral Wilson Brown, commander of the Scouting Force, left in the heavy cruiser *Indianapolis* for Johnston and Palmyra Islands, where he was to study methods of landing on defended atolls. Next morning, Friday, December 5, his subordinate, Vice Admiral J. H. Newton, left with the *Lexington* task force for Midway. Besides the big carrier, Admiral Newton had with him the heavy cruisers *Chicago* (flag), *Astoria*, and *Portland* and a division of destroyers. With Halsey still at sea, the fortunate result was that our only two carriers in the area and no less than seven heavy cruisers with the attendant destroyers were to be absent on the morning of December 7 and were thus to be preserved intact for future battles. Halsey had happened to be present with Kimmel when the November 27 warning had come in, and he had sailed with shotted guns. Brown afterward recalled that he had learned of the warnings, but neither he nor anyone else had troubled to inform Newton of them; and the latter was allowed to depart on a voyage that would carry him some thousand miles directly toward Japan without knowledge of the warning messages. Because of the generally critical situation he took the precaution of flying an anti-submarine patrol ahead and zigzagging during the daytime, but his planes were not bombed-up and ready as were Halsey's. As he was going up one side of the Hawaiian chain, Nagumo was coming down the other; indeed, on his own side, Newton was actually sighted by one of the big Japanese submarines arriving to take her station off Oahu. But the submarine's time for attack had not yet arrived, and she was not detected by the task force.

It was also on Friday that the first of the two Army B-24's, which were to make the photographic reconnaissance over the Mandates, flew into Pearl. It turned out that she had come without "adapters" for her machine guns, and the War Department had issued strict instructions that the two planes were to be fully armed for their mission. There was nothing for it except to hold the bomber and message the mainland for the mechanisms to be sent in her consort. In the result the first B-24 was destroyed in the attack, while the second, fortunately, never came.

Late on Friday information reached Admiral Bloch's 14th District headquarters that the Japanese in the Honolulu consulate were burning their confidential papers. The earlier intercepts had revealed that instructions in that sense had gone to the Manila, Washington, London, and southwest Pacific consulates, but had said not a word about Honolulu. If the Honolulu consulate was now following suit, it would certainly be a significant danger sign. But still the truth did not invade minds which were simply closed against it. The information made no greater impression on Bloch than the messages about the destruction of codes had made on Kimmel. In the early hours on Saturday morning a dispatch went over Bloch's signature to Washington:

> Believe local consul has destroyed all but one system although presumably not included in your eighteen double five of third [i.e., although the Honolulu consulate was presumably not included in the Japanese orders, which had been conveyed to Kimmel in the message referred to].

That seems to have ended the matter. Kimmel afterward remembered that he had been told something about this, but that the information had come to him merely as a report that "they were burning papers outside the Japanese consulate," and that he had paid no attention to it.

It was an hour or two after the dispatch of Bloch's message that Admiral Hart (at 2:25 A.M. Saturday by Hawaiian time) filed his telegram announcing the discovery of the Japanese off Cape Cambodia. It was routed to both Kimmel and Bloch for information; but presumably it was no more than they had been expecting.

II ☜

In his headquarters at Camp Stotsenburg, in central Luzon, General Wainwright was turning in at the end of a long but relatively good day, unaware of the news that Hart had sent off a couple of hours before. After days of automobile travel, the general had got in some horse exercise in the morning, riding over to Clark to have a look at Brereton's B-17's. In the afternoon he had inspected the 26th Cavalry and a battery of field artillery—the Stotsenburg garrison—and he now had a Sunday before him. He went to bed "about 11 o'clock that Saturday night and I had many occasions later on to remember that I got a good night's sleep. It was the last decent sleep that I was to have for three years and eight months."

As the general closed his eyes, it was still only Saturday morning in Washington. Hart's and Winant's dispatches were arriving, and Mr. Welles was multiplying the odds against peace by a thousand. Crisis, obviously, was coming. According to London's estimate as reported by Winant, the Japanese convoys when discovered had been only fourteen hours' steaming from the Kra. If correct, that would put them ashore within another few hours; by 1 o'clock that same afternoon (Washington time) the invasion of the Kra Isthmus might be under way. On top of everything else—the transparent Japanese evasions and delays, the destruction of codes, the clear evidence that the United States was to be involved from the beginning—this surely meant that the moment for incisive action had come. But there was no plan to act upon. Our own commanders had been warned. There was no provision for joint operation with the British and Dutch. There was no agreement on detailed strategy. There was no unity of either military or diplomatic command. For this the President was primarily responsible. One cannot refrain from adding that the Republican members of the Pearl Harbor inquiry were afterward to spend an inordinate amount of time and money in the effort to prove that there had been such a plan or system; and that if the effort had succeeded they would have crucified the President's memory before the altars of neutrality. But it did not; the inquiry was forced to absolve Mr. Roosevelt from the crime of doing what to many today would seem to have been the one effective and foresighted thing he could have done.

Mr. Roosevelt, vividly aware of the divisive and isolationist forces around him (the *Chicago Tribune* had just supplied an object-lesson), couldn't declare war on Japan. He could not even accept Mr. Churchill's suggestion and issue a warning that a further advance would mean war. With really nothing that he could do, he was forced back to the gesture which he had been considering for days—the appeal to the Japanese Emperor. A draft had been ready in the State Department for a week. The telephones were set busy; and in the course of the late morning or early afternoon the White House and the State Department between them reworked and expanded the draft. Just after 3 there came another message from Winant: "Triple priority, most urgent." The Admiralty had been debating the Japanese convoy movement, and now was in doubt whether the probable destination should be taken as the Kra Isthmus or only Bangkok. At some time during the day there also appeared the draft of a proposed warning to be sent by Britain and the Dominions:

> His Majesty's Governments . . . feel bound therefore to warn the Japanese Government in the most solemn manner that if Japan attempts to establish her influence in Thailand by force or threat of force she will do so at her own peril. . . . Should hostilities unfortunately result the responsibility will rest with Japan.

But the President could not go anything like as far as that; and he wanted to try the effect of his own appeal first. There is evidence indicating that late in the afternoon the Australian minister, Mr. Casey, was orally informed from the President that the latter had decided to send his own message to Hirohito at once; that he would wait for an answer until Monday evening, and that if none came he would issue an American warning on Tuesday afternoon or evening. The British warnings were not to be sent until Wednesday. Such, apparently, was the understanding. The message for Hirohito was sent over to the State Department with a memorandum:

> Dear Cordell: Shoot this to Grew—I think can go in gray code —saves time—I don't mind if it gets picked up. F.D.R.

The draft still required emendation, however, and after some changes it was returned to the White House. Promptly it went back again:

> C.H. O.K.—send the amended p. 3 to the British ambassador & send a copy to me. F.D.R.

The day was waning by this time. In the service departments meanwhile there had been little to do. Unable, unwilling, or unprepared to order any specific counter-action, it was a question still of waiting upon the Japanese. Evidence survives to suggest that during the day Naval Intelligene got wind of the fact that the Japanese embassy in Washington had burned its codes and ciphers the night before. Late in the afternoon a dispatch from the Chief of Naval Operations went direct to Kimmel:

> In view of the international situation and the exposed position of our outlying Pacific islands you may authorize the destruction by them of secret and confidential documents now or under later conditions of greater emergency. . . .

But even so, there was no great sense of urgency about it. The message was not given top priority, and Kimmel could not recall that he saw it until after the attack.

At the State Department they had got the Hirohito message in order by dinnertime. Most of Washington had long since knocked off for the Saturday half-holiday; the evening parties were beginning; people were thinking about the theater or the movies, and countless officers and officials with a hard week's work behind them were looking forward to a leisurely Sunday morning. Perhaps among them were the small group of scientific men who had attended a secret section meeting that day in the Office of Scientific Research and Development. Dr. J. B. Conant, speaking for the director, Dr. Vannevar Bush, had told them that the government intended to put an "all-out" effort behind the development of an atomic bomb.

Just at 8 o'clock the State Department got a pilot message on the wires for Ambassador Grew: "An important telegram is now being encoded to you containing . . . text of message from the President to the Emperor." At the White House at the same moment the President, momentarily relieved of the day's cares, was sitting down with a large but mainly unofficial list of dinner guests. The doubtless cheerful patter went around the table—the President was always a lively host —while across the street the code clerks labored in the State Department. At 9 o'clock the main message went off to the Tokyo embassy:

> Almost a century ago the President of the United States addressed to the Emperor of Japan a message extending an offer of

friendship. . . . That offer was accepted, and in the long period of unbroken peace and friendship which has followed, our respective nations, through the virtues of their peoples and the wisdom of their rulers have prospered. . . . Developments are occurring in the Pacific area which threaten to deprive each of our nations and all humanity of the beneficial influence of the long peace between our two countries. . . . Both Japan and the United States should agree to eliminate any form of military threat. . . .

During the past few weeks it has become clear . . . that Japanese . . . forces have been sent to southern Indo-China in such large numbers as to create a reasonable doubt on the part of other nations that this continuing concentration in Indo-China is not defensive in its character. . . .

I am sure that Your Majesty will understand that the fear of all these peoples [of the southwest Pacific] is a legitimate fear. . . . I am sure that Your Majesty will understand why the people of the United States in such large number look askance at the establishment of . . . bases manned and equipped so greatly as to constitute armed forces capable of measures of offense.

It is clear that a continuance of such a situation is unthinkable. None of the peoples whom I have spoken of above can sit either indefinitely or permanently on a keg of dynamite.

There is absolutely no thought on the part of the United States of invading Indo-China. . . . I address myself to Your Majesty at this moment in the fervent hope that Your Majesty may, as I am doing, give thought in this definite emergency to ways of dispelling the dark clouds. . . .

The fact that such a message was being sent, though not its text, had been given to the correspondents, and they were busy finishing up the stories soon to blossom on the radio and under big headlines in the Sunday morning papers. At the White House the President had withdrawn from the dinner party and gone to his study on the second floor, where he was sitting with his close friend and advisor, Mr. Harry Hopkins. At about 9:30 there was an usher at the door with Lieutenant L. R. Schulz, the junior naval aide on duty. Lieutenant Schulz had with him a locked pouch which had just come from "magic." It was something which the President should see at once; and the President seemed to have been expecting it. The officer unlocked the pouch and handed Mr. Roosevelt a bulky message. While Mr. Hopkins paced the room, the President went through the papers.

Since noontime a hidden drama had been unfolding in the ultra-secret recesses of "magic"—the Army's Signal Intelligence Service and the Navy's Communications Intelligence Unit. The two normally divided the work, the Army doing the decrypting and translating of all intercepts on even days of the month, the Navy on odd days. Each, however, was continuously responsible for its share of the distribution of the material, the Navy disseminating it to the White House, Knox, Stark, and the top naval staff officers, the Army delivering it to the State Department, Stimson, Marshall, and the other authorized Army recipients. Saturday, the 6th, was the Army's day for decoding, and around noon there emerged from the Army's code machine a message from Togo to Nomura of the liveliest interest:

> 1. The Government has deliberated deeply on the American proposal of the 26th of November and as a result we have drawn up a memorandum for the United States contained in my message #902 (in English).
>
> 2. This separate message is a very long one. I will send it in fourteen parts and I imagine you will receive it tomorrow. However, I am not sure. The situation is extremely delicate, and when you receive it I want you to please keep it secret for the time being.
>
> 3. Concerning the time for presenting this memorandum to the United States I will wire you in a separate message. . . . Make every preparation to present it to the Americans just as soon as you receive instructions.

So it was coming at last—the answer to the Ten-Point note, the one missing piece in the pattern. There is evidence that the Army got this, the "pilot" message, to the State Department by 3 in the afternoon; the times of its distribution elsewhere are less clear. The pilot message meant nothing, of course, until the main message should arrive, but it would seem that by late Saturday afternoon various high officials were aware that the Japanese reply was to be expected at any moment.

In the "magic" offices they were on the alert for it. But this was Saturday afternoon, and the Army was still working to Civil Service rules and closing down at 1 on Saturdays. The Navy was organized to work around the clock if need be, and normally kept open until 4:30. Around 1 o'clock the Army appealed to Captain L. F. Safford, commander of the Navy unit, to take over the watch, which was done. At about 3, Lieutenant Commander A. D. Kramer, subordinate to Safford and in immediate charge of the translation and distribution, checked to see whether he should further retain the translators whom he had kept on duty. At that moment a message was arriving which showed in its first sentence that it was Part 8 of the fourteen-part reply announced by the pilot message. Commander Kramer held his staff.

The minutes went by; more parts appeared. As 4:30, the usual closing hour, approached it occurred to Captain Safford that he had efficient men at work and that there was nothing he could do "but get in your way and make you nervous." Unhappily for his place in history, Captain Safford went home at 4:30, and then made the further mistake of going out on a late Saturday evening party. As a result, the captain took no more part in the proceedings, and at 2:30 on the following afternoon he was just having breakfast in his pajamas.

The second hands swept stolidly around the clock dials, telling off the fateful minutes; Admiral Nagumo's propeller shafts were spinning with them, telling off the fateful miles as the task force, now at high speed, raced on a southeasterly course down the Hawaiian chain. At some time before 5 Captain Beardall, the President's naval aide, seems to have been notified that an important message was coming. Captain and Mrs. Beardall had a dinner engagement that evening at the home of Admiral Wilkinson, chief of Naval Intelligence. General Miles, the admiral's opposite number, and Mrs. Miles were also to be there. Captain Beardall left the White House about 5:30, but he ordered Lieutenant Schulz to remain in order to receive the message, and left the pouch key with him. Around 6 the Navy unit found that the intercepts were swamping its code machine, and appealed to the Army to reopen its own. Army complied. Around 7:30, with both units working, they had drafts of thirteen of the parts; the fourteenth and presumably most important had not appeared. As there was no sign of it, Kramer had the thirteen parts smoothed up and prepared for distribution.

It was about a quarter of 9 when Kramer, according to custom, began telephoning the prospective recipients to locate them and let them know that he was coming. He also called his wife to ask her to act as chauffeur. It appeared that Admiral Stark could not be reached; for his Saturday evening's diversion he had gone to a performance of the *The Student Prince* at the National Theater. Admiral Turner of War Plans was also unavailable. But the others were in; and with Mrs. Kramer at the wheel he set out shortly after 9 o'clock. The first stop was the White House, where Kramer handed Schulz the locked pouch with instructions that it was to reach the President immediately. The Kramers then drove on.

Behind them, in the second floor study of the White House, the President read through the dispatch while Mr. Hopkins paced and the young lieutenant waited. From the opening sentences it was obvious that Japan's answer to the November 26 note was not a favorable one. "It is the immutable policy of the Japanese Government to insure the stability of East Asia and to promote world peace. . . . However, both the United States and Great Britain have resorted to every possible measure to assist the Chungking regime so as to obstruct the establishment of a general peace between Japan and China. . . . Those countries have strengthened their military preparations, perfecting an encirclement of Japan, and have brought about a situation which endangers the very existence of the Empire."

The note went on, reviewing with an increasing truculence of tone the negotiations of the preceding months. "Finally, on November 26, in an attitude to impose upon the Japanese Government those principles it has persistently maintained, the American Government made a proposal totally ignoring Japanese claims, which is a source of profound regret to the Japanese government." The note stressed Japan's "fairness," "moderation," and "spirit of conciliation exhibited to the utmost degree," contrasting these with the American government's adamant refusal "to yield an inch on its impractical principles." To "attempt to force their immediate adoption" was only a "Utopian ideal." Our proposals were reviewed and bluntly rejected. The suggested Indo-China non-aggression pact, "which is patterned after the old concept of collective security, is far removed from the realities of East Asia." Our proposal relating to the Tri-Partite Pact was apparently designed "to restrain Japan from fulfilling its obligations" under that pact, "and as such it cannot be accepted by the Japanese Government."

As the President read on the tone grew more hostile still. "The American government, obsessed with its own views and opinions, may be said to be scheming for an extension of the war. . . . It is impossible not to reach the conclusion that the American Government desires to maintain and strengthen . . . its dominant position it has hitherto occupied not only in China but in East Asia as well. . . . The Japanese Government cannot tolerate the perpetuation of such a situation." And then, in Part 13: "The proposal in question ignores Japan's sacrifices in the four years of the China Affair, menaces the Empire's existence itself, and disparages its honor and prestige. Therefore, viewed in its entirety, the Japanese Government regrets that it cannot accept the proposal as a basis of negotiations." That disposed of the November 26 note. A few more sentences included Britain and the Netherlands in Japan's displeasure. At that point, Part 13 ended. What, if anything, Japan proposed would be in the missing Part 14.

The President passed the papers to Mr. Hopkins; he read them and handed them back. "This," the President said in substance, "means war." Hopkins agreed. The two talked it over for a time. They spoke of the Japanese deployment in the southwest and the indications that Japan was preparing to strike when she was ready, at the most opportune moment. The President mentioned his message of the afternoon to Hirohito. It occurred to Mr. Hopkins to say that since war was undoubtedly coming it was too bad that we could not strike the first blow. The President nodded and then said, in effect, "No, we can't do that. We are a democracy and a peaceful people." Then he raised his voice, and the lieutenant definitely remembered his saying: "But we have a good record"; we would have to stand on it and simply wait for what was coming. The President thought of calling "Betty" Stark, but the word came back over the telephone that the admiral was at the National Theater, and the President postponed the call as he did not want to cause public alarm by summoning him from the performance. The lieutenant could not recall that anything was said about reaching anyone else or about possible warnings to the field commanders, and he was quite sure that Pearl Harbor was not mentioned. The papers were handed back to him and he withdrew. He had heard that they "meant war." But nothing in the conversation suggested that either the President or Hopkins thought that war was coming the next day.*

Truculent and uncompromising as it was, the message, after all, was not yet complete and it was being sent under orders to Nomura to hold it until further instructions. Mr. Roosevelt,

* The testimony of Captain Harold D. Krick, Admiral Stark's flag secretary, seems to establish the fact that the admiral talked with the White House after his return from the theater that evening and learned that the situation was critical. Stark himself had no recollection of this, or of any of his activities on Saturday evening.

like the others who read the thirteen parts that night, might well have felt that there was a little time still before the crisis would break. None that evening, at any rate, seems to have evaluated the thirteen parts as a call to immediate action. Commander Kramer had gone on to his next stop, Secretary Knox's apartment at the Wardman Park. He found the Secretary with Mrs. Knox and a civilian newspaper associate. Mr. Knox drew to one side and went through the message. The presence of the others precluded much conversation, but the Secretary exchanged a few words with Kramer on certain points. Kramer recalled that the Secretary then stepped out to the telephone; when he returned he told the officer that a meeting of Hull, Stimson, and himself had been arranged for 10 next morning at the State Department, and that Kramer was to report there with Part 14 or anything else that might have come in.*

Kramer returned to the car, where his wife was waiting for him, and they drove out to Arlington to find Admiral and Mrs. Wilkinson's party in full swing. General Miles and Captain Beardall were both there; and since these, with Wilkinson, were authorized to receive "magic," all four men went into a side room to study the papers. This was the first that General Miles or any others on the Army list saw of the message. The Army's "magic" people seem to have taken a less urgent view of the matter than had Commander Kramer, and when they found the message still incomplete that evening they apparently† decided to call it a day and leave their distribution until the morning when the missing part might be in. Even now that Miles had the Navy's copy in his hands, it didn't

* There is some conflict of evidence as to the precise origin of this unusual Sunday conference. While it was apparently inspired by the arrival of the Japanese note, it may have been first suggested earlier in the evening, perhaps as a result of the pilot message, or simply by the Japanese troop movements.

† Again there is direct conflict of evidence on the point. This seems to the present author to be the most probable interpretation.

strike him as of primary "military significance" and he made no effort to reach General Marshall or even to find out whether the message had been delivered to Secretary Hull. Admiral Wilkinson was concerned to assure himself that Kramer had got it to the White House, and Beardall called to check with Schulz. Wilkinson also did some telephoning, and may at this time have mentioned the matter to Admiral Turner of War Plans. But to the group at Wilkinson's house it seemed mainly a business for the diplomats. Kramer was not directed to make any further efforts that night to get the message to Stark or Turner. Indeed, all four rejoined the party and the patient Mrs. Kramer was invited in from the car to chat for a while. At about 12:30 the Kramers drove away. The commander stopped to return the documents to the "magic" office, checked with the watch officer, and found that nothing more had appeared; and then went home to catch a little sleep against what he realized was likely to prove a strenuous day.

III ☞

By 1:30 o'clock, Sunday morning, December 7, most of Washington was, presumably, asleep. At Hamilton Field, San Francisco, it was 10:30 Saturday evening, and a flight of six B-17's was just thundering down the runway and rising off over the Pacific. They were bound for Oahu, 2,400 miles away, as their first stop on the long road to Manila. Six others had left an hour before; and the twelve represented the first element of the 7th Bombardment Group, for which Brereton and MacArthur had been so impatiently waiting. They had been held up by weather and other delays; everyone was in a fever to see them off, and General "Hap" Arnold was there in person to hurry them on their way. General Arnold, who like everyone else had a great deal more to learn about air power than he realized at the time, was "sure in my own mind" that if only he could get enough of the big bombers "out there we could make an attack upon the Philippines unsuccessful." The Commanding General of the Army Air Force himself briefed the squadron leaders and staffs. "I told them at that time that they might run into trouble. I told them that they should have their guns ready and that they might have a fight on their hands." But the only "trouble" which the general envisaged was that which might be encountered beyond Pearl Harbor. To insure a safe gasoline supply for the long initial hop the planes were, as usual, dispatched with no ammunition whatever, with skeleton crews and with the guns in cosmoline. One B-17 was forced to turn back during the night; the remaining eleven droned on toward an early morning arrival at Pearl.

As the last of them was taking off from Hamilton Field, Admiral Nagumo's task force was racing on its southeasterly course into the deepening night. It would be another hour and a half until they came to their turning point, where they were to alter course to due south and head straight in at top speed for the flying-off position, 200 miles north of Oahu. In Nagumo's flagship, *Akagi,* they had the radios tuned to the Honolulu local station, thinking that if their approach were discovered they would hear signs of alarm. The normal succession of commercials, music, and patter flowed unsuspectingly along. It was 8 o'clock on a Saturday night in Hawaii; the week's military activities were largely suspended; the cocktail and dinner parties were well along. That south Pacific war crisis was 6,000 miles away around the curve of the great globe, and tomorrow was the day off.

This is not to imply that the Saturday at Pearl had been free from cares. For the past week Admiral Kimmel, thorough as always, had been making up a memorandum each morning: "Steps to be taken in case of American-Japanese war within the next twenty-four hours." That Saturday he brought it up to date as usual in accordance with current dispositions. It began: "(1). Send dispatch to Pacific Fleet that hostilities have commenced," and continued, listing various moves to be taken. "Patrol plane plans," it noted, "will become effective without special reference."

Admiral Kimmel had spent most of the morning going over the whole situation with his second-in-command, Vice Admiral Pye, commander of the battleships. In the afternoon he had "spoiled a couple of golf games" by keeping his planning and operations officers for further discussions. One important matter was Hart's dispatch reporting the Japanese off Cape Cambodia. Kimmel ultimately sent it over to Pye, in the latter's quarters in the *California*, by his Fleet Intelligence officer, Layton. But Pye and his staff were inclined to the view that though Japan was apparently about to strike, she would not initially take on the United States by striking at the Philippines or Guam. Not one of them seems even remotely to have imagined that Japan might at that moment be on the point of attacking Pearl Harbor.

Over at Fort Shafter the Army had been proceeding in a more routine way. The usual Saturday morning staff conference, presided over by Colonel Phillips, Short's chief of staff, had been held. The purpose of these meetings was to bring up "any points of information or of interest" that had arisen during the week, and Lieutenant Colonel George W. Bicknell, the assistant G-2, had one point that might seem to have been of considerable interest. The Navy had not seen fit to pass on through official channels its information about the Japanese destruction of codes, but Colonel Bicknell had established close relations with Navy Intelligence and the F.B.I. and had learned of the matter a day or two before. At this Saturday conference he reported that he had information "to the effect that the Japanese consuls were burning their papers; and to me that had very serious intent; it would at least show that something was about to happen, somewhere." But to the rest it just seemed a "routine matter"; neither his immediate chief, Fielder, the G-2, nor Phillips appeared to be particularly impressed and there was no discussion.

One of the Army's mobile radar sets, designated as the

Opana Station, had been installed up an isolated wood track on the precipitous north slope of Oahu, some thirty miles from Shafter. Around noon, with the arrival of two relief men, the regular crew had closed it down and departed for the week end. The primary duty of the relief men, Privates Joseph L. Lockard and George E. Elliott, was to guard the instrument. Lockard, however, had received training as an operator, and the two were under orders to man the set during the prescribed hours from 4 to 7 on Sunday morning. Lockard and Elliott made themselves comfortable until that time should arrive.

The bulk of the Army's fighter planes, at Wheeler Field, were ranked on the aprons. At Bellows, on the east side of the island, the fighter squadron which had been doing target practice had parked its planes, emptied the gas tanks, removed the guns for cleaning, and given week-end leave to many of its pilots. The squadron at Haleiwa, on the northwest coast, was in much the same state. Admiral Bellinger's PBY fleet was secured for the week end, most of those at Pearl having been hauled out on the ramps, those at Kaneohe (next to Bellows) being moored in rows in the harbor as there was insufficient room ashore to receive them. The season's biggest local football game was played that afternoon (the Japanese in Nagumo's ships no doubt followed it with interest on their radios) and there were numerous parties afterward.

About 4 in the afternoon Colonel Bicknell received a telephone call in his quarters. It was Mr. R. L. Shivers, local head of the F.B.I., saying that he had "something of immediate importance." Bicknell jumped into his car and drove to his office, which had been established in rooms adjoining Shivers' in a downtown Honolulu office building. Shivers handed him a rather odd document, the transcript of a transocean telephone conversation between a certain Dr. Mori, a Japanese dentist in Honolulu, and someone in Tokyo. It had been intercepted a day or two before, and they had just completed an English translation. It was a strange kind of conversation on which to spend oceanic telephone tolls. While there was a lot in it about flying conditions at Oahu, the number of troops and seamen on the streets, and so on, all that seemed rather innocuous. But one or two apparently quite innocent passages about the varieties of flowers then in bloom in Honolulu had a highly suspect look. The whole thing seemed funny, but was difficult to evaluate. Bicknell got his superior, Fielder, on the telephone and said that he had something which he must show to Fielder and to General Short at once.

The G-2 was unenthusiastic. He and Short were on the point of setting out for a dinner at Schofield; the thing had better wait until morning. But Bicknell was insistent, and was finally told that if he could get back to Fort Shafter in ten minutes, the general and his G-2 would wait for him. Bicknell stepped on the gas and made it in the ten minutes, handing over the transcript. Short couldn't make anything out of it; neither could Fielder, but they saw no reason to get excited over it. They seemed to think that their energetic assistant G-2 was "rather perhaps too 'intelligence conscious' "; they handed back the paper and went their way to the dinner party.*

The calm Pacific evening fell. Short did not stay late at his dinner at Schofield; no doubt he was finishing his coffee and preparing to depart by 9:30, just as Nagumo's task force

* This follows Bicknell's account; Fielder's was somewhat different. In fairness, moreover, it must be pointed out that there is no evidence as to what was the real significance of the Mori message, if any. And it may be added that two messages which were highly significant, intercepted that day by "magic," were not translated until it was too late. They were from the consul in Honolulu. One said, "Considerable opportunity left to take advantage of a surprise attack"; the other, "It appears that no air reconnaissance is being conducted by the fleet air arm." By a grim irony, they were intercepted by an Army monitoring unit at Honolulu and they were in a code which the Navy District Intelligence unit at Pearl Harbor was able to read. But there was no liaison between the two, as "magic" operations were strictly controlled from Washington.

was making its turn south and beginning the final run in to the fly-off. The B-17's from Hamilton Field were well out over the Pacific by that time. At Oahu, while many were enjoying the relaxations of Saturday evening, there were many on duty. The battleships, neatly moored two by two along Ford Island, were in "Condition 3" with about a quarter of the anti-aircraft batteries manned, with the rest capable of being put promptly into action, and with all watertight doors closed except, unfortunately, in *California*, whose compartments had been opened up for maintenance. The net vessels were tending the anti-submarine gates at the harbor entrance. The Army's anti-sabotage guards were walking their beats; and the two privates at Opana had been duly provided with an automatic pistol with which to repel unauthorized visitors. *U.S.S. Ward*, duty destroyer on patrol off the harbor entrance that night, was cruising in her assigned station, all hands alert. Shortly after midnight two minesweepers, *Condor* and *Crossbill*, stood down the channel to perform the prescribed nightly sweep of the entrance.

Pearl Harbor, as the public relations officers had told the reporters, was "virtually on a war footing"—yet Pearl Harbor was also profoundly at peace. By a long, complicated collocation of accident, custom, mischance, misunderstanding, overconfidence, and want of imagination, our great Pacific fortress and the fleet which was the one key to Pacific mastery had been brought to a condition in which both were about as completely exposed to the impending attack as would have been possible short of actual treason. There had been no change in the week-end routines. Virtually the entire fleet (with the fortunate exception of the Wake and Midway task forces) had been brought into harbor and moored where it would offer the surest and simplest target. About one-third of its captains and one-third to one-half the officer personnel were ashore. There were no barrage balloons and no torpedo baffles. There was no reconnaissance; there were no offshore patrols of any kind. The one working means whereby adequate warning might have been given—the Army's radar—was in a purely training status. The only planes which could have acted upon a warning were parked wing to wing, on four hours' notice. The naval vessels did have their anti-aircraft weapons in a reasonable state of readiness; but the Army's anti-aircraft artillery had most of its 3-inch guns, the major reliance, in the gun-parks with their ammunition in the magazines. To draw the latter and get the guns in firing position was a matter of between one and four hours.

With the best will in the world, and bent only on the efficient discharge of their great trust, the three responsible guardians of Pearl Harbor—Kimmel, Short, Bloch—had somehow managed to violate nearly every precept of history and of military security, and thus to lay the great base as open as possible to the precise form of attack which all of them had recognized, theoretically, as the most to be feared. And they had managed to do this on the very evening when, as Hart's dispatch plainly told them, war in the Pacific could be expected to break out within a matter of hours.

The midnight passed. Nagumo's propellers were racing now; the planes would soon be warming up on the flight decks. The B-17's were reeling off the uneventful miles beneath the stars. On *Condor's* bridge the watch officer, a reserve ensign, R. C. McCloy, was peering into the dark waves as the sweep proceeded. In the little camp at Opana, Lockard and Elliott would soon start to bestir themselves for that 4 to 7 watch. The enlisted men of the central plotting crew would soon be preparing to report at the "shack" at Fort Shafter. Lieutenant Kermit A. Tyler, one of Major Bergquist's young fighter pilots, would soon be turning out to go down to the Information Center, stand the 4 to 7 trick, and learn whatever he thereby could about the "set-up." And some 2,300 men, more or less, who had less than twelve hours to live were in merciful ignorance of the fact.

Some time before 4 Lieutenant Tyler got his car and drove off for the Information Center at Shafter. The night was pleasant; he had his radio turned on, and as he drove along it continued even at that late hour to emit soft Hawaiian airs. Lieutenant Tyler remembered that a friend serving with the bombers had told him that the B-17's for the Philippines used the Honolulu commercial station to "home" on in the run from the mainland. Hearing it so late, it occurred to him that another B-17 flight must be coming in.

IV ☞

It was some hours before this that Commander Kramer had gone home to get some sleep, leaving Lieutenant F. M. Brotherhood in charge of the "graveyard shift" at the Communications Intelligence Unit in the Navy Department. Lieutenant Brotherhood's recollections of the events of the ensuing historic hours were afterwards, unfortunately, somewhat hazy. It seems to have been shortly after 5 (Washington time) that the teletype produced what was to prove the missing fourteenth part of the Japanese reply. Though most of it came out, upon decoding, in English,* Japanese was used for address, times, punctuation, and so on, and the message consequently had to be processed by the translators. As there were none in the Navy section, Brotherhood sent the message down the hall to the Army's section of "magic." Presently a couple of more messages showed up; when these emerged from the code machine they proved to be entirely in Japanese, and Brotherhood likewise sent them along to the Army for translation. A couple of hours passed. No one seems to have felt any great sense of haste. In those days one hardly expected to find top civilian officials or the high brass—the only authorized recipients—functioning at 6 o'clock on a Sunday morning.

* Togo had sent the text of the note in English to avoid errors—or possibly any softening by Nomura—in translation.

Up to this point the one man who does seem to have felt a sense of urgency was Commander Kramer. Though he cannot have turned in much before 1 o'clock, he was at his office again by 7:30. As he arrived he found either complete or in process of completeion the missing text of Part 14. The very fact that the Japanese had delayed its tranmission for some twelve hours after the dispatch of the other thirteen parts alone signaled its importance; and a glance at the wording should have been enough for anyone even generally familiar with the negotiations:

> Obviously it is the intention of the American Government to conspire with Great Britain and other countries to obstruct Japan's efforts toward the establishment of peace through the creation of a New Order in East Asia, and especially to preserve Anglo-American rights and interests by keeping Japan and China at war. . . . Thus the earnest hope of the Japanese Government to adjust Japanese-American relations and to preserve and promote the peace of the Pacific through co-operation with the American Government has finally been lost.
>
> The Japanese Government . . . cannot but consider that it is impossible to reach an agreement through further negotiations.

About the only recipient then available was Commander A. H. McCollum, chief of the Far Eastern section of Naval Intelligence, and Kramer took it to him shortly after 8. Back in his own office he had the whole fourteen parts assembled, together with some further "magic" material that had meanwhile come in, and placed in fresh folders ready for distribution. At about a quarter of 9 Kramer heard that Admiral Wilkinson had arrived, and he knew that Admiral Stark was expected, so he took two of these folders along to McCollum. It was apparently not until around 9 o'clock that the Army section began to get into action. Kramer, meanwhile, was working up additional material for the folders. About 9:30 he set out. His first stop was at Admiral Stark's office, where the Chief of Naval Operations had now arrived; he then hurried up to the White House, left the folder for Captain

Beardall, and crossed to the State Department. He got there at ten minutes before 10, just as the Army courier was arriving with his copy of the fourteen-part message for Secretary Hull. Secretary Knox appeared within five minutes; Kramer gave him his folder and then hastened back to the Navy Department.

Beardall meanwhile had carried the fourteen parts up to the President's bedroom. Mr. Roosevelt went through the whole message without apparent excitement. Beardall remembered his saying that "it looks as though the Japs are going to break off negotiations," but could not recall anything implying that the message meant immediate war. In the Navy Department Stark, Ingersoll, Turner, and Wilkinson were all on deck, hashing over the fourteenth part. Wilkinson thought that these were "fighting words" and suggested the advisability of a further warning to the Philippines, but Stark did not respond.

Shortly before 10:30 the industrious Kramer was back at his office. The first thing he saw was the translation of one of the Japanese-language messages that had come in early that morning:

> Re my #902
> Will the ambassador please submit to the United States Government (if possible to the Secretary of State) our reply to the United States at 1:00 P.M. on the 7th, your time.

Here was the tip-off.

The message had been intercepted by the monitoring station on the Pacific coast at 4:37 that morning (Washington time). To teletype it to Washington, decode it, translate it, and get it into the hands of an officer capable of understanding its crucial importance had taken just about six hours. The fatal moment to which it pointed was now but two and a half hours away. (Nagumo, had they only known it, was but one and a half hours from his fly-off point.) In the few minutes which it took his yeoman to type up the message and get it in the folders, Kramer sketched a "time circle" on a scrap of paper. It showed him at a glance that 1:00 P.M. at Washington would be an hour after midnight on the Kra Isthmus and shortly after dawn at Oahu. He hurried down the corridor to Admiral Stark's office.

General Marshall, who had presumably remained at his home at Fort Myer, had heard nothing on the preceding evening about the Japanese reply. The Chief of Staff was usually early at his office on weekdays, but on Sundays he allowed himself more leisure. Unwarned that anything crucial was impending, on this particular Sunday he had breakfasted and then gone out, in accordance with a frequent custom, for a horseback ride. There is more conflict among Army witnesses as to the exact times of that morning's events than is the case with the Navy's witnesses; but at any rate it seems plain that as the general was cantering through the Virginia woods, probably between 8:30 and 9:00 o'clock, the Army Intelligence people began to awake to the seriousness of what they had on their hands.

Colonel Rufus S. Bratton, McCollum's opposite number as chief of the Far Eastern section of Military Intelligence, also had duties corresponding to those of Kramer in the custody and distribution of "magic." Before 9 o'clock Colonel Bratton, was, according to his own account, trying furiously to reach General Marshall (who might easily have been warned the night before) on the telephone. The orderly at Fort Myer said the general had gone horseback riding. Bratton told the orderly to find him at once: "Get assistance if necessary, and find General Marshall, ask him to—tell him who I am and tell him to go to the nearest telephone, that it is vitally important that I communicate with him at the earliest possible moment." If this search was actually organized it failed in its mission. The general completed his ride, still unsuspecting, returned to his quarters, and was taking his shower when word finally came that Bratton was trying to reach him. As Bratton remembers it, it was nearly 10:30 when the general telephoned the War Department. By that time the colonel presumably had the "1 o'clock" message. But he could not discuss "magic" secrets over the telephone. He offered to drive at once to Fort Myer, but the general said no, he was on his way in.

In the meanwhile Bratton had been telephoning Miles and Gerow, chief of War Plans, hastening their Sunday morning shaves and breakfasts. The Navy had been in conclave for some time when the Army high command at last began to assemble. Apparently, it was not until after 11:00 o'clock that the Chief of Staff finally reached his office in the War Department and saw, for the first time, the long fourteen-part Japanese reply. Some twenty-three hours had elapsed since the translation of the pilot message which had announced its coming.

At about 10:30 Kramer had hurried to Stark's office with the "1 o'clock" message, as well as some further intercepts, in which the Washington embassy was instructed to destroy its last codes. McCollum came to the door; Kramer gave him the folder and hastily indicated the concidence of the hour named with the Pacific times. McCollum, a trained naval officer, "reacted instantaneously," and in a few seconds Kramer was on his way back to the State Department. He was there in another ten minutes. Secretary Knox was still in conference with the two other secretaries. Perforce Kramer had to turn the folder over to a State Department attaché for delivery in the conference room; but the naval officer was concerned to get his point about the times to Mr. Knox who, being a civilian, might not, he thought, grasp their significance as readily as McCollum had done. He gave the State Department man a quick take on the matter. But like everyone else even Kramer, at that moment, had his mind focused on the Kra. It had occurred to him as he sketched his "time circle" that the indicated 7:30 at Pearl on a Sunday morning—just the moment when naval crews were normally piped to breakfast—would be the "quietest time of the week." But he did not claim afterward (and it adds to one's respect for his testimony) that he did more than mention Pearl "in passing"; it was in the early morning hour at Kota Bharu of which he was thinking. Kramer hastened on to the White House and thence back to the Navy Department. He saw nothing more of the high officers; his efficient role in that historic hour was done.

The "1 o'clock" message had failed to energize the naval high command. When at 11:25 Miles, accompanied by Bratton bearing the "1 o'clock" message, entered General Marshall's office, they found the Chief of Staff still engrossed in the fourteen-part message—which took time to read, especially if one had not seen it before and were trying to weigh the implications of every phrase. Miles and Bratton tried to interrupt in order to call attention to the new intercept, but interrupting a four-star general isn't so easy. It was not, perhaps, until 11:30—with the fatal moment then only an hour and a half away—that Marshall actually saw the vital message which had been intercepted at 4:37 that morning.

By still another of the innumerable ironies of the story—ironies that almost convince one that Pearl Harbor was decreed by a remorseless predestination—the Navy, which had displayed the greater alertness on the lower echelons, had run into lethargy at the top level; the top levels of the Army, on the other hand, which were now to prove themselves capable of action, had been left in ignorance by inertia in the lower echelons. It was not until about 11:30, when Marshall called Gerow into his office, that the chief of War Plans first saw the fourteen-part reply or even heard of the "1 o'clock" message. But at that moment it came home to all of them—Marshall, Gerow, Miles, and Bratton—that a Pacific war was almost certainly going to start somewhere in another hour and a half.

Marshall caught up the telephone and got Admiral Stark. Ought they not advise the Pacific commanders? The Chief of Naval Operations was unresponsive; he thought they had sent enough war warnings already. Marshall dropped the telephone and started writing a message in long-hand for MacArthur * and Short. In a few minutes the telephone rang; it was Stark who, on thinking it over, had perceived that there might be something in the suggestion. He did not offer to send a message of his own, but asked that the Army message include instructions that it be passed on to the naval commanders.† Marshall wrote on:

> 529 7th Japanese are presenting at 1 P.M eastern standard time today what amounts to an ultimatum also they are under orders to destroy their code machine immediately. Just what significance the hour set may have we do not know but be on alert accordingly. Inform naval authorities of this communication. MARSHALL

Another minute or two went to the question of whether it should be sent to War Plans to be typed up, but the clock hands answered that one. Bratton was sent down the hall with the penciled telegram to the Message Center. When he returned, Marshall asked how soon it would be transmitted, and Bratton went back to find out. The duty officer at the Message Center told him that it would be on its way in ten minutes and would be delivered at Manila and Pearl Harbor within half an hour. That would still provide at least thirty minutes' warning. Marshall did not resort to the "scrambler" telephone, which, as he afterwards contended, was of doubtful security. According to the Message Center notation, the telegram was filed at exactly 12 noon. It was finally delivered

* Miles's memorandum, contemporary but set down after the attack: "There was some discussion as to whether the Philippines should be included or not." Marshall's testimony, on the other hand, indicates that the Philippines were the first consideration and Hawaii the afterthought.

† This is the account as given by both officers. It has been noted, however, that the two calls, one at 11:30 and one at 11:40, shown on the records of the White House switchboard as passing between Marshall and Stark at this time were both logged as originating with Marshall. The first call from Stark to Marshall is logged at 12:10, after the dispatch of the message.

at General Short's headquarters on Oahu eight and a half hours later—eight and a half hours in which the whole course of history had changed. The message was filed in one era of our world civilization. When it was delivered another had begun.*

At 12 noon in Washington the first of Nagumo's 360 aircraft were just roaring off the flight decks in the dawning light 200 miles north of Oahu. Had the message gone instantly upon the writing it would have been too late; in the hour or so remaining neither Short nor Kimmel could have done much to put themselves in a posture of defense. Even if it had gone six or seven hours earlier, when the "1 o'clock" intercept came into the "magic" offices, one may still wonder whether it would have made much difference. Six hours would have given ample time to alert the command, but in the prevailing psychology at Pearl Harbor would either Short or Kimmel have realized the necessity for doing so? It is another question which is in its nature unanswerable.

Secretaries Hull, Stimson, and Knox were still in conference when Kramer sent in the "1 o'clock" message shortly before 11. Whatever the State Department attaché may have conveyed to Knox concerning the time, that was patently the business of the military rather than the civilian heads. It seems rather clear that the civilian secretaries were concerned with a different aspect of the problem. They were still worried by the question of whether, when the expected attack upon the British took place, the United States could be immediately brought in. Mr. Stimson was sufficiently struck by his col-

* After giving its assurance to the Chief of Staff, the Message Center discovered that it could not raise Pearl Harbor over the Army radio, because of static difficulties. The message was sent to Western Union for commercial transmission. The Honolulu office, at some distance from Fort Shafter, confided the telegram to a messenger boy who set off on his bicycle. He was pedaling on his way when the first bombs fell, and not unnaturally spent the next couple of hours in a roadside ditch.

leagues' remarks to get them to call in a stenographer and dictate memoranda. Secretary Hull's began:

> The Japanese Government, dominated by the military fire-eaters, is deliberately proceeding on an increasingly broad front to carry out its long-proclaimed purpose to acquire military control over one-half of the world. . . .

Secretary Knox's was even more to the point:

> We are tied up inextricably with the British in the present world situation. . . . Any serious threat to the British or the Dutch is a serious threat to the United States. . . . I think the Japanese should be told that any movement in a direction that threatens the United States should be met by force. . . .

And so on. "The main thing," according to Mr. Stimson's own diary note on the meeting, "is to hold the main people who are interested in the Far East together." It was nearly noon when the secretaries ended their deliberations. Mr. Stimson went home to lunch. Mr. Knox departed for his office. As they were leaving there was a telephone call from the Japanese ambassador. Admiral Nomura requested an interview with the Secretary of State for 1:00 P.M. that day.

The minutes dripped away. Presently there was another call from the Japanese embassy; it was forced to request that the meeting be postponed until 1:45, as the ambassador was not quite ready. Mr. Hull may have grimly wondered whether the Japanese, after all the code-burning they had been doing, were having more trouble decoding their own dispatches than we had experienced. The 1 o'clock hour passed. The half hour passed. Mr. Stimson was finishing his luncheon. Mr. Knox was on the point of ordering a lunch for himself in his office. And then, at 1:50, there came suddenly out of the unfathomable ether into the Navy radio station at Washington a dispatch so astounding, so totally unlooked-for, as to be almost incredible:

From: C-in-C Pacific Fleet
Action: C-in-C Atlantic Fleet, C-in-C Asiatic Fleet, Chief of Naval Operations
AIR RAID ON PEARL HARBOR. THIS IS NOT DRILL

Stark and Turner were both in Knox's office as the dispatch was brought in. "My God!" Knox exclaimed, "this can't be true! This must mean the Philippines."

"No sir," said Stark. "This is Pearl."

EIGHT

A VERY UNFORTUNATE THING

I ☞

As the "magic" rooms were really getting into action around 9 o'clock on Sunday morning at Washington, it was 3:30 A.M. at Oahu. *U.S.S. Condor*, continuing her routine sweep, was a mile or two southwest of the Pearl Harbor entrance buoy shortly after 3:30; and from her bridge Ensign McCloy, USNR, was scanning the dark surface of the surrounding waters as a good watch officer should. Suddenly his eye was caught by a fleck of white against the darkness. He thought it was a breaking wave; but as he studied it, it did not seem to act like a wave. He picked up the binoculars, at the same time calling over the quartermaster to have a look. The phenomenon was not over 50 yards away, and both men were convinced that what they were peering at was the periscope of a submerged submarine, trailing its telltale white "feather" behind it. In that submarine-conscious command no more dramatic a sight could possibly have met the eyes of a reserve ensign.

The captain was called. The destroyer *Ward*, pursuing her patrol, was not far away, and at about five minutes to 4 *Condor* signaled her by blinker light that she had spotted a submerged submarine. In that area such a vessel could only be hostile. *Ward* immediately went to general quarters and closed up with the minesweeper, but listening as intently as they could they were unable to get a sound contact. The submarine, if it really was a submarine, had vanished. There was some brief conversation between the two vessels by voice radio; this was picked up on shore, but it was not the duty of the shore operators to report overheard messages of the kind. At 4:35 *Ward* thanked *Condor* for her information, asked to be notified if they got anything more, and said that she would continue the search. Neither ship reported the incident. Alleged submarine sightings or contacts were always rather suspect. *Condor's* captain did not feel wholly sure of his young ensign's report. *Ward's* captain sensed this dubiety in *Condor;* he thought that what they had actually seen was possibly a stick or a buoy. Ordering the search kept up, *Ward's* captain himself turned in. Pearl Harbor slept on through the peaceful night.

Pearl Harbor slept, except, of course, for those on duty. Over at Kaneohe they were warming up three PBY's for the usual morning anti-submarine patrol and four more were preparing at Ford Island for exercises they were to carry out at Lahaina that day. At 4:00 A.M. Privates Lockard and Elliott, in their lonely eyrie on Oahu's north shoulder, had put the Opana radar set into operation. Methodically, Lockard swept the unseen levels of the sea before him while Elliott kept the plot. Nothing of consequence appeared in the oscilloscope. In the "shack" at Fort Shafter, at the same time, young Lieutenant Tyler was somewhat idly observing the work of the enlisted telephonists and plotting crew as they received what reports came in from the five operating sets. It was only his second tour at the Information Center and he understood that his duties were still primarily to learn what he could about the system. For that, the outlook was scarcely promising as he found himself the only officer present.

In combat operation the room would have been in command of a control officer. The field reports came in to the enlisted crew over their telephone headsets; these men plotted the reports on the board. The controller, following events on the board, would have general direction over all necessary measures. It was his function to alert air and anti-aircraft commands and the Navy, to order interceptor squadrons into action, to guide and correlate all operations in defense. Under him he was supposed to have a Navy officer, an anti-aircraft officer, a "pursuit" officer, and so on to transmit his orders to the various commands and to keep him informed of what they were doing. This was the very minimum of organization essential to the functioning of the center, especially since at that time we had no "FFI," the ingenious British invention which enabled the searching radars to distinguish instantly between friend and foe. The plotted reports were virtually meaningless in the absence of liaison officers who would know where our own aircraft were and would thus, between them, be able either to identify a reported plane or to determine it to be a stranger. This kind of liaison was particularly necessary at Pearl Harbor, since the security-minded Navy never told the Army what it was up to or when its patrol and carrier-borne aviation might appear in the air.

Nothing of this organization existed on that Sunday morning. The Navy had never got around to assigning any liaison officers at all for the work. There was no controller present. The industrious Major Bergquist, who would normally have acted as a controller, had evidently allowed himself a Sunday of leisure. There was no officer there except Tyler, and while he was technically "pursuit officer," he knew virtually nothing about the job. His later testimony was illuminating:

Q: You really had no conception of what your duties were?
A: I had very little, sir.
Q: This was purely a practice run, to your knowledge?
A: Yes, sir.
Q: There was actually no one stationed in readiness that Sunday morning?
A: No.
Q: There was nothing in readiness?
A: No, sir.

As General Short was afterward to explain, since his fighter aviation was on four hours' notice at best, and since his radars could not be expected to give more than thirty minutes' warning, the only reason for operating them at all that morning was "largely because it was new and they needed training in it more than any other element of the command."

Lieutenant Tyler whiled away the time watching the enlisted men. Dawn would be coming around 6, and an hour afterward the radar watch would be over. Pearl Harbor continued to sleep. *U.S.S. Ward* continued her patrol. Shortly after 6 *U.S.S. Antares*, an ancient "Hog Island" freighter converted to the humble duties of tending targets, came plodding by with a target barge in tow, standing toward Honolulu harbor. *Ward* exchanged signals with her and passed her on. The light was brightening by that time across the graying levels and *Ward's* helmsman, his eye no doubt following the receding *Antares*, all at once noticed that there was something in her wake. He called it to the attention of the j.g., Lieutenant Goepner, who had the deck at the time. It looked like a buoy, but as they watched it appeared to be pursuing *Antares* at a round speed, which was very unusual behavior for a buoy. Goepner turned and rapped on the door of the emergency cabin just behind him: "Captain, come on the bridge!" *Ward's* captain, Lieutenant Commander W. W. Outerbridge, bounded out "as fast as I could." The night's submarine alarm had made them all alert. A short study convinced Outerbridge that the buoy-like object was the conning tower of a submarine running awash and apparently trying to slip into Honolulu under cover of *Antares*. *Ward* went to general quarters at 6:40; the engines were rung full ahead and she charged down, her gun muzzles searching on to the target.

At 6:45 A.M., December 7, *U.S.S. Ward* fired the first shots of the Pacific war. Her 4-inch rifles barked, and on the second salvo one shot landed squarely at the base of the conning tower. It disappeared. *Ward* raced past and dropped a salvo of depth charges where the submarine had been. One of the

PBY's that had been put into the air from Kaneohe appeared and dropped bombs.* But *Ward* had another preoccupation. At almost the same time that they had discovered the submarine they had sighted "one of these large white sampans" of the kind used for fishing by the local Japanese colony, lying to in the forbidden area off the harbor entrance. Turning, *Ward* bore down on the sampan, while her executive officer got off a message to the 14th Naval District, "We have dropped depth charges upon subs operating in defensive sea area." The sampan, now under way, seemed to be trying to escape. She was, of course, readily overtaken; but as *Ward* came boiling up the sampan's master appeared on deck "waving a white flag," which struck Commander Outerbridge as a "funny" procedure for even a transgressing fishing skipper in time of peace. It flashed through Outerbridge's mind that a mere report of dropping depth bombs might, in view of the current skepticism about all submarine contacts, convey an inadequate idea of the unusual events that had been taking place off the entrance to Pearl Harbor. "Well, now," he thought, "maybe I had better be more definite." Depth bombing might imply only a blackfish or a whale, but gunfire was something else. At 6:53 he sent a second message:

> We have attacked, fired upon, and dropped depth charges upon submarine operating in defensive sea area.

And he added a moment later: "Stand by for further messages."

At 6:53 the first wave of Nagumo's bombers, although already air-borne, was still almost exactly an hour away. Kimmel, in a recent confidential circular to his command, had himself

* Just as these were the first shots of the war, here were almost certainly its first casualties. As we were soon to learn, the Japanese midget submarines had no closure between the conning tower and the body of the boat, consequently, *Ward's* hit must have flooded the hull, and the two-man crew now presumably lies in their steel coffin off the entrance to Pearl Harbor.

stressed the importance of any action with even a single submarine, for it might imply the presence in the immediate vicinity of an enemy fleet with fast heavy ships and carriers. Commanders were impressed with the necessity, in such an event, for at once gathering their forces and preparing to meet or search for the possible enemy main body. Something (although admittedly not much) could still have been done in that last remaining hour after the dispatch of *Ward's* report to the 14th Naval District. But Fate was implacable. The great, the inevitable, chasm between even the best theory and the corresponding practice remained to be bridged, and most of that hour went to the bridging of it.

It was, for one thing, early on a Sunday morning. There was, for another thing, all the complicated interlocking machinery of radio communications, duty officers, staff officers, the Commander of Inshore Patrol, the Boom and Net Defense, the 14th District, the Pacific Fleet, and "Cincpac"—Kimmel himself—to be set in motion. At 6:53 Sunday morning this whole massive mechanism seems to have been represented, for all practical purposes, by a middle-aged reserve lieutenant-commander and one telephone operator, the latter of Hawaiian extraction and with a deficient command of English. Lieutenant-Commander Harold Kaminski, duty officer in the 14th District, had been an enlisted man in the first World War; he had taken an interest in the reserve during the intervening years and had volunteered for active duty about a year before. His telephone operator he regarded as "perfectly useless." It was to these two that there came, at twelve minutes past 7 (according to Kaminski's notation), the *Ward's* report.

For two or three weeks past Commander Kaminski "had not liked the look of things." With this message he "knew we were in it." He also appears to have known his duty. He tried at once to get hold of Admiral Bloch's aide, but could not raise him. He called Kimmel's duty officer and read him the dispatch. He messaged the reserve duty destroyer, *U.S.S. Mo-*

naghan, to get under way at once and "contact" the *Ward*. He ordered a copy of this message sent to *Ward*. He tried to raise Captain J. B. Earle, Bloch's chief of staff, but that (as Kaminski remembered it) "took me quite a while," perhaps five or ten minutes. When Earle (who did not recall any such delay) was reached, he was incredulous; "he was quite astounded and said he could not believe it," and ordered that confirmation be secured from *Ward*. Earle first told Kaminski to call Admiral Bloch, but the duty officer's hands were full and the chief of staff undertook to notify the District commander. Kaminski called the District War Plans officer. It was then about 7:30.

Captain Earle reached Admiral Bloch over the telephone at about the same time and "talked the situation over with him for some time with a view to deciding what other action should be taken. Our reaction was that it was probably a mistake as we had had numerous reports of sighting of submarines, but that if it were not a mistake the *Ward* could take care of the situation and the relief destroyer could lend a hand, while the Commander-in-Chief [Kimmel] had the necessary power to undertake any other action which might be desired. Mainly, we were trying definitely to determine what had happened." So one possible channel through which warning might have gone collapsed. Meanwhile, Kimmel's duty officer had raised the admiral himself by 7:30 or 7:40. Admiral Kimmel was told of *Ward's* report, of the dispatch of *Monaghan* to her assistance, and of the orders which had gone out to *Ward* to confirm the contact. At 7:40 "Patwing 2" called to report that its PBY had bombed the submarine. But there was still no "confirmation." "In my judgment," as Admiral Kimmel later testified, "the effort to obtain confirmation, . . . was a proper preliminary to more drastic action in view of the number of such contacts which had not been verified in the past." It is true that they had had a number of false alarms in the preceding weeks. None, however, had reported gunfire on the supposed submarine. Twenty minutes later Admiral Kimmel was still waiting for confirmation of *Ward's* report.

Army was, of course, in total ignorance of all this. Even if it had occurred to any of the naval officers to impart such esoteric matters to the Army command, there would have been no particular machinery through which to do so. Army and Navy were each trusting the other to attend to its "own" business, and Army had been peacefully pursuing its appointed routines. The dawn brightened over Oahu; sunrise was coming. At 7 o'clock sharp, Lieutenant Tyler at the Information Center saw the plotting men take off their headphones, pick up their gear, and decamp for breakfast. Only the lieutenant (whose orders, for some unfathomable Army reason, required him to remain until 8) and one telephone operator were left. The "problem" was over. There was nothing to do but kill time until the relief arrived. The lieutenant was doing so when, a few minutes after 7, the telephone rang and the operator answered it.

Thirty miles away at the Opana Station Private Lockard had started to close down the radar set. Private Elliott protested. Although the "problem" was over, their relief had not come. Elliott wanted instruction in the operation of this fascinating gadget; why not keep it going and give him a chance to work it? Lockard consented, and Elliott sat down at the oscilloscope. Almost immediately there sprang up out of the dancing line of light a "blip" so big as to suggest that the machine must be out of order. Lockard displaced Elliott, tested the controls, found nothing wrong. There was the "blip" still shimmering before them, telling them that there was something out there bigger than they had ever picked up before and far beyond the greatest range at which they had ever previously got an indication. Bearing three degrees east of north, it was 137 miles away; and though the radar of that time afforded no means of telling just what it was, it looked like a lot of airplanes, perhaps as many as 50 or more.

Elliott was pretty excited about it. This was the best thing their new radars had done yet, and he wanted to send in a report. Lockard told him, in effect, not to be silly; the exercise was over and it was no more of their business. But Elliott insisted. Entertaining a grossly exaggerated idea of the real capabilities of the Information Center, he thought that this might be a bunch of Navy planes about which the Army knew nothing, and that if the report went in it might give Army a chance for a nice bit of practice in the technique of interception. Lockard finally told him to go ahead if he wanted to. The "blip" had been obediently recording the approach of the planes; they had come down to 132 miles and were still advancing at a fair speed. The direct telephone lines to the plotting board had been shut down by that time, but Elliott called the center over the service line used for routine business. The operator said there was nobody there. But Elliott continued to insist, and the note of excitement in his voice bestirred the operator to say that he would find the officer and get him to call back. Violating orders, the operator left the switchboard to hunt up the lieutenant. Tyler called back. Lockard, answering the telephone, reported the news. It was all more or less incomprehensible to Tyler. Whatever these guys at Opana were seeing in their oscilloscope, Tyler had no means of knowing what it was. It might be anything. It might be a flight of Navy planes off a carrier. It might be—and Tyler remembered listening to the Hawaiian music on the radio as he had driven in to the center—another flight of B-17's from the mainland. Probably was.* Tyler told Opana to forget it, hung up, and stepped out into the fresh morning air. It was then about 7:20, just as the Navy was beginning to be really aroused over the submarine contact. Tyler found the morning pleasant, but with a good deal of low-hanging cloud, especially over the mountains.

* The B-17's from Hamilton were flying individually, not in formation. Some of them had, in fact, got north of their course; they actually came in on almost the same bearing as the Japanese planes and at almost the same time.

Though snubbed from headquarters, Lockard and Elliott still thought they had made quite an interception, and continued to plot the advancing planes until, at about twenty miles out, the latter entered the "dead space" of the machine and the "blip" broke up among the echoes from the neighboring heights. The two privates then secured the set and made a copy of their record to show their commanding officer. About 7:45 their relief appeared. Lockard and Elliott climbed into the car, made their way down the wood road to the highway, and set off for their barracks some nine miles away. As they tooled cheerfully along, they saw one of the trucks of their own Air-Craft Warning company tearing up the road toward them. It appeared to have the accelerator on the floorboards; it was filled with their comrades from the company, and the men were apparently provided with full battle equipment. Lockard and Elliott honked politely. The truck thundered past without response. Lockard and Elliott thought it rather strange.

II ☞

The first plane, a dive bomber, streaked in low over Pearl Harbor at 7:55 A.M., coming in from the south with its consorts close behind it. Two reconnaissance float planes had been catapulted from the Japanese cruisers before them, but if they reached Oahu they were not observed. The first wave of the main body, 189 aircraft in all, had been flown off the carrier decks at 6:00 A.M., Hawaiian time. As they sighted the north point of Oahu, at ten minutes before 8, they split up. In accordance with sound air warfare doctrine, the first objective was the American defensive aviation. One dive bomber unit, swerving only a little to the right, went in from the north over the ranked and helpless Army fighters on Wheeler Field. Another, swinging wide around the west coast of the island, came up from the south against the Army bombers on Hickam Field and the Navy

PBY's on Ford Island. Immediately behind these were 40 torpedo bombers, launching their deadly missiles from a low altitude at the "sitting ducks" in Battleship Row. Fifty horizontal bombers were on the heels of the torpedo planes, in case the first should fail against nets or baffles; and after them all there came 45 fighters, to put down any opposition which might get into the air or, failing that, to polish off the remains at Wheeler and Hickam, at Ford Island, Kaneohe, and the Marine base at Ewa.

The whole of this massive force was flung within the space of a few minutes at virtually every prominent naval and air installation on Oahu. The Japanese pilots knew that an hour behind them a second wave of 171 aircraft—54 horizontal bombers, 81 dive bombers, and 36 fighters—was on its way in support. But most of the damage was done within the first quarter of an hour. The Ford Island air station and the 29 PBY patrol planes parked there were a shambles within a few minutes, the planes blazing and exploding. This one attack finished Ford Island, and the Japanese did not return. The Marine field at Ewa, to the westward, was worked over more methodically with dive bombing and strafing; and at the end of a rather leisurely fifteen minutes all the 49 planes there—fighters, scout bombers, and utility types—had been either totally destroyed or put out of action. At Kaneohe, the Navy patrol base on the east coast, there were two principal attacks, one at 7:55 and the second about twenty-five minutes later. Of the 33 PBY's there, most of them moored out in the bay, 27 had been destroyed by the end of the second attack and the remainder put out of commission. Save for the seven PBY's which were out on local patrol or maneuvers when the attack began, the Navy and Marine Corps did not get a single plane into the air from Oahu during the action.

At just about 8 o'clock 25 Japanese dive bombers roared low—not more than 50 or 75 feet from the ground—over the long lines of parked fighter planes on the Army's main fighter base at Wheeler Field, in the center of the island. The bursting bombs, the rattle of the enemy machine guns, and the red ball insignia on the wings were the first intimation of war that anyone had at Wheeler. In a few moments the parked aircraft, many with their gas tanks filled, were blazing; great clouds of oily smoke were rolling up on the still air to obscure everything and hamper the frantic efforts to pull the planes apart and get them armed. They managed to put six operable fighters into the air by 8:30 and a couple more just before the Japanese returned, in lesser strength, around 9, while another half dozen or so got up in the final minutes of the action. But that was the extent of Wheeler's contribution to the defense. Forty-two planes were totally destroyed at Wheeler; and out of the 126 modern or fairly modern fighters on the field at the start, only 43 were listed as in commission afterward.

Hickam Field, like Ford Island, was a shambles within the first five minutes, and repeated attacks thereafter did a pretty thorough job. But since most of the planes there were the obsolete B-18 bombers, it did not matter so much. Of Short's twelve B-17's, as luck would have it, four were still serviceable after the attack and only four were destroyed. The Japanese had given a low priority to Bellows Field, across the island next to Kaneohe, and it was not until 8:30 that a single enemy plane made one ineffective pass at the parked aircraft of the fighter squadron which was there for gunnery practice. But although they were thus warned, the planes were without gas or ammunition and it took time to ready them. It was not until about 9 that they were taxi-ing for a take-off; and just at that moment seven Japanese appeared. Two American fighters got into the air, but were shot down as they did so. One pilot was saved, but that ended Bellows' contribution.

Meanwhile, two American air elements had flown, utterly unsuspecting, into the middle of the action. At dawn Admiral Halsey, returning from Wake Island with the *Enterprise* task force, was some 200 miles west of Pearl. He flew off a squadron of scout bombers to perform the usual patrol ahead of the ships, but with orders to continue on in and land at Ewa. One pilot, on the extreme left wing of the patrol, was heard suddenly speaking over the voice radio circuit: "Don't shoot, this is an American plane!" and was never heard from again. Another, seeing the sky over Pearl filled with anti-aircraft bursts, wondered what crazy nonsense the Army was up to, holding anti-aircraft drills on a Sunday. When the truth dawned on him, he could not clear his machine gun; the plane, however, managed to land. In all, seven planes of this squadron were shot down; eight of the fourteen men in them were killed and others wounded. The eleven B-17's from the mainland, though completely unarmed, had better fortune. One, trying to get into Bellows, was hit, set on fire, and destroyed just as she landed, but most of the crew were saved. Six managed to land amid the wreckage at Hickam; one landed at Wheeler, one on a golf course, and two got into the Haleiwa airstrip.

The Japanese missed only one of all our air elements—the fighter squadron at Haleiwa, about which the enemy apparently knew nothing. They were likewise unready, but the commander, Major George S. Welsh, got into the air with one wing man about 8:15 and three more pilots got up later. Major Welsh claimed four Japanese; and the others, together with the fighters which took off from Wheeler and the *Enterprise* scout bombers, got a number more. But the net result was that in the first fifteen minutes of the action the Japanese had successfully destroyed or paralyzed virtually the entire air strength of Oahu. In the same space of time they had gone far toward the accomplishment of their main objective, the destruction of the United States Pacific Fleet.

Seven of Kimmel's eight battleships were moored along the southeasterly face of Ford Island, at big concrete bollards or mooring posts set just off the shore line. *California* was at the southern end of the row, then the tanker *Neosho*, full of aviation gasoline, then *Maryland* and *Oklahoma* side by side with *Oklahoma* outboard, then *Tennessee* and *West Virginia* with

PEARL HARBOR
ANCHORAGE PLAN, DEC. 7, 1941

the latter outboard, then *Arizona* with the repair ship *Vestal* outboard of her, then *Nevada* alone. *Pennsylvania,* the eighth battleship, was in the big drydock at the Navy Yard across the channel, together with a couple of destroyers ahead of her in the same dock. Several cruisers were in relative security in the Navy Yard slips; but the modern light cruiser *Helena* was moored at "10-10 Dock," the long quay paralleling the channel on the eastern side, with the old converted minelayer *Oglala* outboard of her. Around on the northwesterly side of Ford Island there was another row of four ships lying at bollards. In order from the north end these were the light cruiser *Detroit,* the light cruiser *Raleigh,* the old battleship *Utah* converted into a target ship, and the seaplane tender *Tangier.* Most of the destroyers were anchored in nests in the broad basin of East Loch, north of Ford Island, and the submarines were in slips at their base.

Over this great fleet the 40 Japanese torpedo bombers broke like a storm just before 8 o'clock. They came from every direction, each pilot carefully briefed on the particular angle from which to launch his torpedo in order to get the best run and cause the maximum confusion in the defense. Taking the gunners by complete surprise, they were almost impossible to hit; in a few moments the harbor was crisscrossed by the white wakes of their missiles, and tremendous explosions were leaping up against the steel sides of the battleships. The horizontal and dive bombers were immediately behind them; and the bombs were landing even as the torpedoes went home. Every one of the five outboard battleships took one or more torpedo hits in the first few minutes, and the two inboard ships, *Maryland* and *Tennessee,* were hit by bombs. Other torpedo planes and bombers were at the same time attacking the ships moored along the northwest face of the island. The old target ship *Utah,* lying in a berth often used by the aircraft carriers, took two torpedoes, turned over, and sank at 8:13, the first total casualty. The light cruiser *Raleigh,* lying just ahead of her, received one torpedo and later a bomb hit, and only heroic measures kept her from turning turtle.

In Battleship Row, the repair ship *Vestal*, lying alongside of *Arizona*, had afforded the latter slight protection. Two torpedoes streaked past the smaller vessel to reach the battleship,* while a heavy armor-piercing bomb found its way to *Arizona's* forward magazine, and she blew up with a terrific detonation. The whole forward half of the ship was a total wreck, through which tremendous oil fires now poured up their flames and great billows of smoke. Just south of her *West Virginia* had taken four or five torpedo and bomb hits. Enormous rents had been torn in her plating; there was a fierce fire amidships, and she was settling now to the bottom, fortunately on an even keel. *Tennessee*, lying inboard, was not too badly damaged; but she was pinned against the bollards by the sinking *West Virginia* and was imperiled by the oil fires raging in the *Arizona* and across the water between them. South of this pair, the old *Oklahoma*, lying outboard of *Maryland*, had received four torpedo hits in the first minutes; she was soon listing extravagantly, and at 8:32 she rolled completely over and lay, like an immense whale, with her bottom and propellers showing to the now densely smoke-filled sky.

Meanwhile, a single torpedo plane, streaking in from the west, had loosed its "fish" against 10-10 Dock; passing under *Oglala*, the torpedo exploded against the bottom of *Helena*, lying inboard of the old minelayer. The light cruiser was severely damaged, but *Oglala* had her whole side stove in. Tugs dragged her away from *Helena* in time, but presently she went over, sinking on her beam ends. Across from 10-10 Dock the battleship *California*, alone at the southern end of the row, had taken two torpedoes and bomb hits; there were fires in her; the fact that her compartments had been open hindered damage control, and she was slowly settling at her moorings.

* This is uncertain. Later investigation was to throw doubt on the question of whether *Arizona* was torpedoed, but it was so reported at the time.

All this had been accomplished in the first half hour of the attack, and most of it in the first ten or fifteen minutes. The torpedo planes, their missiles expended, faded away. There were still horizontal and dive bombers ranging unhindered over the scene, but for another fifteen or twenty minutes there was something like a "lull" in the action.

As the fact of the attack sank in, the ships had opened with their anti-aircraft; most of the fleet's anti-aircraft batteries were in action within four or five minutes, and all of them, including those of the destroyers (with which the Japanese for the most part did not trouble), within some seven minutes. The Army was firing with machine guns, rifles, and even pistols, and with the few fixed 3-inch A-A batteries in the forts, which had their ammunition ready. But the Army's 60 mobile 3-inch A-A guns were of little help; most of them were not in position and ready to fire until hours after the attack.

About 8:40, as the first onslaught dwindled, the stunned and shattered ships were beginning to revive. Just before the attack began the destroyer *Monaghan* had been ordered to get under way and join *Ward*, and she was now standing down the channel to the west of Ford Island. Sighting one of the midget submarines—almost certainly the only one of the five to penetrate the harbor—*Monaghan* rammed and sank it and continued on out. Other movement began. The battleship *Nevada*, at the north end of the row, was under command of a reserve lieutenant-commander, as her captain was ashore. In spite of bomb and torpedo hits, this reserve officer got her under way and headed down channel. The repair ship *Vestal* freed herself from *Arizona's* appalling wreck (*Vestal's* captain had been blown overboard by the explosion but swam back to his ship) and was successfully beached. Near the southern end of the line the tanker *Neosho* managed by skillful ship handling to get clear between the capsized *Oklahoma* and the sinking *California* and to remove herself and her perilous cargo from the holocaust.

Then at 8:50 the second great wave of Japanese horizontal

and dive bombers (there were no torpedo planes in this echelon) sighted Oahu, split up like the first, and swept in to finish the kill. The anti-aircraft fire was better now; there were a few American fighters in the air, and there was not a great deal left for the support wave to do. But though the second attack was consequently less effective than the first, it put in some further heavy blows. The Japanese saw *Nevada* standing down the harbor, pounced upon her, got in seven or eight additional bomb hits, and started serious flooding. There was a great danger of her sinking in the narrow entrance channel, and thus blocking all ingress or egress. Whether by accident or design, she was grounded on Hospital Point, just at the head of the channel. Tugs afterward got her off and beached her on the opposite shore, clear of the fairway.

Another bomber landed a direct hit on *Pennsylvania*, but the damage was not great, and since the battleship was already safe in drydock repairs were comparatively simple. But the two destroyers just ahead of her in the same dock were thrown off the blocks; fires were started which set off the torpedoes in one of them, and both were reduced to wrecks. Another destroyer, *Shaw*, was in a near-by floating dock. Bomb hits riddled the dock and set fires which reached *Shaw's* forward magazine. She went up in a great explosion which blew off her whole bow as the dock sank under her. Strangely enough, from the bridge aft the damage was only minor. The torso of the ship was refloated; so was the dock, and a month later *Shaw* went back into this same dock to have a temporary bow fitted. She returned to the mainland under her own power, was rebuilt and ultimately rejoined the fleet.

The heavy cruiser *Honolulu*, in one of the Navy Yard slips, took a bomb hit at this time, but the damage was relatively light. By and large, the Japanese job had been done; and by 9:45 the last of the raiding planes had faded into the silent skies. Twenty-four hours before Admiral Kimmel had been noting what he must do if war came within twenty-four hours, and perfecting the plans which were to crown his naval career.

War had come. The plans had vanished forever; the career, like General Short's, was in utter ruin. Twenty-four hours before the admiral had at his command eight great battleships, "the backbone of the fleet." He now had none. Two, *Pennsylvania* and *Maryland*, could be restored to service fairly quickly and a third, *Tennessee*, was not very much worse off, although before she could be repaired it would be necessary to blast away the massive concrete bollards against which she had been wedged by the sinking *West Virginia*. Two of the remaining five, *Oklahoma* and *Arizona*, were total losses. The three others were ultimately salvaged and restored to service. But it was nearly five months before *Nevada*, which presented the least difficult problem, was floated and sufficiently patched to be sent back to the mainland; and it was a much longer time still before *California* and *West Virginia*, after truly heroic exploits of salvage engineering, were at last sent on their way to rehabilitation.

Three cruisers—*Raleigh*, *Helena* and *Honolulu*—had been more or less seriously damaged and three destroyers wrecked; the lives of 2,086 naval officers and men had been lost.* The subsequent history of the war was to suggest that the battleships were actually, perhaps, of less critical importance than both we and the Japanese supposed at the time; and hindsight could take some solace from the fact that the true damage was much less than it seemed to be in that first appalling moment. The carriers and the heavy cruisers were the vessels that afterward bore the main brunt of the Pacific naval war, and these the Japanese missed. Our airplane losses were almost trivial by comparison with the immense air fleets which the war would demand and which were at that time already beginning to come from the assembly lines. It has also been suggested that the really vital targets at Pearl Harbor were the base and dockyard facilities and in particular the exposed oil storage, to which the Japanese paid no attention. Had they

* The Army lost 237 lives. The total casualties, in killed, wounded, and missing for both services, were finally placed at 3,435.

gone after the fuel instead of the ships, they might have rendered Pearl Harbor useless as a base for many months, driven the ships themselves back to the California coast for their oil supplies, and thus largely freed Japan's operations from the persistent opposition and the ultimate counterattack which were built up from Pearl in the ensuing months.

Yet one cannot overcome the fact that the Japanese had, in one hour and forty-five minutes, knocked the heart out of the United States Pacific Fleet. Morally as well as materially, they had paralyzed American naval action in the Pacific for a period of many weeks, which was exactly what they had set out to do. And they had accomplished it at a cost to themselves of just 29 aircraft, five midget submarines, and one fleet submarine. In the wild confusion at Pearl, in the absence of any proper liaison between the Army and Navy, between the radar net and the ships and bomber planes, the retreating enemy returned without interference to their flight decks and Admiral Nagumo's 1st Air Fleet slipped rapidly away to the westward, undetected from beginning to end.

The midget submarines were a failure. They were a suicidal weapon to begin with, and nine of the ten young men who manned them successfully achieved death for the Emperor, though probably nothing else. *Ward* got one before the beginning of the action. *Monaghan* rammed the one that entered the harbor; she had discharged both her torpeodes but both were misses. Another destroyer, *U.S.S. Helm*, had been under way in the harbor when the attack came and was one of the first vessels to get outside. She saw one of the midgets apparently stranded on the reefs just off the entrance and opened fire, but the midget slipped from the reef and disappeared. Her discouraged commander then took her, for some reason, all the way around the south coast of Oahu, finally stranding on another reef a mile off Bellows Field.* His machinist was lost, but the commander reached shore alive

* A chart of Pearl Harbor was recovered from this submarine, and on it a track had been laid out around Ford Island, with times entered

to become Prisoner of War No. 1. He was the sole survivor. The fate of the two other midgets is unknown, but it was learned after the war that the Japanese never recovered them. Nor did they hear again from one of the big I-type submarines that had lain off the entrance. In American records she appears as having been sunk on December 10 by carrier planes.

III ☞

In the early morning quiet in the American embassy at Tokyo a telephone was ringing. All over the globe for the past hour or so the telephone bells had been carrying the tidings; the excited radio broadcasts had been spreading the news; the telegrams had been humming over the wires; the shocked voices at luncheons, dinners, and breakfasts had been repeating, incredulously: "The Japanese have bombed Pearl Harbor!" Of all this Ambassador Grew was in total ignorance.

On the preceding evening—it was the evening of Sunday, December 7, in Tokyo—Mr. Grew had been listening to the news broadcast from San Francisco. Surprisingly, he had heard the announcer declare that the President of the United States was sending an urgent personal message to the Emperor of Japan in the interest of maintaining peace. It was the first that Mr. Grew had learned of anything of the kind. The State Department's pilot message, announcing the coming of the President's telegram, had been filed at 8 o'clock Saturday evening, which was 10 o'oclock, Sunday morning, by Tokyo time. It was not until about 10:30 that evening, after Mr. Grew had heard the San Francisco broadcast, that this pilot message arrived at the American embassy. But Mr. Grew

as if recording a circuit of the harbor. This gave rise to the belief that the midget had actually got into Pearl a day or two before the attack; but the evidence now seems convincing that the plotted track represented an intention rather than an actual performance.

noticed that it carried a notation indicating that it had been received in the Tokyo telegraph office at 11 in the morning. The ambassador called in his councillor, Dooman, and the two waited for the main message. As it began to arrive around 11:30 Dooman called Togo's secretary at the Foreign Office and requested an immediate interview. The secretary demurred on account of the lateness of the hour, but the Americans insisted and the appointment was made. Grew reached the Foreign Minister's residence at 12:15 Monday morning (this was less than two hours before Nagumo's fly-off against Pearl Harbor) and read the President's message to Togo. The ambassador asked an immediate audience with the Emperor. The Foreign Minister intimated that he would have to study the document, but the ambassador pressed him most urgently, and Togo agreed to take it up with the Throne . Mr. Grew left at about 12:30, and turned in for his night's sleep. It was 7 o'clock in the morning (Pearl Harbor by that time was a smoking wreck) when the ambassador was awakened by the telephone. Togo's secretary asked him to come at once; he had been trying to get hold of the ambassador ever since 5. The fact that the embassy telephone had not rung during the preceding two hours seemed to indicate that this was just more of the peculiar Japanese idea of protocol; but at any rate, the ambassador hurried into his clothes and was at the Foreign Minister's residence by 7:30.

Togo handed him a long document which was, he said, the Emperor's reply to the President's message. Actually, it was a copy of the fourteen-part note, which had been started to Washington even before the President's message had been put upon the cables. Grew saw that its substance lay in the final announcement that negotiations were broken off. But he was not particularly concerned; negotiations had been broken off after the invasion of southern Indo-China, and he hoped that again they would be restarted. The Foreign Minister, without a word about Pearl Harbor, made "a little pleasant speech" thanking the ambassador for his co-operation in the cause of peace, and bowed him out. Mr. Grew returned to the embassy, shaved, breakfasted, and started to work up his report. At that moment they heard an Extra being called in the streets; they sent out for one and learned that Japan was at war with the United States. An hour or so later a polite Foreign Office official arrived to present, with hands trembling in excitement, the official notification; and on his heels there came the police, who closed the embassy gates and immured its personnel. According to Lauterbach, it was not until that morning that Prime Minister Tojo brought to the Emperor the declaration of war, and not until 11:30—eight hours after the launching of the attack—that the Imperial brush-stroke was affixed to the instrument. The Emperor "was not entirely happy."

Many telephones had been ringing in those hours. One sounded in General Brereton's quarters at Manila at about 4 o'clock on that grim morning. The Operations Officer answered, and looked up from the instrument: " 'General, Pearl Harbor's been bombed. . . . Sutherland's on the phone and wants to talk to you.' I grabbed the phone and talked to General Sutherland. It came as a surprise to no one." Not far away at the same moment an aide was waking Admiral Hart with an intercepted dispatch originating at Pearl: "Air raid on Pearl Harbor. This is not drill." Hart paused only long enough to get assurance that it was authentic. He was told that it was recognizably a Pearl Harbor operator's hand upon the sending key. Still sitting on his bed, he wrote out a message to all ships and stations under his command:

> Priority dispatch. Japan started hostilities. Govern yourselves accordingly.

At Stotsenburg General Wainwright was wakened by a telephone ringing insistently in the pitch darkness of the next room. He reached the instrument; it was MacArthur's G-3: "Admiral Hart has just received a radio dispatch from Admiral Kimmel informing him that Japan has initiated hostilities."

Dressing with one hand, Wainwright jiggled the telephone with the other to get hold of his aide:

"Johnny!"
"Hello. . . . Yes, General."
"The cat has jumped."

The cat had jumped. But it had not yet landed in the Philippines. For most of them there was little that could be done except to wait for the lethal claws to strike home. The Navy was already dispersed or on station. The raw Filipino recruits soon were being started into the beach defenses, there to await the onslaught. The one weapon capable of an offensive-defensive which MacArthur possessed was represented by the 35 B-17's of the 19th Bombardment Group. But there was no plan for their employment in the crisis. One-third of them had, fortunately, been sent south to Del Monte in Mindanao. The others were ready on Clark Field. But they were without orders, without a considered mission, without even adequate target data. The minutes passed. The tropic dawn and sunrise broke. Nothing happened.

Five hundred miles away, on the airfields of southern Formosa, other telephones had been ringing as well. The 360 aircraft of the Japanese 21st and 23rd Naval Air Flotillas were poised on the runways, their motors warm, their crews ready, their supreme hour at hand—and the monsoon weather rendering a take-off impossible. They were supposed to strike on the instant they got the Pearl Harbor news. They had the news; they were thoroughly briefed, excellent photographic reconnaissance had told them just where the blows should be delivered, and a dense fog over southern Formosa pinned them to the ground. At any moment they expected the American aviation to break through the cloud layers upon them. They took every precaution they could; they even prepared themselves for gas attack. But there was no attack of any kind. The precious hours passed; the fog began to lift; the

Americans did not appear. At 10:15 (9:15 by Manila time) the two air flotillas took off for Luzon.

The Americans had not appeared because there had been no orders to do so.* At 5 o'clock General Brereton had arrived at MacArthur's headquarters at Fort Santiago—that massive, moss-grown pile of seventeenth-century Spanish masonry which had stood at the Pasig's mouth through so many wars—to get authority for offensive action. General Sutherland, the chief of staff, authorized him to prepare the big bombers, but there were no instructions to send them off. Fully alerted and burning to show what they could do, the Far Eastern Air Force was to spend that morning milling around in a tragic futility. The Iba radar reported an approaching force; the fighters were sent up to intercept, and the radar plot

* The following account is based on *The Brereton Diaries*, on the "Memoranda" concerning air events in the Philippines, printed in the *Joint Committee Record*, Pt. 11 p. 5316 *ff.*, and on Ind's *Bataan: The Judgment Seat*. The publication of General Brereton's book in the fall of 1946 elicited a minatory statement from General MacArthur, declaring that Brereton on December 8 "never recommended an attack on Formosa to me and I know nothing of such a recommendation having been made," adding at considerable length and with evident asperity that any such attack would have been quite impossible and that "I" had given orders "several days before" for the removal of the B-17's to Del Monte. This does not accord with Brereton's account of the orders to remove part of the B-17's. Without entering into the relative accuracy of the two generals, one may still observe that MacArthur was the commanding officer, that the B-17's were the best weapon he had, that if a strike on Formosa was not possible it was his duty to see that they were conserved for employment in accordance with some strategic plan that was possible, and that there is nothing to indicate that any such plan existed. If MacArthur in fact received "no recommendation" as to the use of the B-17's on December 8, one is still forced to ask why he did not demand one. The four-engine bombers had been sent to the Philippines, at a time when they were desperately needed elsewhere, as the backbone of the islands' defense. A single newspaper statement is hardly sufficient to relieve the commanding general of responsibility for the fact that they were frittered away without effect.

indicated that they had done so perfectly. Unfortunately, the radar of that day had no means of distinguishing altitudes, and although the Americans were on the correct course they passed the Japanese at a different level without seeing them. The B-17's were ordered to bomb up, and then ordered not to bomb up. Around 8 the Operations Officer at Clark put them into the air, without bombs, for "reconnaissance" and to get them out of danger. They spent the next three hours circling over the mountains and through the cloud banks "unsuccessfully seeking traces of the enemy."

At 9:10, according to Brereton, the commander of the fighters reported that he had 54 ships in the air and another 36 in reserve but that they were not accomplishing anything. Then about twenty minutes later, Iba reported a large enemy formation coming in over Lingayen Gulf. The fighters were disposed to cover both Manila and Clark Field against the onslaught; the Japanese, however, turned sharply left and dropped their bombs on Baguio, the Philippine "summer capital" in the northern Luzon hills. It was the first heavy attack, and the enemy escaped without interception. The fighters were called in to refuel, and Brereton appealed to Sutherland.

He had to use the B-17's for something, or they would simply be destroyed on the field. Lieutenant Colonel E. L. Eubank, commander of the 19th Bombardment Group, flew down to Nielson Field to consult with Brereton. MacArthur sent word that they could undertake "reconnaissance" of the Formosan fields. Eubank flew back to Clark and ordered the B-17's in to refuel. MacArthur sent word that "bombing missions" would be permitted, and Brereton called Eubank to tell him to bomb up. At just about that moment the Iba radar recorded the approach of another big attack. But also at just about that moment, the feeble communications system failed, whether because of sabotage (as was believed at the time) or simple overstrain; and as the fighters were maneuvering to intercept, the hostile formation was lost. At 12:13 P.M. (some eleven hours after the opening of the attack on Oahu) a powerful force of Japanese bombers and strafing planes swept unopposed over Clark Field. They destroyed or put out of commission everything there.

Twelve B-17's had been sent to Del Monte and were thus to survive for a few more days or weeks. One from Clark Field was still out on patrol and so escaped the holocaust. Of the 22 which were at that moment on the ground at Clark, most were destroyed and the rest "filled with bullet holes." They were able to get "two or three" of them back into operation next day. But for practical purposes, that ended the power of the Far Eastern Air Force—and of the great Flying Fortresses on which Mr. Stimson had put so much confidence—as effectively as the power of the Pacific Fleet had been ended a few hours before. In all the vast reaches of the western and southwestern Pacific, there now remained but one serious threat to Japanese expansion. That was the British battle fleet at Singapore. Two days later Admiral Sir Tom Phillips sortied with *Prince of Wales* and *Repulse* against the reported Japanese landings at Kota Bharu—the operation which had given the first real alarm. His movement was discovered by Japanese submarines; and he was overwhelmed by the Japanese 22nd Naval Air Flotilla from the neighborhood of Saigon. With a loss of only four planes, the Japanese sank both battleships and their admiral with them.

IV ☜

The rest belongs to the story of the Pacific war, rather than to the story of what led up to it. Most adult Americans retain their own vivid memories of Pearl Harbor Day, of how the news first came to them, of the first rumors and excitements, of Secretary Hull's meeting with the two Japanese ambassadors, of the President's summons to Congress, of the German and Italian declarations of war, of all those first, half-scared hours and days. Even the events at Pearl Harbor, in the Philippines, and in the Gulf of Siam have here been only briefly sketched; the many details of these desperate actions, the heroism that was displayed, the skill and stamina that were summoned up in that hour of extreme crisis, belong to the story which was beginning rather than to that which had reached its end.

Only a final observation remains. Exactly as they had planned, the Japanese had destroyed the three keys to the mastery of the western Pacific—the United States Pacific Fleet, the heavy bombers in the Philippines, and the British battle squadron at Singapore—within a few hours of the opening of the war. The path of conquest lay clear before them. Rarely has there been so brilliant a success in the history of warfare. Perfectly designed in its power, its surprise, its successful deception, there was only one defect in this politico-military masterpiece. It is a defect common to such exploits. It worked too well.

The onslaught proved so easy, the first great conquests of Hong Kong, of Singapore, of the Philippines, of the Netherlands East Indies, of New Guinea, and the northern Solomons came so readily, that there seemed no reason to stop. The plan, so grandiose at the beginning, was enlarged. Indeed, it compelled its own enlargement. To protect the conquest of the southwest Pacific, it became essential to take India on one side and the Aleutians, Hawaii, and Australia on the other. And that compulsion was fatal. Of the six carriers which launched the paralyzing attack on Oahu in December, 1941, four—*Akagi, Kaga, Hiryu* and *Soryu*—perished off Midway in June, 1942. Admiral Nagumo, who led them to their initial success, also led them to this disaster; he survived it, but only to die, apparently by suicide, in the American capture of Saipan in July, 1944. Admiral Yamamoto, who conceived the grand design, was shot down in flames over Rabaul. Of the crack pilots who smashed Kimmel and Brereton and destroyed Phillips, hundreds were lost at Midway or in the long, bloody attrition of the Solomons, and could never be adequately replaced. Japan did not possess the reserves of men and material to meet the counterattack which she deliberately invited.

The United States, on the other hand, was just reaching the point in December, 1941, at which her tremendous resources could produce new ships, airplanes, guns, and trained men in all but unlimited numbers. The Japanese onslaught served only to forge our sprawling, confused, uncertain democracy at one blow into the most powerful and best integrated instrument of war which the world has ever seen. A final word on Pearl Harbor has been well said by a Japanese, Lieutenant General Ija Kawabe, who told the United States Strategic Bombing Survey :

> The national potential wouldn't allow Japan to build up a military force adequate for a war on this scale, so the bold beginning at the outbreak of the war was just a very unfortunate thing.

INDEX

(Ranks and titles as of 1941)